NOT TO BE REMOV[ED]
FROM THE LIBRAR[Y]

KV-429-467

WITHDRAWN FROM
THE LIBRARY

UNIVERSITY OF
WINCHESTER

KA 0156456 0

MEDIEVAL TEXTS

GENERAL EDITORS
V. H. Galbraith, Sir Roger Mynors and C. N. L. Brooke

ANGLO-SCOTTISH RELATIONS
1174–1328
SOME SELECTED DOCUMENTS

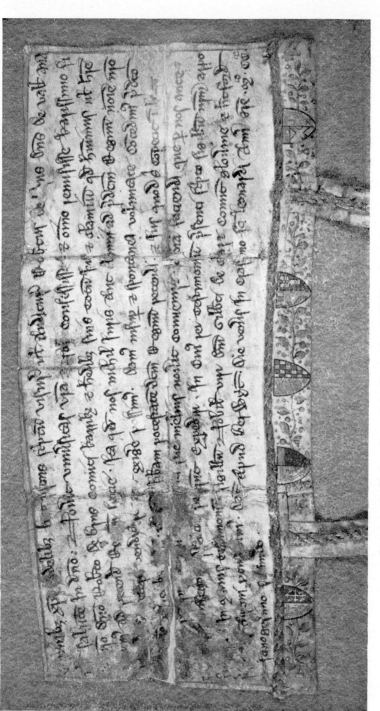

Quitclaim by Robert Bruce 'the Competitor' (1292). See below, p. 58.
(British Museum, Cotton Charters, xviii, 48; size of original 8″ by 3¾″. The decoration at the foot is probably attributable to Sir Robert Cotton)

Anglo-Scottish Relations
1174-1328

Some Selected Documents

edited and translated by
E. L. G. Stones
Professor of Mediæval History,
University of Glasgow

NELSON

THOMAS NELSON AND SONS LTD
36 Park Street London W1
Parkside Works Edinburgh 9
10 Warehouse Road Apapa Lagos
P.O. Box 25012 Nairobi Kenya

THOMAS NELSON (AUSTRALIA) LTD
117 Latrobe Street Melbourne C1

THOMAS NELSON AND SONS (AFRICA) (Pty) LTD
P.O. Box 9881 Johannesburg

THOMAS NELSON AND SONS (CANADA) LTD
81 Curlew Drive Don Mills Ontario

THOMAS NELSON AND SONS
Copewood and Davis Streets Camden 3, N.J.

SOCIÉTÉ FRANÇAISE D'ÉDITIONS NELSON
97 rue Monge Paris 5

———

First published 1965
© E. L. G. STONES 1965

KING ALFRED'S COLLEGE
WINCHESTER.

REF

941·02
STO

61516

Printed in Great Britain by
Thomas Nelson (Printers) Ltd, London and Edinburgh
for Thomas Nelson and Sons Ltd, 36 Park Street, London W.1.

CONTENTS

TO THE MEMORY OF
CHARLES HENRY MORRIS
1907–1964

PREFACE AND ACKNOWLEDGMENTS

MY interest was first aroused in the documents from which this collection is chosen, when I attempted, some fifteen years ago, to assemble the evidence for the diplomatic career of Sir Geoffrey le Scrope, who took part in a number of the English missions which treated with the Scots between 1319 and 1328. It soon became obvious that a number of important documents, including even a complete Chancery Roll (C 71/12), had been unknown to Rymer, Palgrave, Stevenson, and Bain, and therefore to all the writers of secondary works upon Anglo-Scottish relations. It was also clear that no scholar had attempted to study the origins and the composition of the records as a whole, in the manner in which the records of Anglo-French relations have been studied, to the great profit of all future students, by Professor George Cuttino, Dr Pierre Chaplais, and others. The present book does not challenge comparison with their work, but I hope that it will be judged mainly as a contribution to our understanding of an important, and from this point of view neglected, group of mediaeval archives. Archives have been well described as ' secretions of an organism '. With this in mind, the reader may find it possible to dismiss the prejudices which have for so long impeded the study of Anglo-Scottish relations in the middle ages, and to read the texts as the work of bureaucrats of long ago, whose opinions can hardly be regarded now as the material for anything more than purely academic controversy.

I am indebted to the Keeper of the Public Records, and the Controller of Her Majesty's Stationery Office, for permission to print unpublished crown-copyright documents, and to reprint no. 11, which occurs in the official edition of the

Close Rolls ; to the University of Glasgow for permission to print no. 15 ; to the editor and the publishers of the *Scottish Historical Review* for permission to reprint documents which I have previously printed in that journal ; and to the Trustees of the British Museum for permission to reproduce the frontispiece. I trust that all other formal obligations have been recorded in the footnotes. I have received invaluable assistance from many archivists and librarians, and in particular from the officials of the British Museum, the Public Record Office, the Scottish Record Office, the National Library of Scotland, and the Library of Glasgow University. I cannot attempt to name here all the friends who have come to my aid, but I should have been rash, as one who has no intimate knowledge of Scottish history, genealogy, and topography, to proceed without the advice of Professor G. W. S. Barrow, who has read the proofs with great care, and saved me from many errors. He is not committed thereby to any of my views, and I am sure that his forthcoming life of Robert Bruce will further elucidate many of the documents here printed. The proofs have also been read by Mr Grant Simpson and Mr Bruce Webster, and by Mr W. J. Cook, who has in addition had the great kindness to prepare the index. Mr R. E. Latham has helped me greatly with the Latin texts, and Miss Dominica Legge with those in Anglo-Norman. I owe much also to the late Professor W. Croft Dickinson, and to Professor Andrew Browning, Professor C. J. Fordyce, Dr Cyril Wright, Dr Godfrey Davis, Mr H. C. Johnson, Mr John Imrie, the Rev. Charles Burns, Dr Pierre Chaplais, Dr Donald Watt, Dr Constance Fraser, Mr Richard Stones, and Miss R. N. Stewart. The general editors, and the publishers have been most generous in allowing me scope to deal as I wished with the texts, which present certain problems which are new to this series, and Dr Gweneth Whitteridge has devoted great learning and care to the final preparation of the typescript and proofs. The errors which

remain are mine alone. Finally, I acknowledge with gratitude all that I learned from the advice and criticism of the late Sir Maurice Powicke, since I first read nos. 28 and 30 in his Oxford seminar, twenty-five years ago, and the indispensable help which my wife has given in manifold ways, and at every stage, in the preparation of the book.

E. L. G. STONES

INTRODUCTION

I

THE intercourse between the kingdoms of England and Scotland is one of the main political themes of British history until 1603, and indeed the existence of ' two kings in one poor island ' [1] gives the subject a place of special interest in the history of Europe, even at periods when there was no ' auld alliance ' with France, and no intervention by the Holy See. The relevant Scottish records for the medieval period are now woefully meagre; but the English collections are exceptionally well preserved, and in fact among the archives of English foreign relations in the middle ages they come second in quantity only to those concerning France.[2] The present volume attempts to give a representative selection of official documents from all available sources, but the reader must always remember that our main impression of events has to be derived from English materials, which naturally express the English point of view. Hence the particular value of documents such as nos. 16, 28, 31, and 40, which give direct or indirect evidence of what Scotsmen were thinking or arguing at critical points of the story. It is noteworthy that two of these four examples have been found only within the last few

[1] Sir Walter Scott, *The Talisman*, ch. 3 : ' How mean you,' said the Eastern soldier. ' Have you then two kings in one poor island ? ' ' As thou sayest,' said the Scot, for such was Sir Kenneth by birth, ' it is even so.'

[2] Bain's well-known *Calendar of Documents Relating to Scotland* summarises roughly 8,000 documents in its four volumes. This figure *excludes* all the material in the manuscript collections of the British Museum, and in the 1560 folio pages (double columns of small type, with ' record-type ' abbreviations) of *Rotuli Scotiae* ! An analogous figure for France is not available, and it is a moot point whether to regard Gascony as ' foreign '. If it be so regarded, the figure would doubtless be much larger than for Scotland.

years ; probably others still remain to be discovered in unpublished manuscripts.

It is impossible, of course, to include here more than a very small fraction of the surviving texts, and in making our selection, we have given preference to those which throw special light on contemporary views of the questions at issue, or on the conduct of medieval diplomacy and international relations. We have also given preference to documents which were hitherto unprinted, or available only in bad printed texts or in very inaccessible books. It has been necessary, for reasons of space, to exclude a number of famous documents, and in order to assist the reader we give a list of these below, with a note of where their texts, and if possible translations, may be found.[1] It is hoped that the collection will encourage the habit, which is still not by any means the rule in this branch of history, of consulting the sources before proposing theories. Some readers may find, as the editor has done, that they learn much from these documents which is not suggested, and is sometimes even obscured, by the well-known secondary authorities.

Scotland emerges from relative isolation (and from historical obscurity) towards the end of the eleventh century. One single event was largely responsible : the marriage of King Malcolm III (1058–93 ; the ' Malcolm ' of Shakespeare's *Macbeth*) to Margaret, a great-niece of Edward the Confessor, about the year 1070. Margaret, who was a woman of great energy and determination, did everything in her power to open her husband's kingdom to influence from England and abroad, and her three sons who ruled Scotland in succession from 1097 to 1153, and especially the youngest, David I, continued the same policy. In consequence the English chroniclers became more interested in, and better informed about, Scotland, as may be seen by any reader who turns to Dr A. O. Anderson's collection entitled *Scottish Annals from English Chroniclers*. We

[1] See below, pp. xlix-l.

must attempt here to draw attention, very briefly, to the most significant changes which become apparent in the relations between the two kingdoms during the century before our selections begin.

In the first place, Anglo-Norman civilisation penetrated deeply into Scotland, and affected both church and state to such a degree that in the lowlands, at any rate, society came to resemble very closely that of contemporary England.[1] Inter-marriage drew together the two royal families, and baronial houses, like those of Balliol and Bruce, held lands on each side of the border. The close connexion between the two realms is well seen in the career of St Ailred, an Englishman who spent his early years at the court of David I, gained the position of a steward in the Scottish king's household, and ended his life as abbot of Rievaulx, in Yorkshire.[2] Secondly (and in some measure this was a result of the closer ties between the two kingdoms),[3] the political relationship between England and Scotland entered a more difficult phase. For various reasons the territorial boundaries of Scottish power moved southwards, until David I (1124–53) was in control of Northumberland, Cumberland, and Westmorland (not to speak of the enormous honour of Huntingdon). The Scottish occupation of the northern counties did not long survive David I, but the Scottish claim remained as a source of trouble until its formal abandon-ment in 1237 (no. 7). Another difficulty concerned the nature of the relation between the two crowns. Were they inde-pendent, or did the king of Scots owe homage for his realm to the king of England? To this matter we shall return at a later point in this introduction. Thirdly, as the Scottish church

[1] See R. L. G. Ritchie, *The Normans in Scotland* (1954).
[2] See *Life of Ailred of Rievaulx*, ed. Powicke (Nelson's Medieval Texts, 1950), pp. xxxiii ff. ; *Acts of Malcolm IV, King of Scots*, ed. G. W. S. Barrow (1960), pp. 32-3.
[3] Marriage alliances across the border, for example, provided excuses for royal intervention on behalf of relatives in difficulty, as well as claims of the kind which inspired David I to demand Northumberland.

moved from the isolation of its ' Celtic ' period to become manifestly a province of the Western church, the need became evident to decide where its allegiance lay. Since it had no archbishop of its own, either it must be subject directly to the Holy See, or it must acknowledge the claims (for which there was some rather ambiguous historical authority) of the metropolitan see of York. In the first half of the twelfth century the papacy was inclined, on the whole, to support the claims of York; subsequently it changed its position, and soon after the point at which our selections begin, it declared that the Scottish church was a *filia specialis* of the Holy See.[1]

It would be logical to begin our collection of documents at a date where these main themes—the penetration of Anglo-Norman civilisation, the disputes over territory and homage, the relations between the two churches—first come clearly into view, and this would certainly be many years before our actual starting-point. But we possess no relevant and suitable official document before the treaty of 1174 between Henry II and William the Lion, and we have no choice but to make our beginning there. Fortunately this, the first extant treaty between the two kingdoms, illustrates very well the general tendencies of which we have spoken. It states uncompromisingly the English demand for the homage of Scotland, it hints at English claims upon the subjection of the Scottish church, and in the very names of a number of the Scottish sureties it reveals the presence, in the entourage of the king of Scots, of members of Anglo-Norman families.[2] It is well to remember, however, that this treaty was not in itself an event of profound significance in the relations of the two countries. It lasted for only fifteen years. Curiously enough, the last treaty in our collection, the so-called Treaty of Northampton, was repudiated by Edward III after an even shorter time. The

---

[1] In 1192; see below, p. 14, *n.* 2.
[2] Ritchie, *The Normans in Scotland*, pp. 156, *n.* 4; 285, *n.* 1; 291, *n.* 1

traditional emphasis upon it seems so unjustifiable, that we should have preferred to avoid paying it the compliment implied in giving it so prominent a position; and in any case there are many documents later than 1328 which we should have liked to include.[1] Nevertheless, in the space available here it has seemed best to concentrate attention on the period which ends in 1328, because that period comprehends a high proportion both of the most memorable events, and of the most interesting documents, in the history of the relations between England and Scotland in the middle ages.

It should be observed that any selection of official documents dealing with this subject is bound to emphasise strife and controversy, and to give very inadequate illustration to the ordinary peaceful relationships between the two countries. From 1296 to 1323, indeed, war was almost the rule, but in the predominantly peaceful years before 1296, it is only in the provisions of 1194 for the visits of the king of Scots to England (no. 3) and in the grateful letter of Alexander III to Edward I after receiving Edward's condolences upon his bereavement (no. 13) that our texts give a clear picture of the sort of intercourse between the two kings and realms which was, no doubt, habitual, except at times of crisis. Historical text-books have brought up generations of people, especially perhaps in Scotland, to think only of the invasions of one realm by the armies of the other, of periodic English demands for homage, and of Scottish resistance to them. Thus we easily forget that relations between the two lands were not confined to war and politics, or even to the activities of their governments. The same kind of civilisation was established on both sides of the border, and (as we have said) many leading personalities, royal and baronial, lay and ecclesiastical, were closely connected across the frontier by ties of kindred and common interest. Our

---

[1] We have added one supplementary document of 1401 (below, pp. 173-82) for special reasons explained in the notes. It should be said that some scholars would attach much greater importance to the treaty of 1328.

B

selection cannot illustrate these things at all fairly, but they must be constantly kept in mind.[1]

II. THE HISTORICAL BACKGROUND TO THE DOCUMENTS

It will be appreciated that no attempt can be made here to give even a brief continuous account of the relations of England with Scotland between 1174 and 1328, and what follows is more in the nature of a commentary on some of the principal texts in our collection, and on the most important topics with which they deal. As might be expected, the main element of continuity is to be found in the recurrent claim of the king of England that the king of Scots held his realm as a vassal of the king of England. In the first document selected, the treaty of 1174, William the Lion admits the claim in words that leave no doubt, though he was under coercion as a prisoner. In no. 6 the pope urges Alexander II to fulfil his undertakings as a vassal of Henry III. No. 16 gives the reply of the Scots to Edward I's demand for recognition of his rights as overlord of Scotland. In no. 30 we find the fullest statement ever given of the English defence of these rights, in no. 31 a report of the Scottish counter-claims, and in no. 41a the short-lived renunciation of the English claim, issued in the name of the young Edward III by the government of Isabella and Mortimer. Obviously both sides set great store by this matter, and it has been endlessly debated in more recent times, often with unreasonable heat,[2] and with too little recognition of the assumptions which governed medieval thinking on such questions.

[1] cf. the foundation of Arbroath abbey by William the Lion in 1178 in honour of St Thomas of Canterbury; and the request of the chapter of Glasgow, c. 1259, for details of the liberties and customs of Salisbury (*Reg. Episcopatus Glasguensis* (1843), I, 169-71).

[2] Two examples must suffice: (i) The order by the Scots parliament that William Atwood's pamphlets of 1704-5, on the homage question, should be burned by the common hangman; (ii) the fierce criticism in 1882 of the first volume of Bain's *Calendar*, on account of certain features considered to be derogatory to Scotland (cf. *The Scotsman*, 18 January 1882, p. 9; S.R.O. Historical Dept., Office Record, III, ff. 4, 11ᵛ).

We must begin by reminding ourselves that medieval thinkers had no conception of evolution. To us it is clear enough that the progress of time inevitably brought changes in the relative positions of the two countries, in the degree to which one could impose its will on the other, and in the practical implications of feudal theories. In the middle ages, on the other hand, the past was commonly regarded as a witness to unchanging inherent rights and obligations. Thus the records of the past could, if studied with sufficient care, provide a definite answer to any question of title, and one which was perpetually valid. Hence Edward I, in his letter to Boniface VIII, traces feudal relationships back to the time of the Trojan war (no. 30)! Some modern writers seem seriously to have imagined that they could establish or confound the English claim by historical argument: in other words, that there is a ' correct ' answer to the question whether Scotland was feudally subject to England, and one which is equally true for all periods of the middle ages. But if we look candidly at the documents, we shall see that the inherent rights of the parties are really as imaginary as the supposed terms of the Social Contract. There was not even a fundamental treaty between the countries, like that of 1259 between England and France, to use as the starting-point for argument. Further, the problem never received the continuous study which the Anglo-French controversy did in the eighty years after 1259 ; it arose only at intervals, when homage had to be done at the beginning of a new reign, or when there was some other special reason for difficulty. There were only two occasions—in 1291, and in 1300–1—when the question was considered at all systematically. In short, the position is an impossible one to debate in modern terms. If it were not for the intense national feelings which the subject has aroused, it would long since have been realised that historians are not called upon to settle a controversy of this kind, any more than they are expected to decide

between the theoretical claims of the medieval papacy and the empire.

If we once admit that the legal rights of the case are shadows which historians have pursued in vain, we shall at the same time shed the extreme nervousness which partisan writers have felt lest an admission of *de facto* subjection at any point in time should prejudice their position in general. There need be no embarrassment, therefore, in accepting Professor Duncan's recent contention that the Scottish kings were in practice subject to the kings of England in the later eleventh and the early twelfth centuries.[1] We have seen already that the closer connexion between the kingdoms after *c.* 1070 had naturally raised the question whether a feudal relationship existed between them. When William Rufus lent military support to Duncan II and Edgar in 1094 and 1097, it was an understandable, though not a necessary, conclusion for an English observer to draw, that Rufus was acting as their feudal superior. In 1126 we find the archbishop of York assuring the pope that ' the king of Scots was the king of England's man for Scotland '; and obscure as are the details of the homages of Malcolm IV some thirty years later, we can hardly doubt that many English observers must have interpreted them in the same sense.[2] Then in 1174, at the beginning of our period, a lucky chance, which some observers interpreted as an act of divine favour, and which brought William the Lion as a prisoner into the hands of Henry II, gave Henry the opportunity to force from William a written acknowledgment of his subjection in the Treaty ' of Falaise ' (no. 1).[3] In 1189 Richard I restored the *status quo* by the Treaty of Canterbury (no. 2). A damaged exemplar survives in the Register House, Edinburgh, and since no. 1 is

---

[1] A. A. M. Duncan, ' The Earliest Scottish Charters ', *SHR*, xxxvii (1958), 103-35

[2] *Hugh the Chantor*, ed. Johnson (Nelson's Medieval Texts, 1961), p. 126; Poole, *Domesday Book to Magna Carta*, pp. 275-6

[3] This name is traditional, but it will be observed that the version which we print was executed at Valognes. See below, p. 1, n. 1.

extant only in transcripts, this is the oldest original of an Anglo-Scottish treaty in existence. It is very difficult to tell the exact significance of the Treaty of Canterbury, partly because we know so little of the practical use which Henry II had made of William's subjection,[1] and partly because our whole knowledge of Anglo-Scottish relations in the later years of William the Lion is, in any case, so fragmentary.[2] A well-informed English chronicler of the time thought that in 1189 Richard had released William ' and his heirs from all allegiance for the realm of Scotland '.[3] This is not what the text of the treaty (no. 2) says,[4] and it does not correspond with William's attitude, so far as we know it, during the rest of his reign (e.g. nos. 3 and 4). One suspects that to William the restoration of the *status quo* meant chiefly the return of the Scottish castles still in Henry's hands. This was the first item in the treaty of 1189, and it is particularly stressed by William of Newburgh, who was also a very careful and well-informed chronicler.[5] In addition, no doubt, William the Lion wished to abolish the direct homage and fealty of the Scottish magnates to the English crown, which had been enforced in 1174.[6] Otherwise, his conduct suggests that he was not unwilling to accept English suzerainty.[7]

The leaders of the Scottish church in this period seem to have been more anxious for independence than was the crown ;[8]

---

[1] See G. W. S. Barrow, in *SHR*, xxxvi, 138-43.

[2] See below, pp. xlv-xlviii.

[3] ' Benedict of Peterborough ' (ed. Stubbs, RS, 1867), II, 98, 102-4. *Chronica de Mailros*, p. 98, may be asserting the same thing in vaguer language. cf. John Allen, *Vindication of Ancient Independence of Scotland* (1833), p. 29 ; but it is dangerous to assume, as Allen does, that a chronicler's statement is conclusive evidence of the contemporary interpretation of a treaty. Chroniclers sometimes give very garbled reports of treaties.

[4] Hence the spurious passages added later to the Scottish text F (see no. 2, textual notes).

[5] *Chronicles of Stephen, Henry II, and Richard I* (RS, 1884-5), I, 304. This, of course, must be treated with the caution suggested in the above note.

[6] Below, pp. 1-2

[7] Below, nos. 3 and 4. cf. Stubbs, *Constitutional History of England*, I (6th ed., 1897), 595-7 and notes.

[8] This is also true at a later period ; cf. the prominent part played by churchmen during the War of Independence (e.g. Wishart and Lamberton,

or perhaps it would be truer to say that their education gave
them a better understanding of written undertakings and a
keener desire for exact definition of their rights. The see of
York, as we have already seen, had an ancient claim to archiepiscopal jurisdiction over Scotland. The Treaty of Falaise
bound the Scottish church, in rather ambiguous terms, to
' owe such subjection to the church of England as it should do
and was accustomed to do ',[1] and no doubt the English intention was that the claim of York should now be met; but this
was not to be. In 1192 the pope issued a privilege (the original
has not survived) granting independence to the Scottish church
as a *filia specialis* of the Holy See. The terms of this grant were
repeated in the splendid privilege of 1218 which is still extant
in the Register House, Edinburgh, and which we give as no. 5.

The papacy was willing, nevertheless, to support English
claims to secular dominion over Scotland. In no. 6, Gregory
IX writes to Alexander II, reminding him of the homage and
fealty which he owes to the king of England (1235). One
English demand, however, the papacy would not support: the
claim that a Scottish king must not be anointed or crowned
without the permission of the English king (no. 9). Clearly
this demand trespassed on the rights of the Holy See (*talia
concedere sedes apostolica minime consuevit*). Yet it is to be observed
that no Scottish king was anointed at his inauguration until a
papal grant of this privilege was made in 1329. The story
behind this matter is not fully known, but it is to be suspected
that papal concern for English feelings was sufficient to delay
the grant of unction, though not to make the pope accept the
principle that the English should control the use of the privilege
if once granted.

Relations between Alexander II, who succeeded William
the Lion in 1214, and Henry III were for many years under

cf. nos. 34 and 35 below). See, however, G. W. S. Barrow, ' The Scottish
Clergy (etc.) ', *SHR*, XLI (1962), 1-22.
   [1] Below, p. 2

some strain, in spite of Alexander's marriage to Henry's sister in 1221. Henry can hardly have forgotten that Alexander had sided with the English rebels during the English civil war of 1216–17. Then, when Henry was securely on the throne, Alexander chose to revive the old claim of the Scottish kings to Northumberland, Cumberland, and Westmorland.[1] A treaty was eventually concluded, with the help of the papal legate Otto, at York in 1237 (no. 7). Alexander abandoned his territorial claims, but was given some lands in England in compensation. So ended the dispute over the three northern counties of England. The details of this document provide an interesting commentary on the minor problems of the existence, side by side, of the two separate kingdoms.

After Alexander's death in 1249 there was a royal minority of thirteen years, during which the relations of the two countries were especially close, because the young Alexander III married a daughter of Henry III, who showed much care and anxiety about the welfare of the young people. No. 10 records the establishment of a new Scottish council of government at the instance of Henry, who had come north to rescue Alexander from certain ' rebel ' councillors[2] (1255). In no. 11 (1258) Henry declares his approval of a new regime, set up in Scotland as the aftermath of a *coup d'état*, in which Alexander had been seized by a party acting at the instigation of the Comyn family. The events of these years are less well-known than they should be. They anticipate in some ways (as Sir Maurice Powicke has remarked) the supervision of Scottish affairs by Edward I after the death of Alexander III. They must have been remembered, when that crisis arose, by Edward himself, and by some of the guardians of 1286–91 ; and among the competitors for the Scottish crown in 1291, Bruce, at least, was old enough to

---

[1] See above, p. xv.
[2] Such is the interpretation of Fordun (pp. 296-7) ; but it is fair to say that the chronicle of Melrose regards the episode in a different light, and depicts some of these ' rebels ' as patriots (pp. 180-1).

remember them well, and to several others they must have been known by family tradition. It is very possible that Alexander III, when he came to be of age, looked back with gratitude upon the help which he had received from England during his minority.[1] Certainly there is no other period in the middle ages when the personal relations of the two kings are known to have been so good as they were during the maturity of Alexander III. We possess a considerable number of letters from Alexander to Edward, and a few from Edward to Alexander. The former, in view of their interest for the diplomatic of Scottish royal correspondence, deserve close study.[2] Many are in a very damaged or illegible state, and the letter which we have selected (no. 13) is one of these (1284). Its special interest, however, makes it an inevitable choice: Alexander writes to thank Edward, in moving terms, for his letter of consolation after the death of his son, Edward's nephew. There are not many sadder things in British history than the extinction, by the premature deaths of Alexander in 1286 and of his granddaughter in 1290, of this promise of abiding friendship between the two kingdoms.

It is remarkable how little feeling of crisis seems to have arisen after the death of Alexander III. Less than two months afterwards, Edward I set out for Gascony, where he stayed, with apparent unconcern, for three years. We know very little of what was happening in Scotland during that time, but the regents, acting on behalf of the Maid of Norway, seem to have kept the peace without difficulty. After Edward's return, in 1289, elaborate arrangements were made for a marriage between the Maid and the future Edward II which would, if all went well, bring about the union of the two kingdoms.[3]

---

[1] This is a matter of opinion, depending on the view taken of the episodes of 1255 and 1258 already mentioned.

[2] Fortunately these long-neglected letters of Alexander III will be printed in vol. IV of *Regesta Regum Scottorum*, to be edited by Mr Grant G. Simpson.

[3] It has not been possible to include these famous treaties here; for references see below, p. xlix, nos. 2 and 3.

The death of the Maid in the autumn of 1290, when all these cherished schemes had been finally ratified, is the beginning of a period of eight critical months which is very dark in the records. It is not well enough realised how dark it is.[1] We have no document in which the Scots actually ask Edward to settle the disputed succession, no record of his acceptance, and none of whatever summons he issued to the claimants, and to the magnates of both realms, to assemble for the hearing of the ' Great Cause '. In these circumstances it is rash to be dogmatic at any point. From May 1291, on the other hand, when the ' Great Cause ' began, we are almost overwhelmed with records, but here the story is full of difficulties of another kind : the evidence is contradictory and the bulk of the materials has disguised the fact that some important events are imperfectly recorded, or not recorded at all.

The documents which we give here from the period of the ' Great Cause ' are seven in number. (1) The appeals of the seven earls of Scotland (no. 14). Whatever we make of this strange document, it cannot be the missing request for Edward's intervention, to which we have referred. It is a complaint to Edward against the behaviour of the bishop of St Andrews, John Comyn, and John Balliol. The real cause of dispute can hardly be what appears on the surface : the infringement by the guardians of the alleged rights of the earls. It is more likely that the guardians were already manœuvring in favour of Balliol as king, and that their conduct was resented by the complainants. This document, which has been well described as 'the first in the great series relating to the "Great Cause"',[2] survives only in a transcript, and we have no evidence of its

---

[1] The assumption of some Scottish historians that Edward planned the subjugation of Scotland from the first is hardly borne out by the evidence of his inactivity in these crucial months. The absence of records is probably due in the main to his preoccupations, especially with the illness, death, and funeral of his beloved wife, Eleanor, after which he actually went into retirement for five weeks. See F. M. Powicke, *Henry III and the Lord Edward*, (1947), II, 733-5.

[2] *110th Report of Deputy-Keeper of Public Records* (1950), p. 19

date, or of the circumstances of its presentation to Edward. We print it in a more complete form than has hitherto been available. (2) A speech which appears to give the original version of what was said by Roger Brabazon, justice of the king's bench, when he opened the ' Great Cause ' at Norham in May 1291. It is here printed for the first time (no. 15). (3) A statement made by the Scottish representatives at Norham, concerning Edward's demand for the homage of Scotland (no. 16). (4) ' The award of Norham ', a sealed acknowledgment by the competitors of Edward's lordship over Scotland (no. 17). (5) A charter in which Bruce the competitor surrenders his rights in the Scottish succession to his son (no. 18). This document was issued at a point where it was plain that the older Bruce had no hope of success; but his precise purpose in making the grant is not clear. It has hitherto been available in print only in an exceedingly rare seventeenth-century book : this is one reason for its reproduction here. (6) An extract from the fullest record of the climax of the ' Great Cause ', when judgment is given in favour of Balliol (no. 19). (7) A notarial instrument (hitherto unprinted in this form) recording the homage of Balliol to Edward I after his coronation (no. 20). No attempt can be made here to discuss the intricate problems of the documents of the ' Great Cause ', which still await comprehensive treatment.[1]

The ' Great Cause ' was the occasion of the first and better-known of Edward I's essays in historical research into the claims of his predecessors to the homage of Scotland.[2] Though we do not print any of the documents concerned with this episode, we are bound to mention here an enterprise which contributed most of the historical materials to be found in Edward's famous letter to Boniface VIII in 1301 (no. 30). It seems always to have been assumed that the whole of the

---

[1] See E. L. G. Stones in *SHR*, xxxv, 89-109.
[2] The second was in 1300–1 ; see no. 30 and notes.

historical evidence quoted in John of Caen's ' Great Roll '
came from returns submitted by the monasteries. Closer study
of the text shows that Edward's clerks almost certainly possessed
texts of some complete chronicles, and the appeal to the
monasteries for information in March 1291,[1] only two months
before the opening of the ' Great Cause ' at Norham, seems to
have been a last-minute enterprise, inspired by their discovery
that the material in the chronicles which they possessed, and
that which was available in the royal archives, was insufficient.[2]
Probably, therefore, the well-known historical summary in
Caen's ' Great Roll ' was not ready in time to be produced at
Norham in May 1291, though it was to prove invaluable to the
English government ten years later, when their case had to be
made good to the pope.[3]

When Balliol had been settled on the throne of Scotland,
Edward would have been wise to allow his own claims to
recede into the background, to be revived only at the inauguration of Balliol's successor. He must have known, from his
experience as duke of Guienne, the discomfort which he was
creating for Balliol by insisting on his right to hear appeals
against Balliol's judgments in Scotland. The situation is
illustrated in the case printed as no. 21. The end was bound
to be war, but before a vassal could make war on his lord he
had to sever the feudal bond in a formal ' diffidatio ' (no. 23,
here printed for the first time in this notarial version). In April

---

[1] Not March 1290, as often stated ; the date 1290 is based on a misdated
text in Palgrave, *Documents*, p. 89, where *anno regni nostri decimo octavo* is an
error.

[2] Even the treaty ' of Falaise ', though available in transcripts in the
exchequer, had to be cited from an imperfect chronicle text, and this has
influenced the textual history of the treaty down to modern times (see below,
p. 1, *n.*). An illustration of the hurried searches of 1291 is to be seen
in the record of payment to a messenger who had ' hastened to the king
with a letter of William king of Scotland touching the homage which he did
to king John ' (a document which may be no. 4 below, or perhaps the lost
treaty of 1209, see p. xlv). This was only a few days before the opening of
the ' Great Cause ' (Stevenson, *Documents*, I, 225 : 4 May 1291).

[3] Caen's ' Great Roll ' cannot be proved to have been in existence
before 1297 (Stones, *SHR* xxxv, p. 93).

1296 Balliol was defeated, and had to surrender his realm, by a document under his great seal (no. 24),[1] and to go to England as a prisoner. There followed a long series of documents recording the fealty of individual Scotsmen to Edward (commonly called the *Ragman Rolls*) which are here represented by a little-known text which shows that the elder and the younger Bruce submitted on 25 March 1296, before Edward had even crossed the frontier of Scotland (no. 22). A year later William Wallace rose to power, ruling (with a colleague) in the name of the exiled John Balliol. Two documents issued by him in this capacity are given as no. 26. We set beside them, as an appropriate commentary on this use of Balliol's name, a very little-known text in which the same Balliol declares that he will never return to a kingdom which he had found so little to his liking. Edward was clearly in little danger now from Balliol's ambition, though a few years later there seems to have been a passing alarm about his return with French support.[2] But the Franco-Scottish alliance of 1295 (the ' auld alliance '), a direct result of Edward's policy during Balliol's reign, had made it possible for Philip IV of France to exploit Edward's difficulties in Scotland; and in 1299 Pope Boniface VIII also entered the field. In a famous bull, the splendid original of which survives in the Public Record Office, he claimed Scotland as a papal fief, and ordered Edward to withdraw from its borders (no. 28).

This bull, and the documents which arose from it, are of singular interest, since we find there (*a*) a statement of the Scottish case against Edward, (*b*) the advice given to Edward I by his clerks about a reply (no. 29), (*c*) Edward's reply, sent in May 1301 (no. 30), (*d*) a report describing the comments[3] of the Scots upon Edward's reply (no. 31). The rival view-points

---

[1] It was later alleged that this surrender was a forgery; see below, p. 73, *n.*

[2] cf. E. L. G. Stones in *SHR*, xxxiv, 122-34.

[3] For the full text of these comments see *Scotichronicon*, II, 192-218.

are thus well represented. As events turned out, however, Edward had no immediate cause to worry. The pope soon ceased to support the Scots, and Edward continued his war. At some uncertain date in 1301 or 1302, Robert Bruce (the grandson of the competitor of 1291), who had been involved in the rebellion of 1297 and had not subsequently been reconciled, came back to his allegiance, under terms which have recently been discovered (no. 32) ; he fought for Edward at the siege of Stirling in 1304, and was present at the Westminster parliament of February 1305. In the same year a lengthy ordinance was issued which was intended to secure peace (no. 33). From the English point of view, everything seemed to be set for a fair future.

With this document in mind we can more readily understand the shock caused to Edward's plans by Bruce's rebellion in the spring of 1306, after his murder of Comyn. Some of our very meagre information about Bruce's coronation at Scone in March of that year comes from the confession of Lamberton, here printed for the first time (no. 35). As Mr Charles Johnson showed, many years ago,[1] we also possess an important account of Bruce's movements, during the period before his coronation, in a Cottonian MS. This text is here given (no. 34) in a form which is more complete and (it is hoped) more accurate than the existing printed version.

The remainder of our texts illustrate the rise of Bruce from the state of a hunted fugitive to that of a king acknowledged in both realms. One of them is a formal declaration of the Scottish clergy in his favour (no. 36).[2] In 1323 the earl of Carlisle negotiated a peace with Bruce without reference to Edward II (no. 39). For this offence he was hanged, but it is noteworthy that his agreement in some ways foreshadowed the peace which came in 1328. Bruce's terms (discovered only a

---

[1] Charles Johnson in *EHR*, xxxiii, 366-7
[2] On the chronological difficulties see below, p. 140, *n*.

few years ago) for entering upon the negotiations which led to the peace of Northampton are given as no. 40. It is often implied that the peace was an abject surrender by the English. It must indeed have seemed to many Englishmen that the marriage of their king's sister to the son of a late rebel (p. 165), and the surrender of the ancient claim for homage (no. 41 *a*), entitled the agreement to be called a *turpis pax*. The modern reader, while applauding the good sense of the decision to end a fruitless war, is puzzled rather by the willingness of Bruce to pay £20,000 for the recognition which he had won by the sword. It *may* be that he was in fact granting the English government something to atone for the sum which he had exacted from northern England as blackmail during the previous twenty years.[1] Perhaps we should also remember that until quite modern times it was considered reasonable that men should not be asked to surrender what they held to be their legal rights, without material compensation.[2] Some credit should be given to the English negotiators (perhaps to Queen Isabella in particular) for gradually moving Bruce from his firm stand against restoration of Scottish estates to the ' disinherited ' adherents of Edward III.[3] A document recording such a restoration to Henry Percy of Alnwick, which seems hitherto not to have been used in discussions of this matter, is given as the last of our series.

Bruce's triumph, however, was mainly personal, and not based on a settled power. His death in 1329, followed by a minority, and by the renewal of English aggression in 1332, made this very evident ; and the terms which David was

---

[1] See Jean Scammell, *EHR*, LXXIII (1958), 385-403. But it must be noted that in 1323 Bruce was willing to pay the larger sum of 40,000 marks (below, p. 156).

[2] cf. payment of 10,000 marks in 1189 (below, p. 6, *n*. 1) ; the financial terms of the Anglo-French treaty of 1259 (Rymer, I, i, 383-4) ; and perhaps we might add the protest of Lord Mansfield and other peers against the Reform Bill of 1832 (Grant Robertson, *Statutes, Cases and Documents 1660–1832*, p. 346).

[3] On the possible rôle of Isabella see Stones, *SHR*, XXIX (1950), 34-5.

prepared to accept from Edward III in 1363 [1] show that the
independence of Scotland was by no means assured, and
that there were not a few prominent Scotsmen who were
but little concerned to maintain it. The supplementary
document on pp. 173-82 displays the demand for homage as
late as 1401, though it was now beginning to take on the
character of a mere opening move in formalities which normally
petered out in the making of a truce. The old tradition died
hard. John Hardyng, the poet and chronicler, thought it
worth while to forge new and more convincing documents for
Henry V and Henry VI, in support of the ancient claims of
England,[2] and nearly a century later it was still possible for
Henry VIII to renew the old demand for homage.[3] It was left
for his realistically-minded younger daughter to abandon it,
tacitly but finally, in 1560.[4]

III. The Archives

The great majority of the documents concerning Anglo-
Scottish relations in the middle ages are now in the Public
Record Office and the British Museum. The remainder are
in the General Register House, Edinburgh, the Archives
Nationales, Paris, and a variety of other places. It is easy to
forget, in our regret at the poverty of materials in Edinburgh,
that the really remarkable thing is not the amount which
Scotland has lost but the amount which England has preserved.
The documents in the Archives Nationales, for example, bearing
on Franco-Scottish relations between 1295 and 1326, must be a
mere fragment of what once existed. It is not too much to say
that whatever documents Edward I removed from Edinburgh
had a better chance of survival among the English records than
those which remained in Scotland. We know, for instance,

[1] Rymer, III, ii, 715-16
[2] Palgrave, *Documents*, pp. cxcvi-ccxxiv ; *DNB*, *sub nomine* Hardyng
[3] J. D. Mackie, ' Henry VIII and Scotland ', *TRHistS*, xxix (1947),
104-5   [4] F. W. Maitland, *Selected Historical Essays* (1957), p. 185

that the original of 41 *a* was still in existence in Scotland in the early fifteenth century, but it has now disappeared. A certain amount of myth has been allowed to grow around this whole subject. Statements have been made about removals of Scottish records by Edward I which have no foundation in the documentary evidence, and there is even one document that has been 'returned' at some modern date from London to Edinburgh, though it is indubitably an English record, and could never have been 'removed' from Scotland by Edward I, or by anyone else.[1] Bruce has been credited with demanding the 'return' of records by the treaty of 1328, though a reasonably careful reading of its text shows that he was only making a request, common in diplomatic negotiations,[2] for the surrender of obsolete documents which bore on the questions in dispute, and a number of these, perhaps even the majority, would not be 'Scottish' records at all.[3] Moreover he was prepared to send them back again to England if the marriage alliance were not fulfilled! These facts disprove any assertion that Bruce was interested in retrieving Scottish muniments as such.[4] In point of fact our collection contains five documents now preserved in Edinburgh (nos. 2, 3, 5, 36, 41 *c*) of which three (nos. 2, 3, 5) were transmitted from London, by Act of Parliament, in 1937.[5]

[1] This is the indenture of 30 December 1292 between Edward I and Balliol, printed in *APS*, I, 113-17 [red]. The seal of Balliol shows that this is the *English* counterpart; it has therefore no claim to be a Scottish record, and (on the assumptions which have prompted certain agitations in Scotland) it should doubtless be transferred to the Public Record Office. How it came to be in Edinburgh is unknown. It has also been argued that no. 6 below, simply because it is addressed to the king of Scots, must have come originally from the Scottish archives, but there is excellent evidence that the exemplar now in the P.R.O. was in England before Edward I went to war with Scotland. It may be a duplicate of the exemplar sent to Scotland (cf. the bulls of Urban IV addressed in 1263 to the bishop of St. Andrews, now in the Archives Nationales : Teulet, *Inventaire chronologique* (Abbotsford Club, 1839), pp. 1-2). See also p. 44 below, note on text.

[2] e.g. pp. 7, 24 below

[3] e.g. nos. 17, 22, 24. cf. E. L. G. Stones, *History*, XXXVIII, 56-61.

[4] cf. pp. 167-8 below.

[5] The ' Public Records (Scotland) Act ' of that year. For subsequent

It should be stressed, however, that the scarcity of the documents in the Scottish national archives ought not to deter searchers in other Scottish collections. Though there is perhaps little hope of the discovery of unknown originals, the possibility of fresh materials being found in transcripts among the private archives, or in the public or private libraries of Scotland, must not be neglected: witness the important charter bearing upon Henry II's overlordship of Scotland discovered by Professor Barrow,[1] and the manuscript in Glasgow, from which we have taken nos. 15 and 16. Nor should we overlook the lesser-known English collections, and archives overseas. Recently the chapter library of Exeter cathedral has proved to possess an unknown exemplar of Andrew de Tange's ' Great Roll '.[2] As for overseas collections, the Bergen MS mentioned on p. 154 below, and the remarkable discovery by Mr Simpson in the archives at the Hague,[3] make it clear that a thorough search of foreign archives is unlikely to prove vain; and it is hard to believe (giving only one instance) that Edward I's consultation of French lawyers at the time of the ' Great Cause ' has left no trace at all in records outside Great Britain.[4]

We may treat the documents at the British Museum and those in the Public Record Office as one collection, since the former are almost all in the Cotton collection, and must be regarded as ' strays ' from the ill-guarded public records of Cotton's day. It would be well to begin by looking at the matter from the viewpoint of the medieval English clerks. Scottish affairs were never, so far as we know, placed in the hands of a specific official, like the *custos processuum* who looked

transfers see *110th Report of Deputy-Keeper*, pp. 4-5, 16-21. The record evidence for removals of records from Scotland between 1296 and 1323 is given on pp. 75-6 below; and cf. p. 116 below.

[1] p. 1 below, *n.* 1
[2] E. L. G. Stones in *SHR*, xxxix, 86-7
[3] Grant G. Simpson in *SHR*, xxxvi, 111-24
[4] The opinions of certain French lawyers are given in *Scotichronicon*, II, 139-45, but this is the only known reference to the episode in any source (B.M. MS Additional 47214 gives the same material in a separate form).

after documents relating to France during the reigns of Edward I, II, and III.[1] The Chancery kept no *Rotuli Scotiae* until 1291, and even after then the series was often discontinued if Scottish business seemed sufficiently small to enable it to be entered on the Patent and Close Rolls. The lack of ready means of reference must have become evident in 1291, when Edward had to write to the monasteries for information which could in part have been had in his own archives ;[2] and this experience may well account for the opening of *Rotuli Scotiae* by the Chancery, the preparation of a section styled *Scotia* in the great register Liber A, then nearing completion,[3] and the compilation of John of Caen's superb ' Great Roll ' of the ' Great Cause '. The matter was taken up again in the reign of Edward II, when Andrew de Tange prepared a new ' Great Roll ',[4] covering the events of 1291–6, and when a section was assigned, in Bishop Stapledon's calendar of documents,[5] to records relating to Scotland. The sections in Liber A and in Stapledon's calendar, so far as we know, are the only surveys of Scottish documents which were made. When Henry IV wished for information, in 1400, on his rights in Scotland, the relevant folios of Liber A were removed from the book and sent to him (never, it may be noted, to return ; the volume still lacks them).[6] At the same time he was supplied by the Chancery with fifteen original Chancery Rolls, relating, in the main, to Scottish affairs.[7] It seems, therefore, that by the fifteenth century, though the Chancery clerks had no indexes that we know of to help them, they could produce, on demand, a surprising number of relevant documents.

The next attempt at classification came in the seventeenth

[1] G. P. Cuttino, *English Diplomatic Administration* (1940), pp. 19-48
[2] See above, p. xxvii ; below, p. 1, note on text.
[3] E. L. G. Stones in *SHR*, xxxv, 98-9 and refs. Note that the *Scotia* section had no documents earlier than 1291.
[4] Stones, art. cit., p. 102
[5] On Stapledon's calendar see Cuttino, op. cit., pp. 82-3.
[6] Stones, art. cit., p. 99
[7] Palgrave, *Kalendars*, iii, 361-3

century, when that redoubtable student of the records, Arthur
Agarde, compiled a catalogue of the documents relating to
Scotland which were then kept in the chapter-house at Westminster.[1] It is arranged in chronological order, beginning with
a (forged) document of 1065, and continuing to 1586. The
arrangement in sacks and boxes, as it was in his own day, is
recorded; but who was responsible for it is not clear. Comparison with Stapledon's inventory shows considerable changes
in the materials before 1323; a great deal of Stapledon's
material has vanished, and a few new documents have appeared
which escaped Stapledon's notice. This list of Agarde's is
important because the documents there given are the nucleus
of the present Public Record Office series called *Scottish Documents, Exchequer* (E 39). Archivists since Agarde have added
other documents to it, but without destroying its essential
character as a medieval ' archive-group '. A considerable
number of the documents bear the original endorsements of
Stapledon's clerks. The collection has suffered grievously,
since Agarde's time, from damp and from vermin, and some
of the documents have disappeared altogether. It is now
arranged almost entirely in separate membranes rather than
in files, and this system renders any extensive research in E 39
a somewhat tedious matter, though the poor condition of the
documents probably makes it unavoidable.

The great use made of this series E 39 in the printed works
of Rymer and Palgrave bears witness to its importance.[2] But
precisely because of its use by Rymer and Palgrave, and
because it was the only series to have been listed at an early date,
it has tended unduly to overshadow the other materials. The
Rotuli Scotiae, it is true, were printed as early as 1814–19, but

---

[1] Ayloffe, *Calendars*, pp. 287-325
[2] The following texts in this volume are taken from E 39, or depend
partly upon it: nos. 2, 3 (both now in Edinburgh), 14, 17, 20, 22, 24, 35.
In Agarde's time no. 6 (now classified under ' Papal Bulls ') was kept in the
same collection, and probably nos. 5, 9, 18, 23, 28, and 31 belong originally
to the same series.

their concern is mainly with English administration in matters concerning Scotland, and their value can easily be over-estimated. The rich materials for Scotland in the *Chancery Miscellanea* (C 47) and in *Ancient Correspondence* (S.C. 1) on the other hand, were little known until Joseph Bain began to work upon them in 1879.[1] The *Chancery Miscellanea* is an ill-defined accretion, from which the Scottish materials have been arbitrarily separated, in modern times, to form bundles 22 and 23. Over 200 letters in the sixty-two volumes of *Ancient Correspondence* relate to Scotland.[2]

The collections which we have mentioned do not, of course, exhaust the resources of Scottish material in the Public Record Office. There are many categories of record which Bain did not search, and others in which he missed things of great importance.[3] It would be rash to say that no further major discoveries remain to be made; those who have said this in the past have too often been proved to be wrong.

We have already twice had occasion to refer to the work of Joseph Bain. His *Calendar of Documents Relating to Scotland*,[4] published between 1881 and 1888, was a pioneer work of paramount importance for the study of Scottish history, and is still the first book to which the student working among the great collections of Anglo-Scottish documents will normally turn. For this very reason it is important, and not out of place here, to draw attention to defects in Bain's work which the circumstances of its compilation made inevitable, and which it might seem churlish to mention, were it not for the too implicit reliance which historians continue to place upon it. This is in no way to detract from Bain's achievement. If we

---

[1] Joseph Stevenson had printed two of the thirteen files comprising the Scottish section of C 47 in his *Documents* of 1870.

[2] Nos. 4, 8, 13, and 38 *a* to *h* below belong to *Ancient Correspondence*.

[3] Below, p. xxxvii.

[4] Bain (1826–1911, not in the *DNB*) matriculated at Glasgow University in 1842, and for a time practised as a solicitor in Glasgow; but he worked in London from *c.* 1876. See C. Rogers, *Family of Bain* (1871), and E. L. G. Stones, 'Joseph Bain', *Archives*, VI (1963–4), 78–84, 172–7.

appreciate something of the handicaps under which he was working, at a time when the Public Records were enormously more difficult of access than they are to-day,[1] and when, in the very nature of his work, it was necessary to read not one homogeneous single category of documents, but virtually the whole range of the relevant medieval archives, we shall marvel that any man was able to complete the work in so short a time, with no more defects than there actually are.

The main points to be remembered in using Bain's *Calendar* are as follows :

(1) A number of important documents in the Public Record Office are omitted; for example nos. 29, 32, and most of 38 below. Here it should be noted that Bain never professed to have read through the huge bulk of the Exchequer Memoranda Rolls after 1327; he had to rely on the medieval ' repertories ', which are entirely inadequate for a search of this kind.[2]

(2) False datings of documents. In a chronological calendar, undated documents have either to be assigned a date, or put in an appendix without a date. It might have been better for posterity if Bain had chosen the latter course. His guesses are often right, but where they are wrong they have frequently caused great confusion.

(3) Misreadings of the script, and mistranslations of the original languages, are common enough to demand constant care by the modern user. This is particularly true of documents in French; no doubt the notorious shortcomings of Anglo-Norman scholarship in England in Bain's day go far to account for this.

(4) A forgivable, but dangerous foible, is his tendency to

---

[1] A. E. Stamp, ' The Historical Student and the P.R.O.', *TRHistS*, xi (1928), 17-37, especially 24-5.
[2] Nor did he explore ' Diplomatic Documents, Chancery ' (C 47, bundles 27-32), a collection curiously neglected by students of Anglo-Scottish relations, witness, e.g., no. 29 below.

confuse a new document with an old one already in print, and to put the reader off the scent by giving a misleading reference to the old one.[1]

If the modern student wishes to use ' Bain ' extensively, he would be well advised to take his own copy to the Public Record Office, and to enter in it the corrigenda which have been carefully made during the period since Bain's time, in the search-room copies.[2] He will also, of course, find there all the modern apparatus of reference to documents whose references in ' Bain ' are now obsolete.[3] Used with precautions such as these, Bain's *Calendar* is still an invaluable work. Without them, it is full of dangers for the student.

It may be helpful to end this survey of the archive material with some comments on the principal editions in which documents concerning Anglo-Scottish relations can be found *in extenso*. The first (drawn entirely from the records of the Chancery) was edited by Prynne, in vol. III of his famous *Exact Chronological Vindication* . . . (1670). Some of his materials have disappeared since they were printed, for example the original of no. 27 below. Prynne also printed our nos. 28, 29, 30, and 33. His transcripts are, in general, exceedingly accurate. Next came Rymer's *Foedera* (1704–17), on which comment is not called for here, except to observe that Rymer printed a large selection from the materials in E 39, many of which have become illegible since his day, and for which therefore he is a prime authority. He knew hardly anything of C 47 and little of *Ancient Correspondence*; but he printed a great deal of Scottish material from the Chancery Rolls, including the Scottish Rolls. The latter were printed by the Record Commission in full, except for certain ' vacated ' instruments, and letters of protection; omissions which now seem unfortu-

---

[1] For examples see Stones, ' Records of Great Cause ', p. 97.
[2] cf. C. R. Cheney, *Records of Medieval England* (1956), p. 11.
[3] It is desirable to avoid the inconvenient practice of citing Bain's obsolete references, such as ' Tower Miscellaneous Rolls '.

nate. The Commission's new edition of Rymer (1816–69) added a good deal of new material, including the long-lost indentures of the Treaty of Northampton. Sir Francis Palgrave made available from E 39 a great mass of new documents of the time of Edward I in his *Documents and Records* of 1837. Unfortunately his introduction completely ignored the complementary evidence of the C 47 material, and the misconceptions so caused have hindered criticism of the sources even until the present day. Thomas Thomson printed the *Ragman Roll* (a notarial transcript of the homages done to Edward in 1296) in 1834. The last big accession of material *in extenso* came in 1870, when the veteran scholar Joseph Stevenson published two volumes of documents from the period of Edward I, selected from a wide range of materials in the Public Record Office and elsewhere.[1] Since then, apart from some documents printed in full in appendices to Bain's *Calendar*, the main additions of such documents have been in periodical publications.[2]

It is unfortunate that Stevenson and Palgrave selected their documents almost exclusively from the reign of Edward I. We may readily admit the special interest of Edward's reign, which in fact supplies rather more than half the contents of the present volume; but it is most regrettable that the materials [3] which Palgrave assembled for a continuation of his *Documents* beyond 1307 were never printed. Nowadays it is too much to expect that such an enterprise can ever be resumed. Yet a part of the same purpose might be achieved, if the plans which the Public Record Office is understood to have for documents relating to France could be extended to include Scotland. These plans involve (it is believed) printing in full all those diplomatic documents in the class C 47 of which satisfactory

---

[1] Unfortunately these useful volumes abound in misreadings, as may be seen from the corrected search-room copies in the Public Record Office.

[2] Listed in bibliography, pp. li-lv below

[3] These transcripts are now P.R.O. 31/7, vols. 61-4. They seem to have been made in 1834.

texts do not already exist in print.[1] If the Scottish documents
in C 47 could be added to such a scheme, and the unsatisfactory printed texts from E 39 treated in the same way, it
would help to redress the balance between the reign of Edward
I and other periods, and in a manner which is not inconsistent
with modern principles in the publication of archives.

IV. SECONDARY WORKS

An adequate discussion of secondary works on our subject
is impossible within the space of this introduction, but we would
draw attention to the special value of Lord Hailes's *Annals of
Scotland*, published in 1776–9. Hailes has been superseded only
where records have come to light which were unknown to him ;
and he knew so well the records that were in print in his day
that some serious errors could have been avoided by later
historians if they had noted him more carefully.[2] After Hailes
we need scarcely look for any major advance until the publication of Bain's *Calendar* (1881–8) made available so great a mass
of new material. Unfortunately the invitation which Bain's
work gave for a systematic and comprehensive study of Anglo-
Scottish relations has never been accepted. It was too special-
ized a topic to be dealt with as part of a *History of Scotland* ;
and in any case Hill Burton died in the year of Bain's first
volume, Andrew Lang was not versed in medieval records,
and Hume Brown was writing a text-book, in which the
medieval period was given relatively short shrift.[3] We still

---

[1] *115th Report of Deputy-Keeper* (1953), p. 24
[2] For example, the speculations whether the Declaration of Arbroath
ever reached the pope seem to have been made in ignorance not only of the
pope's reply, published in 1864, but of Hailes's observation that ' the pope
. . . employs the very expressions of the Scottish manifesto ' (*Annals*, s.d.
1320). See Gordon Donaldson, ' The Pope's Reply to the Scottish Barons
in 1320 ', *SHR*, xxix (1950), 119.
[3] J. H. Burton, *History of Scotland* (2nd ed., 1873, reprinted 1897) ;
P. Hume Brown, *History of Scotland* (2nd ed., 1911) ; Andrew Lang, *History
of Scotland* (1900–7). Tytler's history was written, of course, long before
Bain's volumes appeared.

await a treatise on *Anglo-Scottish Relations in the Middle Ages* which will do justice to the wealth of the evidence.

V. Method of Editing

(a) *The Latin and French Texts*

With a very few exceptions, which are recorded in the textual notes, every document has been edited from the original manuscripts. No attempt has been made to record all the variant readings, but it is hoped that the most important have been cited in the notes. On a few occasions, which are all mentioned in the notes, the manuscript text has been emended by the editor.

Some difficulty has arisen in dealing with mutilated and illegible passages in the MSS. To indicate exactly what can be read, and what has been conjectured by the editor, is not easy without using elaborate devices which would be out of place in this edition ; and it is difficult, in any case, to show the exact size of gaps, even when the original allows it to be calculated. The following system has been adopted :

(1) Square brackets denote editorial conjectures. When the original reading is known from a trustworthy transcript or early printed text, this is inserted without square brackets. Text no. 14 is a special case, and the notes explain its particular problems. It may be remarked here that we use square brackets also to indicate editorial extensions of heavily abbreviated names in witness-lists, and in similar passages.

(2) Asterisks (*) denote the ultimate degree of conjecture, when the editor has had to supply a word or words with no clue at all except the context and the amount of space to be filled. Where they are found, the reader is warned to exercise all due scepticism.

(3) Dots indicate gaps, but their number does not show the size of the gap ; as a rule an arbitrary number of ten is inserted,

unless it is obvious that only a few letters are missing. If any indication of the size of the gap can be given, it is made in a footnote, or by an estimate in square brackets, e.g. [*one or two words*]. Where this is not practicable, we have on occasion marked the place where new lines begin with a solidus [/], so that the reader may make his own calculation from the number of words to a line. Where dots are found with none of these indications, the reader may take it that it is not profitable for him to speculate without looking at the MS for himself.

When a document has been printed before, the reference is given, but no attempt is made to list the previous editions completely. Only a selection is given of the misreadings of Rymer and other editors. The spelling used for the Latin and French texts requires some explanation, since it differs from that of previous volumes in the series in using the modern distinction between *i* and *j*, and between *u* and *v*. In the French documents it seemed best to follow in this matter the usage of the 'Anglo-Norman Text Society' and of French official record publications, especially since one may presume that something like the same distinction was used in pronunciation by the writers of our texts. If this system be adopted for the French texts, it is logical to do the same for the Latin, and it must be confessed that whatever may be the best orthography for classical Latin, the modern usage looks more convincing for the administrative and official texts which are printed here.

As regards spelling, punctuation, and extension, the following points should be noted. No attempt has been made to reproduce the punctuation and the use of capitals which are found in the manuscripts. The spelling *ci* has been adopted in the Latin for both *ci* and *ti* when followed by another vowel (for example *convencio* is so spelled here, whether the MS reads *conventio* or *convencio*; in many cases it is very difficult to tell which the clerk meant). Abbreviations are extended whenever there is no real doubt; some readers may perhaps feel that we

have been over-cautious in hesitating to commit ourselves with certain place-names. The suspension *q'* is given as *qui* or *que*, unless there is evidence that the scribe would have written *qi* or *qe* if he had troubled to give the word in full.[1]

(b) *The Translation*

The general principle has been adopted that since the reader has the original on the opposite page, the translation is not bound to be literal. We have attempted to make it readable by adopting modern forms of expression as far as possible. This is often very difficult with ecclesiastical Latin, and we do not profess to have solved the problem of making the higher literary flights of papal bulls intelligible without very wide departures from the original. Where it is possible to supply in the translation the obvious sense of missing passages in the original, this has been done, and the addition shown by square brackets. Gaps which cannot be dealt with thus are indicated by an arbitrary number of ten dots, whatever the extent of the gap, unless it is so small that this number would be misleadingly large. Place and personal names have, so far as possible, been modernised. Finally, we have, as a rule, omitted words for which no precise equivalent can be found in modern English (e.g., the titles *dominus* and *monsire*), or words whose equivalents in modern English are generally avoided, except in archaic and legal usage (e.g., *idem, predictus*).

(c) *Footnotes*

The notes are arranged to give, in a preliminary section, the necessary references to MSS, to Bishop Stapledon's calendar, and (with no attempt at completeness) to previous printed editions. An attempt is then made to indicate the special interest of the document, and the circumstances of its issue.

---

[1] See, for example, no. 39; but it is rare to be so certain. It may be added that *mons'* has always been extended as *monsire*.

The textual and explanatory notes follow the general usage of this series; but in some cases textual points have had to be discussed in the explanatory notes, because the editor has felt that there were special reasons why the reader of the translation should have his attention drawn to them.

NOTE ON THE LOST TREATIES OF
1209 AND 1212

THERE is a great deal of uncertainty about the relations of
England and Scotland between the treaties of 1174 and 1237.
Very few documents have survived; and unfortunately these
do not include the treaties of 1209 and 1212 (it may be remarked
that we possess even those of 1174 and 1237 only in transcripts).
It will help in the understanding of the earlier documents in
this volume, if we assemble here what can be ascertained about
these missing texts.

It is certain that there was a treaty between King John and
William the Lion in 1209. Negotiations were in progress in
1205.[1] They were no doubt delayed[2] by John's campaign
in France and the quarrel with Innocent III, but they were
concluded by August 1209. We learn from a document of
7 August 1209[3] that William bound himself to pay 15,000
marks to John ' for his goodwill, and for fulfilling the agreement
which was made between them, *and confirmed by our charters*'.
This refers to an agreement which no longer exists.[4] We know
that it included the names of hostages,[5] and that William
surrendered two of his daughters to John.[6] So much for record
evidence of contemporary date. If we may accept the statements of the chronicler Fordun (writing a century and a half
afterwards) the treaty also provided for the demolition of the
castle at Tweedmouth, the maintenance of the ' honours '

---

[1] Bain, I, no. 368
[2] Bain, I, no. 450 (April 1209), speaks of the coming settlement of matters
long discussed.
[3] Rymer, I, i, 103
[4] cf. *Flores Historiarum* (RS), II, 139 : 'pax scripto mediante sollempni
confirmata est '.
[5] Rymer, loc. cit. : ' obsides in predictis cartis nominati '
[6] ibid.

provided in our document no. 3,[1] and for the marriages of
William's daughters to John's sons, the future Henry III and
Richard of Cornwall.[2]   The charge made against Hubert de
Burgh in 1239 implies that some such marriage agreement had
existed, though Hubert denied all knowledge of it, and we
depend on the same charge for the statement that in return for
the marriage William not only gave John 15,000 marks, but
also surrendered the ancient Scottish claims to Northumberland, Cumberland, and Westmorland.[3]   It seems that the
young Alexander was at the same time invested with all the
lands which his father had held of the king of England, and
that a similar arrangement was intended for every heir to the
Scottish crown in future.[4]

The treaty of 1212 is more obscure.   From no. 4[5] we learn
that between 22 July 1211 and 8 February 1212, William the
Lion agreed to grant the marriage of his son and heir, Alexander,
to John, and that both he and his son swore to be faithful to
John's son Henry, as their liege lord, after the death of John.
This is all the contemporary record evidence.   We know that
the two daughters of William were still in England, and un-
married.[6]   Fordun says that the kings met at Norham in
February 1212 and that a peace was made and confirmed by
charters.[7]   He says nothing at all of its terms.   We depend
therefore on some rather vague later references :

(a) In Magna Carta, John promised ' to do to Alexander,
king of Scots, concerning his sisters, and the rendering of his
hostages, and his liberties, and his right, after the manner in
which we shall act towards the other barons of England, unless

---

[1] Below, pp. 9-11
[2] Fordun, p. 277.   cf. *DNB* under William ' the Lyon '.
[3] Matthew Paris, *Chronica Majora* (RS), VI, 70-2.   cf. Kate Norgate,
Minority of Henry III (1912), p. 127 ; but her reference to a ' copy of the
treaty of Norham ' is misleading ; it is merely a subsidiary document.
[4] Fordun, loc. cit.
[5] Below, p. 12
[6] Bain, I, nos. 530, 544, etc.
[7] Fordun, p. 278

we ought to do otherwise, according to the charters which we have from his father William '.[1] We can infer that these matters had been agreed upon in 1212, and that by 1215 Alexander had reason to complain of John's failure to keep some, at least, of his promises.

(b) According to Matthew Paris, Alexander complained in 1236 that he could prove by charters that John had promised him the hand of John's daughter, Joan, and Northumberland as dowry.[2] The marriage had taken place in 1221, but we seem to know nothing more of its having been contemplated in the time of John, and the promise of Northumberland seems not to be mentioned elsewhere.

(c) In November 1219, Honorius III referred to a peace between William the Lion and John, which the king of Scots had asked him to examine.[3] It seems impossible to be sure whether this was the peace of 1209 or that of 1212; Miss Norgate took the former view and Sir Maurice Powicke the latter.[4] Whichever it was, the pope had received from it (as Sir Maurice observes) the impression that the king of Scots was the vassal of the king of England.[5]

(d) Finally, there are allusions in the treaty of 1237[6] which *may* be to the treaty of 1212. They are too vague for it to be certain that they are relevant.

The next agreement seems to be that of June 1220, which luckily does survive.[7] It is concerned solely with marriages: Alexander II is to marry Joan (Henry III's sister) or her younger sister, Isabella; the unfortunate ladies Margaret and Isabella, who had now been in England for eleven years, were to be married honourably, or promptly returned to Scotland.

---

[1] Magna Carta (1215 text), cap. 59
[2] Matthew Paris, *Chronica Majora* (RS), III, 372-3, and cf. 363
[3] Rymer, I, i, 157
[4] Norgate, *Minority of Henry III*, p. 126; Powicke, *Thirteenth Century*, pp. 594-5
[5] *Cal. Papal Letters*, I, 83; Rymer, I, i, 157.
[6] Below, pp. 19-26   [7] Rymer, I, i, 160-1

It is noteworthy that the 1237 treaty asserts [1] that Henry had not kept a promise made to Alexander that he, Henry, would marry Margaret. There is no such promise in the text of 1220, though there may have been a verbal understanding.[2]

The loss of the originals of these documents is probably to be explained by their surrender after the treaty of 1237 (cf. below, p. 24), and the fact that even transcripts have not survived is possibly due to the complete loss of the Close Rolls for 10–13 John, and of the Patent Rolls for 11–13 John.

---

[1] Below, p. 20

[2] In fact Margaret was married in 1221 to Hubert de Burgh, and Isabella to the earl of Norfolk in 1225. In 1231 Henry III wanted to marry another Margaret (or Margery), the sister of this first Margaret (Powicke, *Henry III and Lord Edward*, II, 768).

LIST OF SOME IMPORTANT DOCUMENTS OF 1174–1328 WHICH ARE NOT GIVEN IN THIS COLLECTION

	Date	Description	Printed
(1)	1284	The Scottish magnates recognise Margaret as heir to the throne	Rymer, I, ii, 638
(2)	1289	Treaty of Salisbury	Rymer, I, ii, 719-20
(3)	1290	Treaty of Birgham (confirmed at Northampton later in the year)	Stevenson, *Documents*, I, 162-73
(4)	1290	Letter of bishop of St Andrews to Edward I on rumour of death of Margaret	Rymer, I, ii, 741
(5)	1291–3	The 'Great Roll' by John of Caen [no. 20 is in substance identical with the corresponding portion of this Roll]	Rymer, I, ii, 762-84
(6)	1291–6	The 'Great Roll' by Andrew de Tange	Prynne, pp. 487-543
(7)	1291–2	Original Pleadings in the 'Great Cause' before Edward I	Palgrave, *Documents*, pp. 21-52
(8)	1291	*Inspeximus*, by two Scottish bishops, of undertakings by Edward I	Unprinted as yet; contained in Duchy of Lancaster, *Cartae Miscellaneae* (D.L. 36), vol. I, f. 60
(9)	1296	The 'Ragman Rolls' by Andrew de Tange [no. 22 is substantially an extract from one of these]	*Instrumenta Publica* (Edinburgh 1834), pp. 59-176
(10)	1301	Letter from English barons to the pope	Rymer, I, ii, 926-7
(11)	*c.* 1301	Instructions to Scottish proctors at papal court, and the process of Baldred Bisset	*Scotichronicon*, II, 192-218
(12)	1303	Letter from Scottish envoys in France to the community of Scotland [this exemplar, now in the Public Record Office was captured by the English *en route* for Scotland, but P.R.O. C 47/30/2, m. 14 (*c.* 1333),	Rymer, I, ii, 955-6 ; see also *EHR*, LXXX (Jan. 1965).

which reveals this, suggests
that more than one copy was
sent, and so the message may
have reached Scotland]

(13) 1320 Letter from Scottish barons to   *APS*, i, 474-5 (red),
the pope ('Declaration of Ar-   and with transla-
broath')   tion in T. M.
Cooper, *Supra Cre-*
pidam, (1951), pp.
61-71

(14) 1323 Truce of Bishopthorpe [see under   Rymer, ii, i, 521
Johnson, Charles, in biblio-
graphy, p. lii]

(15) 1328 Notarial Instruments and Inden-   *SHR*, xxix (1950), 44-
ture forming part of the Treaty   50; Rymer, ii, ii,
' of Northampton '   741-2

Translations, in whole or in part, of many of these documents will be
found in *Source Book of Scottish History*, ed. Dickinson, Donaldson, and
Milne, i (1958).

SELECT BIBLIOGRAPHY AND
LIST OF ABBREVIATIONS

ALLEN, John : *Vindication of the Ancient Independence of Scotland* (1833)

ANDERSON, E.S. : *Early Sources of Scottish History, A.D. 500–1286*, translated by A. O. Anderson (1922)

ANDERSON, James : *Historical Essay, Showing that the Crown of Scotland is Free and Independent* (Edinburgh 1705)

ANDERSON, S.A. : *Scottish Annals from English Chroniclers, A.D. 500–1286*, translated by A. O. Anderson (1908)

APS : *Acts of the Parliaments of Scotland* (vol. I, 1844)

AYLOFFE, Joseph : *Calendars of the Ancient Charters, and of the Welch and Scottish Rolls* [etc.] (1774)

BAIN : Joseph Bain : *Calendar of Documents Relating to Scotland Preserved in Her Majesty's Public Record Office* (Edinburgh 1881–8). In spite of its title, this work contains at the end of vol. IV some documents from the British Museum ; note should also be taken of the *addenda* in the same volume.

BARBOUR, John : *The Bruce*, ed. W. M. Mackenzie (1909)

BARRON, E. M. : *The Scottish War of Independence* (2nd ed., 1934)

BARROW, G. W. S. : *Feudal Britain* (1956)
‘ A Writ of Henry II for Dunfermline Abbey ’, *SHR*, XXXVI (1957), 138-143. ‘ The Scottish Clergy in the War of Independence ’, SHR, XLI (1962), 1-22.

B.M. : British Museum

BROWNE, G. F. : *Echt-Forbes Family Charters* [etc.] (1923). This book has facsimiles of notarial signs found on some documents in the present collection.

BURTON, J. H. : *History of Scotland* (Edinburgh ed. of 1897)

Cal. Charter Rolls, Patent Rolls, Papal Letters etc. : *Calendars* of these and similar series, published by the Public Record Office

Chron. Ed. I and II : *Chronicles of Reigns of Edward I and II*, ed. Stubbs (RS, 1882–3)

CUTTINO, G. P. : *The Gascon Calendar of 1322* (Camden 3rd Series, 1949). Valuable for study of contemporary nomenclature and arrangement of the archives. References in index under *Scots* and *Scotland* are important.
English Diplomatic Administration 1259–1339 (1940)

DALRYMPLE, David [Lord Hailes] : *Annals of Scotland* (edition in three vols., Edinburgh 1819)

DICKINSON, *Scotland* : W. Croft Dickinson, *Scotland from the Earliest Times to 1603* (1961)

DICKINSON, DONALDSON, and MILNE : *Source Book of Scottish History*, I (to 1424). 2nd ed., 1958.

DNB : *Dictionary of National Biography*

DUNBAR : A. H. Dunbar, *Scottish Kings, a Revised Chronology of Scottish History 1005–1625* (2nd ed., 1906)

Écoles Françaises d'Athènes et de Rome : Registres of Gregory IX, Innocent IV, and subsequent popes. Not yet complete for period of this volume (Paris 1884–)

EHR : *English Historical Review*

FORDUN : *Johannis de Fordun Chronica*, ed. W. F. Skene (Edinburgh 1871)

GOUGH, H. : *Itinerary of King Edward I* (1900) ; an expanded and corrected version is kept in the Round Room at the Public Record Office

GRAY, Sir Thomas : *Scalacronica* (ed. Stevenson, Edinburgh 1836)

' Great Rolls ' : See ' Rolls '

HADDAN and STUBBS : *Councils and Ecclesiastical Documents*, ed. A. W. Haddan and W. Stubbs, vol. II, pt. i (1873)

HAILES : See Dalrymple

HEMINGBURGH : *Chronicle of Walter of Guisborough, previously edited as that of Hemingford or Hemingburgh* (ed. Rothwell, Camden 3rd Series, 1957)

HUNTER, Joseph : ' King Edward's Spoliations in Scotland in 1296 ' in *Archaeological Journal*, XIII (1856), 245-55

INNES, Thomas : *A Critical Essay* [etc.] (1729)

Instrumenta Publica, sive Processus super Fidelitatibus et Homagiis Scotorum Domino Regi Angliae Factis, A.D. 1291–96 (Bannatyne Club, 1834)

JAFFÉ : Jaffé, P., *Regesta Pontificum Romanorum . . . ad annum . . . 1198* (2nd ed., Leipzig 1885-8)

JOHNSON, Charles : ' Robert Bruce's Rebellion in 1306 ', *EHR*, XXXIII (1918), 366-7
' A Preliminary Draft of the Truce of Bishopthorpe, 1323 ', *EHR*, XXXV (1920), 231-3

JORDAN FANTOSME : *Chronique de la guerre entre les Anglois et les Ecossois*, ed. Michel (Surtees Society, 1840)

KENNEY, Barnaby C. : ' The Medieval Idea of the State ; the Great Cause, 1291-2 ', *Toronto Law Journal*, VII (1949), 48-71

KNIGHTON, *Chronicon Henrici*, ed. J. R. Lumby (RS, 1889–95). The edition is notoriously bad.

Lanercost, Chronicon de, ed. Stevenson (Edinburgh 1839) ; has an extensive and most important appendix of documents from the Public Record Office and British Museum.

Lists and Indexes published by the Public Record Office :
Vol. XV : *List of Ancient Correspondence* (1902)
  XXXV : *List of Exchequer Accounts, Various* (1912)
      [Important for Diplomatic Missions, Military Expenses, etc.]
  XLIX : *List of Diplomatic and Scottish Documents, and Papal Bulls* (1923)

McKISACK, M. : *The Fourteenth Century, 1307–99* (Oxford History of England, 1959)

Mailros, Chronica de : ed. Stevenson (Edinburgh 1835)

MARSHALL, D. W. Hunter : ' Two Early English Occupations in Scotland ',
  SHR, xxv (1927), 20-37
MOORE, M. F. : *The Lands of the Scottish Kings in England* (1915)
MUNCH, P. A. : ' Concordia Facta inter Anglicos et Scotos, 3 January
  1322/3 ', *Proceedings of Society of Antiquaries of Scotland*, III (1857-60),
  454-62
Nat. MSS Scotland : *National Manuscripts of Scotland*, 3 vols. (1867-73)
NEILSON, George : ' Bruce *versus* Balliol, 1291-2 ', *SHR*, xvi (1918), 1-14
NICOLSON, William : *English, Scotch, and Irish Historical Libraries* (1736, and
  later editions)
O.E.D. : *Oxford English Dictionary*, 1884-1928
PALGRAVE, *Documents* : Sir Francis Palgrave, *Documents and Records Illustra-
  ting the History of Scotland* I [all that was published] (1837)
PALGRAVE, *Kalendars* : Sir Francis Palgrave, *Antient Kalendars and Inventories
  of the Exchequer*, 3 vols. (1836)
Passio Scotorum Perjuratorum, ed. Marquis of Bute, in *Proc. Society of Antiquaries
  of Scotland*, xix (1885), 166-92
POOLE, A. L. : *Domesday Book to Magna Carta, 1087-1216* (Oxford History
  of England, 1951)
POTTHAST : Potthast, A., *Regesta Pontificum Romanorum inde ab Anno post
  Christum Natum 1198 ad annum 1304* (Berlin 1874-5)
POWICKE, F. M. : *King Henry III and the Lord Edward* (1947)
  The Thirteenth Century, 1216-1307 (Oxford History of England, 1953)
PRYNNE : William Prynne, *Exact Chronological Vindication of our Kings'
  Supreme Ecclesiastical Jurisdiction* (etc.), III (1670) [sometimes called
  ' Prynne's *Records* ' or his ' *History of King John, Henry III, and Edward I* ']
P.R.O. : Public Record Office
' Ragman Rolls ' : see ' Rolls '
RAMSAY, J. H. : *The Angevin Empire 1154-1216* (1903)
  The Dawn of the Constitution 1216-1307 (1908)
  The Genesis of Lancaster 1307-99 (1913)
R.C.A.M.S. : Royal Commission on the Ancient Monuments of Scotland
Registers of English Bishops, especially :
  Canterbury and York Society Series : John of Halton (Carlisle), Robert
    Winchelsey (Canterbury)
  Surtees Society Series : York Archiepiscopal Registers from 1215
Registrum Palatinum Dunelmense, ed. Duffus Hardy (RS, 1873-8)
Reports of Deputy-Keeper of the Public Records, no. 110 (1950) [for transfers of
  records from London to Edinburgh]
RICHARDSON, H. G. and SAYLES, G. O. : ' Scottish Parliaments of Edward
  I ', *SHR*, xxv (1928), 300-17
RISHANGER : *Willelmi Rishanger . . . Chronica et Annales*, ed. Riley, (RS, 1865)
RITCHIE, R. L. G. : *The Normans in Scotland* (1954)
ROBERTSON, Joseph : *Statuta Ecclesiae Scoticanae* (1866)
' Rolls, Great ' : (i) Duplicate rolls by John of Caen containing narrative
  of the ' Great Cause ' (Rymer, I, ii, 762-84)
  (ii) Triplicate rolls containing narrative of the ' Great Cause ' and

continuation to 1296, the whole by Andrew de Tange, and compiled 1315–18 (Prynne, pp. 487-543, see Stones, *SHR*, xxxv (1956), 92-5)

'Rolls, Ragman': Triplicate rolls, giving transcript of Scottish homages to Edward I in 1296, compiled by Andrew de Tange in 1300–6 (*Instrumenta Publica* [q.v.], pp. 59-176 b). [See Stones, *SHR*, xxxv (1956), 95.] Also sometimes used to describe the original deeds of homage.

RS : Rolls Series

RYMER : *Foedera, Conventiones*, etc., ed. T. Rymer; cited in new edition by Record Commission (1816–69)

SAYLES, G. O. : ' The Guardians of Scotland and a Parliament at Rutherglen in 1300 ', *SHR*, xxiv (1927), 245-50

' Ancient Correspondence ', *SHR*, xxiv (1927), 325-6

Scotichronicon: *Joannis de Fordun Scotichronicon cum Supplementis et Continuatione Walteri Boweri*, ed. Goodall (1759) [to be distinguished from ' Fordun ' above]

SHR : *Scottish Historical Review*

SIMPSON, Grant G. : ' The Claim of Florence Count of Holland to the Scottish Throne, 1291–2 ', *SHR*, xxxvi (1957), 111-24

S.R.O. : Scottish Record Office, H.M. Register House, Edinburgh

STAPLEDON's Calendar : Bishop Stapledon's Calendar of Documents, printed in Palgrave, *Kalendars*, I, 1-155

STEVENSON, *Documents* : Joseph Stevenson, *Documents Illustrative of the History of Scotland . . . 1286–1306* (1870)

STEVENSON, J. : *Illustrations of Scottish History . . . from MSS. in the British Museum and the Tower of London* (1834)

Documents Illustrative of Sir William Wallace (1841)

STONES, E. L. G. : ' The English Mission to Edinburgh in 1328 ', *SHR*, xxviii (1949), 121-32

' An addition to the Rotuli Scotiae ', *SHR*, xxix (1950), 23-51

' The Anglo-Scottish Negotiations of 1327 ', *SHR*, xxx (1951), 49-54

' The Submission of Robert Bruce to Edward I, c. 1301 ', *SHR*, xxxiv (1955), 122-34

' The Records of the Great Cause of 1291–92 ', *SHR*, xxxv (1956), 89-109

' Historical Revision: The Treaty of Northampton, 1328 ', *History*, xxxviii (1953), 54-61

' A New Exemplar of Andrew de Tange's " Great Roll of Scotland " at Exeter Cathedral ', *SHR*, xxxix (1960), 86-7

' An Undelivered Letter from Paris to Scotland (1303) ? ' (to appear in *EHR*, lxxx (Jan. 1965))

' Joseph Bain (1826–1911), and the Origin of the *Calendar of Documents relating to Scotland* ', *Archives*, vi (1963–4), 78-84, 172-7.

TEULET, A. : *Inventaire chronologique des documents relatifs à l'histoire d'Ecosse conservées aux Archives du Royaume à Paris* (Edinburgh 1839)

THEINER : A. Theiner, *Vetera Monumenta Hibernorum et Scotorum Historiam Illustrantia* (Rome 1864)

THOMSON, J. Maitland : *The Public Records of Scotland* (1922)

TRHistS : *Transactions of Royal Historical Society*
TRIVET, Nicholas, *Annales*, ed. T. Hog (1845)
TYTLER, P. F. : *History of Scotland* (2nd ed., Edinburgh 1841–3)
WYCKOFF, C. T. : *Feudal Relations between the Kings of England and Scotland* (Chicago 1897)

CHRONOLOGICAL TABLE

1124–53   *David I, king of Scots*
1153–65   *Malcolm IV, king of Scots*
1165–1214 *William the Lion, king of Scots*
1174   Capture of William the Lion by the English; treaty ' of Falaise ' (no. 1)
1189   Treaty of Canterbury (no. 2)
1209   Treaty (lost) between John and William the Lion
1212   Treaty of Norham (lost) between John and William the Lion
1214–49   *Alexander II, king of Scots*
1237   Treaty of York (no. 7)
1249–86   *Alexander III, king of Scots*
1286–90   *Margaret, queen of Scots* (' Maid of Norway ')
1289   Treaty of Salisbury
1290   Treaty made at Birgham, and confirmed at Northampton
1290   Death of Margaret; interregnum in Scotland until 1292
1291–2   Adjudication between the claimants by Edward I (' Great Cause ')
1292–6   *John Balliol, king of Scotland*
1296–1306 Interregnum in Scotland
1297   Battle of Stirling Bridge
1305   Execution of Wallace; ordinance for the government of Scotland (no. 33)
1306   Bruce [1] murders Comyn and claims the Scottish throne
1306–29   *Robert I, king of Scots*
1314   Battle of Bannockburn
1328   Treaty of Edinburgh, confirmed at Northampton (no. 41)

[1] A note on the various Robert Bruces who appear in this volume will be found on p. 49 below.

LATIN AND FRENCH TEXTS

with

ENGLISH TRANSLATION

I

Carta ª Convencionis et finis facta inter H[enricum]
regem Anglorum filium Matilldis imperatricis et Willelmum regem Scotorum.ᵇ

HEC ¹ est convencio et finis quem Willelmus rex Scotorum ᵇ fecit cum domino suo Henrico rege Anglorum ᵇ
filio Matilldis imperatricis. Willelmus rex Scottorum ᵇ
devenit homo ligius domini regis contra omnem hominem
de Scocia et de omnibus aliis terris suis, et fidelitatem ei
fecit ut ligio domino suo sicut alii homines sui ipsi facere
solent. Similiter fecit homagium H[enrico] regi ² filio
suo et fidelitatem salva fide domini regis patris sui.
Omnes vero episcopi et abbates et clerus terre regis
Scottorum et successores sui facient domino regi, sicut
ligio domino,ᶜ fidelitatem de quibus habere voluerit
sicut alii episcopi sui ipsi facere solent, et H[enrico] regi
filio suo et heredibus ᵈ illorum.ᵉ Concessit eciam rex

Text : There being no contemporary MS, we depend on two later transcripts,
(i) Red Book of Exchequer (P.R.O. E 164/2), f. 166, r and v, (early 13th
cent.) (A) ; (ii) Little Black Book of Exchequer (P.R.O. E 164/12), ff. 7v
and 8r (early 13th cent.) (B). To illustrate chronicle versions we also give
some readings of Roger of Howden's text, from Haddan and Stubbs, II, i,
237-40 (H). The document has had an unfortunate history. The original
in the English archives was no doubt surrendered to the Scots, after the
treaty of 1189 (see below, p. 7) and is not extant. When Edward I's
clerks prepared their historical survey in 1291, they resorted perforce to a
text obtained from a monastic chronicle (see above, pp. xxvi-xxvii) and this
unsatisfactory text was printed by Rymer (*Foedera* I, i, 30-1 (R)) ; his
cryptic reference to an exchequer roll means in fact John of Caen's ' Great
Roll of Scotland '. B was printed by Hearne (*Liber Niger Scaccarii* (1728), I,
36-40) and A calendared by Bain I, no. 139, but the present edition seems
to be the first critical text. It follows B unless otherwise stated. Only the
more important textual variants are cited in the notes.

ª *Title from* B ; *none in* A
ᵇ *At this date the royal styles were* rex Anglorum *and* rex Scotorum. *In
Scotland the usage never changed, except under John Balliol, but in England* rex
Anglie *was adopted permanently in* 1199. *After* 1199 rex Scot' *in the hand of an*

I

Text of treaty and settlement made between Henry, king of the English, son of the Empress Matilda, and William, king of Scots.

THIS [1] is the treaty and settlement which William, king of Scots, has made with his lord, Henry, king of the English, son of the Empress Matilda. William, king of Scots, has become the liegeman of the king against all men, for Scotland, and for all his other lands, and has sworn fealty to him as his liege lord in like manner as his other men are accustomed to do to him. Likewise he has done homage and sworn fealty to King [2] Henry, his son, reserving the fealty due to the king his father. All the bishops, abbots, and clergy of the realm of the king of Scots from whom he wishes to receive it, and their successors, shall swear fealty to the king as liege lord, as his other bishops are accustomed to swear to him, and to King Henry his son, and to their heirs. The king of

---

English clerk is ambiguous, because of the analogy of English usage. Here, though the MSS are after 1199, there is no doubt, because of the date of the treaty and the occasional spelling Scott', but in many of our later texts the correct extension is doubtful. In the present document B usually has Scott' or Scot', and A has Scocie.

    [c] domino suo A   [d] heredum A   [e] eorum A

    [1] This, the earliest Anglo-Scottish treaty of which the text has survived, was a result of the capture of William the Lion by the English in 1174. It is usually called the 'Treaty of Falaise', on the evidence of the chronicle versions (see H and R), but we know that the text of B was issued at Valognes, and we know of a confirmation at York in 1175 (cf. below, p. 101). Probably a first submission, at Falaise, was repeated at Valognes, and definitively affirmed with the maximum of publicity, at York. For the circumstances see A. L. Poole, *Domesday Book to Magna Carta*, pp. 276-8, and the references there cited, to which should now be added G. W. S. Barrow's remarks in *SHR*, XXXVI, pp. 141-2 ; and cf. above, pp. xvi and xx-xxii.

    [2] Henry, Henry II's eldest son, had been crowned during his father's lifetime (1170).

Scottorum et David frater ejus[a] et barones et alii
homines sui domino regi,[b] quod ecclesia Scot'[c] talem
subjeccionem amodo faciet ecclesie Angl' qualem illi
facere debet[1] et solebat tempore regum Anglorum predecessorum suorum. Similiter Ricardus episcopus sancti
Andree et Ricardus episcopus de Duncoldre[d] et Gal-
fridus abbas de Dunfermelin[e] et Herebertus prior de
Goldingeham concesserunt[f] quod eciam ecclesia Angl'
illud jus habeat in ecclesia Scot' quod de jure habere
debet,[1] et quod ipsi non erunt contra jus ecclesie Angl'
et desicut ligiam fidelitatem fecerunt domino regi et
H[enrico] filio suo eos inde assecuraverunt. Hoc idem
facient alii episcopi et clerus Scot'[g] per convencionem
inde inter[h] dominum regem et regem Scottorum et
David fratrem suum et barones suos factam.[2] Comites
eciam et barones et alii homines de terra regis Scotorum
de quibus dominus rex habere voluerit, facient ei homagium contra omnem hominem et fidelitatem ut ligio
domino sicut alii homines sui facere solent, et H[enrico]
regi filio suo et heredibus suis salva fide domini regis
patris sui. Similiter heredes regis Scottorum et baronum
et hominum suorum homagium et liganciam facient
heredibus domini regis contra omnem hominem.

Preterea rex Scottorum et homines sui nullum amodo
fugitivum de terra domini regis pro felonia receptabunt
in Scocia vel in alia terra sua nisi voluerit venire[1] ad
rectum in curia domini[j] regis et stare judicio curie, sed

---

[a] suus A
[b] domino regi *om.* A
[c] Scott' B; Scot' (or Scoc') A
[d] *So* AB; Dunkelden H
[e] Dunremel' A
[f] *om.* A
[g] Scott' B; Scocie A
[h] inde inter H; de inter B; inter AR
[i] *So* A; *om.* B
[j] *So* A; domini sui regis B

Scots, and David his brother, and the barons, and his other men, have also granted to the king that the church of Scotland shall henceforward owe such subjection to the church of England as it should do,[1] and was accustomed to do in the time of his predecessors as kings of England. Likewise Richard, bishop of St Andrews, Richard, bishop of Dunkeld, Geoffrey, abbot of Dunfermline, and Herbert, prior of Coldingham, have granted that the church of England shall also have the right in the church of Scotland which it lawfully should,[1] and that they will not oppose the right of the church of England, and as they have sworn liege fealty to the king and Henry his son, they have made themselves pledges for this. This same thing shall the other bishops and clergy of Scotland do, by agreement made on this between the king, and the king of Scots, and David his brother, and their barons.[2] The earls, and barons, and other men of the realm of the king of Scots from whom the king wishes to receive it, shall do him homage against all men, and swear fealty to him, as their liege lord, as his other men are wont to do, and to King Henry his son, and to their heirs, reserving the fealty due to the king his father. Likewise the heirs of the king of Scots, and of the barons, and of their men, shall do homage and swear allegiance to the heirs of the king against all men.

Further, the king of Scots and his men shall hereafter receive no one into Scotland, or into their other territory, who is fleeing as a felon from the realm of the king, unless he is willing to come to trial in the court of the king and to submit to the judgment of the court, but the

[1] Note the ambiguity here; cf. above, pp. xxi-xxii, for the claims of the English church upon Scotland.
[2] In 1176 the pope released the Scottish bishops from their promise Haddan and Stubbs, pp. 245-6).

rex Scotorum et homines sui quam cicius poterunt eum
capient, et reddent domino regi vel justic' aut ballivis
suis in Anglia. Si autem de terra regis Scotorum aliquis
fugitivus fuerit [a] pro felonia in Anglia, nisi voluerit venire
ad rectum in curia regis Scotorum vel [b] domini regis
et stare judicio curie, non receptabitur in terra domini
regis sed liberabitur hominibus regis Scotorum per ballivos domini regis ubi inventus fuerit. Preterea homines
domini regis habebunt terras suas quas ipsi habebant et
habere debent de domino rege et de hominibus suis [c] et
de rege Scotorum et de [d] hominibus suis, et homines
regis Scotorum habebunt [e] terras suas quas habebant et
habere debent de domino rege et de hominibus suis.[e]

Pro ista vero convencione et fine firmiter observando
domino regi et H[enrico] filio suo et heredibus suis a rege
Scotorum et heredibus suis, liberavit rex Scotorum
domino regi castellum de Rokesburc et castellum de
Berewic et castellum de Godewrth et castellum Puellarum [1] et castellum de Strivelin in misericordia domini
regis, et ad castella custodienda assignabit rex Scotorum
de redditu suo mensurabiliter ad voluntatem domini
regis. Preterea pro predicta convencione et fine exe-
quendo, liberavit rex Scotorum domino regi David
fratrem suum in obsidem,[f] comitem Dunekan, comitem
Waldevum,[g] comitem Gilbertum,[h] comitem de Anegus,[i]
Ricardum de Moreville constabularium, Nes filium
Willelmi, Ricardum Cumin, Walterum Corbet, Walterum Olifard, Johannem de Vaus, Willelmum de

---

[a] fugerit in Anglia pro felonia A
[b] vel in curia domini regis HR
[c] et de hominibus suis H; *om.* AB   [d] de AH; *om.* B
[e] habebunt *to* suis; A *replaces by* similiter
[f] H *and* R *add* et *after* obsidem *and between all names*; A *after* obsidem *and*
Dunekan *only*   [g] Waldevum H; Waler' B; Waleram (?) A
[h] *So* A; Willelmum B
[i] Danegusum AB   de Anegus H

king of Scots and his men shall take him as soon as they can, and render him to the king, or his justices or bailiffs in England. But if anyone from the land of the king of Scots is a fugitive in England, on account of felony, unless he is willing to come to trial in the court of the king of Scots or of the king, and to submit to the judgment of the court, he shall not be received in the realm of the king, but shall be delivered to the men of the king of Scots, by the bailiffs of the king, where he is found. Further, the men of the king shall have their lands which they had, and ought to have, of the king and of his men, and of the king of Scots and of his men. And the men of the king of Scots shall have their lands which they had, and ought to have, of the king and of his men.

To guarantee to the king, and Henry his son, and their heirs, that this treaty and settlement will be strictly observed by the king of Scots, and his heirs, the king of Scots has delivered to the king the castles of Roxburgh, Berwick, Jedburgh, Edinburgh [1] and Stirling, to be at his complete disposal, and for maintaining the castles the king of Scots will assign proportionally from his revenue, as the king may desire. Further, as hostages for executing the treaty and settlement, the king of Scots has delivered to the king his brother David, Earl Duncan, Earl Waltheof, Earl Gilbert, the earl of Angus, Richard of Morville the constable, Ness son of William, Richard Comyn, Walter Corbet, Walter Olifard, John de Vaux,

---

[1] The usual Latin name for Edinburgh in the middle ages. See refs. in R.C.A.M.S. *City of Edinburgh*, p. xxxv, *n.* 5.

Lindes', Philippum de Coleville, Philippum de Valoniis,
Robertum Frembert, Robertum de Burneville, Hugonem
Giffard, Hugonem Ridel, Walterum de Berkelai, Willelmum de Haia, Willelmum de Mortemer. Quando
vero castella reddita fuerint, Willelmus rex Scotorum et
David frater ejus liberabuntur. Comites quidem et
barones prenominati, unusquisque postquam liberavit
obsidem suum scilicet filium legitimum, qui habuerit, et
alii nepotes suos vel propinquiores sibi heredes, et castel-
lis, ut dictum est, redditis, liberabuntur.

Preterea rex Scotorum et barones sui prenominati
assecuraverunt quod ipsi bona fide et sine malo ingenio
et sine omni occasione facient quod episcopi [a] et barones
et homines terre sue qui non affuerunt quando rex
Scotorum cum domino rege finivit, eandem [b] liganciam
et fidelitatem facient domino regi et H[enrico] regi filio
suo quam ipsi fecerunt, et quod barones et homines sui
qui non [c] affuerunt obsides liberabunt domino regi de
quibus habere voluerit. Preterea episcopi [d] comites et
barones convencionaverunt domino regi et H[enrico]
regi filio suo quod si rex Scotorum aliquo casu recederet
a fidelitate domini regis et filii sui et [e] a convencione
predicta, ipsi [f] cum domino rege tenebunt, sicut cum
ligio domino suo, contra regem Scotorum et contra
omnes homines domino regi inimicantes. Et episcopi [g]
sub interdicto terram regis Scotorum ponent donec ipse
ad fidelitatem domini regis redeat.

Predictam itaque convencionem firmiter observandam
bona fide et sine malo ingenio domino regi et Henrico
regi filio suo et heredibus suis a Willelmo rege Scotorum

---

[a] episcopi AHR; ipsi B   [b] *So* A; eamque B
[c] non *om.* HR   [d] *om.* A
[e] *So* A; *om.* B
[f] *So* A; quod ipsi B
[g] episcopi AH; ipsi B

William Lindsay, Philip of Colleville, Philip of Valognes, Robert Frembert, Robert of Bourneville, Hugh Giffard, Hugh Riddel, Walter of Berkeley, William Hay, and William Mortimer. When the castles have been surrendered, William, king of Scots, and David, his brother, will be released. The earls and barons named, one and all, will be released after they have given a hostage, that is a legitimate son, if they have one, and from others their nephews or nearest heirs, and (as has been said) after the castles have been surrendered.

Further, the king of Scots and his barons have guaranteed that in good faith, and without ill intent, and without making excuse, they will cause the bishops and barons and men of their realm who were not present when the king of Scots made his agreement with the king, to swear the same allegiance and fealty to the king, and to King Henry his son, as they themselves did, and that those of the barons and their men who were not present, from whom he wishes to have them, shall deliver hostages to the king. Further, the bishops, earls, and barons have agreed with the king, and King Henry his son, that if the king of Scots by any chance withdraws from his fealty towards the king and his son, and from this agreement, then they will adhere to the king as their liege lord against the king of Scots, and against all men hostile to the king. And the bishops will place the realm of the king of Scots under interdict, until he shall return to his fealty towards the king.

The king of Scots himself, and David his brother, and all their barons aforesaid, have given security that this agreement will be kept strictly, in good faith, and without ill intent, by William, king of Scots, and David

E

et a David fratre suo et a baronibus suis predictis et ab heredibus eorum, assecuraverunt ipse rex Scotorum et David frater suus et omnes barones sui prenominati desicut devenerunt ligii homines domini regis contra omnem hominem et H[enrici] regis filii sui, salva fidelitate domini regis patris sui.

Testibus [a] Ricardo Abrinc' episcopo [1]; Johanne Sar' decano; Roberto abbate Malmesberi'; R[adulpho] abbate de Munteburg; Hereberto archidiacono Norhamt'; Waltero de Custanciis; Rogero [2] capellano [b]; Osberto de camera [c]; Ricardo filio domini regis, comite Pict'; Galfrido filio domini regis, comite Britannie; comite Willelmo de Essex; Hugone comite Cestr'; comite Mell'; Ricardo de Humet constabulario; Jordano Teisun; Humfredo de Bohun, constabulario; Willelmo de Curci, senescallo [d]; Willelmo filio Aldel', senescallo; Alured de sancto Martino, senescallo; Gislberto Malet, senescallo; Reginaldo de Curtenai; Fulcone Painel; Galfrido de Pertica; Willelmo de Humet [3]; Jordano de Humet [3]; Engelramo de Humet [3]; Radulfo Teisun; Rogero fratre illius; Roberto Bertram; Ricardo de Vernun; Willelmo Vavasur; Roberto de Mortemer; Roberto filio Bernardi; Rannulpho Puher'; Bertramo de Verdun; Rogero Bacun. Apud [4] Valoniis.[e]

---

[a] *A reads* testibus ex parte regis Anglie pluribus. Huic carte appendent sigilla Willelmi regis Scocie, episcopi sancti Andree, episcopi Duneceldensis, Simonis de Toni episcopi Morinie (*sic*), David fratris regis Scocie, comitis Dunekan, comitis Walteri, comitis Danegus, et Ricardi de Moreville *and so ends, with no date or place*
[b] capellano regis HR
[c] clerico de camera HR
[d] *om. all witnesses after* Curci, *save* Malet, HR
[e] Apud Falesiam HR ; *for* A *cf. n. a above.*

[1] Most of the witnesses and others named in the text are identified and described in L. Delisle, *Recueil des actes de Henri II*, Introd. (1909), 351 ff.

his brother, and his barons aforesaid, and by their heirs, towards the king and King Henry his son and their heirs, inasmuch as they have become liegemen of the king against all men, and of King Henry his son, reserving the fealty due to the king his father.

Witnesses : Richard, bishop of Avranches [1] ; John, dean of Salisbury; Robert, abbot of Malmesbury; Ralph, abbot of Montebourg ; Herbert, archdeacon of Northampton ; Walter of Coutances ; Roger the chaplain [2] ; Osbert of the chamber ; Richard, son of the king, count of Poitou ; Geoffrey, son of the king, count of Brittany ; William, earl of Essex ; Hugh, earl of Chester ; [Robert] count of Meulan ; Richard of Le Hommet, constable ; Jordan Taisson ; Humphrey de Bohun, constable ; William of Courcy, steward ; William Fitz-Aldelin, steward ; Alfred of St Martin, steward ; Gilbert Malet, steward ; Reginald of Courtenay ; Fulk Painel ; Geoffrey of Perche ; William of Le Hommet [3] ; Jordan of Le Hommet [3] ; Ingelram of Le Hommet [3] ; Ralph Taisson ; Roger, his brother ; Robert Bertram ; Richard of Vernon ; William Vavasour ; Robert Mortimer ; Robert FitzBernard ; Ranulph Puhere ; Bertram of Verdun ; Roger Bacon. At [4] Valognes.

---

[2] Probably Roger of Howden, the chronicler, whence no doubt his possession of the text.

[3] It has been noted that the constable, Richard of Le Hommet, probably brought these relatives as witnesses to Valognes from Le Hommet nearby (Douglas and Greenaway, *English Historical Documents 1042–1189* (1953), p. 416, *n.* 1).

[4] No date ; we have indicated 1174 on chronicle evidence.

2

Carta regis Ricardi per quam adquietavit regi Scocie homagium suum et castra expressa contra priores convenciones.[a]

Ricardus [1] dei gracia rex Anglorum, dux Normannorum, Aquitanorum, comes Andegavorum, archiepiscopis episcopis abbatibus comitibus baronibus justic' vicecomitibus et omnibus ballivis et fidelibus suis, salutem. Sciatis nos [b] karissimo consanguineo nostro Willelmo eadem gracia regi Scocie [c] reddidisse castella sua [de] [d] Rokesburc [e] et Berwic [2] tanquam ejus propria jure hereditario ab eo et heredibus suis in perpetuum possidenda. Preterea quietavimus ei omnes pacciones quas bonus pater noster Henricus rex Anglorum per novas cartas et per capcionem suam extorsit, ita videlicet ut nobis faciat integre et plenarie quicquid rex Scocie Malcolmus frater ejus antecessoribus nostris de jure fecit [f] et de jure facere debuit,[3] et nos ei faciamus quicquid antecessores nostri

Text: Printed from the transcript in P.R.O. Red Book of Exchequer (E 164/2) f. 166v (early 13th cent.) (A).   Original (E), now largely illegible, was in P.R.O. until 1937 (E 39/1/19), when it was removed to S.R.O.; facsimile in *Nat. MSS Scotland*, i, no. xlvi, gives many readings not now visible; the accompanying transcript is untrustworthy. The 1282 inventory of the Scottish archives (Rymer, i, ii, 616) records an exemplar which is probably, but not certainly E.   No trace survives of the ' promissory letter ' of Richard I, mentioned in the same inventory (Rymer, loc. cit.).   Printed (from E) in Rymer, i, i, 50 (R).   Calendared by Bain, i, no. 196.   Versions also in ' Benedict of Peterborough ' (ed. Stubbs, RS), ii, 102-4 (P), and Roger of Howden (ed. Stubbs, RS), iii, 25-7 (H).   Spurious passages were subsequently added in a Scottish version given by Fordun (i, 272-3) (F). Their purpose was obviously to remove the ambiguity of the genuine text.

  [a] Title from A
  [b] nos R; *om.* A; E *illegible*
  [c] Scocie AE; Scottorum PH
  [d] de *om.* AERPH; *possibly proper names are genitives or adjectives.*
  [e] Rokeborc R, *by misreading ligatured* sb
  [f] *add* pro terris suis in Anglia F

2

Charter of King Richard, by which he quitclaimed
to the king of Scots his homage, and certain specific
castles, despite previous agreements.

RICHARD,[1] by the grace of God king of the English, duke
of the Normans and of the men of Aquitaine, and count
of the Angevins, gives greeting to his archbishops, bishops,
abbots, earls, barons, justices, sheriffs, and to all his
bailiffs and faithful subjects.   This is to inform you that
we have restored to our well-beloved cousin William, by
the same grace king of Scotland, his castles of Roxburgh
and Berwick,[2] as his own by hereditary right, to be held
for ever by him and by his heirs.   Furthermore, we have
released him from all agreements which our good father
Henry, king of the English, exacted from him by new
charters and by his capture, so that (in fact) he shall do
for us fully and completely whatever his brother Malcolm,
king of Scotland, did of right, and ought to have done of
right,[3] for our predecessors, and we shall do for him
whatever our predecessors did for Malcolm of right, and

[1] This ' Treaty of Canterbury' restores the *status quo* as it was before
no. 1, but it is studiously vague about the obligations so implied for the
Scottish king.   No mention is made of the 10,000 marks known to have been
paid to Richard for his concessions (J. Anderson, *Diplomatum Scotiae The-
saurus* (1739), no. xxvi; *Chronica de Mailros*, p. 98).   In general, see above,
pp. xx-xxi.
[2] cf. above, p. 3; Edinburgh Castle had already been returned to
the Scots in 1186, but nothing is known about any transfers of Jedburgh and
Stirling since 1174–5.
[3] It is obvious that there was ambiguity in this definition of what the
king of Scots was to do.

predicto Malcolmo de jure fecerunt et facere debuerunt
scilicet et de conductu in veniendo ad curiam et in
morando in curia et in redeundo a curia et in procura-
tionibus et in omnibus libertatibus et in dignitatibus et
honoribus eidem jure debitis secundum quod recog-
noscetur [1] a quattuor proceribus nostris ab ipso Willelmo
rege electis et a quattuor proceribus illius a nobis elec-
turis.[a] Si autem marchias regni Scocie aliquis nostrorum
hominum postquam predictus rex Willelmus a patre
nostro captus fuit injuste usurpaverit, volumus ut integre
restituantur et ad eum statum reducantur quo erant ante
ejus capcionem.

Preterea de terris suis quas habet [b] in Anglia seu
dominicis seu feodis, scilicet in comitatu Huntendon' [2]
et in omnibus aliis, in ea libertate et plenitudine possideat
et heredes ejus in perpetuum qua prefatus rex Malcolmus possedit vel possidere debuit nisi jam dictus rex
Malcolmus vel heredes sui aliquid postea infeodaverint,
ita tamen quod si aliqua postea infeodata sunt ipsorum
infeodatorum servicia ad eum et ad ejus heredes perti-
neant. Et terram quam pater noster prescripto regi
Willelmo donavit, in eadem libertate qua ipsam ei dedit
ipsum et heredes suos perpetuo jure possidere volumus.
Reddidimus etiam ei ligancias hominum suorum quas
pater noster receperat et omnes cartas [3] quas pater noster
de illo habuit per capcionem suam, et si que forte per
oblivionem retente vel invente fuerint, eas penitus carere
viribus precipimus.

---

[a] *add* postquam Willelmus Bastard conquestor dicti regni Anglie et
heredes sui dictum regnum Anglie optinuerunt F
[b] h̄t A ; E *illegible* ; habet PF ; haberet R

[1] cf. below, pp. 9-11.
[2] For the history of the possessions of the Scottish kings in England see
Margaret F. Moore, *The Lands of the Scottish Kings in England* (1915).

ought to have done, that is in regard to coming to our court and staying at our court and returning from our court, and in provisions, and all liberties, dignities, and honours rightly due to him, according to what shall be certified [1] by four of our nobles appointed by King William, and four of his nobles to be appointed by us. But if any one of our subjects has unjustly usurped possession of the marches of the realm of Scotland since King William was taken by our father, we desire that they be restored completely, and brought back to the state in which they were before his capture.

Moreover, as for the lands which he has in England in demesne or in fee, namely in the county of Huntingdon [2] and in all other counties, he and his heirs shall possess them for ever in the liberty and fullness with which King Malcolm possessed, or ought to have possessed them, unless King Malcolm or his heirs shall since have made any enfeoffments, provided that if any enfeoffments have since been made, the services of those enfeoffed lands shall belong to him and to his heirs. And the land which our father gave to King William we wish him and his heirs to possess by perpetual right, with the same liberty with which he gave it to him. We have restored also to him the allegiances of his men, which our father received, and all the charters [3] which our father had from him as a result of his capture, and if by chance any shall have been retained by forgetfulness, or shall be found, we command that they shall be entirely invalid.

---

[3] Hence perhaps the absence of any original of no. 1 from the English archives now, and apparently as early as 1291. If *omnes* has any definite meaning, it probably refers to the texts of the successive submissions at Falaise, Valognes, and York (above, p. 1, *n.* 1).

Sepedictus vero Willelmus rex leggius homo noster
devenit de omnibus terris [a] de quibus antecessores sui
antecessorum nostrorum ligii homines fuerunt,[1] et nobis
atque heredibus nostris fidelitatem juravit. Ut autem
ratum et firmum sit istud et perpetuum, presenti carta
et sigillo nostro id roboravimus. Testibus [b] B[aldewino]
Cantuariensi W[altero] Rotomagensi J[ohanne] Dublinensi archiepiscopis, H[ugone] Dunolmensi H[ugone] [2]
Lincolniensi G[odefrido] Wintoniensi H[uberto] Saris-
beriensi Reg[inaldo] Bathoniensi episcopis, domino
J[ohanne] fratre nostro, R[oberto] comite Leicestrie,
H[amelino] comite Warennie, H[ugone] Bardolf, Stephano de Longo Campo dapifero nostro, et aliis multis.
v die Decembris. Dat' per manum Willelmi Eliensis
electi, cancellarii nostri, apud Cantuariam, regni nostri
anno primo.

   [a] terris in Anglia F
   [b] Teste meipso anno domini MCXC (sic) et regni nostri anno primo F
(no witnesses)

   [1] cf. above, p. 6, n. 3.
   [2] i.e. St Hugh of Avalon

King William has become our liegeman for all the lands for which his predecessors were liegemen of our predecessors,[1] and has sworn fealty to us and our heirs. In order to ratify and establish this agreement for ever, we have confirmed it by this charter, and with our seal. Witnesses : Archbishops Baldwin of Canterbury, Walter of Rouen and John of Dublin ; Bishops Hugh of Durham, Hugh of Lincoln,[2] Godfrey of Winchester, Hubert of Salisbury, and Reginald of Bath ; the lord John, our brother, Robert earl of Leicester, Hamelin earl of Warenne, Hugh Bardolf, Stephen of Longchamp our steward, and many others. Canterbury, 5 December, by the hand of William, bishop-elect of Ely, our chancellor, in the first year of our reign [1189].

3

Litera regis Anglie de feodo prestando regi Scocie vel de conductu.[a]

RICARDUS [1] dei gracia rex Anglorum, dux Normannorum, Aquitanorum, comes Andegavorum, archiepiscopis episcopis abbatibus comitibus baronibus justic' vicecomitibus senescallis prepositis ballivis et omnibus ministris et fidelibus suis tocius terre sue, salutem. Noverit universitas vestra nos concessisse et presenti carta nostra confirmasse Willelmo illustri regi Scottorum, karissimo amico et consanguineo et fideli nostro et heredibus suis in perpetuum, de nobis et heredibus nostris omnes libertates et rectitudines plenarie [b] quas antecessores sui habere solebant eundo ad curiam antecessorum nostrorum et stando ad curiam et redeundo a curia antecessorum nostrorum, scilicet: unaquaque die postquam de mandato nostro transierit fines regni sui versus curiam nostram centum solidos sterlingorum, et in reditu suo a curia nostra singulis dicbus tantumdcm quousque in terram suam venerit, et singulis diebus ex quo venerit ad curiam nostram usque ad recessum suum versus terram suam triginta solidos sterlingorum, et duodecim de domi-

---

Text: Original (E) in S.R.O. (in P.R.O. until 1937, as E 39/2/19) is now illegible in many places, and much of the text has to be supplied from Rymer, I, i, 62-3 (R), Palgrave, *Documents* [' Illustrations '], pp. xxviii-xxix (P), and Ayloffe, *Calendars of Ancient Charters* (1774), pp. 347-8 (A; styled ' Astle's Calendars ' by Palgrave). The 1282 inventory of the Scottish archives (Rymer, I, ii, 616) records two exemplars; see comments below. Calendared in Bain, I, no. 226. Chronicle version in Roger of Howden (ed. Stubbs, RS) III, 244-5 (H).

  [a] *Title from 1282 inventory, omitting final words* et est dupplicata. *A partly illegible endorsement on E seems identical with the 1282 description. Hence it seems fairly certain that E was in the Scottish archives in 1282, with a duplicate now lost.*
  [b] *So E clearly;* ita plenarie R

3

Letter of the king of England about providing the payment due to the king of Scotland, and about his escort.

Richard,[1] by the grace of God king of the English, duke of the Normans and of the men of Aquitaine, and count of the Angevins, gives greeting to his archbishops, bishops, abbots, earls, barons, justices, sheriffs, stewards, reeves, bailiffs, and all his ministers, and to his faithful subjects of his whole realm. This is to inform all of you that we have granted, and by this our present charter confirmed to William, the illustrious king of Scots, our well-beloved friend and cousin, and our liegeman, and to his heirs for ever, all the liberties and rights due from us and our heirs in full, as his predecessors were accustomed to have them when going to the court of our predecessors, dwelling at the court, and returning from the court of our predecessors, namely :

On each day after he has crossed the bounds of his realm, when coming to our court at our behest, 100/- sterling, and on his return from our court the same amount each day, until he has come to his own country, and each day from his arrival at our court until his departure towards his own land, 30/- sterling, and twelve

---

[1] The relation of this document to the inquest mentioned on p. 7 above cannot be determined. There is some ambiguity in the implication of *de mandato nostro* ; it may mean only that Richard was not bound to the terms of the document if the king of Scots came to England at his own desire, or it may suggest that Richard regarded him as a vassal for Scotland. Here, as with the previous document, it is unwise to attempt to be clearer on the point than contemporaries were. In general, see R. L. G. Ritchie, *The Normans in Scotland* (1954), pp. 385-6.

nicis [1] guastellis [2] nostris, et totidem de simenellis [3] nostris dominicis, et duodecim sextercia [4] vini, quatuor videlicet de dominico vino nostro unde nobis servitur, et octo sextercia [a] de vino unde domui nostre servitur, et [a] duas petras cere vel quatuor cereos [5] et quadraginta candelas [5] de dominicis candelis unde nobis servitur, et duas libras piperis et quatuor libras cimini.[6]

Et preterea conductus quos antecessores sui habere solebant eundo usque ad curiam nostram et redeundo a curia nostra, scilicet quod episcopus Dunelmensis et vicecomes et barones Norhumbrie ad ipsum venient in finibus regni sui et ibi eum recipient et conducent usque ad Teise, et ibi venient ad eum archiepiscopus Eboracensis et vicecomes et barones Ebor' et ibi eum recipient et conducent usque ad episcopatum Lincoln', et ibi ad eum venient episcopus Lincoln' et vicecomes et barones provincie et eum recipient et per ballivas suas [b] conducent, et sic deinceps episcopi et [b] vicecomites provinciarum per quas ipse transierit quousque ad curiam nostram venerit.[7]

Quare volumus et firmiter precipimus quod prefatus rex Willelmus et heredes sui omnia prescripta habeant de nobis et heredibus nostris in perpetuum, et in expensis et in conductibus et in fugitivis qui de felonia se defendere voluerint ad curiam nostram in pace sua ducendis, et in omnibus aliis sine aliqua diminucione, firmiter precipi-

---

[a] sextercia *to* et : A *and* P *defective* ; *text from* R, *with which* E *agrees, so far as legible*

[b] suas *to* et *om.* R, *with marks of lacuna* ; E *defective, text here from* A

[1] *dominicus*, like Old French *demaine* (below, p. 133), can mean ' one's own ' as well as ' the lord's '.

[2] *wastel* = ' bread of the finest flour ' (*O.E.D.*)

[3] *simnel* = ' a kind of bread or bun made of fine flour and prepared by boiling ' (*O.E.D.*)

of our own ¹ wastel ² loaves and the same number of our
own simnel ³ loaves, and twelve sesters ⁴ of wine, that is
four of our own wine, as it is served to us, and eight
sesters of the wine with which our household is served,
and two stone of wax, or four [wax ?] ⁵ candles and
forty [tallow ?] ⁵ candles of our own, as they are served
to us, and two pounds of pepper, and four pounds of
cummin.⁶

Furthermore we have granted the escorts which his
predecessors were accustomed to have in going to our
court and returning from it, namely that the bishop of
Durham and the sheriff and barons of Northumberland
will come to him at the frontier of his realm, and receive
him there and take him to the Tees. There the archbishop of York, and the sheriff and barons of Yorkshire,
will come to him, receive him, and take him to the
bishopric of Lincoln. There the bishop of Lincoln, and
the sheriff and barons of the shire will come to him, and
receive him, and take him through their territory, and
so in turn the bishops, and the sheriffs of the shires
through which he goes, until he arrives at our court.⁷

Therefore it is our will and firm command that King
William and all his heirs shall have of us, and of our
heirs for ever, all the things mentioned above, both
expenses and escorts, and the right of bringing in his
peace, to our court, fugitives who wish to clear themselves of felony, and all else without diminution. We

---

⁴ A fluid measure : see *O.E.D.*, *s.v.* ' sester '.
⁵ The distinction between *cereos* and *candelas* here is not entirely certain,
nor is it clear whether a comma is to be understood after *cereos*.
⁶ Cummin seeds used for flavouring
⁷ For instances of these escorts in subsequent years cf. Bain, I, nos. 803,
1349, 1484, *etc.*

entes ut prefati episcopi vicecomites et barones ei predictos conductus facient et omnes alias rectitudines et libertates suas conservent, et ut vicecomites predicti in bailliis suis prescriptas expensas in eundo ad curiam nostram, et redeundo a curia nostra, plenarie inveniant donec in terram suam venerit.

Testibus hiis : Huberto Cantuar' [a] archiepiscopo, H[ugone] Dunelm' R[icardo] Londinensi H[ugone] Linc' S[effrido] Cicestr' G[ilberto] Rovecestr' W[illelmo] Hereford' H[enrico] Wigorn' episcopis, R[anulfo] comite Cestr', H[amelino] comite de Warr[ennia], R[icardo] comite de Clare, R[ogero] Bigod comite Norffolc', comite David, W[illelmo] comite de Ferariis, W[illelmo] Marescallo, W[illelmo] de Stutevill', Eustachio de Vesci, Gaufrido filio Petri, Hugone Bardolf, W[illelmo] Briwer et multis aliis. Datum per manum Willelmi Eliensis episcopi, cancellarii nostri, apud Wintoniam, xvij die Aprilis,[1] anno quinto [b] regni nostri.

---

[a] *Many of names illegible in* E *and supplied from* P *and* A ; *spelling therefore may not be that of* E.

[b] P *marks lacuna after* quinto *but gap in* E *is normal spacing out of final words to fill last line.* H *dates at Northampton,* 11 *April.*

[1] The day of Richard's second coronation, at which William was present.

strictly order the bishops, sheriffs, and barons who have
been mentioned, to perform their escort-duties to him,
and to maintain all his other rights and liberties, and
the sheriffs in their bailiwicks, to meet in full the expenses
incurred in going to our court and returning, until he
arrives in his own realm.

Witnesses: Hubert, archbishop of Canterbury;
Bishops Hugh of Durham, Richard of London, Hugh of
Lincoln, Seffrid of Chichester, Gilbert of Rochester,
William of Hereford, and Henry of Worcester; Ranulf
earl of Chester, Hamelin earl of Warenne, Richard earl
of Clare, Roger Bigod earl of Norfolk, Earl David,
William earl of Ferrers, William Marshall, William de
Stuteville, Eustace de Vescy, Geoffrey FitzPeter, Hugh
Bardolf, William Briwer, and many others. Winchester,
by the hand of William bishop of Ely, our chancellor,
17 April,[1] in the fifth year of our reign [1194].

4

WILLELMUS [1] dei gracia rex Scottorum omnibus fidelibus [2] has litteras visuris vel audituris, salutem. Sciatis quod concessimus [3] karissimo domino nostro Johanni illustri regi Anglie, ut maritet Alexandrum filium nostrum sicut hominem suum ligium, infra sex annos proximos sequentes post diem cinerum anni regni ejusdem domini regis Johannis tercii decimi, ubi voluerit ad fidem ipsius domini regis, ita quod non disparagetur. Concessimus eciam eidem domino nostro Johanni regi Anglie quod quicquid de ipso contingat, nos et Alexander filius noster Henrico filio ejus tanquam ligio domino nostro contra omnes mortales fidem et fidelitatem tenebimus, et juvabimus eum pro viribus nostris ad tenendum ipsum in regno suo salva fide qua predicto domino nostro regi Johanni tenemur. Et [ad] [a] hec predicta firmiter et fideliter observanda nos et Alexander filius noster tactis sacrosanctis [4] juravimus, et ad majorem hujus rei securitatem

---

Text: P.R.O. Ancient Correspondence (S.C. 1) 2/24 (S). Facsimile in Rymer 1, i, opp. p. 104. Printed by Rymer, loc. cit. (R). Calendared by Bain, 1, no. 508. Listed by Stapledon (Palgrave, *Kalendars*, 1, 128).

  [a] *om.* S ; *supplied by* R, *but for similar omission cf. p. 24 below.*

  [1] S seems to have been accepted as the original, but the hand is probably not less than 30-40 years later than 1211–12. S shows no trace of sealing; its genuineness cannot be taken for granted in the present state of knowledge of the Scottish Chancery under William the Lion. But there are no obviously suspicious features. On the lost text of a treaty made between William and John at about the same time as this letter see above, p. xlvi. No. 4 was cited in the historical survey made for Edward I in 1291 (Rymer, 1, ii, 771).

4

WILLIAM,[1] by the grace of God king of Scots, gives greeting to all loyal persons [2] who shall see or hear this letter. This is to inform you that we [3] have granted to John, our well-beloved lord, the illustrious king of England, the marriage of our son Alexander, as his liegeman, within six years after Ash-Wednesday in the thirteenth year of John [8 February 1212] and at John's entire discretion, provided that Alexander be not disparaged. We have granted also to John our lord, king of England, that whatever may happen to him, we and Alexander our son will maintain faith and fealty to his son Henry as our liege lord against all mortals, and will help him, so far as we have power, to support himself in his realm, reserving the faith by which we are bound to our lord King John. We, and our son Alexander, have touched the Holy Gospels [4] and sworn to maintain this agreement strictly and faithfully; and to give greater

---

[2] If William were addressing only his own subjects, one would expect *fidelibus suis*, but a wider audience is more appropriate, and perhaps we should delete *fidelibus* or read *Christi fidelibus*.

[3] The plural style, adopted by the English royal Chancery under Richard I, seems to have come into use in the Scottish Chancery late in the reign of William the Lion.

[4] Translation assumes that *evangeliis* is understood, but *sacrosancta* is recorded in the sense of ' relics ' (cf. p. 41 below).

F

nos et dominus Willelmus episcopus sancti Andree et
dominus Walterus episcopus Glasguensis et dominus
Johannes electus Dunkeldensis et comes Patricius et
Alanus filius Roll[andi] constabularii et [Philippus] ᵃ de
M[ubr]ay et Walterus Ol[ifard] huic scripto sigilla
nostra apponi fecimus et Alexander filius noster cum
miles ¹ . . . . ᵇ [sig]illum suum apponet.²

ᵃ Philippus *conj. Mr N. F. Shead* ; Alanus R ; S *mutilated*
ᵇ *Two or three words missing from* S

¹ Alexander was knighted by King John on 4 March 1212.
² The date must be later than the election of John II to the see of
Dunkeld on 22 July 1211, and presumably earlier than Ash Wednesday
(8 February) 1212.

security in this matter we, with William bishop of
St Andrews, Walter bishop of Glasgow, John bishop-
elect of Dunkeld, Earl Patrick, Alan son of Roland the
constable, Philip [?] of Mowbray, and Walter Olifard,
have caused our seals to be affixed to this document, and
Alexander our son, when [he has been] knighted,[1] will
[also] affix his seal.[2]

5

Bulla Honorii pape quod ecclesie Scoticane immediate sint subjecte summo pontifici et confirmacio privilegiorum regis et regni.ᵃ

HONORIUS EPISCOPUS SERVUS SERVORUM DEI CARISSIMO IN CHRISTO FILIO ALEXANDRO ILLUSTRI SCOTORUM REGI EJUSQUE SUCCESSORIBUS IN PERPETUUM.¹

CUM universi fideles apud sedem apostolicam patrocinium invenire debeant et favorem, illos tamen specialius convenit ejus proteccionis munimine confoveri quorum fidem ac devocionem in pluribus est experta, ut ad ipsius dileccionis fervorem tanto amplius provocentur et ejus reverencie devociori affeccione subdantur, quanto benivolencie ipsius et gracie pignus se noverint cercius assecutos. Eapropter, carissime in Christo fili, reverenciam ac devocionem quam ad Romanam ecclesiam a longis retro temporibus te ac predecessores tuos habuisse cognovimus attendentes, presentis scripti pagina ad exemplar felicis recordacionis CELESTINI et INNOCENCII ² predecessorum nostrorum Romanorum pontificum districcius

---

Text: Original bull (E), now in S.R.O. (in P.R.O. until 1937, as S.C. 7/18/32). Facsimile in Rymer, I, i, 152-3, and *Nat. MSS Scot.* I, no. xlvii. Printed in Rymer, loc. cit. and Theiner, no. xviii. Calendared in Potthast, no. 5924, and *Cal. Papal Letters*, I, 60; not calendared in Bain; not in Stapledon's calendar. An exemplar is mentioned in the 1282 inventory of the Scottish archives (Rymer, I, ii, 615).

ᵃ *Title from inventory of 1282. E is probably the actual exemplar then in the Scottish archives.*

¹ This bull is a ' solemn privilege ', the most impressive type of document produced by the papal chancery, both in external appearance (E measures 30″ × 25″) and in dignity of language (see Cheney and Semple, *Letters of Innocent III* [Nelson's Medieval Texts], pp. xviii-xix, and references there cited). On the general significance of this bull see above, pp. xxi-xxii.

5

Bull of Pope Honorius stating that the Scottish churches are directly subject to the supreme pontiff, and confirming the privileges of the king and the realm.

HONORIUS, BISHOP AND SERVANT OF THE SERVANTS OF GOD, TO HIS WELL-BELOVED SON IN CHRIST, ALEXANDER, THE ILLUSTRIOUS KING OF SCOTS, AND TO HIS SUCCESSORS FOR EVER.[1]

ALTHOUGH all of the faithful should receive support and favour from the apostolic see, it is right that those in particular should be encouraged by her strong defence, whose faith and zeal she has in many ways experienced. So may they be moved all the more to love her fervently, and constrained to a more devout feeling of reverence for her, by the knowledge that they have gained a pledge of her goodwill and approval. Therefore, well-beloved son in Christ, bearing in mind the respect and the zeal which we know that you and your predecessors, from times long past, have had for the Roman church, we follow, in this present document, the example of our predecessors CELESTINE and INNOCENT,[2] Roman pontiffs of happy memory, and strictly forbid that anybody

---

[2] The present bull is substantially a repetition of two earlier bulls. The first was probably issued by Celestine III in 1192 (Jaffé 16836); the second by Innocent III at an uncertain date (*Scotichronicon*, I, 522; apparently not registered). There has always been some doubt whether Celestine III's predecessor, Clement III, had not anticipated Celestine; but the mention of Celestine, not Clement, in our text, is a strong argument that the earliest bull was that of Celestine. Cf. R. K. Hannay, 'The Date of the *Filia Specialis* Bull', *SHR*, xxiii (1926), 171-7; A. O. Anderson, 'The Bull *Cum Universi*', *SHR*, xxv (1928), 335-41; and the important note in *Chronicle of Holyrood* (Scottish Hist. Soc.), 1938, pp. 160-1.

inhibemus ut cum Scoticana ecclesia sedi apostolice, sicut filia specialis, nullo medio sit subjecta,[1] in qua hee sedes episcopales [2] esse noscuntur, ecclesia videlicet sancti Andree, Dumblenensis, ecclesia Glascuensis, Dumkeldensis, Brechinensis, ecclesia Aberdenensis, ecclesia Murevensis, ecclesia Ros[s]ensis et ecclesia Katenensis nemini liceat nisi Romano pontifici vel legato ab ipsius latere destinato in regnum Scocie interdicti vel excommunicacionis sentenciam promulgare, et si promulgata fuerit, decernimus non valere. Adicimus eciam ut nulli decetero qui de Scocie regno non fuerit, nisi quem apostolica sedes propter hoc de corpore suo specialiter destinaverit, licitum sit in eo legacionis officium exercere. Prohibemus autem ut controversie que fuerint in regno ipso de possessionibus ejus exorte ad examen extra regnum positorum judicum non trahantur nisi ad Romanam fuerit ecclesiam appellatum. Si qua vero scripta contra hujus libertatis statutum apparuerint impetrata vel in posterum istius concessionis, mencione non habita, contigerit impetrari, nullum tibi tuisve successoribus vel ipsi regno circa hujus prerogative concessionem prejudicium generetur. Preterea libertates et immunitates tam tibi quam regno tuo et ecclesiis in eodem regno constitutis ab ecclesia Romana concessas et hactenus observatas, ratas habemus et eas futuris temporibus illibatas manere sancimus, salva tamen sedis apostolice auctoritate. Nulli ergo omnino hominum liceat hanc paginam nostre concessionis prohibicionis et confirmacionis infringere, vel ei ausu temerario contraire. Si quis autem hoc attemptare presumpserit, indignacionem

---

[1] The point here is the desire of the Scottish church to be free from the claims of the see of York over Scotland (above, pp. xxi-xxii).

[2] The pope omits the sees of Galloway, Orkney, Argyll, and the Isles. Galloway was at this time subject to York, and Orkney and the Isles to Trondheim, and so these dioceses were not part of the *ecclesia Scoticana*;

except the Roman pontiff, or his legate sent *a latere*, should publish a sentence of interdict or excommunication in the kingdom of Scotland, and if it has been published we declare it to be invalid; for the Scottish church (in which it is well-known that there exist the following episcopal sees [2]: the churches of St Andrews, Dunblane, Glasgow, Dunkeld, Brechin, Aberdeen, Moray, Ross, and Caithness) is subject to the apostolic see, with no intermediary,[1] as being a specially privileged daughter. We add that no person who does not belong to the realm of Scotland shall in future be allowed to exercise the office of legate there, unless the apostolic see has specially sent one of its own number for the purpose. If any disputes arise in that realm about its possessions, we forbid that they be referred to the scrutiny of judges outside its borders, unless appeal is made to the Roman church. If any documents are found which have been obtained contrary to this declaration of liberty, or chance to be obtained afterwards, which do not make mention of it, let no prejudice arise to you or your successors, or to the realm, concerning the grant of this privilege. Moreover we ratify the liberties and immunities granted by the Roman church to you and your realm and to the churches in the realm, and hitherto observed, and decree that they shall remain undiminished in future, reserving, however, the authority of the Holy See. Let no man whatever, therefore, be allowed to infringe this text of our grant, prohibition, and confirmation, or presume to defy it. If anyone should dare to try this, he should

---

but the omission of Argyll (founded about 1200) can only be explained by the copying of the names from the bulls of Celestine and Innocent.

omnipotentis dei et beatorum Petri et Pauli apostolorum ejus se noverit incursurum. AMEN, amen, AMEN.

[Rota] ¹ Ego Honorius catholice ecclesie episcopus subscripsi.² Benevalete.³

✠ Ego Guido, Prenestinus episcopus subscripsi

✠ Ego Petrus, Sabinensis episcopus subscripsi

✠ Ego Leo, tituli sancte crucis in Iherusalem presbiter cardinalis subscripsi

✠ Ego Stephanus, basilice duodecim apostolorum presbiter cardinalis subscripsi

✠ Ego Gregorius, tituli sancte Anastasie presbiter cardinalis subscripsi

✠ Ego Thomas, tituli sancte Sabine, presbiter cardinalis subscripsi

✠ Ego Guido, sancti Nycolai in carcere Tulliano diaconus cardinalis subscripsi

✠ Ego Octavianus, sanctorum Sergii et Bachi diaconus cardinalis subscripsi

✠ Ego Gregorius, sancti Theodori diaconus cardinalis subscripsi

✠ Ego Stephanus, sancti Adriani diaconus cardinalis subscripsi

✠ Ego Alebrandinus, sancti Eustachii diaconus cardinalis subscripsi

✠ Ego Egidius, sanctorum Cosme et Damiani diaconus cardinalis subscripsi

Datum Laterani per manum Ranerii sancte Romane ecclesie vicecancellarii, xj kal. Decembris, indiccione vij, incarnacionis dominice anno Mᵒ Cᵒcᵒxviij, pontificatus vero dompni HONORII pape tercii anno tercio.

---

¹ The rota is a circular figure characteristic of a solemn papal privilege. See R. L. Poole, *Papal Chancery* (1915), pp. 101-5.

² This does not imply that the pope and the cardinals wrote the whole subscription in autograph; cf. C. R. Cheney, ' Some Papal Privileges for

know that he will incur the anger of Almighty God, and
of SS. Peter and Paul his apostles. AMEN, amen, AMEN.

[Rota] ¹ I, Honorius, bishop of the Catholic Church,
have subscribed.² Farewell.³

✠ I, Guy, bishop of Palestrina, have subscribed.

✠ I, Peter, bishop of Sabina, have subscribed.

✠ I, Leo, cardinal priest of the title of Santa Croce in
Gerusalemme, have subscribed.

✠ I, Stephen, cardinal priest of the title of the Santi XII
Apostoli, have subscribed.

✠ I, Gregory, cardinal priest of the title of Sant' Anas-
tasia, have subscribed.

✠ I, Thomas, cardinal priest of the title of Santa Sabina,
have subscribed.

✠ I, Guy, cardinal deacon of San Nicola in Carcere
Tulliano, have subscribed.

✠ I, Octavian, cardinal deacon of Santi Sergio e Bacco,
have subscribed.

✠ I, Gregory, cardinal deacon of San Teodoro, have
subscribed.

✠ I, Stephen, cardinal deacon of Sant' Adriano, have
subscribed.

✠ I, Hildebrand, cardinal deacon of Sant' Eustachio,
have subscribed.

✠ I, Giles, cardinal deacon of Santi Cosma e Damiano,
have subscribed.

At the Lateran, by the hand of Ranerius the vice-
chancellor of the Holy Roman church, 21 November,
indiction 7, A.D. 1218, in the third year of the pontificate of Pope HONORIUS III.

Gilbertine Houses ', in *Bull. Instit. Historical Research*, XXI (1946), pp. 49 ff.
³ Written as a monogram ; cf. R. L. Poole, op. cit., p. 105.

6

Bulla Gregorii pape ix per quam supplicat regi
Scocie quod observet composicionem factam inter ipsum
et regem Anglie, videlicet homagii et fidelitatis, et quod
non insurgat contra regem Anglie.[a]

GREGORIUS [1] episcopus servus servorum dei carissimo in
Christo filio .[2]. illustri regi Scocie salutem et apostolicam
benediccionem. Si tua, ut credimus, celsitudo consideret
quod carissimo in Christo filio nostro .[2]. illustri regi
Anglie vinculo specialis dileccionis astringimur, teque
sincera diligimus et amplectimur caritate, per consequens
recognosces quod nec debemus nec possumus [b] preterire
maxime requisiti quin ad pacem inter te ac ipsum perpetuo conservandam paterno intendamus affectu, et
opem impendamus ac operam efficacem, sperantes et
fiduciam firmam habentes quod utrique regno de hujusmodi concordia magna debeat utilitas provenire ; sane
idem rex in nostra nuper fecit presencia recitari [3] quod
jam dudum inter clare memorie H[enricum] avum et
J[ohannem] patrem suum ex parte una, et W[illelmum]
Scocie regem ex altera composicio amicabilis intercessit,

Text: Printed from P.R.O. Liber A (E 36/274), f. 81v, a transcript of the
time of Edward I (A).   Original bull, P.R.O. E 39/91/7, is now almost
totally illegible because of damp and mutilation (E) ; was listed by Stapledon
(Palgrave, *Kalendars*, I, 22, item 89), whose note ' duppl[icata] ' in margin
may refer to E 39/91/6, a version addressed to the archbishop of York and
the bishop of Carlisle, and also transcribed in Liber A.   Printed (from E ?)
by Rymer, I, i, 215 (R) ; Theiner, no. lxxiii (T).   Calendared in Bain, I, no.
1266 ;   *Cal. Papal Letters*, I, 142 ;   Potthast 9815 ;   *Registres de Grégoire IX* (ed.
Auvray), no. 2337.   On the presence in the English archives of a bull
addressed to the king of Scots see above, p. xxxii, *n.* I.   Since Liber A was
completed before 1296, E (from which A is copied) was in England too
early for it to have been one of the documents removed from the Scottish
archives in that year (see below, pp. 75-6).

    [a] *Title from margin of* A, *where described as* bulla sub filo canabi (*cf.*
Letters of Innocent III, *ed.* Cheney and Semple, *p. xix*).
    [b] *So* RT ; possimus A

6

Bull of Pope Gregory IX in which he urges the king of Scotland to observe the agreement made between him and the king of England namely for homage and fealty and not to rebel against the king of England.

GREGORY,[1] bishop and servant of the servants of God, gives greeting and apostolic benediction to his well-beloved son in Christ .[2]. the illustrious king of Scotland. If, as we believe, your highness reflects that we are bound by a tie of particular affection to our well-beloved son in Christ .[2]. the illustrious king of England, and that we cherish and embrace you also with sincere love, you will realize in consequence that we should not, and cannot fail, especially when we have been so invited, to strive with fatherly compassion to keep peace for ever between him and you, and to furnish effectual help and assistance, hoping, and maintaining the firm belief, that from a union of this kind, great benefit may arise to either realm. Now that same king recently caused it to be recounted in our presence [3] that once there was a friendly agreement between Henry his grandfather and John his father, of renowned memory, on the one hand, and William king of Scotland on the other, as a result of which William

---

[1] For general comments on this bull see above, p. xxii.

[2] The dots are the *gemipunctus*; see L. C. Hector, *Handwriting of English Documents* (1958), p. 46. and Cheney and Semple, op. cit., p. xxxvii.

[3] This seems to be our only information about this English complaint to Gregory IX.

per quam ipse W[illelmus] predictis avo ᵃ et patri ac
eidem regi, et tu patri et sibi ligium homagium et fidelitatem fecistis,¹ que tenentur successores tui, comites
barones Scocie ipsi et suis successoribus exhibere, ac
comites et barones predicti esse cum regibus Anglie contra
reges Scocie si composicionem eandem forsitan non serva-
rent.² Quod si unius homines fugerent ᵇ ad regnum alterius metu criminum commissorum, ille ac homines sui
eos in terra sua receptare non debent.³ Et utriusque regis
homines terras quas in regno alterius ante composicionem
habuerant optinebunt. Unde idem rex nobis humiliter
supplicavit ut prefatam composicionem apostolico digna-
remur munimine roborare. Quocirca serenitatem regiam
rogandam duximus propensius et hortandam, quatinus
ad ea que pacis sunt intencionem tuam dirigens et ea
prudenter evitans que ad scandalum vel discordiam
pertinerent, predictam composicionem sicut provide
facta fuit et ab utraque parte sponte recepta studeas
observare, maxime cum dicatur paci et tranquillitati
utriusque regni plurimum expedire.

Datum Perusii ij non' Januarii, pontificatus nostri
anno octavo.

ᵃ avuo A
ᵇ fugerint T

¹ The pope here gives an obviously garbled account of events, but
probably he is condensing a description (supplied by English envoys) of
Anglo-Scottish treaties since 1174. For the lost treaties of 1209 and 1212
between William and John see above, pp. xlv-xlviii, and Powicke, *Thirteenth
Century*, pp. 594-5.
² cf. above, p. 4.
³ cf. above, pp. 2-3.

did liege homage and swore fealty [1] to the aforesaid grandfather and father, and to the present king, and you did the same things to the latter two; and your successors, and the earls and barons of Scotland, are bound to offer the same to him and his successors, and the earls and barons are to support the kings of England against the kings of Scotland, if perchance the latter should keep not the agreement.[2] If the subjects of the one should flee to the realm of the other, in fear of punishment for the crimes which they have committed, the latter and his subjects ought not to receive them in his land.[3] The subjects of either king shall hold those lands, in the realm of the other, which they had before the agreement. Therefore the king has humbly begged us to lend weight to this agreement by giving it the support of the Holy See. Hence we have readily decided to admonish your royal serenity to direct your attention to those things which make for peace, and (in your wisdom) to avoid those which make for scandal or discord, and to study to observe the agreement in the prudent manner in which it was made, and freely accepted, by each side, especially since it is said to be most expedient for the peace and quietness of each realm.

Perugia, 4 January, in the eighth year of our pontificate [1235].

7

Carta Convencionis inter Regem Anglie et Regem Scocie[a] de Comitatibus Norhumberlandie Cumbrelandie Westmorlandie et de quibusdam terris.[b]

SCIANT [1] presentes et futuri quod ita convenit in presencia venerabilis patris domini Ott[onis] sancti Nicholai in carcere Tulliano [2] diaconi cardinalis et tunc apostolice sedis legati apud Eboracum, inter dominum H[enricum] regem Anglie et dominum A[lexandrum] regem Scottorum[a] super omnibus querelis quas idem rex Scocie[a] moverat vel movere poterat contra dominum regem Anglie, usque ad diem veneris proximam ante festum sancti Michaelis anno gracie MºCCºxxxvijº, scilicet super comitatibus Northumberlandie, Cumberlandie, Westmerlandie, quas idem rex Scocie[a] peciit sicut hereditatem suam [3] a dicto rege Anglie. Et preterea de quindecim milibus marcis argenti quas illustris rex J[ohannes] pater predicti H[enrici] regis Anglie receperat a domino Willelmo quondam rege Scocie patre predicti A[lexandri] regis Scocie, pro quibusdam convencionibus [4]

Text: P.R.O. Red Book of Exchequer (E 164/2), ff. 174v-176r (contemporary transcript) (E) ; P.R.O. Patent Roll 21 Henry III (C 66/47), m. 2d (badly disfigured by galls) (C) ; whence Rymer, I, i, 233-4 (R). Calendared by Bain, I, no. 1358. The original chirographs are apparently not extant, despite the remarks of Hall, *Red Book of Exchequer* (RS), I, p. cii ; but one existed in the Scottish archives in 1291 (*APS*, I, 112 [red]). Printed here from E, except where otherwise noted.

[a] *On* rex Scocie/Scotorum *see above, p. 1, n. b. In* E *the scribe almost always writes* Scocie *(in full) or* Scott' *(which must mean* Scottorum*). His usage is followed here, but the form intended by the lost original remains in doubt.* C *seems usually to read* Scoc'*, with an occasional suspicion (never a certainty) of* Scot'*.*

[b] *Title from* E

7

Text of a Treaty between the king of England and the
king of Scotland about the counties of Northumberland,
Cumberland, and Westmorland, and about certain
[other] lands.

T HIS [1] is to inform men now, and in time to come, that
the following agreement was made at York, in the
presence of the venerable father Otto, cardinal deacon
of San Nicola in Carcere Tulliano,[2] and at that time
papal legate, between Henry, king of England, and
Alexander, king of Scots, about all the complaints which
the king of Scotland had raised, or was able to raise,
against the king of England up till Friday next before
Michaelmas [25 September] in the year of grace 1237.
That is to say about the counties of Northumberland,
Cumberland, and Westmorland which the king of Scotland sought from the king of England as his inheritance ; [3]
further, about 15,000 marks of silver which the illustrious
King John, father of King Henry of England, had
received from William, formerly king of Scotland, father
of Alexander, king of Scotland, in return for certain
agreements [4] between the kings which Alexander, king

---

[1] On this treaty see above, p. xxiii ; Dickinson, *Scotland*, p. 81 ; Powicke,
Thirteenth Century, pp. 586-7, 594-5 ; Ramsay, *Dawn of the Constitution*, p. 83.
  [2] On the mission of Otto see D. M. Williamson, 'The Legate Otto ',
SHR, xxviii (1949), 14-20, and ' Some Aspects of the Legation of Otto ',
EHR, lxiv (1949), 145-73.
  [3] On this Scottish claim see Dickinson, *Scotland*, pp. 75 ff., and above,
p. 000.
  [4] This reference and that on the following page are made obscure by the
loss of the treaties of 1209 and 1212. They raise problems which are discussed on pp. xlv-xlviii above. For the payment of 15,000 marks see Rymer,
I, i, 103.

inter dictos reges initis que a dicto rege Johanne non fuerant observate, ut idem Alexander rex Scocie dicebat.
Et de convencionibus factis ¹ inter dictum H[enricum]
regem Anglie et dictum A[exandrum] regem Scottorum
super matrimonio contrahendo inter eundem H[enricum]
regem Anglie et Margaretam sororem dicti A[lexandri]
regis Scocie, quod ex parte dicti H[enrici] regis Anglie
non fuit observatum, sicut idem rex Scottorum dicebat,
et de omnibus aliis querelis quas dictus A[lexander] rex
Scottorum movit vel movere potuit pro se vel pro antecessoribus suis contra dictum regem Anglie usque ad
terminum predictum, videlicet : quod dictus A[lexander]
rex Scottorum remisit et quietum clamavit pro se et
heredibus suis dicto H[enrico] regi Anglie et heredibus
in perpetuum dictos comitatus Northumberlandie, Cumberlandie, Westmerlandie et totam predictam pecuniam,
et omnes convenciones factas inter predictum J[ohannem]
regem Anglie et predictum W[illelmum] regem Scottorum super conjugiis faciendis inter predictum H[enricum]
regem Anglie vel Ricardum fratrem suum et Margaretam
vel Isabellam sorores predicti A[lexandri] regis Scottorum, et similiter convenciones factas inter dictum
H[enricum] regem Anglie et dictum A[lexandrum]
regem Scottorum super matrimonio contrahendo inter
ipsum H[enricum] regem Anglie et Margaretam sororem
dicti A[lexandri] regis Scottorum. Pro hac autem re-
missione et quieta clamancia predictus H[enricus] rex
Anglie dedit et concessit dicto A[lexandro] regi Scottorum ducentas libratas terre infra dictos comitatus Norhumberlandie et Cumberlandie,² si predicte ducente
librate terre in ipsis comitatibus, extra villas ubi castra

---

¹ See above, p. 19, *n.* 4.
² This grant was the subject of a charge against Hubert de Burgh in
1239 ; cf. Matthew Paris, *Chronica Majora* (RS), VI, 70-2. The lands were
not actually assigned until 1242, when Alexander received seisin of the

of Scotland, asserted that King John had not kept; about agreements [1] made between Henry, king of England, and Alexander, king of Scots, concerning a marriage to be contracted between Henry, king of England, and Margaret, sister of Alexander, king of Scotland, which, according to the king of Scots, had not been kept by the king of England; and about all other complaints which Alexander, king of Scots, raised, or was able to raise, on his own account, or that of his predecessors against the king of England up to the date mentioned; namely:

Alexander, king of Scots, remitted and quitclaimed for himself and his heirs, to Henry, king of England, and his heirs, in perpetuity, the counties of Northumberland, Cumberland, and Westmorland, and all the money mentioned above, and all of the agreements made between John, king of England, and William, king of Scots, about the marriages to be contracted between Henry, king of England, or his brother Richard, and Margaret or Isabel, sisters of Alexander, king of Scots, and also the agreements made between Henry, king of England, and Alexander, king of Scots, about the marriage to be contracted between Henry, king of England, and Margaret, sister of Alexander, king of Scots. In return for this remission and quitclaim Henry, king of England, gave and granted to Alexander, king of Scots, two hundred pounds' worth of land in the counties of Northumberland and Cumberland,[2] if two hundred pounds' worth could be found in those counties outside towns where there are castles. If there be anything

---

manors of Langwathby, Salkeld, Scotby, Sowerby, and Carlatton, with £60 worth of land in the manor of Penrith (Bain, I, no. 1575).

G

sita sunt, possint inveniri, et si quid inde defuerit ei
perficietur in locis competentibus et propinquioribus
dictis comitatibus Norhumberlandie et Cumberlandie,
habendas et tenendas et in dominico retinendas eidem
A[lexandro] regi Scottorum et heredibus suis regibus
Scottorum de dicto H[enrico] rege Anglie et heredibus
suis, reddendo inde annuatim unum osturum sorum [1]
ipsi regi Anglie et heredibus suis apud Karleol' per
manum constabularii castri Karleol', quicumque fuerit,
in festo Assumpcionis beate Marie, pro omnibus serviciis
consuetudinibus et aliis demandis que pro eisdem terris
exigi possint, ita libere quod predicti rex Scottorum et
heredes sui habeant et teneant dictas terras et homines
dictarum terrarum cum omnibus libertatibus et liberis
consuetudinibus et quietanciis suis, in bosco et plano in
pratis et pasturis in aquis et molendinis in viis et semitis
in stagnis et vivariis in mariscis et piscariis, cum soc et
sac thol et theam infangenethef utfangenethef ham-
sokne grithbreche blodwite fihtwite ferdwite hengwite
leyrwite flemenesfrith murdro et latrocinio forstal, infra
tempus et extra tempus, et in omnibus locis.[2] Et quod
ipse rex Scottorum et heredes sui et omnes homines sui
de predictis terris sint liberi et quieti ab omni scotto
geldo et omnibus auxiliis vicecomitum et omnium minis-
trorum suorum et de hydagio carucagio danegeldo horn-
geldo excercitibus (*sic*) wapentaciis scutagiis tallagiis
lestagiis stallagiis sciriis hundredis wardis [a] wardpeny
averpeny hundredespeny borghalpeny [b] tethingepeny, et
de operibus castellorum parcorum poncium clausuris et

---

[a] ward' C ; warda E
[b] *So* C; brokenalpeny E
[1] *Sore*: 'a hawk of the first year that has not moulted' (*O.E.D.*); a
common form of nominal rent

lacking, it shall be made up, in suitable places near to the counties of Northumberland and Cumberland. These lands are to be had, and held, and kept in demesne by Alexander, king of Scots, and his heirs, the kings of Scots, of Henry, king of England, and his heirs, by rendering for them every year a ' sore ' [1] falcon to the king of England and his heirs, at Carlisle by the hands of the constable of Carlisle castle, whoever he be, on the feast of the Assumption of St Mary [15 August], as being all the services, customs, and other demands that can be exacted for those lands. They are to be so freely enjoyed that the king of Scots and his heirs shall have and hold the lands, and the people of the lands, with every liberty and free custom and immunity, in woodland and open land, in meadows and pastures, in waters and mills, in roads and paths, in ponds and fish-pools, in marshes and fisheries, with soc and sac, tol and team, infangenethef and utfangenethef, hamsoken, grithbreche, bloodwite, fihtwite, ferdwite, hengwite, leyrwite, flymenafyrmth, murder, theft and forestall, in season and out of season, and in all places.[2] The king of Scots, and his heirs, and all his men in those lands, shall be free and quit from every scot and geld, and from all aids of sheriffs and of all their servants, and from hidage, carucage, danegeld, horngeld, military services, wapentakes, scutages, tallages, lastages, stallages, shires, hundreds, guards, wardpenny, averpenny, hundredpenny, burghalpenny, tithingpenny, and from maintenance of castles, parks, bridges, and

---

[2] For explanations of these terms see F. E. Harmer, *Anglo-Saxon Writs* (1952), pp. 73-85 ; Pollock and Maitland, *History of English Law* (2nd ed., 1898), I, 574 ff. The translation converts some of them into more common forms than those of the MSS.

omni cariagio ᵃ summagio navigio et de domuum rega-
lium edificacione et omnimoda operacione.¹ Et quod
predicti rex Scottorum et heredes sui habeant omnia
animalia que dicuntur wayf ² inventa in predictis terris,
nisi aliquis ea sequtus fuerit qui possit et velit probare
quod sua sint.

Concessum est eciam a dicto rege Anglie quod omnia
placita que in dictis terris de cetero emergent et que
coram justiciariis in banco vel coram ipso rege Anglie
in itinere suo ³ teneri consueverunt, de cetero placitentur
in curia ipsius regis Scottorum et heredum suorum infra
predictas terras et ibi terminentur per ballivos ipsius
regis Scottorum et heredum suorum per returnum brevis
ipsius regis Anglie et heredum suorum quod ᵇ vicecomites
ipsorum eisdem ballivis habere facient, si placita illa per
legem Anglie ibi teneri et terminari possint. Et placita
que ibi coram predictis ballivis per legem terre terminari
non poterunt, coram justiciariis dicti regis Anglie et
heredum suorum itinerantibus ad primas assisas infra
comitatus in quibus terre ille fuerint teneantur et terminentur in primo adventu ipsorum justiciariorum priusquam aliqua alia placita tencantur, secundum quod
justum fuerit, presente senescallo dicti regis Scottorum
et assidente tanquam justiciario ad illa placita tenenda,
ita quod ballivi vel homines ipsius regis Scottorum de
predictis terris pro nulla summonicione vel aliquo placito
exeant comitatus in quibus predicte terre fuerint. Si
qua vero terra assignata fuerit dicto regi Scottorum de

ᵃ kareio C
ᵇ quod C (?) R ; q̅m̅ E
¹ See above, p. 21, *n.* 2.
² A legal term (probably of Scandinavian origin) for property without
apparent owner
³ The reference is not to the general eyre (as supposed by Bain) but to

closes, and from all carriage, summage and navage, and
from the building of royal houses, and every kind of work-
service.[1] The king of Scots and his heirs shall have all
the animals which are called ' wayf ' [2] found in the lands,
unless somebody has followed them who can prove, and
wishes to, that they are his own.

The king of England has also agreed that all pleas
which arise in future in the lands, and which previously
have been held before the justices of the bench, or before
the king of England himself on his journeys,[3] shall in
future be pleaded in the court of the king of Scots himself, and that of his heirs, within the lands aforesaid, and
shall be determined there by the bailiffs of the king of
Scots, and of his heirs, by the return of the writ of the
king of England, and of his heirs, which their sheriffs
shall cause those same bailiffs to have, if the pleas can
be held and determined there by the law of England.
Pleas which cannot be determined there, by the law of
the land, before the bailiffs, shall be duly held and
determined before the justices itinerant of the king of
England, and of his heirs, at the first session in the
counties in which those lands are, on the first arrival of
the justices, before any other pleas are held, according
to what is just, the steward of the king of Scots being
present and sitting as a justice for the holding of those
pleas, so that the bailiffs or men of the king of Scots in
the aforesaid lands do not have to go outside the counties
in which the lands are situated on account of any
summons or plea. If any land shall be assigned to the
king of Scots from the aforesaid two hundred pounds'

---

the migrations of the king's bench with the king, which began again, after
their cessation during the minority of Henry III, in 1234 (Sayles, *King's
Bench under Edward II* (Selden Society 74), pp. xxxviii ff.).

predictis ducentis libratis terre infra metas foreste, nullus forestarius regis Anglie intrabit eandem terram ipsius regis Scottorum ad manducandum vel hospitandum vel aliquid aliud exigendum nisi tantum pro attachiamentis faciendis de placitis ad forestam spectantibus, et hoc per visum ballivi ipsius regis Scottorum, si requisitus interesse voluerit.

Placita vero corone cum in predictis terris emerserint atachientur per ballivum et coronatores regis Anglie, presente ballivo regis Scottorum si requisitus venire voluerit, et placitentur et terminentur eadem placita coram justiciariis itinerantibus et predicto senescallo ad primam assisam, sicut predictum est. De aliis placitis, ubi si aliquis hominum suorum de predictis terris convictus fuerit de felonia, post judicium factum fiat justicia per ballivos et homines ipsorum regis Scottorum et heredum suorum, ita tamen quod non licebit dictis regi Scottorum vel heredibus suis remittere alicui judicato penam ei debitam secundum legem terre, nec heredibus dampnatorum terram per feloniam perditam reddere, nec eciam amerciamenta ª remittere hiis qui amerciati fuerint pro quocumque forisfacto. Omnia eciam amerciamenta et eschaete et proventus de predictis terris ᵇ de anno et die dicti regis Anglie et heredum suorum, tam de terris per feloniam forisfactis quam de omnibus aliis exitibus, tam de placitis foreste quam de omnibus aliis placitis homines predictarum terrarum contingentibus, remaneant ipsis regi Scottorum et heredibus suis inperpetuum. Et si forte contingat aliquo tempore ipsos reges Scottorum vel heredes suos inplacitari de predictis terris vel aliqua parte earumdem, dictus rex Anglie et heredes

worth which is within the bounds of the forest, no
forester of the king of England shall enter that same land
of the king of Scots to eat or to lodge or to make any
other demand, but only to make attachments in pleas of
the forest, and this shall be done under the supervision
of the bailiff of the king of Scots if (on being asked) he
wishes to be present.

When pleas of the crown arise in the lands, they shall
be attached by the bailiff and coroners of the king of
England, in the presence of the bailiff of the king of
Scots if (on being asked) he wishes to come, and those
pleas shall be pleaded and terminated before the justices
itinerant, and the steward, at the first session, as was
previously said. As regards other pleas, whenever any of
his men in the lands is convicted of felony, let justice be
done, after judgment, by the bailiffs and men of the king
of Scots and his heirs, provided that the king of Scots and
his heirs shall not be allowed to remit to anyone so convicted the due penalty imposed on him by the law of
the land, nor to render to the heirs of the condemned the
land lost by felony, nor to remit amercements to those
who have been amerced for any trespass. All amercements, escheats, and revenues of the lands, for a year and
a day, belonging to the king of England and his heirs,
both from lands forfeit for felony, and from all other
profits, both from pleas of the forest, and from all other
pleas touching the men of the lands, shall remain to the
king of Scots and his heirs for ever. And if it chance to
happen at any time that the kings of Scots or their heirs
are impleaded for the lands, or any part of them, the king
of England and his heirs will warrant and defend the

sui easdem terras sicut illas ei dedit ipsis regi Scottorum et heredibus suis warantizabit et defendet inperpetuum, ita quod propter illud placitum non oportebit ipsos regem Scottorum et heredes suos ad curiam regis Anglie accedere ut inde alicui respondeant.

Et dictus rex Scottorum fecit dicto regi Anglie homagium suum de predictis terris et fidelitatem ei juravit. Scripta vero vel instrumenta super predictis maritagiis et convencionibus a predicto J[ohanne] quondam rege Anglie, sive a predicto H[enrico] rege Anglie et a predicto W[illelmo] quondam rege Scottorum vel a dicto A[lexandro] rege Scottorum confecta debent hincinde restitui,[1] eo salvo quod si in ipsis scriptis vel instrumentis aliqua capitula presens negocium non tangencia inveniantur que alterutrius regis utilitatem contingant,[a] debent predicta capitula per utriusque regis literas innovari[2]; similiter autem si que carte super predictis comitatibus possunt inveniri regi Anglie restituantur. Et si forte in posterum aliqua instrumenta inveniantur de predictis comitatibus et convencionibus que non fuerint restituta viribus careant et pro nullo[b] habeantur.

Hanc autem convencionem fideliter tenendam inperpetuum, predictus rex Anglie fecit in animam suam[3] jurare W[illelmum] comitem Warenne. Et dictus rex

[a] contineant EC (?) R ; contingant *conj. Mr R. E. Latham*
[b] nullis C

[1] The restoration of superseded (and compromising) diplomatic documents to their grantors was a recognised practice (cf. above, p. 7 and below, p. 167). This clause probably accounts for the loss of the treaties of 1209 and 1212 (cf. above, p. xlviii, and Powicke, *Thirteenth Century*, p. 594).

[2] This translation seems preferable to ' gone into again ' as suggested in Powicke, op. cit., p. 595.

[3] The practice of vicarious swearing on the soul of a king will be found in several documents in this collection (below, pp. 33, 39, 157, etc.). It has been supposed to have arisen because it was 'inconsistent with the sanctity of an anointed king' to take an oath in person (see Rothwell,

lands, as he gave them to the king of Scots and his heirs, for ever, so that by reason of that plea the king of Scots and his heirs shall not have to go to the court of the king of England and make answer to anyone about it.

The king of Scots has done homage to the king of England for the aforesaid lands, and has sworn fealty to him. The writings and documents concerning the marriages and agreements negotiated by John, formerly king of England, or by Henry, king of England, and by William, formerly king of Scots, or by Alexander, king of Scots, are due to be mutually restored,[1] saving that, if in those writings or instruments there are found any points not touching the present business which concern the interests of either king, these points ought to be set out afresh [2] in letters of each king; likewise if any charters can be found concerning the aforesaid counties, let them be restored to the king of England. If perchance in future any documents be found concerning the counties and the agreements which have not been restored, they shall be of no significance, and be regarded as null.

The king of England has caused William, earl of Warenne to swear on the king's soul [3] that this agreement shall be faithfully kept for ever. The king of Scots like-

---

Edward I's Case against Philip the Fair', *EHR*, XLII (1927), p. 576, *n.* 2). Alexander was not ' an anointed king ', for no Scottish king was anointed at his inauguration until 1331 ; but Alexander certainly *desired* to be anointed, and the papacy had already, in 1221, refused his request for anointing. Cf. below, p. 39, where Alexander III asks to be allowed *as a special favour* to swear by deputy. No such concession was made to John Balliol in 1292 (Rymer, I, ii, 781), but the case is not quite parallel, for he had not yet been inaugurated as king at Scone. By the later fourteenth century the reluctance of sovereigns to swear in person diminished ; cf. Rymer, III, i, 520, and Cosneau, *Grands Traités de la Guerre de Cent Ans* (1889), pp. 98, 114.

Scottorum similiter in animam suam fecit jurare Walterum Cumyn comitem de Meneteth, et preterea idem rex Scottorum fecit comitem Mauculmum comitem de Meneteth Walterum filium Alani Walterum Olifard Bernardum Fraser Henricum de Bayllol G[ilbertum] Marescallum comitem Penbroc H[umfredum] comitem Herefordie David Cumyn David Marscallum Thomam filium Ranulfi Willelmum de Forz Johannem de Baillol et Henricum de Hasting' jurare de pace ista tenenda, in forma literarum patencium quas ipsi regi Anglie inde fecerunt. Preterea idem rex Scottorum et barones predicti jurati posuerunt se jurisdiccioni domini pape sub hac forma, quod si dictus rex Scottorum vel dicti barones sui aliquo tempore contra predictum juramentum suum venirent, debent super hoc a domino papa canonice coherceri, propter quod eciam debent ipse rex Scottorum et barones predicti domino pape literatorie[1] significare ut hanc jurisdiccionem alicui suffraganeorum Cantuariensis archiepiscopi de consensu parcium committat. Ad majorem eciam hujus pacis securitatem facta est hec carta inter dictos reges in modum cyrographi,[2] ita quod uterque illorum alterius parti sigillum suum apposuit. Hiis testibus,[a] venerabilibus patribus W[altero] Ebor' archiepiscopo ; R[adulpho] Cyc', domini regis Anglie cancellario, W[altero] Carl', W[altero] Wigorn', et W[illelmo] de Glasgu, cancellario prefati regis Scotorum, episcopis ; W[illelmo] electo Valencie, R[icardo] comite Pictavie et Cornubie, W[illelmo] comite Warenne, J[ohanne] comite Linc', constabulario Cestrie, W[illelmo] comite Albemarl', R[ogero] comite Winton', S[imone] de Monteforti, G[ilberto] Marescallo, comite

---

[a] E *stops here* ; *remainder given from* C, *and where* C *now illegible, from* R

wise has caused Walter Comyn, earl of Menteith, to
swear on the king's soul, and in addition the king of
Scots has caused Earl Malcolm, the earl of Menteith,
Walter FitzAlan, Walter Olifard, Bernard Fraser, Henry
Balliol, Gilbert Marshall, earl of Pembroke, Humphrey,
earl of Hereford, David Comyn, David Marshall,
Thomas FitzRanulph, William de Forz, John Balliol, and
Henry of Hastings to swear to the keeping of this peace,
in the words of the letter patent on the subject which
they have made for the king of England.   Further, the
king of Scots, and the barons taking the oath, have submitted themselves to the jurisdiction of the pope in this
fashion : that if the king of Scots, or his barons, at any
time infringe their oath, for this they ought to be subject
to canonical censure by the pope, and therefore the king
of Scots and the barons ought also to signify to the pope,
by letter,[1] that he may commit this jurisdiction to one of
the suffragans of the archbishop of Canterbury, with the
consent of the parties.   For the better safeguarding of
this treaty, the present charter was made between the
two kings, in the form of a chirograph,[2] in such a way
that each of them affixed his seal to the other's counterpart.   Witnesses, the venerable fathers Walter, archbishop
of York ;   Ralph, bishop of Chichester, chancellor of the
king of England, Walter, bishop of Carlisle, Walter,
bishop of Worcester, and William, bishop of Glasgow,
chancellor of the king of Scots ;   William, bishop-elect
of Valence, Richard, count of Poitou and earl of Cornwall, William, earl of Warenne, John, earl of Lincoln
and constable of Chester, William, count of Aumale,
Roger, earl of Winchester, Simon de Montfort, Gilbert

---

[1] See Rymer, I, i, 234.
[2] i.e., an ' indenture '

Pembr', comite Patricio, comite de Strathern, comite de Livenath, comite de Angoiz, comite de Mar, comite de Athol, comite de Ros, Willelmo Lungespee, Radulpho de Thaeny, W[illelmo] de Ros, R[oberto] de Ros, W[illelmo] de Ferrariis, R[ogero] Bertram, H. Painel, G[ilberto] de Umframville, Amauricio de sancto Amando, P[etro] de Malo Lacu, magistro Petro de Burdegal' et magistro Att', clericis domini legati, Johanne filio Galfridi, Hugone de Vivon', Stephano ᵃ de Sedgrave, W. de Lanc' ᵇ [?], W. de Say, Ricardo de Gray, Thoma de Furnivall, Johanne de Lexinton, Johanne de Plesseto, Bartholomeo Peche, Willelmo Gernun, Ricardo filio Hugonis, et aliis.¹

ᵃ Stephano de *repeated* C
ᵇ Lacu R, *Bain*

¹ The witness list speaks for itself as evidence of the splendour of this exceptional occasion, when both kings were present at the conclusion of a major treaty.

Marshall, earl of Pembroke, Earl Patrick, the earl of Strathearn, the earl of Lennox, the earl of Angus, the earl of Mar, the earl of Athol, the earl of Ross, William Longsword, Ralph de Tany, William de Ros, Robert de Ros, William Ferrers, Roger Bertram, H. Painel, Gilbert de Umfraville, Aimery of Saint-Amand, Peter de Maulay, master Peter of Bordeaux and master Atho, clerks of the lord legate, John FitzGeoffrey, Hugh of Vivonne, Stephen Segrave, W. of Lanc[aster ?], W. de Say, Richard Gray, Thomas Furnivall, John of Lexington, John du Plessis, Bartholomew Peche, William Gernun, Richard FitzHugh, and others.[1]

8

Excellentissimo [1] domino suo Henrico, dei gracia illustri regi Anglie domino Hybernie duci Normannie Aquitannie et comiti Andegavie, suus humilis Hugo de Bolbec [2] salutem et fidele semper obsequium. Excellencie vestre notificetur me a die sancti Michaelis in quindecim dies, scilicet ad diem a rege Scocie mihi prefixum, cum discrecioribus militibus de comitatu vestro Norhumbrie [3] in propria persona mea usque Revedeneburne accessisse, et ibidem David de Lindesey justiciarium Laoudie et Patricium comitem de Dunbar et plures alios milites a rege Scocie transmissos reperisse, et [a] negocio pro quo ibidem hincinde conveneramus exposito, placuit omnibus nobis in communi primo sex milites ex parte vestra alias juratos, et alios sex milites ex parte regis Scocie eligere, qui rectam perambulacionem facerent inter regnum vestrum Anglie et regnum Scocie scilicet inter Karham et Hawedene.[4] Quo facto prefati sex milites ex parte vestra electi per rectas et antiquas divisas et marchias inter prefata regna unanimi processerunt assensu, prefatis sex militibus ex parte regis Scocie electis in hoc illis omnino dissensientibus (*sic*) et contradicentibus, unde iterum tam predictis justiciario et

---

Text : P.R.O. Ancient Correspondence (S.C. 1) 2/166 (A); probably the original letter. It has no signs of endorsement. The shape of the lower edge suggests that it was sealed *sur simple queue*. Printed in *Royal Letters of Reign of Henry III*, ed. Shirley (RS), 1, 186-8 (S). Calendared in Bain, 1, no. 832, under wrong date 1222, as is obvious from his no. 1676.

    [a] et S; ex A

    [1] This letter describes a perambulation of a small portion of the marches, and is our earliest evidence for the section between Carham and the Cheviots. It is not clear why so short a section (only about eight miles) is covered, and possibly the enquiry was intended only to settle a dispute about the lands of the canons of Carham (cf. Bain, 1, no. 1699) which lay in this

8

To [1] his most excellent lord, Henry, by the grace of God the illustrious king of England, lord of Ireland, duke of Normandy and Aquitaine, and count of Anjou, Hugh of Bolbec [2] his humble servant, offers greeting and ever faithful service. This is to tell your excellency that on the quinzaine of Michaelmas [13 October], that being the day assigned to me by the king of Scotland, I went in person to Reddenburn, with some judicious knights from your shire of Northumberland. [3] There I found David Lindsay, justiciar of Lothian, Patrick, earl of Dunbar, and many other knights sent by the king of Scotland. The business for which we had met at that place was mutually explained, and we all together decided to begin by electing six knights sworn on your behalf already, and six other knights on behalf of the king of Scotland, who would make a true perambulation between your realm of England and the realm of Scotland, that is, between Carham and Hadden. [4] After this the six knights chosen on your behalf proceeded with common assent along the true and ancient bounds and frontiers between the kingdoms, but the six knights chosen on behalf of the king of Scotland entirely disagreed with them, and contradicted them in this.

---

region, and were apparently bounded by the frontier. Unfortunately the topographical details are scanty. See R.C.A.M.S., *Roxburghshire* (1956), 1, 8-9; J. L. Mack, *The Border Line* (1926), esp. chapter 2.

[2] Sheriff of Northumberland

[3] For the names of these twenty-four knights see Bain, 1, no. 1676.

[4] I am grateful to Professor Barrow for pointing out that Carham and Hadden are here not the terminal points of the perambulation, but the lands on the English and Scottish sides respectively, whose junction constituted the disputed frontier. ' Between Carham and Hadden ', therefore, means between the lands of Carham on the English side and of Hadden on the Scottish side. This Hadden was about four miles E.N.E. of Kelso.

comiti quam mihi placuit in communi alios sex milites
ex parte vestra et alios sex milites ex parte regis Scocie
eligere, et prefatis duodecim militibus ad majorem securitatem super predicta perambulacione facienda asociare
(*sic*). Quibus electis et juratis, milites ex parte vestra
electi in dictas consensere, ut prius, divisas, et milites ex
parte regis Scocie electi in alteras ᵃ assenserunt divisas.
Et quia per predictos milites Scocie stetit quominus dicta
perambulacio ibidem [tunc ᵇ] fieret, tunc secundum
tenorem mandati vestri mihi directi viginti et quattuor
discretos et legales milites de predicto comitatu vestro
elegi et jurare feci quod rectas et antiquas marchias et
divisas inter regna predicta recognoscerent, qui scilicet
loca subscripta rectas et antiquas marchias et divisas
inter predicta regna sacramento esse recognoverunt,
videlicet : a Tweda per rivulum de Revedenburne
ascendendo versus austrum usque ad tres karras,¹ et a
tribus karris ¹ linealiter directe ascendendo usque ad
Hoperichelawe ² et de Hoperichelawe linealiter directe
usque ad Witelawe. Quibus sic ire volentibus et predictam perambulacionem sic facere incipientibus, predicti justiciarius et comes cum militibus suis vi illis
resistentes ne dictam facerent perambulacionem minando
impediverunt. Quo facto milites nostri sic impediti
firmiter asserebant predicta loca rectas et antiquas inter
predicta regna marchias esse et divisas. Quod autem
vestro sederit beneplacito, super hiis et aliis mihi si placet
significare dignemini. Valeat excellencia vestra semper
in domino.

ᵃ alteras *corrected from* alias A
ᵇ tunc *almost obliterated* A ; *om.* S

¹ cf. *O.E.D.*, s.v. ' carr ' (from Old Norse).
² ' Hoperichelawe ' has been identified as Hopriglaw, but no such place
is to be seen on the modern map. Cf. 2½ inch Ordnance survey, sheets NT
(36) 73, 82, 83.

Accordingly the justiciar and the earl and I together agreed to choose another six knights on your behalf, and another six on behalf of the king of Scotland, and to join them with the said twelve knights, in order to have greater assurance in making the perambulation. When they had been chosen and sworn, the knights chosen on your behalf agreed on the said boundaries, as previously, and the knights chosen on behalf of the king of Scotland agreed on different boundaries. And since the knights of Scotland were to blame that the perambulation could not take place there at that time, according to the terms of your mandate sent to me I chose twenty-four judicious and lawful knights of your county, and caused them to swear that they would make a declaration of the true and ancient bounds and frontiers between the realms. They made a declaration on oath that the places mentioned below were the true and ancient bounds and frontiers between the kingdoms : from the Tweed by the stream of Reddenburn ascending southwards to ' three marshes ' [1] and from ' three marshes ' [1] by a direct line ascending to ' Hoperichelawe ',[2] and from ' Hoperiche- lawe ' by a direct line to Whitelaw. When they wanted to go and begin to make the perambulation, the justiciar and earl, with their knights, resisted them by force, and by threats prevented them from making the perambula- tion. Then our knights, being hindered thus, firmly declared that these places were the true and ancient bounds and frontiers between the kingdoms. Be good enough, if you please, to tell me what is your pleasure in these and other matters. May your excellency ever prosper in the Lord.

H

9

Bulla Innocencii pape quarti per quam non exaudit peticiones regis Anglie, videlicet quod rex Scocie non possit inungi vel coronari sine licencia sua, et de decima ecclesiasticorum beneficiorum habenda. R[egistrata] in m[agno] libro.ᵃ

INNOCENCIUS ¹ episcopus servus servorum dei, carissimo in Christo filio .². regi Anglie ilustri (*sic*) salutem et apostolicam benediccionem. Ex parte tua fuit nobis cum instancia supplicatum ut tibi ne carissimus in Christo filius noster .². rex Scotie illustris, absque tuo assensu inungi vel coronari posset, cum sit ligius homo tuus tibique homagium fecerit, concedere curaremus. Quia vero talia concedere sedes apostolica minime consuevit, non mireris si te non exaudivimus in hac parte, noveris tamen quod alicui non concederemus aliquid quod redundare crederemus in prejudicium regie dignitatis. Super eo vero quod petebas tibi decimam ecclesiasticorum proventuum in ipsius regno concedi, peticionem tuam, de quo non turberis, non admisimus quia quod hoc in alterius regno concederetur alicui est penitus inauditum. Dat' Lugdun' viij idus Aprilis, pontificatus nostri anno octavo.

Text: From original bull in P.R.O. Papal Bulls (S.C. 7), 20/11 (S). Copy (of time of Edward I) in P.R.O. Liber A (E 36/274), f. 81v (A). Listed by Stapledon (Palgrave, *Kalendars*, I, 22). Printed by Rymer, I, i, 277. Calendared in Bain, I, no. 1798; *Cal. Papal Letters*, I, 270; Potthast 14291; *Registres d'Innocent IV* (ed. E. Berger, Paris 1887), II, no. 5211.

ᵃ *Title is an endorsement on* S, *probably by the clerks of Edward I, and it appears also in the margin of* A. *The* ' *great book* ' *is Liber* A. S *has a second endorsement* (*by the papal clerks*) *not given here.*

¹ On Scottish ' coronations ', and the desire of Scottish kings for unction see Powicke, *Thirteenth Century*, pp. 593-4 and the references cited there, and cf. above, p. xxii, and below, p. 44, *n.* 4. A note by Marc Bloch in *SHR*,

9

Bull of Pope Innocent IV in which he does not
hearken to the requests of the king of England, namely
that the king of Scotland may not be anointed or
crowned without his permission, and concerning the
grant of a tenth of ecclesiastical benefices. (Registered
in the great book.)

Innocent,[1] bishop and servant of the servants of God,
gives greeting and apostolic benediction to his well-
beloved son in Christ .[2]. the illustrious king of England.
It has been strongly represented to us, on your behalf,
that we should proceed to grant to you that our beloved
son in Christ .[2]. the illustrious king of Scotland may not
be anointed or crowned without your consent, since he
is your liegeman and has done you homage. Yet, because the apostolic see is but little accustomed to admit
requests of this kind, you must not be surprised if we
have not hearkened to you in this matter, for we must
explain that we would not make a concession to anybody
which might, in our opinion, tend to prejudice the royal
dignity. Concerning your request for the grant of a tenth
of ecclesiastical revenues in his kingdom, we have not
granted it (and be not distressed at this) because it is
altogether unheard of that any ruler should be granted
this privilege within the kingdom of another sovereign.
Lyons, 6 April, the eighth year of our pontificate [1251].

---

xxiii (1926), 105, shows that Alexander III was at this very time soliciting
the right of unction from the pope, but Bloch apparently did not notice the
present bull. The pope is not here agreeing to grant unction (it was not in
fact granted until 1329) but refusing Henry III's request that English
agreement should be made a condition for it. Alexander III had been
enthroned at Scone two years before the date of this bull.

[2] The *gemipunctus*; see above, p. 17, *n*. 2.

10

De Facto Scocie.[a]

H[ENRICUS] [1] dei gracia rex Anglie etc.,[2] omnibus ad quos presentes littere pervenerint, salutem. Sciatis nos litteras dilecti filii et fidelis nostri Alexandri, dei gracia regis Scottorum illustris, habere in hec verba :

Universis Christi fidelibus ad quos presens scriptum pervenerit Alexander dei gracia rex Scottorum salutem. Noverit universitas vestra quod cum karissimus pater noster et dominus H[enricus] rex Anglie illustris pro honore et utilitate nostra et regni nostri ad marchiam regnorum Anglie et Scocie sui gracia personaliter accessisset, nos ad instanciam ipsius regis et de consilio magnatum nostrorum, scilicet venerabilium patrum in Christo W[illelmi] Glasg' [3] R[icardi] Dunkeld' et P[etri] Abbirden' episcoporum et dominorum [b] G[amelini] electi sancti Andree,[3] de Dunfermel' de Kelchou de Geddeworth de Newebolt, abbatum, M[alcolmi] comitis de Fyf P[atricii] comitis de Dunbar N[igelli] comitis de Carric M[alisii] comitis de Strathern Alexandri senescalli Scocie Roberti de Brus Alani hostiarii [4] Walteri de Morevia David de Lindes' Willelmi de Brechyn Hugonis Giffard Rogeri de Munbray Gileberti de Haya Roberti de Meyners Willelmi de Duveglas Johannis de Vallibus

---

Text: Original lost; transcripts in P.R.O. Charter Roll 39 Henry III (C 53/46 A), m. 8, schedule (C) ; Patent Roll 39 Henry III, part 2 (C 66/69), m. 2 (P), whence Rymer, I, i, 329.   Calendared in Bain, I, no. 2013 ; in *Cal. Charter Rolls 1226–57*, p. 438, and in *Cal. Patent Rolls 1247–58*, p. 426. Printed here from C, except when otherwise stated.

[1] For the occasion of this document see above, p. xxiii; Dickinson,

10

On the affairs of Scotland.

HENRY,[1] by the grace of God king of England, etc.,[2] gives greeting to all whom the present letter shall reach. This is to tell you that we have received a letter from our beloved and faithful son Alexander, by the grace of God the illustrious king of Scots, which reads as follows :

Alexander, by the grace of God king of Scots, gives greeting to all the faithful in Christ whom the present writing shall reach. This is to inform all of you that when our most dear father and lord, Henry, the illustrious king of England, graciously came in person to the border of the realms of England and Scotland, for the honour and the advantage of ourselves and of our realm, we, at the instance of the king himself, and by the advice of our magnates, namely the venerable fathers in Christ, William, bishop of Glasgow,[3] Richard, bishop of Dunkeld, and Peter, bishop of Aberdeen, Gamelin, bishop-elect of St Andrews,[3] the abbots of Dunfermline, Kelso, Jedburgh, and Newbattle, Malcolm, earl of Fife, Patrick, earl of Dunbar, Nigel, earl of Carrick, Malise, earl of Strathearn, Alexander, the steward of Scotland, Robert Bruce, Alan Durward,[4] Walter of Moray, David Lindsay, William of Brechin, Hugh Giffard, Roger of Mowbray, Gilbert Hay, Robert de Meyners, William Douglas,

---

Scotland, pp. 81-2 ; and (for a different view) Powicke, *Thirteenth Century*, pp. 590-1.   Chronicle accounts are in Anderson, *E.S.* II, 580-5, and *S.A.*, pp. 370-3.

[2] To be extended as on p. 27

[3] The inclusion of the bishop of Glasgow and the elect of St Andrews in the first of these lists as advising their own removal, seems inexplicable, except as a mere error.

[4] See *D.N.B.*, s.n. ' Durward '.

Willelmi de Ramesheye et aliorum plurium baronum
nostrorum, amovimus W[illelmum] Glasg' [1] C[lemen-
tem] Dumblan' episcopos G[amelinum] electum sancti
Andree [1] W[alterum] Comyn comitem de Menetyef [sic]
Alexandrum Comyn comitem de Bochan [a] Willelmum
comitem de Mar Johannem de Baylol Robertum de Ros
Aymerum de Makyswell et Mariam uxorem ejus Johannem Comyn Nicholaum de Sules Thomam de Norman-
vill Alexandrum Uviet Johannem de Dundemor David
de Graham Johannem le Blund Thomam filium Ranulphi
Hugonem Gurle et Willelmum fratrem ejus Willelmum
Wyschard archidiaconum sancti Andree fratrem Ricardum elemosinarium de ordine milicie templi David de
Louchor Johannem Wyscard Willelmum de Cadyhou [b]
et Willelmum quondam capellanum nostrum, meritis
eorum exigentibus, ut dicitur, a consilio nostro et balliis
suis, et ipsos aut complices vel fautores suos ad consilia
nostra et negocia regni nostri tractanda, seu ad graciam
nostram vel familiaritatem aliquam nequaquam admit-
temus donec ipsi predicto regi et nobis excessus eis
impositos et imponendos concordia vel judicio ad plenum
emendaverint; ad quod faciendum modis omnibus
quibus justum fuerit eos si necesse fuerit compellemus.
Illud quoque condictum et utrimque concessum est quod
si principem extraneum regnum Scocie invadere vel
impugnare contingat, liceat dictos [c] magnates a nostro
consilio jam ammotos et alios quoscumque ad nostrum
auxilium admittere et invocare.

Ad hec autem, mediante regis predicti consilio et
dictorum magnatum nostrorum, ordinavimus quod

---

[a] Bocham C; Botham P
[b] *So* P; Cadyhav' C
[c] liceat nobis predictos P

[1] See above, p. 30, *n*. 3.

John de Vaux, William Ramsay, and many others of
our barons, have removed the following from their
offices on our council because their faults so demand,
as it is reported : William, bishop of Glasgow [1] and
Clement, bishop of Dunblane, Gamelin, bishop-elect of
St Andrews,[1] Walter Comyn, earl of Menteith, Alexander
Comyn, earl of Buchan, William, earl of Mar, John
Balliol, Robert de Ros, Aymer of Maxwell and Mary his
wife, John Comyn, Nicholas de Soules, Thomas de
Normanville, Alexander Uviet, John de Dundemor,
David Graham, John le Blund, Thomas FitzRanulph,
Hugh Gurle and his brother William, William Wishart,
archdeacon of St Andrews, Brother Richard, almoner of
the order of the Templars, David of Lochore, John
Wishart, William of Cadzow, and William our former
chaplain. We shall not admit them, or their accomplices
and sympathisers, to our counsels, and to the conduct of
the business of our realm, or to our grace, or to any sort
of intimacy, until they have fully atoned, by concord
or by judgment, to King Henry and ourselves, for the
offences imputed, and to be imputed to them. We
shall compel them, if necessary, to do this, by every
sort of just means. This also was settled and granted on
both sides, that if it should happen that the realm of
Scotland is invaded or attacked by an alien prince, we
shall be allowed to admit and invoke the magnates now
removed from our council, and any others whatsoever,
to come to our help.

For this purpose we have ordered, with the advice of
the king and of our said magnates, that the venerable

venerabiles patres Ricardus et Petrus Dunkelden' et
Abbirden' episcopi M[alcolmus] comes de Fyf P[atricius]
comes de Dumbar M[alisius] comes de Strathern N[igellus]
comes de Carric Alexander senescallus Scocie
Robertus de Brus Alanus hostiarius Walterus de Moravia
David de Lindes' Willelmus de Brechyn Robertus de
Meyners Gilbertus de Haya et Hugo Giffard ad consilia
nostra et gubernacionem regni nostri et custodiam corporis
nostri et regine sponse nostre deputati, a consilio
nostro et balliis suis citra terminum septem annorum
completorum et incipiencium ad festum translacionis
sancti Cuthberti anno domini M⁰CC⁰ quinquagesimo
quinto, vel terminum breviorem in quem dictus dominus
rex vel ejus heredes et nos communiter duxerimus consenciendum,
nullatenus ammovebuntur, nisi manifeste
demeruerint quominus ipsis consiliis et regni nostri negociis
debeant interesse.   Quod si ipsorum aliquem vel
aliquos ex causa hujusmodi ammoveri vel in fata concedere
infra dictum tempus contigerit, alius vel alii loco
ipsius vel ipsorum de consilio predictorum episcoporum
comitum et baronum consiliariorum nostrorum vel
eorum qui ex ipsis superstites extiterint substituentur.
Preterea de feodalibus custodiis vel escaetis nostris nichil
fiet nisi de consilio et consensu dictorum consiliariorum
nostrorum, seu eisdem modo predicto substituendorum
et nostro.

   Si vero vicecomites forestarii et ceteri minores ballivi
delinquant per quod debeant a suis balliis ammoveri,
nos per supradictum consilium nostrum alios loco ipsorum
substitui faciemus.   Nec castra nostra ab eis quibus
tempore confeccionis presencium commissa fuerunt resumemus,
nisi per consilium commune eorumdem consiliariorum
nostrorum ad custodiam et gubernacionem

fathers, Richard, bishop of Dunkeld, and Peter, bishop of
Aberdeen, Malcolm, earl of Fife, Patrick, earl of Dunbar,
Malise, earl of Strathearn, Nigel, earl of Carrick, Alexander, the steward of Scotland, Robert Bruce, Alan
Durward, Walter of Moray, David Lindsay, William of
Brechin, Robert de Meyners, Gilbert Hay, and Hugh
Giffard, who have been appointed to our council, the
government of our realm, and the guardianship of our
body, and of that of our queen, shall in no wise be
removed from their offices on our council, before the
expiry of seven complete years, beginning at the feast
of the translation of St Cuthbert [4 September] in the
year 1255, or of a briefer period upon which King
Henry, or his heirs, and ourselves shall have agreed
together, unless they shall clearly have so acted as to be
unworthy to take part in our councils and the business
of our realm. But if it should happen that any one or
more of them is removed for this reason, or should die,
within that time, then another or others may be substituted in his or their place by the advice of the aforesaid
bishops, earls, and barons, our councillors, or of those
among them who survive. Further, nothing shall be
done with our feudal wardships and escheats, except by
the council and assent of our said councillors, or of those
substituted for them in the above manner, and of ourself.

If sheriffs, foresters, and other lesser officials so offend
that they ought to be moved from their posts, we shall
cause others to be put in their place by our aforesaid
council. We shall not take back our castles from those
to whom they were committed at the time when this
letter was made, except by the common counsel of our
advisers, assigned for the wardship and government of

regni nostri et corporis nostri et regine nostre assigna-
torum. Promisimus eciam bona fide prefato domino
regi quod filiam suam reginam nostram affectu maritali
cum honorificencia omnimoda que filiam tanti principis
et nostram decet reginam tractabimus et custodiemus, et
eidem a regno nostro honores debitos et convenientes in
omnibus et per omnia exhiberi faciemus. Obligaciones
eciam et concessiones racionabiles quas predicti episcopi
et magnates nostri fecerunt prefato domino regi ratas
habemus et acceptas, ut eas que de mandato nostro et
voluntate processerunt.

Et ad omnia predicta fideliter et inviolabiliter observanda, jurare fecimus in animam nostram [1] Patricius
comes de Dumbar, subicientes nos cohercioni domini
pape ut si contra predicta in aliquo, quod absit, veniamus,
ipse per censuram ecclesiasticam absque strepitu judiciali
nos ad plenam premissorum observacionem compellat,
presenti scripto, completo predicto termino ut predictum
est, nobis vel heredibus nostris bona fide restituendo, nec
postmodum aliquo tempore valituro. In hujus autem
rei testimonium presenti scripto sigillum nostrum fecimus
apponi. Teste me [a] ipso apud Roke[s]burg' xx die
Septembris anno regni nostri [a] septimo.

Nos vero predicto regi Scottorum promittimus et concedimus bona fide quod expleto termino supradicto, per
ea que in dicto scripto continentur nullum sibi vel
heredibus suis vel regno suo aut libertatibus suis regiis
prejudicium generabitur, et quod in fine termini memorati predictum scriptum nichil valeat et quod nichilominus restituatur, et pro nullo penitus habeatur. In

---

[a] *to* [a] *Scribe of* C *at first wrote* Teste rege . . . . anno regni ipsius domini
regis *as if enrolling a writ* (*as, for example, on p. 36 below*).

[1] cf. above, p. 24, *n.* 3.

our realm, and of our person, and of that of our queen. We have also promised King Henry, in good faith, that we will treat and guard his daughter, our queen, in matrimonial affection, with every sort of consideration which befits our queen and the daughter of so great a prince, and we shall cause due and proper honour to be shown to her, in our realm, in every possible way. We ratify and accept also the reasonable undertakings and concessions which the same bishops and magnates of ours have made to the king, as representing our own command and desire.

We have caused Patrick, earl of Dunbar, to swear on our soul [1] that we shall faithfully and inviolably observe all these provisions, and we subject ourselves to the discipline of the pope, so that if we offend against them in any particular (which God forbid) he may force us by ecclesiastical censure, without recourse to legal proceedings, to make full observance of them. When the stated period is complete, as we have said, the present document is to be restored to us, or our heirs, in good faith, and is not thereafter to have any value. As evidence of this we have caused our seal to be affixed to the present letter. Witness myself, at Roxburgh, 20 September, in the seventh year of our reign [1255].

We have promised and granted to the king of Scots in good faith, that on the expiry of the stated period, no prejudice shall be caused to him, or his heirs, or his realm, or his royal liberties, by the contents of the document, and that at the end of the period the document shall be of no effect, and that it shall be restored none the less, and regarded as entirely void. As evidence of

hujus igitur rei testimonium has litteras nostras fieri fecimus patentes. Teste meipso apud Sprouston xx die Septembris anno regni nostri xxxix°.

Memorandum ᵃ *quod ista littera facta fuit et concessa domino regi Scocie per preceptum domini regis Anglie apud Karham per consilium et visum R[icardi] comitis Glouc' G[alfridi]* ¹ *de Lezinan W[illelmi] de Valencia fratrum regis J[ohannis] Mansel* ² *prepositi Beverl' R[ogeri] le Bigot comitis Norf' marscalli Anglie J[ohannis] de Warenne comitis Surr' W[illelmi] de Fortibus comitis Albemarle Edmundi de Lacy J[ohannis] de Plessetis* ᵇ *comitis War' Hugonis le Bigot Rogeri de Monte Alto senescalli Cestrie* ᶜ *Elie de Raban'* ᵈ *J[ohannis] de Grey R[oberti] Walerand W[illelmi] de Clare et multorum aliorum baronum et consiliariorum regis tunc ibidem existencium.*

. . . .

Memorandum ᵉ *quod litera regis Scocie de convencione tenenda quam fecit cum domino rege Anglie apud Werk'* ³ *remansit in custodia J[ohannis] Mansel* ² *prepositi Beverl'.*

Memorandum quod hec omnia instrumenta ⁴ *de facto Scocie inrotulata sunt in rotulo patencium anni etc. xxxix* ᵐⁱ, *et sic in duobus locis* ⁵ *poterunt reperiri sicut provisum fuit per concilium regis apud Karham.*

ᵃ *This memorandum appears in margin of* P *and in text of* C.
ᵇ *So* P; Plessēt C
ᶜ senescalli Cestrie *om.* P
ᵈ Rabbayne P
ᵉ *This follows after four letters of Henry III which are here omitted.*

¹ For the identification see Rymer, I, i, 327.
² For the career of this very able civil servant see *D.N.B.*, and Powicke, *Henry III and Lord Edward*, p. 294, *n.*
³ This letter seems unknown.
⁴ ' All these instruments ' includes the four letters omitted here.
⁵ It was a common practice to keep important documents in duplicate or triplicate; cf. below, p. 56, *n.*, p. 64, *n.* 1, *etc.*

this, we have caused this letter patent of ours to be written. Witness myself, at Sprouston, 20 September, in the thirty-ninth year of our reign [1255].

Note that that letter was made and granted to the king of Scotland by command of the king of England at Carham, by the advice and under the supervision of Richard, earl of Gloucester, G[eoffrey] [1] *of Lusignan, and William of Valence, the brothers of the king, John Mansel,* [2] *provost of Beverley [minster], Roger Bigod, earl of Norfolk and marshal of England, John de Warenne, earl of Surrey, William de Forz, count of Aumale, Edmund de Lacy, John du Plessis, earl of Warwick, Hugh Bigod, Roger of Mold, steward of Chester, Elias de Rabbayne, John de Grey, Robert Walerand, William of Clare and of many other barons and counsellors of the king, who were present there at the time.*

. . . .

Note that the king of Scotland's letter about the keeping of the agreement which he made with the king of England at Wark, [3] *remained in the keeping of John Mansel,* [2] *the provost of Beverley [minster].*

Note that all of these instruments [4] *about the business of Scotland are enrolled on the patent roll for the thirty-ninth year [of the reign of King Henry III (1254–5)] and thus they can be found in two places,* [5] *as was directed by the king's council at Carham.*

II

De facto Scocie.[a]

REX [1] nobilibus viris et amicis suis dilectis G[amelino], eadem gracia [2] episcopo sancti Andree Johanni de Acre Marie dicta [2] gracia regine Scocie sponse ipsius Johannis [3] Alexandro Comyn comiti de Bouchan Willelmo comiti de Mar' Alexandro senescallo Scocie Alano hostiario Roberto de Meyners et Gilberto de Haya consiliariis karissimi filii sui illustris regis Scocie, salutem. Cum in vos curam regni Scocie assumpseritis, sciatis nos vobis bona fide promisisse quod quamdiu negocia ipsius regni secundum deum et justiciam et ad commodum et honorem predicti filii nostri regis domini vestri et filie nostre predilecte regine Scocie domine vestre atque secundum leges et bonas consuetudines illius regni hactenus usitatas rite tractaveritis, in eisdem negociis, cum indigueritis et a vobis fuerimus requisiti, consilium nostrum et auxilium vobis favorabiliter impendemus, ita quod si vos omnes vel aliqui seu aliquis vestrum super premissis in aliquo deliqueritis, et a nobis requisiti fueritis super emenda exinde facienda, nec infra spacium trium mensium post nostram monicionem super hoc a vobis receptam illud emendaveritis secundum quod debueritis, in nullo extunc vobis teneri volumus. In

---

Text: P.R.O. Close Roll 43 Henry III (C 54/74), m. 15 d, and schedule, whence printed in *Close Rolls Henry III (1256-59)*, pp. 461-2. Calendared in Bain, 1, no. 2140. Not in Rymer, as Bain alleges; but the letter patent of Henry III in Rymer, 1, i, 378 is very close to the first part of the text.

[a] *Title from margin of MS*

[1] For the occasion of this document see Powicke, *Thirteenth Century*, p. 592, and Dickinson, *Scotland*, p. 82 ; and cf. above, p. xxiii. It represents a compromise, in which Gamelin, and the earls of Buchan and Mar, excluded

II

On the affairs of Scotland.

THE [1] king [Henry III] gives greeting to his noble and beloved friends Gamelin, by [God's] grace [2] bishop of St Andrews, John of Acre, Mary, by the said grace [2] queen of Scotland, and wife of the same John,[3] Alexander Comyn, earl of Buchan, William, earl of Mar, Alexander, the steward of Scotland, Alan Durward, Robert de Meyners and Gilbert Hay, counsellors of his well-beloved son the illustrious king of Scotland. Because you have taken upon you the care of the realm of Scotland, we notify you that we have promised in good faith, that when you are in need, and we have been asked by you, we shall favourably grant our counsel and help to you in the affairs of the realm of Scotland, so long as you genuinely conduct them with regard for God and for justice, and for the profit and honour of our son the king, your lord, and of our beloved daughter the queen of Scotland, your lady, and according to the laws and good customs of that realm as hitherto followed. But if all, or any, or one of you fail in any way in the above, and are asked by us to make amends for this, and within the period of three months after receiving our admonition thereupon you have not made amends as you should, we shall thenceforward be under no sort of obligation to

---

for seven years in 1255 (above, p. 31), are accepted again as members of the Scottish king's council.

[2] ' *Eadem* ' and ' *dicta* ' *gracia* are explained by the fact that in the engrossment of the text, as distinct from this enrolment, the opening would be *Henricus, dei gracia rex*. The text, as it stands here, is anomalous.

[3] Mary of Coucy, widow of Alexander II, had married John of Acre, son of the king of Jerusalem, as her second husband.

cujus *etc.*[1] Teste rege [2] apud Westmonasterium vj die Novembris.

Et sciendum quod in forma cedule hic appense debet impetrari littera,[3] *et similiter alia littera sub eodem tenore de sigillo regis Scocie si fieri possit, et cum venerint debent irrotulari; et ad ista negocia prosequenda mittuntur Robertus de Neuvyle et frater Willelmus de Horton' monachus de sancto Albano; et habent litteras regis de credencia directas regi Scocie et regine et predictis consiliariis.*

[*schedule*]

Omnibus hoc scriptum visuris vel audituris G[amelinus], dei gracia episcopus sancti Andree Johannes de Acre Maria dei gracia regina Scocie sponsa ipsius Johannis Alexander Comyn comes de Bochan Willelmus comes de Mar' Alexander senescallus Scocie Alanus hostiarius Robertus de Meyners et Gilbertus de Haya salutem in domino. Cum inter manus nostras curam regni Scocie jam habeamus, noveritis nos fideliter manucepisse quod negocia ipsius regni tractabimus secundum deum et justiciam et ad commodum et honorem domini nostri regis et domine nostre regine ac predicti regni utilitatem, secundum leges et bonas consuetudines illius regni hactenus usitatas, faciendo tam divitibus quam pauperibus equanimiter plenam justiciam exhiberi. Nos autem inter dictum dominum nostrum regem et predictam dominam nostram reginam bonum amorem et unitatem, in quantum diligencius poterimus, procurabimus omni tempore observari, volentes et concedentes

---

[1] The engrossment would read *in cujus rei testimonium*, followed by words describing the mode of execution of the document. The formula suggests that the letter was sent out patent, in spite of being enrolled on the Close Roll; and the circumstances of its issue make this seem likely in any case. cf. Tout, *Chapters in Administrative History*, v (1930), 123-6; Maxwell-Lyte, *Notes on Great Seal of England* (1926), p. 392.

[2] The engrossment would read *Teste meipso*.

you. In [testimony] etc.[1] Witness the king,[2] Westminster, 6 November [1258].

And note that a letter should be obtained [3] in the words of the schedule here appended, and likewise another letter with the same wording under the seal of the king of Scotland, if it can be had, and when they arrive, they should be enrolled; and Robert Neville and Brother William de Horton, a monk of St Albans, are being sent to attend to that; and they have royal letters of credence directed to the king and the queen of Scotland, and to the counsellors mentioned.

[*schedule*]

We, Gamelin, by the grace of God bishop of St Andrews, John of Acre, Mary, by the grace of God queen of Scotland and wife of the same John, Alexander Comyn, earl of Buchan, William, earl of Mar, Alexander, the steward of Scotland, Alan Durward, Robert de Meyners, and Gilbert Hay, give greeting in the Lord to all those who see or hear this document. Since we have now undertaken the custody of the realm of Scotland, we inform you that we have faithfully promised to conduct the government of the realm with regard for God and for justice, and for the profit and honour of our lord the king, and our lady the queen, and the welfare of the realm, according to the laws and good customs of that realm hitherto in use, causing full justice to be shown impartially to rich and poor alike. We shall endeavour, so far as we reasonably can, to ensure that love and unity be always maintained between our lord the king and our lady the queen, and we willingly agree that if all or any

---

[3] Since this letter was not subsequently enrolled, it seems probable that it never was ' obtained '.

I

ut si nos omnes vel aliqui seu aliquis nostrum super premissis in aliquo, quod absit, deliqueremus et ab ipso domino rege Anglie super hoc requisiti infra spacium trium mensium post illam monicionem nobis datam illud non emendaverimus, secundum quod debuerimus, quod ipse dominus rex extunc nobis in nullo teneatur. Preterea autem nos et omnes alii de regno Scocie quos ad hoc faciendum alicere poterimus domino regi Anglie, cum nostro indiguerit adjutorio, et ab ipso fuerimus requisiti, libenter nostrum consilium et auxilium pro nostro posse infra regnum Anglie impendemus. Si vero idem dominus rex non fecerit nobis in premissis ea que nobis facere promisit, prout in litteris suis quas inde habemus plenius continetur, non volumus extunc sibi teneri in premissis.

or one of us shall offend in any way in these things (which God forbid) and shall not make amends (as we should) at the request of the king of England within three months after his admonition to us, the king shall henceforth be under no sort of obligation to us. Further, we, and all others of the realm of Scotland whom we can induce to do so, shall freely render our counsel and aid to the king of England, within the realm of England, so far as we can, when he needs our help, and we are asked to by him. But if the king does not keep his promises to us in these undertakings, as more fully set out in the letter which we have from him about it, we do not wish to be committed to him any longer in the matter.

12

(a)

MEMORANDUM [1] quod in parleamento [*sic*] regis Edwardi apud Westmonasterium, in festo sancti Michaelis,[2] anno regni ejusdem regis sexto, in presencia episcoporum Wynton' Dunelm' Hereford' Norwici prioris provincialis ordinis fratrum predicatorum in Anglia decani Sar' magistri Thome Bek Willelmi de Valencia avunculi regis, comitum Cornubie Glouc' Warennie Warr' et de Karrik [3] Roberti de Tybetot Antonii Bek magistri Roberti de Scardeburg Radulphi de Sandwyco Johannis de Lovetot Walteri de Hopton magistri Galfridi de Aspale Walteri de Wynburne Nicholai de Stapelton Radulphi de Hengham Galfridi de Neubaud Johannis de Cobeham Willelmi de Brompton Philippi de Wyleby Thome de Weyland Walteri de Helyun Ricardi de Holebrok Bartholomei de Sudleye Hugonis filii Ottonis Patricii de Cadurc' Roberti filii Walteri et aliorum multorum, venit Alexander rex Scocie [a] filius Alexandri quondam

---

Text of (*a*) :   P.R.O. Close Roll 6 Edward I (C 54/95), m. 5 d (C).   Printed in Rymer, I, ii, 563, and in John Allen, *Vindication of Independence of Scotland* (1833), pp. 87-8.   Calendared in Bain, II, no. 127.

Text of (*b*) :   National Library of Scotland, MS Adv. 34.1.3a (Cartulary of Dunfermline), f. 39 (N) ; printed in *Registrum de Dunfermelyn*, ed. C. Innes (1842), p. 217.   Attention seems first to have been drawn to this entry by A. O. Anderson in *E.S.* II, 676.   Unfortunately it was made after the War of Independence (it is in the same hand as an adjacent document dated 1320, and was probably copied about 1320–30).   This, in itself, does not condemn the text, whose substance can in any case be traced as early as the end of the thirteenth century (see p. 82 below) ; but it is regrettable that there is no contemporary copy, and all the more so since Edward is known to have expected Alexander to do homage ' unconditionally ', i.e., in terms like those of (a) (see Powicke, *Thirteenth Century*, p. 595, *n*.).

[a] Scoc' *or* Scocie *in full*, C *passim*

12

(a)

NOTE [1] that in the parliament of King Edward at Westminster, at Michaelmas [2] in the sixth year of the king's reign [1278], in the presence of the bishops of Winchester, Durham, Hereford, and Norwich, the prior provincial of the Dominican order in England, the dean of Salisbury, Master Thomas Bek, William of Valence (the king's uncle), the earls of Cornwall, Gloucester, Warenne, Warwick, and Carrick,[3] Robert de Tybetot, Anthony Bek, Master Robert of Scarborough, Ralph of Sandwich, John de Lovetot, Walter of Hopton, Master Geoffrey of Aspall, Walter of Wimborne, Nicholas of Stapleton, Ralph de Hengham, Geoffrey of Newbold, John of Cobham, William of Brompton, Philip of Willoughby, Thomas of Wayland, Walter of Helion, Richard of Holbrook, Bartholomew of Sudeley, Hugh FitzOtto, Patrick of Cahors, Robert FitzWalter, and of many others, Alexander, king of Scotland, son of Alexander,

---

[1] For discussions of this homage see Ramsay, *Dawn of the Constitution*, pp. 322-4 (written in ignorance of text (b)); Dickinson, *Scotland*, p. 148; Powicke, *Thirteenth Century*, pp. 594-5; Anderson, loc. cit. Alexander had in 1251 declined to do homage to Henry III for the kingdom of Scotland until he had deliberated further on the matter (Matthew Paris, *Chronica Majora* (RS), v, 268). The special interest of our texts lies in the two different versions of the words of homage by Alexander. cf. also the statement of Boniface VIII, p. 82 below.

[2] Anderson, *E.S.* II, 676, assumes that this is an erroneous statement that the homage took place on Michaelmas Day (29th September; cf. the date 28 October, given in 12 (b)). But the text simply means that the homage took place during the ' Michaelmas ' parliament, which probably did not meet until well on in October (cf. *Annales Monastici* (RS), IV, 474). Alexander had gone to meet Edward at Tewkesbury a short time before (Bain, II, no. 128).

[3] See below, p. 49, *n.*; this is Bruce ' the elder '.

regis Scocie ad predictum Edwardum regem Anglie apud Westmonasterium, in camera ejusdem regis, et ibidem optulit idem rex Scocie eidem regi Anglie devenire hominem suum ligium [*sic*] et facere ei homagium suum, et [a] illud ei fecit in hec verba :

'Ego Alexander rex Scocie devenio ligeus homo domini Edwardi regis Anglie contra omnes gentes'.

Et idem rex Anglie homagium ejusdem regis Scocie recepit,[a] salvo jure et clamio ejusdem regis Anglie et heredum suorum de homagio predicti regis Scocie et heredum suorum de regno Scocie, cum inde loqui voluerint. Et idem rex Scocie statim post dictum homagium suum sic a prefato rege Anglie captum, optulit eidem regi Anglie fidelitatem suam et supplicavit eidem regi Anglie quod fidelitatem illam facere posset per os [1] Roberti de Brus comitis de Carrik'. Et idem rex Anglie hoc concessit eidem regi Scocie de gracia sua speciali illa vice. Et idem Robertus, rogatus per eundem regem Scocie quod id faceret statim data sibi potestate a predicto rege Scocie jurandi in animam ejusdem regis Scocie juravit regi Anglie nomine et vice ejusdem regis Scocie fidelitatem predictam per hec verba :

'Ego Robertus comes de Carrik' juxta potestatem michi a domino meo rege Scocie traditam in presencia domini regis Anglie et aliorum predictorum [2] prelatorum et procerum jurandi in animam regis Scocie et in pre-

---

[a] *to* [a] *Allen, op. cit., pp. 16, 87, says that these words are written over an erasure, and Ramsay, 'Dawn of the Constitution', p. 324, follows him, apparently without examining the MS. But C has no signs of erasure, and Allen's allegations of fraud seem groundless.*

[1] cf. above, p. 24, *n.* 3. Edward here grants as a favour what had in no. 7 been taken for granted.

the late king of Scotland, came to Edward, king of England, in the king's chamber at Westminster, and there the king of Scotland presented himself to the king of England to become his liegeman, and to do homage to him, and he did it in the following words :

' I, Alexander, king of Scotland, become the liegeman of Lord Edward, king of England, against all men '.

And the king of England received the homage of the king of Scotland, reserving the right and the claim of the king of England, and of his heirs, to the homage of the king of Scotland, and of his heirs, for the realm of Scotland, when they wish to discuss the matter.   And the king of Scotland, straightway after the homage thus received by the king of England, offered his fealty to the king of England, and asked the king of England that he might swear fealty by the mouth [1] of Robert Bruce, earl of Carrick.   And the king of England allowed it to the king of Scotland, as an act of special grace, for that occasion.   Then Robert was asked by the king of Scotland to do this, and thereupon (the king of Scotland having given him power to swear ' on the soul of the king of Scotland ') he swore fealty to the king of England in the name of, and on behalf of, the king of Scotland, in the following words :

' I, Robert, earl of Carrick, by virtue of the power given to me by my lord the king of Scotland, in the presence of the king of England, and of the other aforesaid [2] prelates and magnates, to swear on the soul of the king of Scotland, and in the presence of the king of

---

[2] This word is quite inappropriate in the context ; words meaning ' here present ' are required.

sencia dicti regis Scocie et de precepto suo, juravi fidelitatem domino Edwardo regi Anglie in hec verba :

' " Ego Alexander rex Scocie portabo bonam fidem
domino Edwardo regi Anglie et heredibus suis regibus
Anglie de vita et menbris et terreno honore, et fideliter
faciam servicia debita de terris et tenementis que teneo
de rege Anglie supradicto ". '

Et predictus rex Scocie fidelitatem illam sic nomine
suo et vice sua per predictum Robertum juratam et
factam confirmavit et ratificavit.

(b)

De homagio quod fecit Alexander tercius rex Scocie [a]
Edwardo regi Anglie pro terris suis quas habuit in regno
Anglie.[b]

Memorandum quod anno gracie M°CC°LXXVIIJ° die Apostolorum Symonis et Jude, apud Westmonasterium,
Alexander rex Scocie fecit homagium domino Edwardo
regi Anglie filio regis Henrici sub hiis verbis :

' Ego devenio hominem vestrum [*sic*] de terris quas
de vobis teneo in regno Anglie de quibus homagium
vobis debeo, salvo regno meo '.

Tunc dixit episcopus Norwycensis [1] ' et salvum sit
regi Anglie si jus habeat ad homagium vestrum de
regno '. Cui rex statim respondit et aperte, dicens ' ad
homagium regni mei Scocie nullus jus habet nisi solus
deus nec illud teneo nisi de solo deo '. Tunc Robertus
de Brus comes de Carryk fecit fidelitatem pro dicto
domino rege Scocie, jurando in anima[m] sua[m] sub
hiis verbis :

---

[a] Scoc' ; N *here, and passim*
[b] *Title from* N

Scotland and by his command, do thus swear fealty to Edward, king of England :

' " I, Alexander, king of Scotland, will keep true faith with Edward, king of England, and with his heirs, the kings of England, in matters of life and limb and of earthly honour, and will faithfully perform the services due for the lands and tenements that I hold of the king of England ". '

And the king of Scotland confirmed and ratified the fealty thus sworn and undertaken by Robert, in his name, and on his behalf.

(b)

The homage done to Edward, king of England, by Alexander III, king of Scotland, for his lands which he had in the realm of England.

Note that in A.D. 1278, on the feast of the Apostles Simon and Jude [28 October] King Alexander of Scotland did homage, at Westminster, to King Edward of England, son of King Henry, in the following words :

' I become your man for the lands which I hold of you in the realm of England for which I owe you homage, reserving [the right of] my kingdom.'

Then the bishop of Norwich ¹ said ' and let it be reserved to the king of England, if he should have right to your homage for the kingdom '. The king answered him publicly at once, saying ' nobody but God himself has the right to the homage for my realm of Scotland, and I hold it of nobody but God himself '. Then Robert Bruce, earl of Carrick, swore fealty for the king of Scotland on the king's soul, in the following words :

---

¹ This bishop (William of Middleton) was a lawyer, who might well have had a special interest in the technicalities of this occasion (Powicke, *Thirteenth Century,* p. 481).

' Sic deus me adjuvet et hec sacrosancta,[1] dominus meus rex Scocie qui hic est erit vobis fidelis de vita et menbris et de terreno honore et vestra consilia celabit '. Et tunc rex Scocie adjecit secundum formam homagii quod supra fecit, scilicet, ' de terris quas de vobis teneo in regno Anglie '.[2]   Et rex Scocie concessit quod faceret servicia regi Anglie de illis salvo regno suo debita et consueta de quibus eidem fecit homagium.

[1] cf. above, p. 12, *n.* 4.
[2] If text (b) is contemporary, it seems to be the earliest recorded use of the Scottish plea that the homage was due only for lands in England.

' So may God help me, and these Holy Gospels,[1] my lord the king of Scotland here will be faithful to you in matters of life and limb, and of earthly honour, and will keep your counsels secret'. Then the king of Scotland added, according to the form of homage which he had done above, ' for the lands that I hold of you in the realm of England '.[2] And the king of Scotland agreed to perform the proper and customary services to the king of England for the lands for which he had done homage to him, reserving [the rights of] his kingdom.

13

MAGNIFICO [1] principi domino Edwardo dei gracia regi
Anglorum [a] illustri, domino Hibernie et duci Aquitanie,
fratri suo dilectissimo, suus Alexander, eadem gracia
rex [Scottorum] salutem et o[mne quod] est optimum,
cum dileccione sincera, et parata ad beneplacita voluntate. Quamvis fidelis amicus a dileccione amici sui
recedere [?] non noverit [et] excellencie vestre constan-
ciam ob plura beneficia debeamus per multam experien-
ciam non immerito commendare ; de eo tamen ad
presens quod post tristissimas et intollerabiles angustias
et eventus, quos sensimus et sentimus de morte filii nostri
dilectissimi, nepotis vestri cari, per fratrem Johannem de
sancto Germano, de ordine [fratrum . . . orum,[b] deso-
la]cionis solacium non modicum propinastis, mandantes
quod licet sanguinem vestrum in partibus nostris mors
taliter sustulerit sorte sua, nos tamen [manemus *] [c]
indissolubilis amoris vinculo dante domino nostro perpetuo colligati, celsitudini vestre karissime pre ceteris
curialitatibus et beneficiis ad grates [tradendas?] nos
[tenemur *] ob [san]guinis reverenciam, ad vestram, si
placet, memoriam reducentes quod ex sanguine vestro,
scilicet ex filia nepte vestre, filia nostre karissime quondam bone memorie regine Norwagie, que nunc est

---

Text :   P.R.O. Ancient Correspondence (S.C. 1), 20/162 (S) seems to be
the original letter, though no trace of sealing is now visible. The text is
damaged by holes, stains, and fading ; I am much obliged to Mr R. E.
Latham for help in reading it. Calendared in Bain, II, no. 250.

    [a] *Alexander's clerk writes* Anglorum, *instead of* Anglie, *no doubt because of
Scottish analogy* (*see above, p. 1, n. b*).

    [b] *Either* minorum *or* predicatorum *must have been written.*

    [c] *There may be a small gap after* manemus *.*

13

To [1] the exalted prince Lord Edward, by the grace of God the illustrious king of the English, lord of Ireland, and duke of Aquitaine, and his most beloved brother, Alexander, his friend, and by the same grace king of Scots, sends greeting and every good wish, with true affection, and the desire to do what pleases him. Although faithful friends know not fickleness in their affection, and after our long experience we ought with good reason to praise the faithfulness of your excellency for the many kindnesses that we have received ; yet at present, because after the grievous and unbearable trials and tribulations which we have suffered, and do suffer, from the death of our dear son, your beloved nephew, you have offered no small solace for our desolation by sending brother John of St Germain, of the [Dominican *or* Franciscan] order, to say that although death has thus by his decree borne away your kindred in these parts, we are united together perpetually, God willing, by the tie of indissoluble affection :—we are bound to thank your dear highness, beyond what is due for other courtesies and acts of benevolence, in that you have regard for our kinship, and we would recall, if we may, to your recollection, that in the providence of God much good may come to pass yet through your kinswoman, the daughter of your niece, the daughter, too, of our beloved, the late queen of Norway,

[1] On the Alexander III/Edward correspondence see above, p. xxiv. Edward's letter, to which this is a reply, has been lost.

apparens heres nostra,[1] divina providente clemencia, multa bona poterunt provenire que . . . .[a] fedus indissolubile inter vos et nos contractum, tanquam inter fideles et constantes, nisi morte tantum, nunquam dissolveretur, sicut firmiter confidimus et tenemus. Hinc [?] est quod magnificenciam vestram dilectissimam specialiter deprecamur quatinus hiis que religiosus vir Andreas, abbas de Cupro . . . .[b] dignemini fidem indubitatam adhibere, mandantes nobis cum fiducia per eundem vestre . . . .[c] [Valeat excellencia vestra] [d] per tempora longiora. [Teste meipso apud castrum] [d] Puellarum, xx° die Aprilis, anno regni nostri xxx° quinto.

[a] *Two or three illegible words*
[b] *Nearly half a line illegible here* (*the average number of words to a line in* S *is about 23*).
[c] *One or two illegible words*
[d] *Nothing can be read here, and the text suggested in brackets is based on the analogy of other letters of Alexander.*

[1] Margaret ' the Maid of Norway ', Alexander III's grand-daughter (born *c.* 1283), and also grand-daughter of Edward I's sister, Margaret, who had married Alexander in 1251, was destined to become queen of Scots after Alexander's death in 1286. Her premature death, in 1290, caused the dispute for the succession, which was settled in favour of John Balliol (see below, nos. 14-19).

of happy memory, who is now our heir-apparent,[1]
who . . . . indissoluble bond created between you
and us, as between men who are faithful and constant,
should never be broken, as we firmly maintain and
believe, except by death.   Hence it is that we particularly ask your beloved majesty to be kind enough to give
credence without question to what the monk Andrew,
abbot of Cupar [has to say to you on our behalf?], and
to send us by the same messenger trustworthy [news
concerning?] your own [state?].   [Wishing prosperity
to your excellency] for many years to come.   [Witness
myself at] Edinburgh, 20 April, in the thirty-fifth year
of our reign [1284].

14

Rotulus [1] continens appellaciones septem comitum regni Scocie super jure ejusdem regni ad eosdem comites pertinente coram custodibus dicti regni per dictos comites factas et prolatas [a]

[I] [b] CUM [2] per mortem nobilis memorie domini Alexandri quondam regis Scocie [c] sedes regia regni ejusdem jam ad tempus vacaverit, et per leges et consuetudines regni Scocie a tempore a quo non extat memoria usque in presens ad jus et proprietatem et ad libertates septem comitum [3] regni Scocie et communitatis regni ejusdem pertineat regem in eodem regno facere et in sede regia instituere,[4] et honores ad regimen regni Scocie pertinentes eidem attribuere, quandocumque predicta sedes regia de facto et de jure vacaverit; ne vos, domine

---

Text: P.R.O. Scottish Documents, Exchequer (E 39), no. 89 (E), is now largely illegible, and our text is derived from Palgrave, *Documents*, pp. 14-19 (P), which was printed from E when much more of it could be read. Only the first membrane of E is printed here, for the second (Palgrave, pp. 19-21) is an entirely different document, though in the same hand. Bain (II, no. 465) calendared the text without realising this. Listed by Stapledon (Palgrave, *Kalendars*, I, 132). It seems that misguided attempts have been made in modern times to secure the transmission of E to Scotland, presumably on the assumption that it was the original exemplar, addressed to the Scottish guardians in charge of the realm during the interregnum (cf. *110th Report of Deputy-Keeper of the Public Records*, p. 19). The appearance of E, however, and the nature of the material on membrane 2, make it clear that E is only a copy, written probably by the clerks of Edward I, and not a survivor of the medieval royal archives of Scotland. To judge from the use of *talis* in the text, E was derived from a draft, and not from the exemplar sent to the guardians (if indeed the document ever was sent). We have conjecturally filled a number of gaps by analogy with similar passages elsewhere in E. These additions (marked by square brackets) make the present text more complete than Palgrave's.

[a] *Title from Stapledon's calendar; not, of course, contemporary*
[b] *In E the text is divided into three paragraphs, indicated here by Roman numerals.*
[c] *Damage to E makes reading uncertain, but probably the scribe uses* Scoc' [*for* Scocie] *everywhere.*

14

Document ¹ containing the appeals of the seven earls of the realm of Scotland, made and preferred by these earls before the guardians of the realm, concerning the right in that realm which belongs to the earls.

[I] SINCE ² by the death of Lord Alexander of noble memory, late king of Scotland, the royal throne of the kingdom has been vacant until the present time, and by the laws and customs of the realm of Scotland, from time immemorial up till the present, it is one of the rights and privileges and liberties of the seven earls ³ of the realm of Scotland, and of the community of the realm, to make a king of that realm, and to set him upon the royal throne,⁴ and to confer on him the honours which go with the rule of the realm of Scotland, whenever the said royal throne is vacant in fact and in law; lest you, William, bishop

---

¹ E is not now a ' roll ', though it may have been so before it was repaired in modern times. But medieval clerks often used *rotulus* in the sense of ' a membrane ', and probably this is the strict meaning here.

² This document is a mysterious one, and raises many difficult problems. Its date must be between September 1290 and May 1291. On the general circumstances see above, p. xxv; Powicke (who takes membrane 2 to be part of the appeal), *Thirteenth Century*, pp. 601-2; and Barrow, *Feudal Britain*, pp. 391-2.

³ The ' seven earls ' are not named, apart from those of Fife and Mar; and the difficulty of identifying the remainder has persuaded the editor of the soundness of Professor Barrow's view that the phrase ' the seven earls ' must ' describe a constitutional concept rather than a precise number of actual magnates ' (Barrow, *Feudal Britain*, p. 392). In other words, the party who were responsible for this document are claiming to speak on behalf of the whole body of earls in Scotland in 1290–1.

⁴ This refers to the inauguration ceremony at Scone, of whose nature at this period, in the absence of any text of the rite, we know very little. See P. E. Schramm, *History of the English Coronation* (1937), pp. 243-4; and cf. above, pp. xxii, 29, with notes. It is clear that the central event of the ceremony was the setting of the king upon the stone of Scone.

K

Willelme, episcope sancti Andree, et domine Johannes
Cumyn qui vos geritis et tenetis pro custodibus regni
Scocie,[1] una cum particula communitatis regni Scocie
vobis adherente, aliquem regem ad regimen regni Scocie
optinendum auctoritate vestra propria proficiatis, insti-
tuatis vel . . . .[a] fa[ciatis in prejudicium ?] et
lesionem libertatum et jurium septem comitum Scocie
et communitatis ejusdem eis adherentis, de quibus septem comitibus filius bone memorie Duncani, quondam
comitis de Fyff est unus, a vobis, domine Willelme,
episcope sancti Andree, et domine Johannes Cumyn, et
a particula communitatis Scocie vobis adherente, et
eciam a vobis, domine Johannes de Balliolo, ne vos in
regno Scocie aliquod opus manuale faciatis vel . . . .[b]
[in ?] regimine regni Scocie vos aliquo modo intro-
mittatis in prejudicium et lesionem juris et libertatis
septem comitum Scocie et communitatis ejusdem eis
adherentis, ego *talis*,[2] in presencia vestra constitutus,
vice et nomine predictorum septem comitum, episcoporum, abbatum, priorum, comitum, baronum et libere
tenentium Scocie et communitatis ejusdem eis adherentis,
ad dominum Edwardum dei gracia regem Anglie illus-
trem, et [ad ?] presenciam [3] et ad coronam [3] Anglie
regiam propter injuriam eis a vobis illatam hiis scriptis
appello, et presenciam predicti domini regis Anglie
nomine predictorum comitum et eis adherencium [peto
cum effectu [4] ?], subiciens personas predictorum septem

---

[a] *Only an infinitive missing?*
[b] *Only a word or two missing?*

[1] Six guardians had been appointed to govern Scotland in the name of
' the Maid of Norway ' after the death of Alexander III in 1286. Four
survived at this date : William, bishop of St Andrews, John Comyn,
Robert, bishop of Glasgow, and James the Steward.

of St Andrews, and John Comyn, who are acting and
holding yourselves as guardians of the realm of Scotland,[1]
should, with part of the community of the realm of Scotland supporting you, of your own private authority put
forward, institute or . . . . any king to exercise rule
in the realm of Scotland or should do anything in prejudice of, and to the injury of, the liberties and rights of
the seven earls of Scotland and of the community of the
same who are supporting them (of which seven earls the
son of Duncan, late earl of Fife, of worthy memory, is
one) ; I, *So and so*,[2] appointed in your presence on behalf
of and in the name of the said seven earls, the bishops,
abbots, priors, earls, barons, and free tenants of Scotland,
and the community of the same supporting them, because of the injury you have done to them, do appeal by
this document to the Lord Edward, by the grace of God
the illustrious king of England, and to the help [3] of the
royal crown of England, from you William, bishop of
St Andrews, and John Comyn, and the part of the community of Scotland supporting you, and also from you,
John Balliol, lest you should take any action in the realm
of Scotland, or . . . . should meddle in any wise in
the rule of the realm of Scotland, to the prejudice and
injury of the right and liberty of the seven earls of
Scotland, and of the community of the same supporting
them.   In the name of the seven earls and their adherents I seek urgently [4] the help of the king of England,
placing the persons of the seven earls, and of all the

---

[2] *Talis* indicates that a personal name is to be inserted.   Its use is
evidence that E was copied from a draft.
[3] Treated in translation as a hendiadys.   For sense of *presencia* see
Forcellini, *Lexicon totius Latinitatis*, s.v.
[4] *Cum effectu* is rare in this sense, but sufficiently established (cf. *Statuta
Antiqua Universitatis Oxoniensis*, ed. S. Gibson (1931), p. 68).

comitum et aliorum omnium supradictorum et personas
communitatis regni Scocie eis adherentes, et eciam consanguineorum et [amicorum suorum et omnia?] bona
sua mobilia et immobilia, ubicumque fuerint inventa,
speciali [pace?] protexione et defencione [*sic*] predicti
domini regis Anglie et corone sue regie, ne vos ad predictum ª . . . . gravamen eorumdem aliquo modo
procedatis seu procedere attemptetis.¹

Item quia vos, domine Willelme, episcope sancti
Andree, et domine Johannes Cumyn, qui vos [pro custodibus regni Scocie tenetis, super omnibus?] dampnis
et gravaminibus predictis septem comitibus et suis
supradictis, et omnibus eis adherentibus a [tempore
obitus nobilis?] memorie domini Alexandri quondam
regis Scocie [usque in presens, per vos et per ballivos et
substitutos viros?] illatis, nullas emendas fec[istis vel?]
aliquo modo facere [curav?]istis, [a vobis, domine Willelme episcope sancti Andree?] et domine Johannes
Cumyn [et ab omnibus vobis adherentibus, ad predictum regem Anglie et ad coronam Anglie regiam in
hiis scriptis appello?] . . . . .ᵇ

[II] Cum vos, domine Willelme, episcope sancti
Andree, et domine Johannes Cumyn, qui vos geritis et
tenetis pro custodibus regni Scocie, ad manutenendum
et defendendum jura et libertates et consuetudines regni
ejus[dem] ᶜ approbatas, ... [? quosd]am ᵈ alios
subcustodes vestros fecistis autoritate [*sic*] vestra propria
et substituistis, ad quos substituendos a nobilibus et
magnatibus et communitate regni Scocie nulla fuit vobis

ª predcm̄ P ; E *illegible.   Extent of gap uncertain*
ᵇ *Final bracketed clause is entirely conjectural; and in any case it is uncertain
whether anything followed* appello.
ᶜ ejus P
ᵈ *Gap here must be very small.*

others mentioned, and the persons of those supporting them among the community of the realm of Scotland, and of their kindred and their friends, and all their property, movable and immovable, wherever it is, under the special peace, protection, and defence of the king of England and of his royal crown, lest you should in any way proceed or attempt to proceed to the aforesaid . . . . their injury.[1]

Further, since you, William, bishop of St Andrews, and John Comyn, who are holding yourselves as guardians of the realm of Scotland, have made no amends, nor in any way taken care to make amends, for all the losses and injuries caused by you, and your bailiffs, and your agents, to the seven earls and their people, and all their supporters, from the time of the death of Alexander, of noble memory, late king of Scotland, until the present, I appeal by this document from you, William, bishop of St Andrews, and John Comyn, and from all those supporting you, to the king of England and to the royal crown of England . . . .

[II] Since you, William, bishop of St Andrews, and John Comyn, who are acting and holding yourselves as guardians of the realm of Scotland, to preserve and defend the established rights and liberties and customs of the realm . . . . have substituted others, by your own authority, as your subordinate guardians, for which substitution no authority or power was given by the nobles and magnates and community of the realm of

---

[1] The sense here must be ' proceed, or attempt to proceed, to do anything to the injury of the earls and their adherents ', but it is difficult to suggest a convincing completion of the Latin text. *Predictum* could equally well be read as *predictam*.

auctoritas vel potestas attributa ; qui quidem custodes substituti vestri ad terram Moravie, que est immediate in manu regis Scocie,[1] autoritate [*sic*] et potestate eis a vobis commissa accedentes, terras et villas liberorum hominum domini regis Scocie ibidem destruxerunt et depredaverunt, ac villas predictas et horrea plena de blado exarcerunt [*sic*] et bona omnia eorumdem hominum Moravie secum asportaverunt [et ?] viros mulieres et pueros parvulos quot attingere potuerunt crudeliter interfecerunt, super quibus injuriis dampnis et gravaminibus alique emende per vos vel per substitutos viros aliquando . . . .[a] non sunt facte, propter quod ob defectum vestrum et injuriam predictis hominibus Moravie per substitutos viros illatam, ego *talis* in presencia vestra constitutus, vice et nomine domini Dovenaldi, comitis de Marr'[2] unius de septem comitibus Scocie et eciam nomine predictorum liberorum hominum Moravie consanguineorum, parentum, et affinium et aliorum amicorum suorum et predicti domini comitis de Marr' qui dictas injurias dampna et exarsiones passi sunt, pro remedio optinendo et emendis consequendis a vobis, domine Willelme episcope sancti Andree, et domine Johannes Cumyn, et ab omnibus vobis adherentibus, ob defectum vestrum, et pro eo quod predicta dampna et injurias et exarsiones transsire [*sic*] permisistis impunita et non correcta, ad presenciam domini Edwardi regis Anglie et ad coronam Anglie regiam in hiis scriptis appello, et presenciam ipsius domini regis Anglie peto cum effectu ; supponens predictum dominum Dovenaldum comitem de Marr', omnes consanguineos, affines et amicos suos et omnes sibi adherentes, et eciam homines

---

[a] *There may be no gap after* aliquando.

Scotland ; and these your subordinate keepers, by the authority and power which you have given to them, have gone to the land of Moray, which is directly under the rule of the king of Scotland,[1] and have there destroyed and robbed lands and villages belonging to freemen of the king of Scotland, and have burnt these villages, and barns full of grain, and have taken away with them all the goods of the men of Moray, and cruelly slain as many men, women, and little children as they could find, and for these grievous injuries no amends have ever been made by you or your subordinates : therefore because of your default and the injury done to the men of Moray by your subordinates, I, *so and so*, appointed in your presence, on behalf of, and in the name of Donald, earl of Mar,[2] one of the seven earls of Scotland, and also in the name of the freemen of Moray, their relatives, families, and kindred and other friends, and of those of the earl of Mar who have suffered injuries, losses, and arsons, to secure a remedy and gain redress from you, William, bishop of St Andrews, and John Comyn, and from all your supporters, for your default, and because you have allowed these losses, injuries, and arsons, to pass unpunished and unatoned, I appeal by this document to the assistance of Edward, king of England, and to the royal crown of England, and I seek the help of the king of England urgently ; placing Donald, earl of Mar, and all his relatives, kindred, and friends, and all his supporters, and also the king's men in Moray, and all their

---

[1] The earldom of Moray was not created until 1312.
[2] This is made clearer by the later passage (see next note) which refers to the sufferings of the dependants of the earl of Mar ' in Moray '.

predictos domini regis de Moravia et omnia bona sua et
eorumdem omnium, mobilia et immobilia, ubicumque
fuerint inventa, speciali paci proteccioni et defensioni
predicti domini regis Anglie et corone sue regie, ne eis
vel aliquibus eorumdem aliquod dampnum injuriam vel
gravamen ulterius faciatis vel in aliquo facere presumatis. [Item quia vos ?] domine Willelme, episcope sancti
Andree, et domine Johannes Cumyn, qui vos pro custodibus regni Scocie tenetis super omnibus dampnis
gravaminibus et injuriis predicto comiti de Marr' [con-
sanguineis affinibus et ?] amicis suis supradictis de
Moravia ¹ sibi adherentibus a tempore obitus nobilis
memorie domini Alexandri [quondam ?] regis Scocie
usque in presens per vos et per ballivos et [per substitutos
viros ?] .... propter patienciam vestram ....
ill[atis] .... nullas emendas vel satisfaccionem
facere .... [vel aliquo modo ?] facere curavistis,
a vobis, domine Willelme episcope sancti Andree et
domine Johannes Cumyn, et ab omnibus vobis adherentibus, ad predictum dominum regem Anglie et ad coronam ipsius regiam, iterato in hiis scriptis appello.

[III] Cum vos, domine Willelme, episcope sancte
Andree, et domine Johannes Cumyn, qui vos geritis et
tenetis pro custodibus regni Scocie ad manutenendum
et defendendum leges et consuetudines regni ejusdem ᵃ
approbatas, et ad tribuendum unicuique jus suum quod
sibi de jure deberet competere,ᵇ licet nos Robertus de

ᵃ diu P, *who indicates as corrupt.* E *now illegible, but* ejusdem *seems probable*;
cf. page 46, n. c above.
    ᵇ compectere P, *who seems to read* E *correctly here, but presumably* competere
was intended.

goods, and the movable and immovable property of them all, wherever they are found, under the special peace, protection, and defence of the king of England and of his royal crown, lest you cause any further loss, injury, or damage to them, or any of them, or venture to do so in any way. Further, since you, William, bishop of St Andrews, and John Comyn, who are holding yourselves as guardians of the realm of Scotland . . . . make no amends or satisfaction . . . . nor have cared to make, in any wise, for all the losses, hurts, and injuries done to the earl of Mar, and his relatives and kindred and friends supporting him in Moray,[1] from the time of the death of Alexander of noble memory, late king of Scotland, until the present, by you and your bailiffs and subordinates . . . . because of your forbearance . . . . therefore, by this document, I appeal yet again from you, William, bishop of St Andrews, and John Comyn, and from all your supporters, to the king of England and to his royal crown.

[III] Since you, William, bishop of St Andrews, and John Comyn, who are acting, and holding yourselves, as guardians of the realm of Scotland, to preserve and defend the established laws and customs of the realm, and to render to each person the right which should belong to him by law (though we, Robert Bruce, lord

---

[1] From this it would appear that the earl of Mar had interests outside the territory of Mar proper (i.e. between the Dee and the Don). Little seems to be known of the episode, apart from this passage.

Brus dominus vallis Anandie tanquam heres legitimus et
verus [1] assignatus [in ?] regimine regni Scocie super jure
nostro quod habemus in regno Scocie supradicto clamium imposuimus et prosecucionem juris nostri, prout
tenemur, faciamus cum effectu, vos, unacum aliquibus
de regno Scocie vobis et voluntati vestre consencientibus
et adherentibus in prejudicium nostrum et juris nostri
impedimentum, et eciam in prejudicium et lesionem
juris et libertatis septem comitum Scocie, quod et quam
habent, et a tempore a quo non est memoria habuerunt,
de rege faciendo et in sede regia instituendo in regno
Scocie unacum communitate regni ejusdem eis adherente,
quocienscumque sedes regia Scocie de jure et de facto
vacaverit, dominum Johannem de Balliolo regem in
regno Scocie facere [2] et jura et honores regiminis regni
eidem attribuere intenditis et proponitis ; ideoque nos,
ob defectum vestrum et injuriam per vos nobis et predictis septem comitibus illatam, pro jure nostro quod
habemus in regimine regni Scocie et pro jure predictorum septem comitum prosequendo et optinendo, [ad]
presenciam domini Edwardi dei gracia regis Anglie illustris et coronam Anglie regiam in hiis scriptis appellamus.
Et ne vos in prejudicium juris nostri et libertatis predictorum septem comitum ad aliquem regem faciendum
in regno Scocie, quousque super jure nostro, in presencia
domini regis Anglie predicti, plenum recipiamus judicium,[3] quod a vobis nullo modo recipere volumus, aliquo

---

[1] Three Robert Bruces have to be distinguished in this volume (a) ' the
Competitor' (1210 ?-95), referred to here ; (b) 'the elder' (1253 ?-1304),
son of (a), and earl of Carrick; (c) 'the younger' (1274-1329), earl of
Carrick, later Robert I of Scotland. There has been much confusion
between them; e.g., Dugdale, *Baronage of England*, 1 (1675), 450. It is
convenient to follow the method of *D.N.B.* in calling them Bruce VI, VII,
VIII (numbers based on descent from the Robert Bruce I who came from
Normandy). In claiming to be true heir, Bruce was relying on Alexander
II's declaration in his favour in 1238, when Alexander had no children
(Powicke, *Thirteenth Century*, p. 602).

of Annandale, as the legitimate and true heir [1] designate
to the rule of the realm of Scotland, have put forward a
claim concerning the right which we have in the realm
of Scotland, and are urgently pursuing our right, as we
are bound to do) ; you, with some persons of the realm
of Scotland supporting you, and falling in with your
wishes, intend and propose to make John Balliol king in
the realm of Scotland,[2] and to confer on him the rights
and honours which go with the rule of the kingdom, to
our prejudice and the hindrance of our right, and also to
the prejudice and injury of the right and liberty of the
seven earls of Scotland, which they have, and have had
from time immemorial, with the community of the realm
supporting them, of making the king and setting him on
the royal throne in the realm of Scotland, whenever the
royal throne of Scotland was vacant in law and in fact :
therefore, because of your default and the injury done
by you to us, and to the seven earls, we appeal by this
document to the assistance of Lord Edward, by the grace
of God the illustrious king of England, and to the royal
crown of England, for pursuing and obtaining our right
which we have in the realm of Scotland, and on behalf of
the right of the seven earls.   And lest you should proceed
in any manner, in prejudice of our right, and of the
liberty of the seven earls, to make anyone king in the
realm of Scotland before we receive full judgment of our
right in the presence of the king of England [3] (and this
judgment in no wise do we wish to receive at your hands),

---

[2] John Balliol (born 1249), son of the founder of Balliol College, Oxford.
For the claims of Balliol, and other competitors, to the Scottish throne, see
below, pp. 56-62, and notes.
　[3] One of the very few allusions, before the actual opening of the ' Great
Cause ' in 1291, to the proposal to submit the dispute to the judgment of
Edward.   Unhappily it cannot be dated.

modo procedatis, iterato, ut prius, ad predictum dominum regem Anglie et ad coronam ipsius regiam in hiis scriptis appellamus; supponentes nos specialiter, et septem comites supradictos, et omnes consanguineos affines et amicos suos et nostros speciales nobis et supradictis comitibus adherentes, et omnes terras et possessiones nostras et suas, et omnia bona nostra et sua, mobilia et immobilia, ubicumque fuerint inventa, speciali paci protexioni et defencioni [sic] predicti domini regis Anglie et corone sue regie, ne vos nobis [vel] ᵃ . . . . predictis septem comitibus vel [aliquibus eorumdem?] lo . . . .
. . is . . . . vel s . . . . aliquod dampnum injuriam vel gravamen [ulterius faciatis?] vel aliquo modo inferre presumatis.

Item, quia vos, domine Willelme episcope sancti Andree, et domine Johannes Cumyn, qui vos pro custodibus regni tenetis, super omnibus dampnis gravaminibus et injuriis nobis et nostris a tempore obitus nobilis memorie domini Alexandri, quondam regis nostri Scocie, usque in presens per vos et per ballivos et substitutos vestros illatis, nullas emendas fieri fecistis vel aliquo modo propter patienciam vestram facere curavistis, a vobis, domine episcope sancti Andree, et domine Johannes Cumyn, et ab omnibus vobis adherentibus, ad predictum regem Anglie et coronam Anglie regiam iterato, ut prius, in hiis scriptis appellamus.

ᵃ P *supplies* vel; E *illegible*

we appeal once again, as before, by this document, to the king of England and to his royal crown. We place ourselves, in particular, and the seven earls, and all of their relatives and kindred, and of their and our particular friends who support us and the earls, and all of our and of their lands and possessions, and all of our and of their property, movable and immovable, wherever it is, under the special peace, protection and defence of the king of England and of his royal crown, lest you do any further injury or hurt to us or . . . . to the seven earls or to any of them . . . . or in any way presume to do so.

Further, because you, William, bishop of St Andrews, and John Comyn, who are holding yourselves as guardians of the realm, have caused no amends to be made, or in any way cared to make them, because of your forbearance, for all the losses, hurts, and injuries done to us and to ours, from the death of Alexander of noble memory, our late king of Scotland, until now, by yourselves and your bailiffs and subordinates, we appeal yet again, as before, by this document, from you, the bishop of St Andrews, and John Comyn, and from all your supporters, to the king of England and to the royal crown of England.

15

Coment [1] Edward roi d'Engleterre devant les hauts
hommes d'Escoce qui a sa requeste vindrent a Norham
pur treter d'acunes busoignes touchant la terre d'Escoce
qui feust alors destituyt [2] d'un roi par la mort de Alisandre qui y feust roi, declara la cause de sa venue come
soverein seignor de la terre d'Escoce avantdite.[a]

Nostre [3] seignur le roy regardaunt la pees du roiaume
d'Escoce estre troublé pour [b] la mort du roy Alisandre et
de ses enfantz,[4] qui proscheinz furent a nostre seignur le
roy, dont moult lui poise, il pour l'amour de droiture
faire a touz qui en l'eritage du roiaume d'Escoce rien
purront demander, et pour la pees garder entre la gent
du poeple,[5] vous bone gent [6] du roiaume pria venir icy
pur [c] aucune chose q'il vous voloit moustrer [c]; e il
mesmes de lontaigne pays est cea venuz issint que par la
soveraine seignurie laquele est sowe face droit a touz, et

Text: French text, printed here for the first time, extant only in Glasgow
University Library MS BE 10-y.3, f. 4v (on the MS see remarks by E. L. G.
Stones in *SHR*, xxxv, 1956, 98-100) (G).   Latin text in Hemingburgh, pp.
234-5 (H).

   [a] *Title from margin of* G
   [b] per mortem H ; *read* par la mort *?*
   [c] *to* [c] *these words not represented in* H

   [1] G seems to have been written *c.* 1400, and its rubrics cannot necessarily
be assumed to have existed in the documents which its scribe was copying.
Yet it will be noted that he cannot have borrowed the name ' Norham '
from the text which follows, and other evidence suggests that he had some
manuscript authority for his rubrics.
   [2] cf. ' destitutus ' in ecclesiastical Latin, often used of a benefice which
had no pastor.
   [3] According to H, the speaker is Roger Brabazon (justice of the King's
Bench) and the place Norham parish church.   This may be the original

15

How [1] Edward, king of England, declared the reason for his coming as overlord of the land of Scotland before the magnates of Scotland, who, at his request, came to Norham to negotiate certain business touching the land of Scotland, which was then destitute [2] of a king, because of the death of Alexander who had been king there.

Our [3] lord the king has observed the peace of the realm of Scotland to be disturbed by the deaths of King Alexander and of his children,[4] who were kinsfolk of our lord the king (by which deaths he is greatly distressed) and in his desire to do right to all those who can make any claim to the inheritance of the kingdom of Scotland, and in order to keep the peace among the people,[5] he has asked you, the good people of the realm,[6] to come here, because of a certain matter which he wished to explain to you. He himself has come hither from a distant place, in order that by virtue of the overlordship which belongs to him he may do justice to everyone, and, after all

---

text of the opening speech of the ' Great Cause ' of 1291–2 (see above, pp. xxv-xxvii). The Latin notarial versions (Rymer, i, ii, 762 ; Prynne, 488-9) are much embellished with a rhetoric which can hardly be translated from the French actually spoken. A very close Latin rendering of G appears in H (pp. 234-5), though preceded by a florid passage of ten lines which has no equivalent in G. H adds that William de Hothum (a noted Dominican scholar) had drawn up (*preordinaverat*) the speech. It is not possible to establish the relation between G, H, and the notarial texts, nor to be sure of what was actually said, except that the language was French, a point on which all the Latin texts agree. Possibly G is only a summary.

[4] Possibly it would be better to translate ' enfantz ' as ' progeny ', since Margaret of Norway was Alexander's grand-daughter. H has *mortem prolis sue*.

[5] The phrase ' la gent du poeple ' seems certainly corrupt. H has *pro pace conservanda in populo dicte terre*.

[6] *Bone gent* : equivalent in H is *magnates*. cf. *hauts hommes* of rubric, and below, p. 53, *n*. 2.

que toutes destourbances oustees ferme pees rendre [1] au royaume d'Escoce. Ne il ne entent rien pour prendre noun duement sur nulluy, ne nully droit delayer, ne nully fraunchise destourber ne amenuser, mes a touz faire droit come soverain. Et que ceste chose peuse estre moeve a bone fyn requiert nostre seignur le roy vostre debonere assent et la conisance de la [2] sovereine seignurie et voet ovrer par voz conseils a droit faire et [par]former.[a]

[a] former G, *which is not impossible, but emendation given seems likely.* H *has* ad justiciam perficiendam et servandam.

disturbances have been quelled, may restore [1] settled
peace to the kingdom of Scotland. He does not propose
to take anything from anybody without just cause, nor
to delay any man's receiving of his right, nor to disturb
nor diminish his franchise, but only to do justice to everyone as sovereign. And in order that this matter may be
brought to a satisfactory conclusion, our lord the king
asks for your kind agreement, and for recognition of his [2]
overlordship ; and he wishes to act with your advice in
doing and in executing justice.

[1] If *rendre* is correct, it must depend on *face.*
[2] *la* : possibly corruption of *sa*, as assumed in translation.

L

16

C'est la response fait et doné a le roi d'Engleterre par les hauts hommes d'Escoce touchant la demande du soverein seignurie du roiaume d'Escoce quel le dit roi d'Engleterre ad demandez.[a]

SIRE,[1] la bone gent [2] d'Escoce que l'autre jour viendrent a Norham [3] par vostre requeste et les autres q'il poent avoir dedeinz si brief temps, vous maundent saluz par nous, et vous mercient moult de la bone voluntee que vous avez envers le royaume d'Escoce et la bone gent [2] de la terre et encore averez, si vous plest, qar il entendent[4] q'il ne ount autre chose deservy ne deserviront, si Dieu plest. Et vous maundent, sire, q'ils ount entendu [4] la monstraunce que feust l'autre jour faite en l'esglise de Norham en vostre presence par la bouche sire Rogier Brabazoun vostre chivaler [5] laquele est icele, si come ils ont entendu,[4] que vous ditez que vous estez chief seignur

---

Text : Extant only in Glasgow University Library MS BE 10-y.3, f. 5 (see textual note on no. 15) (G). Printed by E. L. G. Stones, *SHR*, xxxv (1956), pp. 108-9. A very brief summary has long been available in Rishanger (RS), pp. 124-5, but the full text was not known until the discovery of G a few years ago.

[a] *Title from margin of G. On its origin cf. above, p. 51, n. 1.*

[1] For the occasion of this text see Stones, *SHR*, xxxv (1956), pp. 105-7, and Powicke, *Thirteenth Century*, p. 605. Presumably it is the Scottish reply to no. 15, or to the speech of which no. 15 gives the gist.

[2] Here, and in no. 15 above, *bone gent* is translated literally, in order that the reader may interpret the words himself in the light of what is said below. The rubricator of nos. 15 and 16 understood the sense to be ' magnates ' (i.e., clerical and lay nobles), and so did Hemingburgh in his version of no. 15 (above, p. 51, *n.* 6). But a circumstantial narrative printed in Rishanger (ed. Riley (RS), p. 242) categorically asserts that *no* reply came from the magnates, but only from the ' communitas '. *Bone gent* is sometimes used vaguely in the sense of ' faithful subjects ' (e.g., p. 154 below), and on p. 120 below it seems clearly to mean the leaders of the realm. But probably in most recorded instances it does not include ' les grauntz seigneurs ', who are mentioned separately. Yet, as I pointed out in *SHR*, xxxv, loc. cit., it

16

This is the answer rendered to the king of England by the magnates of Scotland, concerning the claim which the king of England has made to the overlordship of the realm of Scotland.

Sir,[1] the good people of Scotland [2] who came to Norham [3] the other day at your request, and the others whom they have been able to [consult] in so short a time, send you their greetings by us, and they thank you very much for the kindness which you show towards the kingdom of Scotland, and the good people [2] of the realm, and will continue to show, if it please you; for they think [4] that they have deserved, and will deserve, nothing less, if it please God. They inform you, Sir, that they have heard [4] the declaration made the other day, in the church of Norham, in your presence, by Roger Brabazon, a knight of yours,[5] which amounts to this, as they understand [4] it: you say that you are overlord of

---

is impossible in the present case to believe that this speech proceeded from a body which excluded the Scottish magnates. Professor Barrow (' The Scottish Clergy (etc.) ', *SHR*, XLI (1962), p. 20), using the Latin equivalent *probi homines* (for which cf. pp. 65, 171, below), is really arguing, like myself, against the exclusion of the magnates in this case, though the linguistic and textual problem is such that our agreement may not be immediately obvious.

[3] According to the accepted dating, based on the ' Great Rolls ', the meeting at Norham ' the other day ' took place on 10 May 1291. An adjournment was allowed to the next day, and then until 2 June, for the Scots to consider their reply. It would be unwise to assign the present document to 2 June without hint of doubt, for the chronology of the ' Great Rolls ' is often suspect (cf. Stones, *SHR*, xxxv, 104). Yet the ' si brief temps ' agrees well enough with an adjournment of three weeks, which gave the Scots too little time to consult their compatriots who were at any great distance from Norham.

[4] The various uses of *entendre* in this text are striking. cf. Collas, *Year Books 12 Edward II* (Selden Society 70), pp. xl-lxiv.

[5] The reference seems to be to p. 51 above (cf. *n.* 3 thereon).

du royaume d'Escoce et que l'avantdit royaume est tenue
de vous en chief, dont vous requistez la bone gent que
la furent q'ils vousissent aerdre [1] a vous come a chief
seignour, et que vous les meyntiendrez en pees et en
quiete solonc les loys et les usages du royaume d'Escoce.[2]
Et pour ce que vous ne entendez ne ne voulez que nul
homme soit desheritez, si volez que les demaundantz qui
droit cleiment eu [3] royaume monstrent en vostre presence
le droit que chescun quide avoir, et vous vostre droit
monstrer volez et par vostre conseil et le conseil de la
bone gent du roiaume resoun et droit ferrez a chescun.[a]

Sire, a ceste monstrance vous respoignent la bone
gent que icy nous ont envoiez, q'ils ne entendent mie que
si grante chose demandroiez si bon droit ne entendisez
avoir, mes de vostre droit rien ne sievent ne par vous ne
par voz auncestres unques demaundé et usé ne ne virent,[4]
dount ils vous respoignent, taunt come en eaux est, que a
vostre monstrance ne ount ils poair a respondre saunz
seignur a qui la demaunde doit estre faite et qui poair en
avera a respondre, car s'il feust ensi que ils se assentissent
a vostre demaunde, rien ne acrestroit a vous de droit ne
de proffit ne decrestroit a lour lyge seignour ; mes bien
volent la bone gent du roiaume que celuy qui roy serra
en l'avantdit royaume face a vous quantque reson et
droiture demaunde, car il poair en avera de respondre et

---

[a] G *has a blank space after* chescun *for the equivalent of ten lines, but inserts marginal lines to show that no discontinuity is intended.*

[1] from Lat. *adherere*

[2] There are phrases in this sentence which cannot be exactly paralleled in no. 15. If no. 15 is not a mere draft or summary, but gives Brabazon's speech in full, we must assume that the text here is explaining what the Scots conceive to be its implications. On this assumption we render *entendu* on p. 53, last line, as ' understand ', rather than ' have heard ', although the authors of no. 16 were probably present at Brabazon's speech.

[3] *eu = en + le*

the realm of Scotland, and that the kingdom is held of
you in chief, wherefore you asked the good people there
present to adhere [1] to you, as overlord, and [you say]
that you will maintain them in peace and quiet, according to the laws and customs of the realm of Scotland.[2]
And since you do not intend or desire that anyone should
be disinherited, you wish that the claimants who assert
that they have a right to the [3] kingdom should exhibit,
in your presence, the right which each one thinks that
he has, and you [also] desire to show your own right;
and by your advice and the advice of the good people of
the realm, you will do to each one what reason and
justice demand.

Sir, to this statement the good people who have sent
us here make answer that they do not in the least believe
that you would ask so great a thing if you were not con-
vinced of your sound right to it. But they have no
knowledge of your right, nor did they ever see it claimed
and used by you or your ancestors [4]; therefore they
answer you, as far as in them lies, that they have no
power to reply to your statement, in default of a lord to
whom the demand ought to be addressed, and who will
have power to make answer about it. For if it should
happen that they agreed to your demand, no right or
profit would accrue to you, nor be lost to their liege lord.
But the good people of the realm earnestly desire that he
who shall be king in the aforesaid kingdom shall do to
you whatsoever reason and justice may demand, for he,
and no other, will have power to reply and to act in the

---

[4] If the evidence of p. 40 above is accepted (to say nothing of general
probability), it must have been known in Scotland in 1291 that Edward had
a *claim* to overlordship; but there was certainly no living recollection of the
' right ' being ' used ', and since the matter had not yet become a subject
for historical research, the earlier precedents may well have been unknown.

faire, et nul autre. Ne lour semble que autre respounce vous purront faire, sauve le serment q'ils firent aprés la mort le roy et la generale sentence donee par evesques, abbés, et autres prelatz sur ceaux qui encontre lour serment viendroient, et a sauver vostre fait et le lour qe fust fet et affermé en vostre presence ¹ a Norhampton.ᵃ Car si autre chose faisent encontre lour serment, parjurs serroient et a desheriter par lour lige seignur. Par quoy ils vous prient qe vous ainsy voulez overir, si vous plest, q'ils ne chisent en grand peril et villeynie reproche,ᵇ desicome ils ount toutz jours assentu a chose que bone vous feust a lour poair, et encore sont apareillez a faire en toute veritee et loiautee.

ᵃ *The text of this sentence may be corrupt.*
ᵇ villeynie reproche *can hardly be explained unless the former word is an adjective.*

matter. It seems to them that they can give you no other answer, saving the oath which they took after the death of the king, and the general sentence [of excommunication] pronounced by bishops, abbots, and other prelates against those who should violate their oath, and to save your deed and theirs, which was executed and affirmed in your presence ¹ at Northampton. For if they did otherwise, against their oath, they would be perjurers, and fit to be disinherited by their liege lord. Therefore they beg you to act in such a way, if it please you, that they fall not into great danger, and shameful disgrace ; for they have always agreed to anything which was to your advantage, so far as in them lay, and they are still prepared to do so, in all truth and loyalty.

¹ This refers to the Treaty of Northampton of 1290 (Stevenson, *Documents*, I, 162-73). cf. below, p. 83.

17

Scriptum [a] per quod petentes jus in regno Scocie obligant se ad petendum et recipiendum jus suum coram rege Anglie tanquam superiore domino Scocie et per quod concedunt quod ipse rex audiat et terminet jura sua in dicto regno, sicut ei qui est superior dominus Scocie competit in hac parte.

A TOUZ [1] qi ceste lettre verront ou orrount, Florence counte de Holand, Robert de Brus seignor du val d'Anaunt, Johan de Baillol seignor de Gaweye, Johan de Hastinges seignor de Bergeveny, Johan Comyn seignor de Badenough, Patrik de Dumbar counte de la Marche, Johan de Vescy por son pere, Nichol de Soules et Willame de Ros, saluz en Dieu. [2] Come nous entendoms avoir droit eu realme d'Escoce, e cel droit moustrer, chalanger et averrer devaunt celui qi pluis de poer, juris-diccion et reson eust de trier nostre droit; et le noble prince sire Edward, par la grace de Dieu roy d'Engle-terre, nous eyt enfourmez par bones et suffisauntes resons qe a lui apent et avoir doit la sovereine seignurie du dit

Text: P.R.O. Scottish Documents, Exchequer (E 39), no. 18 (A) and 88/2 (B) are duplicates, A being sealed on green cords, and B on *doubles queues* of parchment. Eight seals survive on A, the missing one being that of Count Florence; its cord is also missing, but the hole for it is present. It has been inferred from this (wrongly) that Florence was absent from the transaction. All the seals are now lost from B (which is in poor condition), though one still survived in Bain's time. cf. the similar duplication of the document by which Edward received seisin of Scotland from the competitors (E 39/88/1; B.M. Cotton Charters xviii, 40). Since both A and B are damaged, our text is a conflation of them. Transcripts, in the 'Great Rolls of Scotland' and elsewhere, are ignored here. Printed from A by Rymer, I, ii, 755 (R); calendared in Bain, II, no. 488. Listed by Stapledon (Pal-grave, *Kalendars*, I, 131).

[a] *Title from endorsement to* B; *given also by Stapledon*

17

Letter by which those claiming their due in the realm of Scotland undertake to seek and receive it before the king of England, as lord superior of Scotland, and by which they grant that the king may hear and determine their rights in the realm of Scotland, as is fitting in this matter for one who is lord superior of Scotland.

WE,[1] Florence, count of Holland, Robert Bruce, lord of Annandale, John Balliol, lord of Galloway, John Hastings, lord of Abergavenny, John Comyn, lord of Badenoch, Patrick of Dunbar, earl of March, John de Vescy (on behalf of his father), Nicholas de Soules and William de Ros, give greeting in the Lord to all who shall see or hear this letter.[2] Since we consider that we possess a right in the realm of Scotland, and [are entitled] to demonstrate, claim, and urge it before the person who has the most power, jurisdiction and reason to try our case ; and the noble prince, Lord Edward, by the grace of God king of England, has shown us, with good and sufficient reasons, that the overlordship of the realm of

---

[1] This document (sometimes known as ' the award of Norham ') began the judicial process by which the crown of Scotland came to be adjudged to John Balliol. See Dickinson, *Scotland*, p. 149.

[2] For the pedigree showing the descent of these claimants see Dickinson, *Scotland*, p. 151.

reaume d'Escoce et la conissaunce de oir, trier et ter-
miner nostre droit ; nous de nostre propre volunté saunt
nule manere de force ou destresce voloms, otrioms et
grauntoms de receyvre droit devaunt lui com soverayn
seignor de la terre, et voloms ja le meins [1] et promettoms
que nous averoms et tendroms ferm et estable son fet, et
que celui enportera la realme a qui droit le durra devaunt
lui. En tesmoigne de ceste chose nous avoms mys nos
seals a cest escrit. Fet et doné a Norham le mardy
prochein aprés la [a] Assenssion, l'an de grace mil et deus
cens nonaunte primereyn.

[a] la R ; le B ; A *illegible*

Scotland, and the jurisdiction for hearing, trying, and determining our right, belong to him, and that he ought to have them, we, by our own free will, without any kind of constraint or distress, do desire, concede, and grant that we should receive justice before him, as lord superior of the realm. We are willing, moreover,[1] and we promise, that we shall uphold and maintain his decision without dispute, and that the person shall have the realm, to whom justice shall award it in his presence. In testimony of this, we have affixed our seals to this document. Norham, Tuesday next after Ascension Day [5 June], A.D. 1291.

[1] Rare in this sense; but see R. Kelham, *Dictionary* (1779), *s.v.* ' jale-mens '.

18

OMNIBUS Christi fidelibus hoc presens scriptum visuris vel audituris, Robertus de Brus,[1] dominus de valle Anandie, salutem in domino. Noverit universitas vestra nos concessisse et omnino remisisse karissimo filio nostro domino Roberto de Brus [1] comiti Karrik' et heredibus suis, totum jus et clamium quod habuimus vel habere potuimus ad petendum regnum Scocie; ita quod nos nichil juris aut clamii ad predictum regnum nomine nostro petendum de cetero vendicare aut exigere possimus. Damus insuper et spontanea voluntate concedimus predicto filio nostro et heredibus suis plenam et liberam potestatem dictum regnum petendi, et jus quod sibi competit in hac parte nomine suo prosequendi, prout voluntati sue melius noverit convenire, et omnia faciendi que per nos ante tempus confeccionis presencium potuerunt [a] expediri.

In cujus rei testimonium, presenti scripto sigillum nostrum apposuimus, et in majus testimonium sigillum nobilis viri domini Gilberti de Clare, comitis Glovernie et Hertfordie,[2] presentibus apponi procuravimus. Datum apud Berwyc', die veneris in crastino sancti Leonardi,[3] anno gracie M^{o}CC^o nonogesimo secundo.

Text: The original exemplar, B.M. Cotton Charters, xviii, 48 (C), is decorated on the lower edge with five emblazoned shields, and a pattern of foliage, probably all of the time of Sir Robert Cotton. The seals of Bruce and of Gilbert of Clare are attached, each *sur double queue*. (See Frontispiece.) The text and seals were damaged by the Cottonian fire of 1731, and the resulting gaps in the text are supplied from a transcript in Holkham MS 677, f. 405 (H) whose readings I owe to the kindness of Dr W. O. Hassall. Printed hitherto only in the rare *Discoverie of Errours in the First Edition of the Catalogue of Nobility Published by R. Brooke* (1622), pp. 255-6 (B).

[a] poterint H; poternt (?) C (*damaged*); poterunt B; potuerunt *ed.*

18

Rᴏʙᴇʀᴛ Bʀᴜᴄᴇ,¹ lord of Annandale, gives greeting in
the Lord to all the faithful in Christ who shall see or hear
this document. We inform all of you that we have
granted, and totally surrendered, to our well-beloved
son Robert Bruce,¹ earl of Carrick, and his heirs, the
whole right and claim that we had, or could have had,
to sue for the realm of Scotland, so that henceforth we
can assert or propound no right or claim to sue for that
kingdom in our own name. Moreover we give and
grant, of our free will, to our son and his heirs, full and
free power to sue for the realm, and to prosecute in his
own name the right which pertains to him in this matter,
in the way which seems best to him, and to do everything
which we could have set afoot before the writing of this
charter.

As evidence of this, we have affixed our seal to the
present document, and in confirmation we have arranged
for the seal of the noble Lord Gilbert of Clare, earl of
Gloucester and Hertford,² to be affixed to it. Berwick,
Friday, the morrow of St Leonard's day ³ [7 November]
ᴀ.ᴅ. 1292.

---

¹ The grantor is Bruce VI and the grantee Bruce VII (see above, p. 49,
n. 1). The grant was made at the point in the ' Great Cause ' when the
former realised that he had no hope of being awarded the crown of Scotland.
Two days later Bruce VII surrendered the earldom of Carrick to *his* son
(Bruce VIII), the future Robert I (*APS*, i, 449 [red]). The present charter
has been scarcely noticed by Scottish historians. See also above, p. xxvi.

² Earl Gilbert (1243–95), Edward I's son-in-law, was related to Bruce VI
by marriage, and had supported his candidature (Gray, *Scalacronica* [1836],
p. 120).

³ The date 5 November, given in *Scots Peerage*, ii, 431, is wrong.

19

.... DIE ¹ lune sequenti proxima post festum
beati Martini, apud Berewik' super Twedam in aula
castri ejusdem,² anno regni predicti domini regis E[d-
wardi] vicesimo, coram eodem domino rege Anglie
superiore domino dicti regni Scocie, presentibus venerabilibus patribus J[ohanne] archiepiscopo Dublen'
J[ohanne] Winton' A[ntonio] Dunelmensi W[illelmo]
Eliensi .ᵃ. Carleolensi W[illelmo] sancti Andree
R[oberto] Glascuensi M[attheo] Dunkeldensi R[oberto]
Rossensi et Marcho Sodorensi episcopis, H[enrico] de
Lacy comite Linc' Hunfrido comite Hereford' J[ohanne]
comite de Bouczhan ᵇ G[ilberto] comite de Anegus Mal-
lisio comite de Strazern,ᵇ et nonnullis aliis prelatis
comitibus baronibus proceribus et magnatibus utriusque
regni Anglie et Scocie et presentibus eciam quaterviginti ³ predictis de Scocia electis et dicta die assignata
Erico regi Norwagie F[lorencio] comiti Holandie J[o-
hanni] de Balliolo et omnibus aliis petentibus predictum regnum ad audiendum judicium super peticionibus
suis predictis, vocatisque et publice proclamatis omnibus petentibus supradictis, predictus dominus rex per

---

Text : Extract from B.M. MS Cotton Claudius D VI, ff. 160-1 (D) ;
printed from D, as part of his so-called *Annales Regni Scotiae*, by Riley, in
Rishanger (RS), pp. 357-60.

ᵃ *The bishop of Carlisle's name was* John ; *the 'gemipunctus' (above, p. 17,
n. 2) may here indicate that the clerk did not know the name.*

ᵇ C *reads* ' z ' *in these names, but probably the letter* ' yogh ' [ȝ] *was originally
intended in* Bouczhan *and* Goliczly. Strazern *may show a further confusion, the
original* ' thorn ' *for* ' th ' *being confounded with* ' y ', *and then the* ' y ' *with* ' z '.

19

. . . . ON [1] the Monday following, the next after
Martinmas, in the twentieth year of King Edward [17
November 1292] at Berwick-on-Tweed, in the hall of
the castle,[2] before the king of England, lord superior of
the realm of Scotland, in the presence of the venerable
fathers, John, archbishop of Dublin, John, bishop of
Winchester, Anthony, bishop of Durham, William,
bishop of Ely, [John], bishop of Carlisle, William, bishop
of St Andrews, Robert, bishop of Glasgow, Matthew,
bishop of Dunkeld, Robert, bishop of Ross, and Mark,
bishop of Sodor, of Henry de Lacy, earl of Lincoln,
Humphrey, earl of Hereford, John, earl of Buchan,
Gilbert, earl of Angus, Malise, earl of Strathearn
and of many other prelates, earls, barons, nobles and
magnates of the two realms of England and Scotland,
and in the presence also of the eighty elected persons [3]
of Scotland, because that day had been assigned to Eric,
king of Norway, Florence, count of Holland, John
Balliol, and all the others who were claiming the realm,
for them to hear judgment upon their petitions, all the
claimants were called and publicly summoned, and the

---

[1] The *Annales* are written in a hand of *c*. 1300, and contain a narrative
which, though incomplete and disjointed, is often fuller and more credible
than those of the ' Great Rolls '. For fuller discussion see Stones, *SHR*,
xxxv (1956), 89-107; also above, pp. xxv-xxvi. We select here the narrative
of the judgment in favour of Balliol. The corresponding passages in the
' Great Rolls ' are Rymer, I, ii, 780 (R); Prynne, pp. 525-7 (P). Some
differences between R, P, and D are mentioned in the notes.
[2] R adds ' in pleno parleamento '.
[3] On these ' auditors ' see the important article by George Neilson
(above, p. liii).

Rogerum de Brabazun [1] justiciarium suum judicium suum fecit in hunc modum [2] proferri :

Constat [3] vobis omnibus et constare debet qualiter Ericus rex Norwagie, Florencius comes Holandie, J[ohannes] de Balliolo, R[obertus] de Bruis, J[ohannes] de Hastinges, Patricius comes de Marchia, W[illelmus] de Ros, W[illelmus] de Vesci, J[ohannes] Comyn, R[obertus] de Pinkeni, Nicholaus de Soules, Patricius de Golicztly,[a] et Rogerus de Maundevile peticiones suas de regno Scocie et raciones suas per quas asserebant se jus ad idem regnum habere coram quaterviginti electis de Scocia et viginti quatuor nominatis per dictum dominum regem Anglie superiorem dominum regni Scocie proposuerunt. De quibus petentibus antedictus R[obertus] de Pinkeni, Patricius comes de Marchia, Nicholaus de Soules, Patricius Goliczly,[a] W[illelmus] de Ros, W[illelmus] de Vescy, et Florencius comes Holandie peticiones suas retraxerunt. Propter quod dicit eis [4] dominus rex per judicium quod nihil capiant per peticiones suas de eo quod petunt. Et quia Ericus rex Norwagie, J[ohannes] Comyn et R[ogerus] de Maundevile peticiones suas non sunt prosecuti, dicit eis dominus rex per judicium quod propter defectum secte sue nihil similiter capiant per peticiones suas de eo quod petunt. Constat eciam vobis [4] qualiter R[oberto] de Bruis petente predictum regnum Scocie tanquam impartibile racione proximitatis in gradu et J[ohanne] de Balliolo petente similiter idem regnum tanquam impartibile quia ex Margareta filia comitis David primogenita exivit, dictum fuit eidem Roberto de Bruis quod non habuit jus in sua

---

[a] *See p. 59, n. b.*
[1] Brabazon is not mentioned in R or P at the corresponding point.
[2] An indication that the exact words are not given. The speech would

king, by the mouth of his justice Roger Brabazon,[1] caused his judgment to be promulgated in this manner [2] :

You all know,[3] or ought to know, that King Eric of Norway, Florence, count of Holland, John Balliol, Robert Bruce, John Hastings, Patrick, earl of March, William de Ros, William de Vescy, John Comyn, Robert de Pinkeny, Nicholas de Soules, Patrick Golightly and Roger de Mandeville have placed before the eighty persons chosen from Scotland, and the twenty-four nominated by the king of England, the lord superior of the realm of Scotland their petitions for the realm of Scotland, and the arguments on which they based their claim that they had a right to the realm. Of these claimants, Robert de Pinkeny, Patrick, earl of March, Nicholas de Soules, Patrick Golightly, William de Ros, William de Vescy, and Florence, count of Holland, have withdrawn their petitions. Therefore the king says to them [4] in judgment that they shall gain nothing of what they ask in their petitions. Since King Eric of Norway, John Comyn, and Roger de Mandeville have not pursued their petitions, the king says to them in judgment that because of their failure to sue, they too shall gain nothing of what they ask in their petitions. You [4] all know also, how when Robert Bruce claimed the realm of Scotland as impartible, by reason of proximity in relationship, and John Balliol likewise claimed the kingdom as impartible, because he was descended from Margaret, the eldest daughter of Earl David, it was declared to Robert

---

certainly have been made in French, but it is impossible to say how closely the Latin follows the lost original.

[3] R and P have nothing corresponding to this address to the assembly in the next 40 lines.

[4] The alternation between second and third person is remarkable.

M

peticione ad regnum Scocie secundum formam et modum peticionis sue. Constat eciam vobis qualiter Johannes de Hastinges quia de tercia filia dicti comitis David Ada nomine exivit peciit terciam partem totius hereditatis que descendit Margarete filie regis Norwagie per mortem Alexandri ultimi regis Scocie petendo videlicet terciam adquisitorum et eschaetarum que per reges Scocie fuerant adquisita. Similiter dictus R[obertus] de Bruis quia de secunda filia predicti comitis D[avid] exivit propartem suam peciit de grosso et corpore ejusdem regni Scocie et de adquisitis et eschaetis que eidem regno obvenerant.[a]

Unde predictus dominus rex superior dominus regni Scocie auditis et intellectis peticionibus et racionibus predictorum J[ohannis] de H[astinges] et R[oberti] de B[ruis] propartes suas modo predicto petencium et eisdem diligenter examinatis pro jure et per judicium dicit quod dictum regnum Scocie non est partibile nec adquisita per reges Scocie nec eschaete infra idem regnum que ad manus regum devenerant[b] partibiles existunt sed de terris et tenementis que sunt extra regnum Scocie fiat secundum leges et consuetudines regnorum et patriarum ubi terre ille et tenementa consistant. Propter quod predictus rex vobis J[ohanni] de H[astinges] et vobis R[oberto] de Bruis dicit per judicium quod nihil per judicium de propartibus quas petitis infra metas regni Scocie capiatis. Vobis autem[c] Johanni de Balliolo tanquam propinquiori heredi Margarete filie regis Norwagie domine Scocie et neptis quondam Alexandri ultimi regis Scocie jure successionis ad idem regnum

---

[a] obvenert D
[b] devenert D
[c] autem de J. (*interlineated*) Ball' D

Bruce that, having regard to its form and manner, there was no justification for his petition for the realm of Scotland. You know also that John Hastings claimed, as a descendant of the third daughter, Ada, of Earl David, a third of the whole inheritance which descended to Margaret, daughter of the king of Norway, by the death of Alexander, the last king of Scotland, that is by asking for a third of the acquisitions and escheats which accrued to the Scottish kings. Likewise Robert Bruce, as a descendant of the second daughter of Earl David, claimed his share of the realm of Scotland in gross and in sum, and of the acquisitions and escheats which had accrued to the realm.

Therefore the king, the lord superior of the realm of Scotland, after hearing and noting the demands and arguments of John Hastings and Robert Bruce, who were asking for their shares in this manner, and examining them carefully, declares as a matter of law, and by way of judgment, that the realm of Scotland is not partible, and that the acquisitions of the kings of Scotland, and the escheats within that realm which came into the hands of the kings, are not partible; but the lands and tenements outside the realm of Scotland should be dealt with according to the laws and customs of the realms and districts where the lands and tenements are. Therefore the king declares by way of judgment to you, John Hastings, and Robert Bruce, that you shall receive nothing, by this judgment, of the shares which you demand within the bounds of the realm of Scotland. But to you, John Balliol, as the nearest heir of Margaret, daughter of the king of Norway, lady of Scotland, and grand-daughter of the late Alexander, the last king of Scotland—by right of succession to the realm of Scotland,

Scocie optinendum secundum quod est coram predicto domino rege inventum, idem dominus rex reddit predictum regnum Scocie et seisinam ejusdem cum omnibus pertinenciis suis infra idem regnum existentibus et que [a] ad manus ipsius domini regis tanquam ad superiorem dominum predicti regni Scocie post mortem prefate Margarete devenerint [b] salvo jure ejusdem domini regis et heredum suorum cum inde loqui voluerint. Et [1] assignat vobis idem dominus rex diem ad faciendum sibi fidelitatem vestram pro regno Scocie supradicto die Jovis proxima sequenti in festo sancti Edmundi regis et martyris ubicumque tunc fuerit et diem ad faciendum sibi homagium vestrum pro regno Scocie supradicto in die [2] nativitatis dominice ubicumque tunc fuerit in regno suo. Et dictum fuit ei [3] quod sequatur brevia de seisina sua habenda de regno suo supradicto. *Item de eodem in Gallico* : Le rei de Engleterre, soverein seignur du reaume de Escoce, dist que par dreit e par jugement le reaume de Escoce ne est mie partable, ne les aquestz, ne les purchaz de reis, ne les eschetes dedeinz meme le reaume, ne sont mie partables. Mes de terres e de tenemenz que sont hors du reaume de Escoce seit fet solom les leys e les coustumes des reaumes e du pais ou les terres sont

. . . .

---

[a] *Possibly emend to* et ea que

[b] deven<u>er</u>t D

[1] At this point, one exemplar of John of Caen's ' Great Roll ' inserts a warning to Balliol to rule justly, lest Edward should have cause to intervene in Scotland. (Stones, *SHR*, xxxv, 93 and 105.) It was later included in all exemplars of Tange's Roll.

[2] The homage was actually done on 26 December 1292.

[3] Note again the change of person.

as determined before the king—the king renders the
realm and the seisin thereof, with all the appurtenances
which there are within the realm, and what has come
into the hands of the king as lord superior of the realm
of Scotland since the death of Margaret, saving the right
[in Scotland] of the king and his heirs, when they wish
to raise the point. The [1] king appoints next Thursday, the feast of Saint Edmund, king and martyr [20
November], for swearing to him your fealty for the
realm of Scotland, at whatsoever place he may then
be, and Christmas day,[2] wherever he may then be in
his realm, for doing to him your homage for the realm
of Scotland. And he [3] was told to sue out writs to have
seisin of his realm. *The same in French*: the king of
England, overlord of the realm of Scotland, says that
by law and by [his] judgment the realm of Scotland
is in no wise partible, and that the acquisitions and
purchases of the kings, and the escheats within the same
realm are in no wise partible. But the lands and tenements outside the realm of Scotland should be dealt with
according to the laws and customs of the realms and
districts where the lands are . . . .

20

Instrumentum super homagio regis Scocie facto regi Anglie.[a]

IN [1] nomine domini Amen. Anno a nativitate ejusdem millesimo ducentesimo nonagesimo secundo, secundum quod observat ecclesia Anglicana,[2] indiccione sexta et regni magnifici principis domini Edwardi dei gracia regis Anglie illustris vicesimo primo, sexta die exeunte [3] mense decembri, apud Novum Castellum super Tynam in aula palacii dicti domini regis Anglie infra castrum, in presencia mei notarii et testium subscriptorum, egregius princeps dominus Johannes de Balliolo rex Scocie [4] fecit homagium predicto domino regi Anglie tanquam superiori et directo [5] domino regni Scocie de eodem regno et pertinenciis suis presencialiter, verba ipsius homagii proferens ore proprio sermone Gallico hunc habencia litteraliter intellectum :

Domine mi, domine Edwarde, superior dominus regni Scocie ego Johannes de Balliolo rex Scotorum [4] devenio vester homo ligeus de toto regno Scocie cum

---

Text : From P.R.O. Scottish Documents, Exchequer (E 39), 17/8, m. 2 (E) ; part of a very long document prepared in 1298 for the use of the English envoys in France. Calendared in Bain, II, no. 990. Other transcripts in E 39/17/4, and in Paris, Archives Nationales, J 631/6. This particular attestation of the homage (apparently unprinted) preserves the text of one of the three minor instruments known to have been made by John of Caen concerning the ' Great Cause '. Of the others, one is found in all the above MSS, and the other only in Glasgow University MS, BE 10-y.3, ff. 13v-14. The usual assumption that John's ' Great Roll ' was based on the so-called ' protocols ' of Andrew de Tange is certainly an error, and the present text, with its two companions, suggests that John may have prepared a similar series of ' protocols ' of his own (see remarks by E. L. G. Stones in *SHR*, xxxv (1956), 95-7). The text given here should be compared with that in John's ' Great Roll ', printed in Rymer, I, ii, 782 (R).

   [a] *Title from margin of* E

20

Instrument concerning the homage which the king of Scotland did to the king of England.

In [1] the name of the Lord, Amen. In the year A.D. 1292, according to the reckoning of the English church,[2] in the sixth indiction, and the twenty-first year of the reign of the eminent prince Lord Edward, by the grace of God the illustrious king of England, on 26 [3] December, at Newcastle-upon-Tyne, in the hall of the palace of the king of England inside the castle, in the presence of myself (the notary) and of the undermentioned witnesses, the honourable prince John Balliol, king of Scotland,[4] did homage to the king of England, as lord superior [5] of the realm of Scotland, for the realm and its appurtenances, being personally present, and uttering words of homage with his own mouth, in French, which have the following literal purport:

My lord, Lord Edward, lord superior of the realm of Scotland, I, John Balliol, king of Scots,[4] hereby become your liegeman for the whole realm of Scotland

---

[1] Other versions of this homage may be found in Prynne, pp. 530-2, and in Bain, II, nos. 653-5. In general see above, p. xxvi, and Dickinson, *Scotland*, p. 152.

[2] i.e., the custom of beginning the New Year on 25 March, cf. below, p. 164 and *n.* 1.

[3] Reckoning backwards from the last day of the month; a common notarial habit. In R John gives the date as ' St Stephen's day '.

[4] Notice the inconsistency in Balliol's style (above, p. 1, *n.* b). Balliol did, however, use ' Rex Scotorum ' in the legend on his Great Seal.

[5] cf. below, p. 96, *n.* 3.

pertinenciis et omni eo quod appendet, quod quidem regnum teneo et debeo de jure ac clamo pro me et heredibus meis regibus Scocie tenere hereditarie de vobis et heredibus vestris regibus Anglie, et fidem ac fidelitatem portabo vobis et heredibus vestris regibus Anglie de vita et membro et terreno honore, contra omnes homines qui possunt vivere atque mori.

Actum anno, indiccione, die, et loco predictis, presentibus venerabilibus patribus dominis Johanne archiepiscopo Dublinensi et Johanne dei gracia episcopo Karleolensi, necnon et nobilibus viris dominis Henrico de Lascy, Lincolnie, Johanne de Warenna, Surreye, comitibus, Johanne de sancto Johanne, Roberto de Tipetot, Briano filio Alani, Nicolao de Segrave, Gilberto de Thornton, Rogero le Brabanzon, Roberto Malet, Roberto de Hertford, Johanne de Langeton Anglie cancellario, Hugone de Cressingham, Johanne Woghan, magistro Johanne Lovel, Waltero de Langeton canonico Eboracensi et custode garderobe prefati domini regis Anglie, Johanne de Drokenessford et Gilberto de Robery ejusdem domini regis clericis et nonnullis aliis prelatis magnatibus proceribus militibus et nobilibus ac popularibus utriusque regni Anglie et Scocie existentibus tunc ibidem testibus ad hec vocatis specialiter et rogatis. Et ego, Johannes Erturi de Cadamo apostolice sedis auctoritate notarius publicus, premissis que acta fuerunt prout superius continetur omnibus interfui propria manu scripsi, et ad pleniorem evidenciam eorumdem rogatus mei signi annotacione in hanc publicam formam redegi.[1]

---

[1] John of Caen was a notary who acted for Edward I on many occasions after his first undoubted appearance in his service in 1288. His most important productions were duplicate copies of his ' Great Roll of Scotland ', which recorded the ' Great Cause '. The *signum* was the notarial mark of authentication, at the end of the document, and across the joins of membranes. Reproductions of John's *signum* may be seen in *SHR*, xvi (1918), 9,

with its appurtenances and everything that goes with it, and that kingdom I hold, and ought to hold, and claim to hold of right for myself and my heirs, the kings of Scotland, by inheritance, of you and your heirs, the kings of England; and I will maintain faith and fealty to you and your heirs, the kings of England, in matters of life and limb and of earthly honour, against all mortal men.

Transacted in the year, indiction, day and place aforesaid, there being present the venerable fathers John, archbishop of Dublin, and John, by the grace of God bishop of Carlisle, and the noble lords, Henry de Lacy and John de Warenne, earls of Lincoln and of Surrey, John of St John, Robert de Tipetot, Brian FitzAlan, Nicholas Segrave, Gilbert of Thornton, Roger Brabazon, Robert Malet, Robert of Hertford, John Langton, chancellor of England, Hugh Cressingham, John Wogan, Master John Lovel, Walter Langton, canon of York and keeper of the king of England's wardrobe, John of Droxford and Gilbert of Rothbury, clerks of the king, and other prelates, magnates, nobles, knights and men of rank, and common folk of the two realms of England and Scotland who were there at the time, and specially called and summoned as witnesses to these things. And I, John, son of Arthur, of Caen, a public notary, by authority of the apostolic see, was present at all these proceedings, which took place as described above, and have written with my own hand, as requested, and drawn up a record in this public form, marked with my *signum*, as fuller evidence of them.[1]

---

and in Browne, *Echt-Forbes Charters*, plate xii ; also below, p. 72. Since E is a transcript of later date, made by other notaries, this *signum* does not appear there. For an original instrument by John see pp. 70-2 below.

21

.... Et [1] rex Scocie dicit quod ipse est rex regni Scocie nec predicto Magdulpho ad querelam suam nec de aliquo regnum suum tangente ausus est respondere sine consilio proborum hominum [2] regni sui. Et prefatus Magdulphus petit judicium de ipso rege tanquam de indefenso, ex quo presens est in curia regis per adjornamentum ei factum per breve regis quod cognovit se recepisse, nec aliquid ei respondet. Et super hoc dictum est eidem regi Scocie per dominum suum regem Anglie quod idem rex Scocie est homo suus ligius de predicto regno Scocie, de quo fecit ei homagium et fidelitatem, et est coram eo hic adjornatus quod respondeat vel dicat quare nolit vel non debeat hic coram eo respondere.

Et idem rex Scocie dicit, sicut prius dixit, quod de aliquo regnum suum contingente non est ausus nec potest hic respondere inconsultis probis hominibus regni sui. Et super hoc, quia idem rex Scocie dicit quod non ausus est hic respondere inconsultis probis hominibus [2] regni sui, dictum est ei quod requirat alium diem ad consulendum si voluerit, qui precise respondet quod nullum diem requiret, nec aliquod adjornamentum hic

---

Text: Extract from Coram Rege Roll (K.B. 27), 138 (Michaelmas Term 1293), m. 39 (K). Not hitherto printed in this form; but much of the text is identical with *Rotuli Parliamentorum*, I, 113 (Z). Our notes make some comparisons with this, and with Andrew de Tange's ' Great Roll ' (page references to Prynne) (P).

[1] This MacDuff case illustrates Edward I's hearing of appeals by Balliol's vassals. The breach between Edward and Balliol, which led to war in 1296, was the result. See Powicke, *Thirteenth Century*, pp. 610-12 ; Sayles, *King's Bench under Edward I* (Selden Society), II, pp. lxii-lxiii ; Richardson and Sayles in *SHR*, xxv, 308-10 : and cf. above, p. xxvii. The

21

.... [November 1293] AND [1] the king of Scotland says that he is king of the realm of Scotland and dare not make answer at the suit of MacDuff, nor in anything touching his kingdom, without the advice of the people [2] of his realm. And MacDuff demands judgment against the king of Scotland, as against one with no defence, for he is present in the king's court by an adjournment given to him by the king's writ, which he acknowledges that he has received, and yet he makes no answer to him. And hereupon it is said to the king of Scotland by his lord the king of England, that the king of Scotland is his liegeman for the realm of Scotland, for which he performed unto him homage and fealty; and that an adjournment has been given here before the king of England so that he may answer, or say why he will not, or should not, answer before him.

And the king of Scotland says, as he said previously, that he dare not and cannot answer here on any matter touching his realm without consulting the people of his realm. And hereupon, because the king of Scotland says that he dare not answer now without consulting the people [2] of his realm, he is told that he may ask for a delay for consultation if he so desires, and he in reply says plainly that he will seek no delay, nor will he suffer

---

first 37 lines of the entry are omitted here. The previous history of the case is that Macduff of Fife was alleged to have been denied justice by Balliol, and imprisoned. His appeal came before the King's Bench in Trinity 1293 and then went to the English parliament of Michaelmas 1293. Our extract begins with part of the report of what took place in that parliament.

[2] cf. *bone gent*, above p. 53, *n.* 2.

admittet. Postea [1] venit predictus rex Scocie coram
domino rege et consilio suo, et fecit domino regi quandam
supplicacionem ore suo proprio per verba subscripta, et
eadem verba in quadam cedula scripta per manum suam
porrexit, etc. : Sire, jeo suy vostre homme du realme de
Escoce e vous pri que de ceo que vous me avez mys a
devaunt que touche les genz de mon realme ausy cum a
mey, voyllez mestre en suffraunce jeskes taunt que jeo
ey a eus parlé, que jeo ne sey surpris par defaute de
consayl de si cum les genz qui cy sunt od mey ne me
volent ne osent counseyller saunz autres du realme ; et
quant jeo me averey a eus counseillé jeo vous respundray
a vostre primer parlement aprés Paske le counseill que
il me averount donez, et f[e]rey envers vous ceo ke fere
devereye.

Et dominus rex, habito super hoc consilio, ad rogatum
predictum predicti regis Scocie, et eciam ad instanciam
procerum et magnatum de consilio suo, ex gracia sua
speciali et similiter de consensu predicti Magdulphi, concessit ipsi regi Scocie supplicacionem suam predictam et
diem ei dedit ad parleamentum suum post Pascham,[a]
videlicet in crastino sancte Trinitatis etc. in omnibus in
eodem statu [b] quo nunc. Idem dies datus est predicto
Magdulpho etc. Et dictum est regi Scocie quod ibi
habeat brevia domini regis Anglie sibi ex parte ipsius
regis Anglie per vicecomitem Northumbrie directa, et
que se recognovit recepisse etc.[2]

---

[a] *From* Pascham *a line runs to this marginal note*: quere plura in termino
sancte Trinitatis anno xxj° (*i.e., Trinity 1293*).
[b] *Addition of* querela remanente *must be understood.*

any adjournment. Afterwards [1] the king of Scotland came before the king and his council and made a request in person of the king, in the following words, and with his own hand delivered a schedule which bore the same speech in writing : Sir, I am your liegeman for the realm of Scotland, and I pray you to hold in suspense this matter about which you have informed me, which touches the people of my realm as well as myself, until I have had speech with them, that I may not be taken unawares for lack of advice, for the folk who are here with me will not and dare not counsel me without others of the realm ; and when I have taken counsel with them I will report to you, at your first parliament after Easter, the advice that they give me, and I shall do towards you as my duty demands.

And the lord king, after taking counsel on this, of his special grace, and with the agreement of MacDuff, at the request of the king of Scotland and at the instance of the nobles and magnates of his council, granted his petition to the king of Scotland, and assigned him a day to appear at the parliament after Easter, namely on the morrow of Trinity etc. [14 June 1294] everything in the case remaining until then as it is now. The same day was assigned to MacDuff, etc. And the king of Scotland was told that he must bring there the writs of the king of England directed to him on behalf of the king of England by the sheriff of Northumberland, which he acknowledged that he had received, etc.[2]

---

[1] Between *admittet* and *postea*, Z has a long passage in which the council condemns Balliol for denying the implications of Edward's suzerainty, which he had acknowledged during the Great Cause, and declares him to be *in misericordia*.

[2] Here Z concludes, saying that the case was ultimately remitted to the King's Bench.

Ad [a] quem diem predictus rex Scocie in propria persona sua coram ipso domino rege Anglie et consilio suo ad parliamentum suum apud Westmonasterium, videlicet in manerio archiepiscopo Ebor' [1] venit, et similiter predictus Magdulphus qui se optulit versus prefatum regem Scocie de placito predicto. Et quia dominus rex Anglie variis et arduis prepeditus negociis predicte querele predicti Magdulphi versus predictum regem Scocie placitande et terminande intendere non potest,[2] datus est dies predicto regi Scocie coram ipso domino rege Anglie ad parliamentum suum a die Pasche in unum mensem anno regni ipsius regis Anglie vicesimo tercio ubicumque etc.,[3] in eodem statu [b] in omnibus predictam querelam tangentibus in quo statu eadem querela fuit ad predictum crastinum sancte Trinitatis . . . .[c] Postea,[d] a die Pasche in unum mensem, anno xxiij°, dominus rex mandavit hic litteram suam sub sigillo suo privato, que residet in ligula preceptorum de termino Pasche anno xxiij°, pretextu cujus mandati Johannes rex Scocie solempniter vocatus non venit . . . .[e] et super hoc venit Ricardus de Breteville, qui sequitur pro domino rege, et petit judicium de defalto ipsius Johannis regis Scocie . . . .[e] ideo datus est dies predicto Ricardo qui sequitur pro ipso rege a die sancti Michaelis in xv dies ubicumque, etc.[4]

---

[a] *A new hand begins here.*
[b] *Addition of* querela remanente *must be understood.*
[c] *Omission of five lines by editor*
[d] *A third hand begins here.*
[e] *Omission of a few words by editor*

[1] i.e., York Place, where Whitehall Palace later stood. P (p. 536) seems to confound this meeting with that of the parliament of Michaelmas 1293. Its story is much garbled (probably because it was compiled so long after the event [1315–18]).

On that day the king of Scotland appeared in person
before the king of England and his council in parliament
at Westminster, in the house of the archbishop of York,[1]
and so too did MacDuff, who appeared against the king
of Scotland in the plea which has been spoken of. And
because the king of England could not attend to the trial
and decision of the suit of MacDuff against the king of
Scotland, because he was preoccupied with many difficult
matters of business,[2] a day was assigned for the king of
Scotland to appear before the king of England at his
parliament to be held a month after Easter in the
twenty-third year of the king's reign [May 1295]
wherever [3] [the king may be], everything touching the
plea remaining in the same state in which that plea was
on the morrow of Trinity mentioned above . . . .
Afterwards, one month after Easter in the twenty-third
year [May 1295] the king sent his letter here under the
privy seal (it is kept in the bundle of ' precepts ' of Easter
term in the twenty-third year), and by virtue of that
order John, king of Scotland, was formally called upon,
and did not appear . . . . and thereupon Richard
de Breteville, who sues on behalf of the king, came and
asked for judgment by default of John, king of Scotland
. . . . therefore a day is assigned to Richard, who
sues for the king, on the quinzaine of Michaelmas [13
October 1295] wherever [the king may be].[4]

---

[2] P says that the parliament *cessavit sive non tenebatur* (p. 537) ; a confusion probably based on this passage. Edward was now preoccupied with
a Welsh rebellion and a French war.

[3] P (p. 537) has an adjournment to a fictitious parliament ' at Bury
St Edmunds in 1295 ' (Richardson and Sayles, op. cit., p. 309, *n.*).

[4] Nothing more is heard of this case in the records. By Michaelmas
1295, indeed, England and Scotland were on the verge of war.

22

A TUZ ceus qe cestes lettres verront ou orrunt Patryk
conte de la Marche e de Dumbar, Gilbert de Humfra-
ville conte de Anegos, Robert de Brus le veil, e Robert
de Brus le juuene [1] comte de Carryk, saluz. Por ce que
nous sumes e tuz jours avoms esté a la fey e a la volunté
du tres noble prince e nostre chier seignur sire Edward,
par la grace de Dieu roy d'Engleterre, seigneur d'Irlaunde
e duc d'Aquitaine, nous promettoms pur nous e pur nos
heyrs sur peyne de corps e d'aveyr e sur quanque nous
pussoms encoure, qe nous li serviroms bien e lealment
encuntre totes gentz qi purrunt vivre e morir, totes les
foyz qe nous serroms requis ou garniz de par nostre
seignur le roy d'Engleterre avantdit, ou par ses heyrs, e
qe nous leur damage ne saveroms qe nous ne le [a] destur-
beroms a tut nostre poer e le leur faceoms a saveyr.[2] E
a cestes choses tenir e garder nous obligoms nous e nos
heyrs e tutz nos biens. E outre ceo avoms juré sur seintes
ewangeiles. E puys nous tutz e chescun de nous par sey
avoms fet homage a noster seigneur le rey avantdit en
cestes paroles:

Text: P.R.O. Scottish Documents, Exchequer (E 39), 17/2 and 9, ms 6 and
7 (E) (part of a ' homage ' roll, made in April 1298, by the notaries John
Bush and John of Caen). Given also by Hemingburgh, pp. 283-4 (H) and
Knighton (RS), i, 310-11. The date and place present a problem, since the
' Ragman Roll ' of Andrew de Tange has the same text, but dated at
Berwick on *28 August* 1296 (*Instrumenta Publica* (Bannatyne Club, 1834),
pp. 176a-b; it is curious that one of Tange's three exemplars (C 47/23/3,
m. 20) omits it). But Edward is known to have been at Wark on 25 March,
and our text seems undoubtedly authentic. The two Bruces, therefore,
submitted to Edward before the campaign against Balliol had even begun.
For the circumstances see Powicke, *Thirteenth Century*, pp. 613-14; and cf.
above, p. xxviii.

   [a] les E ; le H

22

WE, Patrick, earl of March and Dunbar, Gilbert de Umfraville, earl of Angus, Robert Bruce the elder, and Robert Bruce the younger,[1] earl of Carrick, give greeting to all those who shall see or hear this letter. Since we are, and always have been, faithful to, and subject to the will of the most noble prince, and our well-beloved lord, Edward, by the grace of God king of England, lord of Ireland, and duke of Aquitaine, we promise, on our own behalf and that of our heirs, on pain of forfeiting our lives and our property, and of whatever penalty we can incur, that we shall serve him well and loyally against all mortal men, on every occasion that we are so required or instructed by our lord the king of England, or by his heirs, and that if we come to know of anything hurtful to them, we shall do all in our power to frustrate it, and shall bring it to their notice.[2] We pledge ourselves, and our heirs, and all our chattels, that we shall keep and honour these promises. Further, we have sworn this on the Holy Gospels, and thereafter all of us together, and each of us separately, have done homage to our lord the king aforesaid in these words :

---

[1] On the Robert Bruces see above, p. 49, *n.* 1.
[2] This passage is made intelligible by the Latin of a similar document in Rishanger, pp. 163-4 : ' et quod nos non sciemus damnum eorum quin illud impediemus omnibus viribus nostris, et eos premuniemus '.

N

' Jeo devenk voster home lige de vie e de membre e de terrien honur contre totez gentz qi pount vivre e morir '.

E mesmes celi nostre seigneur le roy l'ad resceu en ceste forme :

' Nous le recevoms des terres dunt vous estes ore seisi, sauve nostre droyt e autry, e forpris les terres lesqueles Johan de Baillol, qi fust roy d'Escoce,[1] vous dona puys qe nous lui eumes renduz le reaume d'Escoce, si nules vous eit donee '.

Estre ceo nous tutz e chescun de nous par sey avoms fet fealté a nostre seignur le roy avantdit en cestes paroles :

' Jeo serray feal e leal e foy e leauté porteray au roy Edward, roy d'Engleterre, e a ses heyrs, de vie e de membre e de terrien honur contre totes gentz qi porunt vivre ou morir, e jammés pur nuly armes ne porteray n'en conseyl n'en eyde ne serray contre lui ne countre ses heyrs en nul cas qe poet avenir, e lealment reconustray e lealment f[e]ray les services qui apartenent as tenementz qe jeo cleim tener de luy, si Dieu me eyde e les seintz '.

En temoignance de queles choses nous avoms fet fere cestes lettres overtes selés de nos seals. Doné a Werk, le vintime quint jour de Marz, l'an du regne nostre seignur le roy d'Engleterre avantdit vintime quart.

' I become your liegeman in matters of life and limb and of earthly honour, against all mortal men '.

And the king, our lord, has received it in this form of words :

' We receive it, for the lands of which you are now seised, reserving our own right and that of anyone else, and excepting any lands which John Balliol, the former king of Scotland,[1] gave you after we handed over the kingdom of Scotland to him, if he has given you any '.

Further, all of us together, and each of us separately, have sworn fealty to our lord the king aforesaid in these words :

' I will be faithful and loyal, and will maintain faith and loyalty to King Edward, king of England, and to his heirs, in matters of life and limb and of earthly honour against all mortal men ; and never will I bear arms for anyone against him, or his heirs, nor give counsel or aid against him, on any occasion which may arise ; and I will loyally recognise and perform the services which are attached to the tenements which I claim to hold of him, so may God help me and the saints '.

As evidence of these things we have caused this letter patent to be written, and sealed with our seals. Wark, 25 March, in the twenty-fourth year of the reign of our lord the king of England [1296].

---

[1] Thus, even before Edward's invasion had begun on 28 March 1296, Balliol is treated as being no longer king of Scotland.

23

Transcriptum littere Johannis de Balliolo de reddicione homagii sui.[a]

In [1] NOMINE DOMINI AMEN.[b] Hoc est exemplum cujusdam littere.. regis Scocie et ex parte ejusdem regis per religiosos viros .. gardianum fratrum minorum de Rokesburg' et socium suum anno domini millesimo ducentesimo nonagesimo sexto, indiccione nona, quinta die intrante [2] mense Aprili, apud Berewyk super Twedam, in castro ejusdem ville domino .. regi Anglie presentate, cujus tenor talis est:

[c] Magnifico principi domino Edwardo dei gracia regi Anglie, Johannes, eadem gracia Scocie [d] rex. Cum vos, ac alii de regno vestro, vobis non ignorantibus, vel saltem ignorare non debentibus, per violentam vestram potenciam nobis et regni nostri incolis graves et intolerabiles injurias, contemptus, et gravamina, necnon et dampna enormia contra nostras et regni nostri libertates ac contra deum et justiciam notorie et frequenter intuleritis, nos extra regnum nostrum ad levem cujuscumque suggestionem pro libito voluntatis vestre citando [3] et

---

Text: B.M. MS Cotton Vespasian F VII, f. 42, an original instrument in the hand of John of Caen, slightly damaged, and in places illegible (C) ; P.R.O. Chancery Miscellanea (C 47) 27/3/12, a damaged copy of the early fourteenth century omitting the authenticating clause (A), whence probably Rymer, 1, ii, 836-7 (R) ; P.R.O. Scottish Documents, Exchequer (E 39), 2/8, a damaged early fourteenth-century copy of Balliol's letter alone (E). A version once existed under the seals of four English bishops (Palgrave, *Kalendars*, iii, 108). The full notarial text is printed here for the first time, from C, with recourse to A, E, and R when C is illegible ; Balliol's letter alone has several times been printed, and is calendared in Bain, ii, no. 722 (from E).

[a] *Title from dorse of* E (*by Stapledon's clerk ?*)   [b] In dei nomine Amen A
[c] E *begins*.   [d] Scoc' C ; Scocie E ; A *illegible*

23

Copy of a letter from John Balliol about the renunciation of his homage.

IN [1] THE NAME OF THE LORD, AMEN. This is a copy of a letter of the king of Scotland, presented on behalf of the said king to the king of England, at Berwick-upon-Tweed, in the castle of that town, on 5 [2] April A.D. 1296, in the ninth indiction, by two friars (the warden of the Franciscans of Roxburgh, and his companion) and its text is as follows:

To the eminent prince, Edward, by the grace of God king of England, John, by the same grace king of Scotland. You yourself, and others of your realm (to your own knowledge, for surely you should not be ignorant of what they do) have (as everyone knows) inflicted over and over again, by naked force, grievous and intolerable injuries, slights, and wrongs upon us and the inhabitants of our realm, and indeed have caused harm beyond measure to the liberties of ourselves and of our kingdom, and in a manner which offends against God and against justice; for instance by summoning us [3] outside our realm at the mere beck and call of anybody, as your own whim dictated, and by harassing us unjustifiably; by

[1] On the circumstances of this ' defiance ' see above, p. xxvii; and cf. Gray, *Scalacronica* (1836), p. 122.
[2] A common notarial form of dating; cf. *die exeunte* below.
[3] cf. above, pp. 65-7.

indebite vexando, castra nostra, terras, et possessiones
nostras ᵃ et nostrorum infra regnum vestrum injuste et
sine nostris demeritis occupando, bona nostra ac subditorum nostrorum tam per terram quam per mare
rapiendo et infra regnum vestrum receptando, mercatores
et alios regni nostri incolas occidendo, hominesque nostros
de regno nostro violenter in regnum vestrum abducendo,
ipsosque ibidem detinendo et incarcerando ¹; super
quibus reformandis nuncios nostros sepe vobis trans-
misimus, que non solum adhuc remanent incorrecta,
verum eciam de die in diem per vos et vestros prioribus
deteriora cumulantur. Vos namque jam cum innumera-
bili armatorum multitudine, exercitu vestro publice con-
vocato ad exheredandum nos et regni nostri incolas ad
fines regni nostri hostiliter accessistis, et ultra progredi-
entes in regno nostro strages et incendia necnon insultus
et invasiones violentas tam per terram quam per mare
commisistis inhumane. Nos dictas injurias contemptus
gravamina et dampna necnon et hostiles impungnacio-
nes [*sic*] ulterius sustinere non valentes, nec in fidelitate
et homagio vestro, licet per violentam inpressionem ᵇ
vestram extortis,² manendo,ᶜ contra vos eciam ad defensionem nostram et regni nostri cujus defensioni et
tuicioni vinculo juramenti sumus astricti nos volentes
erigere, fidelitatem et homagium vobis facta tam a nobis
quam ab aliis quibuscumque regni nostri incolis fidelibus

ᵃ nostras E ; *om.* CA
ᵇ *So* CE ; oppressionem A
ᶜ *So* CA ; E *damaged but seems to read* manendo a . . contra, *possibly for*
ac contra. *There may be some corruption, though the ablative gerund used as a
present participle is well established in later Latin.*

¹ Nothing seems to be known from other sources of these alleged acts of
violence by Edward I before the invasion of Scotland in 1296, but as early

seizing our castles, lands and possessions, and those of
our people, within your realm, unjustly and without any
fault on our part; by taking away, and receiving within
your realm, both by land and by sea, our chattels and
those of our subjects; by slaying merchants and other
inhabitants of our realm; and by forcibly seizing the
men of our realm, taking them into your own, and
keeping and imprisoning them there.[1] We have often
sent our envoys to you to discuss the amendment of
these things, yet, up to the present, the injuries not only
persist as they were, but even have offences added to
them which are worse than the first, by you and your
subjects, as one day succeeds another. For now you have
come to the frontiers of our realm in warlike array, with
a vast concourse of soldiers, and with an army openly
assembled, to disinherit us and the inhabitants of our
realm, and have crossed beyond into our realm, and
brutally committed acts of slaughter and burning, as
well as aggression and acts of violence both by land and
by sea. We cannot any longer endure these injuries,
insults, and grievous wrongs, nor these hostile attacks,
nor can we remain in your fealty and homage (which, be
it said, were extorted by extreme coercion on your part) [2]
and we desire to assert ourselves against you, for our own
defence and that of our realm, to whose defence and safe-
keeping we are constrained by the bond of an oath; and
so by the present letter we renounce the fealty and
homage which we have done to you, and which any
other person among our faithful subjects, the inhabitants

---

as 16 October, 1295 he had confiscated the lands and property held by
Scots in England (Bain, ii, no. 718).

[2] There seems to be no contemporary evidence that the homage and
fealty of the Scots in 1291–2 were extorted by violence.

nostris racione terrarum quas in regno vestro de vobis
tenebant,[1] ac eciam racione menagii seu retencionis
vestre, nomine nostro ac nomine eorumdem omnium et
singulorum vobis reddimus per presentes.[a] [2]

Exemplata et ascultata fuit suprascripta littera anno
et indiccione predictis, quinta die exeunte mense Aprili,
apud Berewyk super Twedam, in domo fratrum de
Carmelo, presentibus venerabilibus viris dominis Johanne
de Langetone prefati domini regis Anglie cancellario,
Willelmo de Hameltone archidiacono Eboracen', et
Roberto dicto Galby, notario publico, qui una mecum
easdem litteras ad autenticas, que sigillo vero supra-
nominati regis Scocie fuerant sigillate, diligenter et
fideliter ascultarunt.[b]

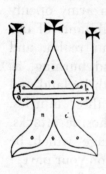

Et ego, Johannes Erturi de Cadomo,
apostolice sedis auctoritate notarius publicus, prout in litteris antedictis inveni ita
fideliter de verbo ad verbum per ordinem
exemplavi, scripsi, et eas ad mandatum
et rogatum memorati domini regis Anglie
ad majorem evidenciam premissorum mei
signi [3] annotacione in hanc publicam formam redegi.

[a] E *ends.*
[b] AR *end.*

of our realm, has done, by reason of the lands which are held of you in your realm,[1] and also by reason of the membership of your household or retinue : this we do in our own name and in the name of each and all of them.[2]

This letter was collated and copied in the year and indiction already mentioned, on 26 April, at Berwick-upon-Tweed, in the house of the Carmelite friars, in the presence of the venerable John Langton, chancellor of the king of England, and William Hamilton, archdeacon of York, and of Robert Galby, notary public, who with me diligently and carefully collated the letter with the original, which was sealed with the seal of the king of Scotland.

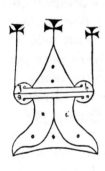

And I, John, son of Arthur, of Caen, notary public by authority of the Apostolic See, have written a faithful copy, word for word, in order as I found it, of the text in the letter, and have drawn it up in the form of this public instrument with the mark of my *signum*,[3] at the request of the king of England, as fuller evidence of the matters aforesaid.

---

[1] John seems almost to suggest that even his homage of 1292 had been only for his lands in England (see above, pp. 63-4).

[2] John's letter has no date, as was noted by the chronicler Cotton (*Historia Anglicana* (RS), 1859), p. 309.

[3] cf. above, p. 64, *n.* 1 ; and see the illustration (reduced from original size) on this page.

24

Litera Johannis regis Scocie per quam reddidit domino Edwardo regi Anglie filio regis Henrici regnum Scocie.[a]

JOHAN par la grace de Dieu rey de Escoce, a touz ceaus qui ceste lettres verront ou orront saluz. Cume nous par mauvoys consail e faus e par nostre simplesce eions grevousement offendu e courecé nostre seignor Edward, par la grace de Dieu roy de Engleterre, seignor de Hirlaunde e duc de Aquitaine en moult des choses, ceo est a saver nous estaunt e demoraunt a sa foy e en son homage, de fere aliaunce au roy de Fraunce contre li qui adonk[es] estoit e encore est son enemy,[b] e a fere mariage ove la fielle son frere sire Charles, e por nostre seignor grever e le rey de Fraunce eider a tot nostre poer par gere e en autres maners; e puis par nostre mauvoys consail avantdit defier [1] nostre seignor le rey d'Engleterre, e nous metre hors de son homage e sa foy par le homage rendre; e ausi noz gens enveer en sa tere d'Engleterre por fere arsons, pries [c] prendre, homicides fere, e autres damages plusors; e la tere de Escoce, la-

---

Text: P.R.O. Scottish Documents, Exchequer (E 39), 100/133: the original letter patent, with the Great Seal of Balliol in white wax, *sur double queue* (E); whence, apparently, Rymer, I, ii, 841-2 (R), where followed by a Latin version from an unidentified MS. Listed by Stapledon (Palgrave, *Kalendars*, I, 132). Hemingburgh (pp. 280-1 : H) and Knighton (RS, I, 308-9) give text, H dating it 10 July, which is also the date of a Latin version in Rishanger, pp. 161-2 (L). The place of issue in H and L is Brechin. Calendared in Bain, II, no. 754. Printed here from E, with its damaged passages restored from R and H. The discrepancies over date and place need not arouse suspicion in themselves, since the text may have been reissued. The surrender was, however, regarded as invalid by the Scottish Guardians (see below, p. 77) and by the king of France, who continued to call Balliol ' king of Scots '. For allegations of forgery against Edward see *Scotichronicon*, II, 218, and Ramsay, *Dawn of the Constitution*, p. 430. But no. 27 below shows Balliol as glad to abandon his thankless position in Scotland.

24

Letter of King John of Scotland, by which he surrendered the realm of Scotland to Edward, king of England, son of King Henry.

JOHN, by the grace of God king of Scotland, gives greeting to all those who shall see or hear this letter. Seeing that we have by evil and false counsel, and our own folly, grievously offended and angered our lord Edward, by the grace of God king of England, lord of Ireland, and duke of Aquitaine, in many ways, in that while we yet owed him fealty and homage we made alliance against him with the king of France, who then was, and still is, his enemy, agreeing to arrange a marriage with the daughter of Charles, the French king's brother, and to harass our lord, and help the king of France, with all our power, in war and by other means ; and in that by the same evil counsel we have ' defied ' [1] our lord the king of England, and have withdrawn ourselves from his homage and fealty by renouncing our homage, and also in that we have sent our men into his land of England to burn, plunder, murder, and do many other wrongs, and have fortified against him the land of Scotland, which is

---

[a] *Title from Stapledon*; *a similar description is partly legible as an endorsement on* E.

[b] einemy R ; E *illegible* ; enemy H

[c] pries R ; E *illegible* ; prayes H

[1] See above, pp. 70-2. The alliance with France is the famous treaty of 1295.

quele est de son fie,[1] de genz armés [a] e en viles, chasteux
e aillors mettre e establir por la terre defendre contre li
e por son fie li deforcer ; por lesqueu [b] choses e trespas [2]
desudiz nostre seignor le rey d'Engleterre avantdit est en
la terre d'Escoce entré, e a force la ad prise e conquise,
nonostant [c] le poer que nous avions mis contre li, laquele
chose il pout fere de droit com seignor de son fie puis
que nous lui avions le homage rendu e fet les choses
avantdites.

Por laquele chose nous estant en nostre plen poer e
nostre fraunche volenté, luy avons rendu la tere de
Escoce e tote la gent ove touz leur homages. En tesmoigne de queue chose nous avons fet fere cestes noz
lettres overtes. Donees a Kyncardyn [d] le secund [e] jour
de Jul', l'an de nostre regne quart.

[a] genz armes R ; E *illegible* ; genz des armes H
[b] queu R ; *end of word illegible* E ; queles H
[c] non ostant R ; E *illegible* ; nonesteant H
[d] Brighine H ; Brithin (*rectius* Brichin) L
[e] disme H ; decimo L

his fief,[1] by putting and maintaining armed men in the towns, castles, and elsewhere, to defend the land against him, and deprive him of his fee: for all these reasons and these many wrongs,[2] our lord the king of England has entered the realm of Scotland and taken and conquered it by force, notwithstanding the army that we had sent against him, a thing which he was rightly able to do as lord of his fee, since we had renounced our homage to him and done the things already described.

Therefore we, acting under no constraint, and of our own free will, have surrendered to him the land of Scotland and all its people, with the homages of all of them. As evidence of this action, we have caused this our letter patent to be written. Kincardine, 2 July, the fourth year of our reign [1296].

[1] Text probably corrupt; L has *contra eum muniendo* after word corresponding to ' fie ', and translation reads accordingly.
[2] *Pro quibus transgressionibus* L

25

(a) : A.D. 1296

. . . . ET [1] memorandum quod, xvij die Septembris, anno xxiiij[to], omnia jocalia infra [2] scripta mittebantur de Berewico usque London' per Johannem Candelarium in tribus cofris cum signis ut supra, et unum magnum cofrum et ij parvos cofros cum diversis scriptis et memorandis inventis in castro de Edeneburgh et unum cofrum cum reliquiis inventis ibidem ; et xix cornua de bucle et unum cornu griffone que liberata fuerunt in garderoba per dominum Robertum Giffard et dominum Hugonem de Robury, que inventa fuerunt in quodam prioratu iuxta Forfare [3] et unum fardellum cum diversis rebus que fuerunt episcopi sancti Andree [4] liberatum in garderoba per dominum J[ohannem] de Swineborn militem et custodem ejusdem episcopatus mense Septembris in principio, et unum discum magnum argen[ti] pro elemosina.[5]

Et omnia ista liberavit dictus Johannes domino Johanni de Drokensford, que idem dominus Johannes deposuit in garderoba Westm'.

Text : (a) Extract from P.R.O. Exchequer, Accts. Various (E 101), 354/9 m. 1, (E). Printed in full by Joseph Hunter in *Archaeological Journal*, XIII (1856), 247-9. Calendared in Bain, II, no. 840.
(b) Extract from P.R.O. Exchequer, T.R., Misc. Books (E 36), vol. 268 [Stapledon's *Calendar*], p. 242 (S). Printed in Palgrave, *Kalendars*, I, 137.

  [1] These texts, together with the statement on p. 116 below, are the only contemporary record evidence for any permanent removal of Scottish records to England by Edward I. Though E testifies to the removal of only three coffers of documents in 1296, S, the conclusion of a list made in 1323, proves the presence by then in the English archives of a considerable bulk of Scottish records.

25

(a) : A.D. 1296

.... Note [1] that on 17 September, in the king's twenty-fourth year, all the jewels in the list overleaf [2] were sent from Berwick to London by John Chandler, in three coffers bearing the marks already stated, and [there were also sent] a big coffer, and two small coffers, with various documents and memoranda found in Edinburgh castle, and a coffer with the relics found there ; and nineteen buffalo horns and a griffin horn, committed to the wardrobe by Robert Giffard and Hugh of Rothbury, which were found in a priory near Forfar,[3] and a bundle with various things which belonged to the bishop of St Andrews,[4] delivered to the wardrobe by Sir John of Swinburne, keeper of that bishopric, at the beginning of September, and a large silver alms-dish.[5]

John delivered all these things to John of Droxford, and the latter deposited them in the wardrobe at Westminster.

---

[2] Refers to the inventory of jewels on the reverse of the membrane, not printed here.
[3] Presumably the Augustinian priory of Restennet
[4] William Fraser, who died in exile in France in 1297.
[5] I cannot find evidence for Hubert Hall's statement that on 17 September 1296 a chest was sent from Berwick to London with ' the Scotch regalia ', and a chest with the records of the fealties and homages of the Scots (H. Hall, *Red Book of Exchequer* (RS), 1 (1896), p. xiii).

(b) : A.D. 1323

. . . . Munimenta regum Scocie et aliorum diversorum ejusdem regni, ut de cartis regiis per reges ejusdem terre diversis factis, ac eciam cartis et scriptis diversorum magnatum et aliorum dicte terre, una cum aliis variis memorandis de quibus hic mencio expresse fieri non potuit pre confusione scripture et propter eorum minimum valorem, set sunt reposita videlicet in duobus forceriis de coreo ferro ligatis, in quatuor hanaperiis de coreo nigro coopertis, in ix forceriis ligneis, in xviii hanaperiis de virgis, et in xxxii pixidibus, preter alia munimenta et memoranda ejusdem terre antea in isto libro [1] per diversas particulas et diversa signa,[2] atque secundum ordinem numeri et secundum eorum facultates intrata et registrata.[3]

[1] i.e., in the preceding pages of Stapledon's *Calendar*.

[2] *Signa* : marks on the containers of each batch of records, reproduced in the margin of Palgrave's edition of Stapledon.

[3] i.e., in addition to the 65 containers mentioned in the text, the ' Scottish ' documents filled 17 other containers of which detailed inventories had been given in the preceding pages ; a total of 82. It is important to realise that much of the contents of these 17 containers consisted of English archives relating to Scotland, not of Scottish archives transferred to England.

(b) : A.D. 1323

[Concluding entry in inventory of the documents concerning Scotland which were at this date in the English
royal archives.]

. . . . Muniments of the kings of Scotland, and
of various other persons of that realm, such as royal
charters made by various kings of that realm, and also
charters and documents of various magnates and other
persons of the same realm, with various other memoranda, of which a detailed inventory could not be given
here because of the disorder of the writing, and because
of their trifling value : they are contained, however, in
two leather forcers bound with iron, in four hampers
covered with black leather, in nine wooden forcers, in
eighteen hampers of wicker, and in thirty-two boxes,
apart from other muniments and memoranda of that
country which have been entered and registered [3]
already in the present book,[1] arranged by their various
bundles and marks of identity,[2] and in their numerical
order and according to their subject.

o

26

Littere Protectorie ᵃ

(a)

ANDREAS ¹ de Moravia et Willelmus Walensis duces exercitus regni Scocie, nomine preclari principis domini Johannis dei gracia regis Scocie ² illustris, de consensu communitatis regni ejusdem, omnibus hominibus dicti regni ad quos presentes littere pervenerint, salutem. Sciatis nos nomine dicti regis priorem et conventum de Hexildesham in Northumbria, terras suas, homines suos et universas eorum possessiones, ac omnia bona sua mobilia et immobilia, sub firma pace et proteccione ipsius domini regis et nostra juste suscepisse. Quare firmiter prohibemus ne quis eis in personis, terris seu rebus malum molestiam injuriam seu gravamen aliquod inferre presumat, super plenaria forisfactura ipsius domini regis, aut mortem eis vel alicui eorum inferat sub pena amissionis vite et membrorum, presentibus post annum minime valituris. Datum apud Hexildesham vij° die Novembris.³

(b)

Andreas etc.⁴ Sciatis quod suscepimus unum canonicum de Hexildesham cum uno armigero et duobus famulis suis in salvum et securum conductum regis nostri

Text: Known only from the transcript in Hemingburgh, pp. 306-7 (H).

ᵃ *Title as in* H

¹ These protections seem to have been given only after Hexham had already been plundered (cf. Hemingburgh, p. 305). See also above, p. xxviii, and Powicke, *Thirteenth Century*, pp. 686-7.

² On the style, see above, p. 63, *n.* 4; notice here the continuing Scottish recognition of Balliol, who was in exile after renouncing his crown (above, p. 73).

26

Letters of Protection

(a)

WE,[1] Andrew of Moray and William Wallace, the leaders
of the army of the realm of Scotland, in the name of
the eminent prince Lord John, by the grace of God the
illustrious king of Scotland,[2] with the agreement of the
community of the realm, give greeting to all of that
realm to whom the present letter shall come. We inform
you that in the name of the king we have duly received
into the firm peace and protection of the king and of
ourselves the prior and the convent of Hexham in
Northumberland, with their lands, and their men, and
all their possessions, and their property, moveable and
immoveable.   Therefore we strictly forbid anyone to
presume to inflict on them, in their persons, lands, or
chattels, any ill, interference, injury, or hurt, on pain
of incurring plenary forfeiture to the king himself; or
to cause the death of them, or of any one of them, on
pain of loss of life and limb.   The present letter is to
be of no value after one year.   Hexham, 7 November
[1297].[3]

(b)

We, Andrew, etc.[4]   We inform you that we have
granted safe-conduct in the name of our king and of
ourselves to one canon of Hexham, and one squire, and
their two servants, to come to us, wherever we may be,

---

[3] The year has to be inferred from the context in the chronicle.
[4] *Etc.* ; to be extended as in (a).

et nostrum, ad veniendum ad nos ubicumque fuerimus quandocumque necesse fuerit et expediens dicte domui. Et ideo vobis omnibus et singulis nomine dicti domini regis mandamus firmiter injungentes quatinus cum aliquis canonicus dicte domus cum predicto armigero et famulis suis presentes literas secum habens causa veniendi ad nos inter vos venerit, ipsos sub salva custodia ad nos ducatis ita quod nullus eos in personis seu rebus molestet in aliquo, sub regis plenaria forisfactura, aut mortem eis vel alicui eorum inferat sub pena amissionis vite et membrorum, presentibus ad voluntatem nostram duraturis.[1]

[1] Presumably the date is the same as that of (a).

whenever it is necessary and expedient for that [religious] house. Therefore, in the name of the lord king, we give command to one and all, strictly ordering that when any canon of that house, with a squire, and their servants, having this letter with him, shall come among you with the intention of journeying to meet us, you shall bring them to us under safe guard, in such manner that nobody may molest them in any way, either in their persons or in their property, on pain of incurring plenary forfeiture to the king; or cause the death of them, or of any one of them, on pain of loss of life and limb. The present letter is to remain in force as long as we so desire.[1]

27

IN [1] nomine Domini Amen. Anno a nativitate ejusdem millesimo ducentesimo nonagesimo octavo, indiccione undecima, prima die mensis Aprilis, in camera hospicii venerabilis patris A[ntonii] episcopi Dunelmensis extra London,[2] ipse de statu et condicione regni Scocie et inhabitancium idem regnum coram nobili viro domino Johanne de Balliolo verba faciens . . . .[a] idem Johannes motu proprio, in presencia mei notarii et testium subscriptorum, inter alia quedam verba dixit et protulit sermone Gallico, hunc habencia intellectum, videlicet quod, dum ipse dictum regnum Scocie ut rex et dominus ipsius regni tenebat atque regebat, tantam invenit in hominibus ejusdem regni maliciam fraudem prodicionem et dolum, propter eorum malignitatem nequiciam dolositates et alia nonnulla execrabilia et detestabilia facta ipsorum, qui eum tunc principem eorum pocionari,[2] sicut veraciter intellexerat, machinabantur, [quod] intencionis sue non est predictum regnum Scocie ingredi vel intrare aliquo tempore in futurum, seu de ipso aut pertinenciis suis per se vel per alium aut alios intromittere ullo modo, nec eciam dictis et aliis multis de causis aliquid habere commune cum Scotis; adjiciens idem dominus J[ohannes] quod alias

---

Text: Extant only in Prynne, p. 665, where it is printed from the notarial instrument which was then (1670) in the Tower of London, but is now apparently lost. We have altered Prynne's spelling and punctuation to accord with the conventions of this volume.

[a] *Prynne has dots here.*

[1] Balliol had been in captivity in England since his surrender in 1296 (above, p. 73). The present declaration may have been influenced by the fact that the French were at this time pressing for his release (cf. Rymer, I, ii, 861, misdated 1297 for 1298).

27

In ¹ the name of the Lord, Amen. In the year A.D. 1298,
the eleventh indiction, and on 1 April, in a room in
the lodging outside London ² of the venerable father
Anthony, bishop of Durham, the bishop said something
about the state and condition of the realm of Scotland
and of its inhabitants, in the presence of the noble lord,
John Balliol . . . . and this John, of his own
accord, in the presence of myself, the notary, and of the
witnesses named below (among other observations which
he made) uttered a statement in French, to this effect:
namely, that when he possessed and ruled the realm of
Scotland as king and lord of the realm, he found in
the men of that realm such malice, deceit, treason,
and treachery, arising from their malignity, wickedness,
and stratagems, and [from] various other execrable and
detestable actions by those who, as he had good grounds
to believe were plotting to poison him,³ who was then
their prince, that it is not his intention to enter or go into
the realm of Scotland at any time to come, or to interfere
in any way with it, or its appurtenances, through his
own agency, or through that of any other person or
persons, or even (for the reasons given and for many
others) to have anything to do with the Scots. And John

---

² Durham House, on the site of the present railway station at Charing
Cross
³ The text seems to provide the only evidence of this alleged attempt on
Balliol's life.

rogaverat prefatum dominum episcopum Dunelmensem
ut magnifico principi et domino suo, domino Edwardo
regi Anglie illustri, hanc suam esse intencionem voluntatem et firmum propositum explicaret, et adhuc sibi
cum instancia supplicat, quatenus premissa eidem
domino regi ex parte sua dignetur et velit exponere ac
plenius aperire.

Actum anno indiccione die et loco predictis, presentibus memorato domino episcopo Dunelmensi et nobili viro Radulpho de Sandwyco constabulario turris
London', et nonnullis aliis existentibus tunc ibidem.

Et ego, Johannes Erturi de Cadomo, apostolice sedis
authoritate notarius publicus, hiis omnibus interfui, propria manu scripsi, et mei signi [1] annotacione in hanc
publicam formam redegi.

---

[1] See above, p. 64, *n.* 1.

added that on another occasion he had asked the bishop of Durham to explain this, his intention, will, and firm resolve to the eminent prince, Edward, the illustrious king of England, and his lord, and he still urgently beseeches him that he may graciously agree to explain, and fully to expound, these things to the king on his behalf.

Executed in the year, indiction, and place, and on the day aforesaid, in the presence of the bishop of Durham and the noble Ralph of Sandwich, constable of the Tower of London, and of various other people who were present there at the time.

And I, John, son of Arthur, of Caen, a public notary by authority of the Apostolic See, was present at all these proceedings, and have written with my own hand and drawn up a record in this public form, bearing the mark of my *signum*.[1]

28

Bulla Bonifacii pape octavi quod rex desistat a guerra
Scocie in qua terra papa dicit se jus habere, et quod rex
deliberare faciat episcopos Glasguensem et Sodoriensem
quos fecit incarcerari.[a]

[i] [b] Bonifacius [1] episcopus servus servorum Dei carissimo in Christo filio Eduardo regi Anglie illustri, salutem
et apostolicam benediccionem. Scimus fili, et longi jam
temporis spacio magistra nos rerum experiencia docuit,
qualiter erga Romanam matrem ecclesiam que te gerit
in visceribus caritatis regie devocionis affectus exuberat
reverencie zelus viget quodque promptus et sedis ejus
votis obtemperas, beneplacitis acquiescis. Quamobrem
firmam spem gerimus plenamque fiduciam obtinemus
quod regalis sublimitas verba nostra benigne recipiat
diligenter intelligat efficaciter prosequatur. Sane ad
celsitudinem regiam potuit pervenisse et in tue libro
memorie nequaquam ambigimus contineri, qualiter ab
antiquis temporibus regnum Scocie pleno jure pertinuit
et adhuc pertinere dinoscitur ad ecclesiam supradictam,[2]
quodque illud sicut accepimus progenitoribus tuis regni

Text: From the original bull in P.R.O. Papal Bulls (S.C. 7), 6/10 (S),
whence Rymer, I, ii, 907-8. The P.R.O. also has transcripts not collated
here, and there are many chronicle copies. Calendared in Bain, II, no.
1069; *Registres de Boniface VIII*, ed. G. Digard, *et al.*, II (Paris, 1904), no.
3343; and *Cal. Papal Letters*, I, 584-5. Listed by Stapledon, Palgrave,
Kalendars, I, p. 22.

 [a] *Title from Stapledon; so far as legible, endorsement on S corresponds.*
 [b] *Paragraph numberings not in* S; *inserted here to correspond with citations in
no. 29 and so facilitate reference.*

 [1] S was presented to Edward I at Sweetheart abbey by Archbishop
Winchelsey in August 1300. Two replies were sent, one by the barons of
England on 12 February 1301, the other by Edward himself on 17 May
1301 (below, pp. 96-109). See Powicke, *Thirteenth Century*, pp. 693-706;
and cf. above, p. xxviii.

28

Bull of Pope Boniface VIII, demanding that the king abandon the war in Scotland, a land in which the pope says that the right belongs to himself, and that the king release the bishops of Glasgow and of Sodor, whom he has imprisoned.

[i] BONIFACE,[1] bishop and servant of the servants of God, sends greeting and apostolic benediction to his well-beloved son in Christ Edward, the illustrious king of England. We know, my son, and experience of events, as our teacher for a long period of time, has taught us by now how ample is the strength of your royal devotion towards the Roman church, the mother who sustains you with the abundance of her charity, how also the fervour of your reverence abounds, and how promptly you submit to the wishes of the Roman see, and acquiesce in her desires. Therefore we firmly hope, and we have every confidence, that your royal highness will receive our words kindly, hear them diligently, and follow them effectively. It may indeed have come to the knowledge of your royal highness, and we can hardly doubt that it is contained in the book of your memory, that from ancient times the realm of Scotland belonged rightfully, and is known still to belong, to the Roman church,[2] and that (as we understand) it was not, and is not, feudally

---

[2] Even the most extravagant interpretation of pp. 14-16 above will not justify this papal claim, for which Boniface gives no real evidence. Indeed, it cannot be reconciled with the earlier papal acceptance of English lordship over Scotland (e.g., above, pp. 17-18), or with Alexander III's claim to hold Scotland from God alone (above, p. 40).

Anglie regibus sive tibi feudale non extitit nec existit,
qualiter eciam clare memorie Henricus rex Anglie pater
tuus tempore discordie sive guerre inter ipsum et
quondam Symonem de Montforti suosque fautores et
complices suscitate a recollende memorie Alexandro
ejusdem Scocie rege ac ipsius Henrici genero auxilium
sibi peciit exhiberi; et ne hujusmodi auxilium jure
cujuslibet subjeccionis aut debiti petitum seu prestitum
notaretur prefatus Henricus eidem regi Scocie suas
patentes duxit litteras concedendas, per eas firmiter
recognoscens predictum auxilium se recepisse vel se
recepturum dumtaxat de gracia speciali.[1] Preterea cum
successu temporis prefati regi[s] Scocie tui sororii tunc
viventis in tue coronacionis solenniis habere presenciam affectares, sibi per tuas patentes cavere litteras
curavisti quod in ipsis solenniis ejus habere presenciam
non ex debito sed tantum de gracia intendebas.[2] Et
cum eciam rex ipse [a] pro Tyndalie ac de Peynerre [3] terris
in regno Anglie positis se ad tuam presenciam personaliter contulisset tibi fidelitatem solitam impensurus idem
in prestacione fidelitatis hujusmodi, multis tunc presentibus, vive vocis oraculo publice declaravit quod pro
terris eisdem sitis tantum in Anglia, non ut rex Scocie
neque pro Scocie regno fidelitatem exhibebat eandem,
quinimmo palam extitit protestatus quod pro regno
ipso tibi fidelitatem [b] prestare seu facere aliquatenus non
debebat utpote tibi penitus non subjecto, tuque sic

---

[a] Cum eciam *over erasure*; *space after* ipse, *filled with line* S.
[b] *Space after* fidelitatem, *filled with line* S.

[1] This letter, if it ever existed, seems not to survive.
[2] Edward was crowned in August 1274; Alexander III was certainly
present, but there is no record of the issue of this letter. The common
statement that Alexander did homage then seems to be wrong; it was
deferred until 1278 (above, pp. 38-41).

subject to your predecessors, the kings of the realm of
England, nor to you; likewise that King Henry of
England your father, of renowned memory, in the time
of the conflict or war which arose between him and the
late Simon de Montfort and his accomplices, sought for
help at the hands of Alexander, of famous memory, the
king of Scotland and son-in-law of Henry and, lest help
of this kind should be regarded as being sought or
afforded by reason of any subjection or obligation, Henry
caused his letter patent to be issued to the king of Scotland, in which he distinctly admitted that he had
received, or was going to receive, this help only as an act
of special grace.[1]   Further, with the passage of time,
because you wanted to have the presence of the king of
Scotland, your brother-in-law, who was then still alive,
at the ceremony of your coronation, you were careful to
protect his interests by your letter patent declaring that
you proposed to have his presence at that ceremony not
of right, but only by grace.[2]   When also the king himself
appeared in person, in your presence, to offer you the
fealty which was usual for the lands of Tynedale and of
Penrith,[3] he publicly declared by word of mouth, in the
presence of many people, in the very act of offering this
fealty, that he offered that fealty only for those lands
situated in England, and not as king of Scotland, nor
for the realm of Scotland; nay he openly declared that
for that realm he ought not in any manner to offer or
swear fealty to you, as being entirely free from subjection
to you, and you received the fealty of this nature so

---

[3] On Penrith see above, p. 20, *n.* The superfluous ' de ' is curious.

oblatam fidelitatem hujusmodi admisisti.[1] A tua quoque
creditur non excidisse memoria qualiter eodem rege
Scocie sublato de medio, quondam Margareta puella
nepte tua tunc minoris etatis herede sibi relicta, non ad
te velud ad dominum regni pervenit custodia memorati
sed certi ejusdem proceres ad ejus electi custodiam
extiterunt quodque postmodum dispensacione ab apostolica sede obtenta super matrimonio contrahendo inter
dilectum filium nobilem virum Eduardum natum tuum
et Margaretam predictam dum viveret si ad id procerum
dicti regni accederet vel haberetur assensus, tu eisdem
proceribus per tua scripta cavisse dinosceris priusquam
vellent hujusmodi matrimonio consentire quod regnum
ipsum penitus liberum nullique subjectum seu quovis
modo summissum imperpetuum remaneret, quodque in
pristinum seu talem ipsius statum restitueretur omnino
si ex hujusmodi matrimonio contrahendo liberos non
extare contingeret, ac nomen et honorem ut prius pariter
retineret tam in suis sibi servandis legibus et preficiendis
officialibus dicti regni quam parlamentis [*sic*] tenendis
tractandis causis in ipso et nullis ejus incolis extra illud
ad judicium evocandis, et quod in tuis patentibus litteris
inde confectis hec plenius et seriosius contineri noscuntur.[2] Prefata insuper Margareta de presenti luce
subtracta et tandem super successione dicti regni Scocie
suborta dissensionis materia inter partes, ipsius regni
proceres metuentes sibi dictoque regno posse occasione
hujusmodi prejudicium generari non aliter ad tuam

---

[1] cf. above, pp. 38-41.
[2] This refers to the negotiations for a marriage alliance between the
future Edward II and Margaret, the heiress of Scotland; the document
mentioned is the treaty of Birgham (July 1290; Stevenson, *Documents*, 1,
162-73).

offered to you.[1] We may also assume that you have not
forgotten how when the same king of Scotland was
removed from human ken, the late Margaret was left as
his heir, a girl who was your niece, and at that time a
minor, and that the wardship of the kingdom did not
devolve upon you, as the lord, but certain of its magnates
were elected for its custody; and that after a dispensation
had been gained from the apostolic see for contracting a
marriage between our beloved son, the noble Edward,
your child, and this Margaret, during her lifetime (if the
agreement of the nobles of the realm were forthcoming
or could be had to that proposal), you are known to have
safeguarded the interests of the nobles, before they were
willing to consent to this marriage, by writing that the
realm should remain for ever entirely free, and subject,
or submitted, to nobody, and in no wise, and that if it
should happen that there were no children of this contemplated marriage, the realm should be entirely restored
to its former state, or to a similar state, and that it should
retain its name and dignity exactly as they were before,
both in the keeping of the laws and the appointing of the
officials of the realm, and in the holding of parliaments
and the trial of causes therein, and in the summoning of
none of its inhabitants outside it for judgment; and that
in your letter patent made on this subject these things
are well known to be set out fully and in detail.[2] Further,
when Margaret departed from this life, and an occasion
arose for conflict among certain parties about the succession to the realm of Scotland, the nobles of the realm
feared that prejudice would arise to themselves and to
the realm by an event of this kind, and would not come

presenciam extra ipsius regni accedere limites voluerunt
nisi per te patenti scripto caveretur eisdem quod id non
fiebat ex debito sed ex gracia speciali quodque nullum
exinde ipsius regni libertatibus posset dispendium i[m]mi-
nere.[1] Et licet ut dicitur super statu ejusdem regni
Scocie ac ejus prius habita libertate regno ipso tunc
carente presidio defensoris per ipsius regni proceres tunc
velud acephalos et ducis vel aurige suffragium non
habentes sive per illum [2] cui prefati regni regimen, licet
indebite,[3] diceris commisisse contra morem solitum aliqua fuerint hactenus innovata, ea tamen utpote per vim
et metum qui cadere poterat in constantem [4] elicita
nequaquam debent de jure subsistere aut in ejusdem
regni prejudicium redundare.

Ceterum nobis nullatenus venit in dubium quin
pocius certi sumus quod cum apostolice sedis precellens
auctoritas per suas litteras in Anglie ac Scocie regnis
simul alicui legacionis committit officium exequendum,
vel pro quavis causa quam racionabilem reputat decime
solucionem indicit, hujusmodi apostolice littere ad prefatum Scocie regnum se aliquatenus [5] non extendunt,
speciali predicte sedis privilegio Scotis indulto penitus
obsistente, prout tempore felicis recordacionis Adriani
pape predecessoris nostri [6] tunc sancti Adriani diaconi
cardinalis et per ipsius sedis litteras simul in regnis ipsis

---

[1] May refer to Bain, II, no. 474, though this was dated *after* the Scots
had crossed the border, and says nothing about *non ex debito sed ex gracia
speciali*.

[2] Presumably alludes to John Balliol, and marks the beginning of the
story that Edward unjustly imposed him on Scotland (cf. below, p. 140).

[3] cf. ' debite ' in Edward's reply, p. 105 below.

[4] See ' A Thirteenth-Century Phrase ' in *Collected Papers of T. F. Tout*,
II, 285-7.

[5] *Aliquatenus* has to be replaced by *ipso facto*, or equivalent words, in
order to make sense of the passage.

to your presence outside the bounds of that realm unless
a recognition were given to them by your letter patent
that this was done not of right, but by special grace, and
that no loss could arise thereby to the liberties of the
realm.¹ And although, as it is said, certain unaccustomed
innovations have taken place, at the time when the realm
of Scotland lacked the protection of a ruler, which affect
the state of the realm and the freedom which previously
it enjoyed, those things have been done by the nobles of
the realm, who were then without a head, and had not
the approval of a leader or guide, or they have been done
by the man ² to whom you are said to have committed
the rule of the kingdom, and in this you acted without
regard for what was fitting.³ Done indeed they have
been through force, and in consequence of the fear
which may assail even a brave man ⁴; and they should
certainly not have any legal effect, nor redound to the
prejudice of the realm of Scotland.

But there is no doubt at all in our mind, and indeed
we are certain of it, that when the supreme authority of
the apostolic see commits to anyone by letter the duty of
acting as legate in the realms of England and Scotland
at the same time, or, for any cause which it deems
reasonable, declares that a tenth is to be levied, the
apostolic letter of this kind does not extend *ipso facto* ⁵
to the realm of Scotland, by reason of the special privilege
of the Holy See granted to the Scots, directly forbidding
such a thing. This was made clear in the time of Pope
Adrian our predecessor,⁶ of happy memory, with whom
we were then on familiar terms, who was then cardinal

---

⁶ Cardinal Ottobono, later pope Adrian V, visited England in 1265–8,
with the future Boniface VIII in his retinue (whence the reminiscence in
the text). See Powicke, *Henry III and Lord Edward*, ii, 526 ff., and T. S. R.
Boase, *Boniface VIII*, pp. 11-13, 209-11.

P

legati cum quo familiariter tunc eramus contigit evidenter. Nam legatus ipse ad prefatum regnum Scocie
aliquatenus admissus non extitit donec per litteras
speciales apostolicas sibi legacionis fuit commissum
officium in eodem.[1] Preterea noscere potest regia celsitudo qualiter regnum ipsum per beati Andree Apostoli
venerandas reliquias, non sine superni numinis grandi
dono, acquisitum et conversum extitit ad fidei catholice
unitatem, qualiter eciam antiquis temporibus Eboracensis archiepiscopus qui tunc erat, mota per eum super
jure metropolitico adversus prelatos Scocie questione in
qua dictum antiquitas fuisse commemorat ' memento
quod sumus tui ' [2] (ut cetera que inde secuntur silencio
relinquamus) pro se sentenciam obtinere nequivit.
Quamvis alia plura et varia que in hac parte raciona-
biliter proponenda se offerunt ex quibus eciam ad hec
tibi scribenda movemur pretereat calamus, ne inde forsitan sensibus regiis tedium generetur.

[ii] Hec profecto fili carissime infra claustra pectoris
sollicite considerare te convenit et attendere diligenter,
ex quibus nulli in dubium veniat regnum Scocie prelibatum ad prefatam Romanam ecclesiam pertinere
quod tibi nec licet nec licuit in ipsius ecclesie ac multorum
prejudicium per violenciam subjugare tueque subicere
dicioni. Cum autem, sicut habet fide digna et nostris
jam pluries auribus inculcata relacio, fameque precu-
rentis [*sic*] affatibus divulgatur tu premissa ut debueras
non attendens neque debita consideracione discutiens et

---

[1] This, as it stands, might imply that Ottobono did enter Scotland; in
fact it seems that he was denied admission, and had to content himself with
a meeting of Scottish clergy in England (*Scotichronicon*, II, 106, 108).
[2] The quotation has not been traced.

deacon of St Adrian and appointed legate in both realms
by a letter of the Holy See, for he was certainly not
admitted as legate to the realm of Scotland until the
duty of the legateship therein was committed to him by
a specific papal letter.[1] Furthermore, your royal highness may know how the realm itself was converted, and
won to the unity of the catholic faith, by the venerable
relics of the blessed Apostle Andrew, with a great out-
pouring of the divine power, and also how in olden times
the archbishop of York of that day, after the question
had been raised by him about the metropolitan right
over the prelates of Scotland, on which occasion anti-
quity records that it was said ' remember that we are
thine '[2] (what follows we leave in silence) was unable to
gain a sentence in his favour. Although there are a
number of other different things which reasonably
suggest themselves to be put forward in this matter
which also influence us in writing these things to you,
our pen must pass them over, lest perhaps weariness be
aroused thereby in your highness's mind.

[ii] It is right, well-beloved son, that you should
straightway think upon these things with care, and
diligently study them in your heart of hearts; and
nobody who considers them can doubt that the realm
of Scotland belongs to the Roman church, and that it
was not, and is not, lawful for you to dominate it by
force and to subjugate it to your rule, to the prejudice
of the Roman church and of no small number of people.
Since, however, as a credible report has already forced
it upon our hearing many times, and as it is divulged by
the tongues of rumour running in advance, you have
not attended to these things as you should, nor investigated
them with proper consideration, and have vehemently

ad occupandum et subjugandum dicioni regie regnum
ipsum tunc regis auxilio destitutum vehementer aspirans,
et tandem ad id exercens potencie tue vires venerabilibus
fratribus nostris Roberto Glasguensi et Marco Sodorensi
episcopis et nonnullis clericis et aliis personis ecclesiasticis
dicti regni, ut dicitur, captis et carceralibus vinculis
traditis [1] quorum aliquos, sicut asseritur, squalor carceris
violentus extinxit ac eciam occupatis castris et, prout
fertur, monasteriis aliisve religiosis locis quampluribus
dirutis seu destructis ac dampnis gravibus ejusdem regni
habitatoribus irrogatis in ejusdem regni partibus officiales
regios posuisti qui prelatos, ceteros clericos, et ecclesiasticas ac eciam seculares dicti regni personas multimodis
perturbare molestiis et affliccionibus variis et diversis
impetere non verentur, in divine majestatis offensam,
sedis memorate contemptum, regie salutis et fame dispendium, juris injuriam, et grave scandalum fidelium
plurimorum : regalem itaque magnificenciam rogamus
et hortamur attente ac obsecramus, in eo qui est omnium
vera salus, quatinus solerter attendens quod ex debito
pastoralis officii nostris humeris incumbentis ad conservanda et gubernanda sollicite bona juraque omnia
ecclesie supradicte tenemur quodque homini plusquam
Deo deferre non possumus nec debemus, predictos
episcopos clericos et personas ecclesiasticas quos adhuc
carcer regius tenet inclusos pro divina et apostolice sedis
ac nostra reverencia, sublato difficultatis et dilacionis
objectu, benigne restitui facias pristine libertati dictosque

---

[1] Robert Wishart, bishop of Glasgow, imprisoned after the battle of
Stirling Bridge in 1297, was subsequently released at an uncertain date, and
taken into custody again in 1306. Nothing is known of the dates of captivity of the bishop of Sodor. The 'chains' are probably metaphorical,
though in his later captivity, after 1306, Wishart was actually put in chains
(Bain, II, no. 1813).

longed to occupy, and to subject to the royal power, a
realm which was then destitute of the help of a king, and
at length, exercising the strength of your power for that
purpose, you have seized and committed to chains [1] and
to prison our venerable brethren Robert, bishop of
Glasgow, and Mark, bishop of Sodor, and certain clergy
and other ecclesiastical persons of the realm (as it is
reported) of whom some, it is asserted, have been killed
by the harshness of their imprisonment ; since you have
also occupied castles and, it is said, monasteries and other
places of the religious orders, and demolished or destroyed
many of them, and brought heavy losses to the inhabitants of the realm, and have established royal officials in
the same realm, who fear not to perturb the prelates
and other clergy and the ecclesiastical and secular
persons of the realm with manifold vexations, and to
assail them with various and divers afflictions to the
offence of the Divine Majesty, the contempt of the Holy
See, the injury of the royal welfare and reputation, the
outrage of justice, and the grave scandal of many of the
faithful : accordingly we request and admonish your
royal highness zealously, and beseech you, by Him who
is the true salvation of all, that—carefully observing how,
out of regard for the pastoral office which rests on our
shoulders, we are bound to cherish and watch over
diligently the property and all the rights of the church,
and that we cannot and should not defer to man rather
than to God—that you kindly cause to be restored to
their former liberty the bishops, clerks, and ecclesiastical
persons whom the royal prison now holds in durance,
out of reverence for God and the apostolic see and ourselves, setting aside all obstacles causing difficulty or
delay, and that you recall those officials from the realm

officiales de regno Scocie revoces memorato. Sic te in hiis, prout speramus et cupimus, promptis et efficacibus studiis habiturus ut apud celestem regem pro minimis grandia rependentem non immerito reddaris acceptior, gracior habearis, et preter laudis humane preconium tibi proinde proventurum apostolice sedis favorem et graciam possis uberius promereri.

[iii] Si vero in eodem regno Scocie vel aliqua ejus parte jus aliquod habere te asseris, volumus quod tuos procuratores et nuncios ad hoc specialiter constitutos cum omnibus juribus et munimentis tuis hujusmodi negocium contingentibus, infra sex menses a recepcione presencium numerandos ad nostram presenciam mittere non ommittas, cum parati sumus tibi tanquam dilecto filio plene super premissis exhibere justicie complementum et jura, siqua habes, inviolabiliter observare. Nos enim nichilominus ex nunc lites questiones et controversias quaslibet inter te dictumque regnum Scocie ac prelatos clericos ac personas seculares ejusdem subortas et que possunt imposterum ex quibusvis causis preteritis exoriri, totumque negocium predicta contingens aut aliquod eorumdem ad cognicionem et determinacionem sedis ejusdem presencium tenore reducimus et eciam reservamus, decernentes irritum et inane si secus scienter vel ignoranter a quoquam in hac parte contigerit attemptari.

Dat' Anagnie, v kal' Julii [1] pontificatus nostri anno quinto.

---

[1] The long delay between this date, and the receipt of the bull in England in the summer of 1300, is strange. Mr Boase suggests that the bull was held up at the curia for some time, until news arrived that Edward was again invading Scotland (Boase, *Boniface VIII*, p. 210, *n.* 2).

of Scotland. You will comport yourself in these matters, so is our hope and desire, with such speedy and effective zeal, that in the eyes of the heavenly king, who grants great rewards for small merits, you may not undeservedly be rendered more acceptable and held more dear, and so that, over and above the measure of human praise which shall come to you thereby, you may more richly deserve the favour and grace of the apostolic see.

[iii] If you do indeed assert that you have a right in the realm of Scotland, or in any part of it, we desire that without fail you send to our presence, within six months reckoned from the receipt of the present letter, your proctors and envoys specially appointed for the purpose, with all your titles and muniments touching this case, for we are ready to grant to you, as our beloved son, full and complete justice in the matter, and to observe inviolably your rights, such as they are. For by this present letter we from now onwards recall and reserve to the jurisdiction and judgment of the Holy See whatever disputes, questions, and controversies have arisen, and in future, from whatever previous causes, may arise, between you and the realm of Scotland and its prelates, clergy, and secular persons, and every matter which concerns this subject, or any part of it; and if it should happen that anything is attempted to the contrary in this matter by anybody, knowingly or unknowingly, we declare his action to be null and void. Anagni, 27 June,[1] in the fifth year of our pontificate [1299].

29

Certificacio magistri Willelmi de Sardene,[1] officialis curie Cantuariensis, etc., super periculis et remediis, et securiori via procedendi ad evitand' pericula infrascripta.

Pericula extracta per clericos de consilio avi [2] domini nostri regis a bulla Bonifacii pape viij dicto avo directa vendicando superioritatem terre Scocie ad ecclesiam Romanam pertinere non solum in spiritualibus set eciam in temporalibus.[a]

Consideratis [3] forma et effectu litterarum apostolicarum, videtur quod nulla causa vel racio sufficiens est expressa, nec eciam omnes simul collecte in eisdem, propter quas regnum Scocie ab antiquo pertinuit ad Romanam ecclesiam, vel debeat pertinere. Quod vere idem regnum Scocie feudale et subjectum extitit et existit regibus Anglie patet satis per informaciones jam scriptas.[4]

Quantum ad secundam partem litterarum apostolicarum predictarum ubi dicit ' hec profecto ' etc.,[5] patet per informaciones prescriptas [4] quod nichil injuriosum rex

---

Text : P.R.O. Chancery Miscellanea (C 47), 31/15 (A), and 31/16 (B), (C), probably all of the early years of Edward III. B and C are badly mutilated, and from B Prynne printed an incomplete text (pp. 885-7 : P). The present seems to be the first complete edition. The relation of the MSS is unknown, but B and C omit a clause found in A (below, p. 94, *n.* a). Printed here from A, except when otherwise stated.

  [a] *Title as in* A, *where on the dorse. Above it are the words* De Scocia ; De periculis et remediis ; De Secunda via et tercia.

  [1] William (a civil lawyer) was in the service of the archbishop of Canterbury at least as early as 1282.
  [2] That is, the MS was copied for Edward III, but the original text had been compiled for his grandfather, Edward I.
  [3] This document contains advice given to Edward I on the problem of answering Boniface's bull printed above (pp. 81-7). It clearly shows the procedural difficulties of Edward's position. It cannot be exactly dated.

29

Advice of Master William of Sardinia,[1] official of the court of Canterbury, etc., upon certain dangers, and the appropriate remedies, and on the safest way of proceeding for avoidance of the dangers described below.

Dangers, noted by the clerks of the council of the grandfather[2] of our lord the king, in a bull of Pope Boniface VIII addressed to the king's grandfather, claiming that lordship over the land of Scotland belonged to the Roman church, not only in spiritual but also in temporal affairs.

EXAMINATION[3] of the form and the purport of the papal letter suggests that no sufficient cause or reason is given, and that even all those contained in the letter are together not enough to show that the realm of Scotland has belonged from ancient times to the Roman church, or that it should so belong. Indeed, the fact that the realm of Scotland was, and is, in fee to and subject to the kings of England is clear enough from the statements already written.[4]

As for the second part of the papal letter, where it says ' these things ' etc.,[5] it is clear from the aforesaid statements[4] that the king of England has tried nothing

---

In September 1300 Edward summoned representatives of the two Universities, and a number of individual scholars, including William of Sardinia (Prynne, p. 884), to a parliament at Lincoln, where they were to give advice on the problems raised by the bull. Our text was perhaps drafted for that occasion. See Powicke, *Thirteenth Century*, pp. 701-2 ; and above, pp. xxvi and xxviii.

[4] One can only conjecture what this other document was ; possibly it was the material collected for the historical sections of no. 30 (below, pp. 97 ff.).

[5] Above, p. 85, para. [ii]

Anglie attemptavit, set jus, possessionem, et statum antecessorum et progenitorum suorum ac suum continuans
prosequens et defendens, rebellionem, contumacias,
offensas, et excessus intollerabiles subditorum suorum,
prout sibi licuit, refrenabat.

Circa terciam partem bulle ubi dicit 'si vero in
eodem regno Scocie jus aliquod', etc.,[1] videtur esse
voluntarium mandatum; similiter ut rex Anglie destitutus
possessione, ut premittitur, de suo jure vel proprietate
contendat et quod sequitur 'volumus' etc., videtur esse
deliberandum cum prelatis et clericis prelatorum an
debeant vim habere denunciacionis, monicionis, citacionis seu artacionis.[2]

Item, habeatur deliberacio circa septem : *Primo*, an
sit mittendum ad papam vel non, juxta formam mandati
apostolici, per procuratores aut nuncios. *Secundo*, supposito quod non, an sit mittendum ad declinandum
judicium vel ad excusandum. *Tercio*, supposito quod
non, an sit mittendum ad informandum papam extra
judicium. *Quarto*, et si sic, utrum informacio sit faciend'
per nuncium cum litteris de credencia. *Quinto*, vel cum
litteris regiis. *Sexto*, vel alio modo. *Septimo*, an nullo
modo sit mittendum.[3]

Circa primum, an sit mittendum ad papam secundum formam litterarum apostolicarum, videtur quibusdam quod periculosum esset mittere secundum formam
mandati, quia sic recognosceretur papa[a] superior et
judex competens in temporalibus. Item,[b] papa esset

---

[a] *One would expect* ut *after* papa.
[b] P *begins here.*
[1] Above, p. 87, para. [iii]

injurious, but has sought for and defended the continuous right, possession, and status of his predecessors and of himself, and has restrained, as he was entitled to do, the rebellion, and the unbearable insults, offences, and excesses of his own subjects.

As for the third part of the bull, where it says ' if you do indeed assert ' etc.,[1] it seems to be an arbitrary command ; and, in order that the king of England, who is deprived of possession, as is said above, may contend for his right or ownership, and because there follows ' we desire ' etc., it seems that there should be consultation with the prelates, and the clerks of the prelates, whether the words properly have the force of a *denunciacio*, a *monicio*, a *citacio*, or an *artacio*.[2]

Next, seven points should be discussed : *First*, whether a mission should be sent to the pope or not, according to the terms of the papal mandate, by proctors or envoys. *Second*, if not, whether anyone should be sent to deny the papal jurisdiction, or to make excuse. *Third*, if not, whether anyone should be sent to inform the pope in an extra-judicial capacity. *Fourth*, if so, whether the statement should be made by an envoy with a letter of credence. *Fifth*, or with a royal letter. *Sixth*, or in another manner. *Seventh*, whether nothing should be sent at all.[3]

On the first point, whether a mission should be sent to the pope, according to the terms of the papal letter, it seems to some that it would be dangerous to send according to the terms of the mandate, because in this way the pope would be admitted as superior, and as a proper judge in matters temporal. Again, the pope

---

[2] These technical words defy translation, and are retained in Latin.
[3] This plan is not strictly followed in the sequel.

judex in propria causa. Item, rex Anglie revocaret in
dubium jus et possessionem suam regni Scocie sic aggre-
diendo litem. Item, si rex mitteret secundum formam
littere supradicte, videretur approbare reduccionem et
reservacionem litium, questionum, et controversiarum
subortarum ᵃ que possent imposterum exoriri ex quacumque causa inter regem et regnum Scocie ad cognicionem et determinacionem sedis apostolice, et eciam
decretum subsequens, per quod decernit irritum et inane
si secus etc.,¹ per que videtur interdicere manum mili-
tarem in suos subditos et rebelles regni Scocie, et auferre
potestatem iurisdiccionem, cohercionem in eosdem et
justiciam faciendi, et sua facta et jura regalia annullare.

Item, cum papa asserat ' in libro memorie regis contineri ipsum regnum Scocie ad Romanam curiam pertinere pleno jure ',² et eciam concludat dictum regnum in
bonis seu de bonis ecclesie Romane esse, periculosum
esset apud sedem apostolicam coram papa litigare,
maxime cum rex contra papam qui papa se asserit
judicem et partem, nullum in curia Romana consilium
vel auxilium inveniret. Et periculosum eciam esset ibi
in[s]trumenta et munimenta deferre que eciam etsi
valida essent, ea contra se et suam assercionem forsan
nullatenus approbaret.

Si ᵇ vero non mittat rex Anglie secundum formam
mandati predicti, deliberandum est cujusmodi possent
ex hoc pericula evenire. Tamen videtur quibusdam
quod si illud verbum ' volumus ' etc. importat vim

ᵃ Add et *after* subortarum (*as in corresponding passage in bull, above, p. 87*) ?
ᵇ C *begins here.*

¹ Above, p. 87   ² Above, p. 81

would be judge in his own cause. Again, by undertaking
a suit in this way the king of England would cast doubt
on his right to, and possession of, the realm of Scotland.
Again, if the king were to send according to the terms of
the letter, he would seem to approve ' the recall and reser-
vation to the jurisdiction and judgment of the apostolic see
of disputes, questions and controversies which have arisen
and which in future may arise, for any cause, between
the king and the realm of Scotland ' ; and to approve the
subsequent decretal by which the pope ' declares anything
to the contrary to be null and void ' etc.,[1] whereby he
seems to forbid military force against the king's rebellious
subjects in the realm of Scotland, to abolish his power of
enforcing jurisdiction and justice, and of taking forcible
action against them, and to nullify his actions, and his
royal rights.

Again, since the pope asserts that ' it is contained in
the book of the king's memory that the realm of Scotland
belongs rightfully to the Roman court ',[2] and also concludes that the said realm is among the property, or part
of the property, of the Roman church, it would be
dangerous to undertake litigation before the pope at the
apostolic see, especially since the king would find no
counsel or aid at the Roman court against the pope, who
says that he is judge, as well as a party, in the dispute ;
and it would also be dangerous to send documents or
muniments there, for even although they be valid, it may
be that the pope would in no wise accept them as evidence against himself, and against his own statement.

If indeed the king of England does not send according
to the terms of the mandate, one must consider what
kind of dangers might arise from this. Yet it seems to
some that if the words ' we desire ', and so forth, have the

denunciacionis, tunc erit hujusmodi ᵃ [?] effectus quod
dominus rex Anglie prosequatur jus suum infra tempus
prefixum alioquin cedat ab accione, ut sicut destitutus
a possessione excludatur a jure. Si vero illa verba
' volumus ' etc. cadant in vim citacionis vel artacionis,
ut quidam opinantur, tunc creditur posse evenire ut sic
rege non mittente juxta formam litterarum predictarum
contracta contumacia vel mittetur ecclesia Romana in
possessione regni Scocie vel excluso rege Anglie a vendica-
cione juris regni Scocie, per decretum declarabit regnum
Scocie ad Romanam ecclesiam pertinere vel ad alias
penas domino regi prejudiciales, tam spirituales quam
temporales saltem de facto usurpando jurisdiccionem
potest extendere manus suas in personam scilicet vel in
rem, presertim cum papa offerat eidem regi plene
exhibere justicie complementum et jura si que habeat
inviolabiliter observare, unde rege non mittente forsan
papa reputaret regem oblate sibi justicie et auctoritatis
sedis apostolice contemptorem et de observacione eciam
jurium suorum similiter oblata nolle curare.

Circa tercium [sic],¹ an sit mittendum ad declinandum
judicium, cognicionem, jurisdiccionem, et forum, vel ad
excusandum quare non mittit secundum formam mandati, deliberandum est ex quibus causis competentibus
rex posset sic declinare vel excusare, et que possent ex
hiis pericula evenire. Et videtur quibusdam quod si rex
declinet papam quod non sit judex suus in temporalibus,

ᵃ hujusmodi *ed.* ; his ABC
¹ The writer is confused ; he means *circa secundum*.

force of a *denunciacio*, then the effect will be of this sort,
that the king of England may prosecute his right within
the time laid down, or otherwise he may withdraw
from the action, so that, like someone deprived of possession he may be excluded from his right. But if the
words ' we desire', and so forth, have the force of a
citacio or an *artacio*, as some hold, then it is believed that
it may turn out that by not sending according to the
form of the letter, the offence of contumacy is committed,
and either the Roman church will be placed in possession
of the realm of Scotland or, the king of England being
excluded from the defence of his right in the realm of
Scotland, the pope will declare by decree that the realm
of Scotland belongs to the Roman church, or the pope
may proceed to inflict other penalties prejudicial to the
king, both spiritual and temporal, if only by usurping
jurisdiction *de facto*, and directed either against his
person or against his possessions. This is all the more
true because the pope offers ' to grant the king full and
complete justice, and to observe his rights inviolably,
such as they are', wherefore if the king did not send, the
pope would perhaps consider that the king despised the
justice offered to him, and the authority of the apostolic
see, and, at the same time, that he was not interested in
the circumspection that was shown about his rights.

On the third [1] point, whether anyone should be sent
to refuse the papal judgment, cognizance, jurisdiction
and authority, or to make excuse for not sending according to the terms of the mandate, it must be considered
for what proper causes the king can so refuse or make
excuse, and what dangers might arise from these. It
seems to some that if the king refuses the pope because
he is not his judge in temporal matters, for the pope

quia papa non debet judicare de laico feudo, et papa
asserat regem Anglie esse vassallum suum, posset forsan
esse periculum quia papa reputans eum negasse vassal-
lagium suum prorumperet in pronunciaciones domino
regi prejudiciales super feudo quod dicit eum tenere ab
ecclesia, et forte declinacionem illam non admitteret cum
asserat regnum Scocie ad Romanam ecclesiam pleno jure
pertinere, et sic ipsum regnum sibi subesse in juris-
diccione temporali, et si sic declinaret, quodammodo
sibi attribueretur cognicio in dubio an sua sit jurisdiccio
cum unus asserat et alius neget. Nec est verisimile quod
papa pronunciaret contra assercionem suam bullatam,
immo pocius pro eadem et ulterius ad alia deteriora et
regi prejudicialia procederet.

Item cum papa reducit[a] ad se omnes questiones et
lites exortas inter regem Anglie et regnum Scocie, et
quascumque personas de regno eodem, et in precedenti-
bus litteris apostolicis narretur de injusta incarceracione
episcoporum prelatorum et clericorum Scocie, et de
destruccione monasteriorum et aliorum locorum religio-
sorum regni ejusdem, et aliis excessibus et dampnis datis,
rege comparente coram papa per procuratores et nuncios
ad hoc specialiter deputatos, sicut in prefatis litteris
apostolicis continetur, quilibet in regno Scocie, ut videtur,
posset contra regem denunciare predicta, et acusare

---

[a] reducit ABC; reducat P, *rightly?*

ought not to be judge of a lay fee, and the pope asserts
that the king of England is his vassal, there might be
danger, because the pope, thinking that the king has
renounced his vassalage, might launch out into judgments which would be harmful to the king, about the
fee which he says that the king holds from the church;
and perhaps he might not admit that refusal, for he
affirms that the realm of Scotland belongs rightfully to
the Roman church, and so, that the realm itself is subject
to him in temporal jurisdiction; and if the king were
thus to decline, cognizance would be attributed to the
pope in some sort, in view of the doubt whether the
jurisdiction is his, since the one asserts it and the other
denies it. Nor is it likely that the pope would give
judgment against his own assertion made in a bull;
rather the contrary, he would decide in its favour, and
would go further, to take other actions against the king
which would be even more harmful.

Again, since the pope recalls to himself all questions
and disputes which have arisen between the king of
England and the realm of Scotland, and certain other
persons of the same realm, and since in the earlier part
of the apostolic letter an account has been given of the
unjust imprisonment of bishops, prelates, and clergy of
Scotland, and of the destruction of monasteries and other
houses of the religious orders in the same realm, and of
other injuries and losses inflicted; if the king appear
before the pope by proctors and envoys specially
appointed for this, as is demanded in the aforesaid
apostolic letter, anybody in the realm of Scotland, it
seems, can make complaint against the king of these
things and accuse him of them, and so he would be

[*sic*] eum de eisdem, et sic haberet necesse omnibus de se conquerentibus respondere in curia memorata.

CIRCA ᵃ QUARTUM ᵃ [*sic*] ¹ si vero se excuset quia jura corone sue non potest in judicium deducere sine consensu procerum et magnatum regni sui, quodam modo videretur eum reputare judicem suum.

Item, si excuset se quia proceres regni sui positi ad racionem concorditer dicunt se nolle permittere regem jura ᵇ corone sue ad quorum conservacionem et defensionem juramenti vinculo sunt astricti contra libertates leges et consuetudines regni Anglie coram papa in judicium deducere, nec jus et possessionem suam regni Scocie que clara sunt et certa in judicium deducere, nec in dubium ac scrupulum questionis ponere quoquomodo, et quod ipsi proceres illud idem ita scribent ²; deliberetur an sit expediens, quia timetur quod papa reputaret istam excusacionem frivolam, et procederet forsitan ad penas prejudiciales prescriptas spirituales et temporales in personam scilicet et rem, supponendo se esse suum judicem competentem.

Circa quintum [*sic*] ³ vero, videlicet de mittendo informaciones conrespondentes litteris apostolicis, si hoc videatur consilio expediens, deliberetur de modo mittendi, an per nuncium cum litteris de credencia qui extrajudicialiter predictas informaciones pape seriatim exponat et de periculis qui possent inde contingere; et videtur

---

ᵃ *majuscules* BC
ᵇ *So* BC ; regem [*one or two illegible words*] corone sue A

¹ Again the number seems wrong, but by now the writer is beginning to diverge somewhat from his plan in any case.
² This letter was in fact written (dated at Lincoln 12 February 1301 ; Rymer, I, ii, 926-7).
³ See note 1, above.

bound to make answer in the court to all those who make complaint against him.

ON THE FOURTH POINT,[1] if indeed he excuses himself because he cannot submit the rights of his crown to judgment without the consent of the nobles and magnates of his realm, in a certain sense he would appear by this action to acknowledge the pope as being his judge.

Again, if he excuses himself because the nobles of his realm, when the matter is posed to them, say unanimously that they will not allow the king to submit the rights of his crown for judgment by the pope (for the keeping and defence of which they are bound by an oath) in despite of the liberties, laws, and customs of the realm of England, nor to submit to judgment his right in and possession of the realm of Scotland, which are manifest and certain, nor to subject them in any way to the doubt and question of controversy, and that the nobles themselves will put that same statement in writing [2]; it should be considered whether this is expedient, because it is feared that the pope would consider this a frivolous excuse, and would perhaps proceed to the prejudicial penalties which have already been mentioned, both spiritual and temporal, and against both the king's person and his possessions, believing that the pope himself is a proper judge in his own cause.

On the fifth [3] point, that is on sending a statement in answer to the papal letters, if this seems expedient to the council, one must consider the manner in which it is to be sent, whether it is to be done by an envoy with letters of credence, who would explain the information in detail to the pope in an extra-judicial capacity, and the dangers which may arise from that: to some there seems to be

quibusdam periculum esse quod cum latum sit mandatum
credencie et incertum per interogaciones subtiles et
astutas faciendas, a papa posset nuncius hujusmodi injuncta sibi excedere, et aliqua prejudicialia forte fateri.
Item, cum nuncius credenciam plenam habens quan-
doque major sit omni procuratore propter generalitatem
credencie posset forsan compelli respondere et alia dicere
quam sibi erant injuncta, quorum nulla vel difficilis valde
foret revocacio in futurum. Item, sic mittendo nuncium
cum talibus informacionibus jus quod habet in regno
Scocie contingentibus, videretur parere quodammodo
mandato ᵃ apostolico et prefixionem termini acceptare,
ipsumque judicem agnoscere quodammodo,ᵃ cum ibi
contineatur quod mittat nuncios cum juribus etc. infra
certum tempus, nec protestaciones ᵇ facto contrarie
valerent. Item forsan papa tali nuncio talia proponenti
prefigeret terminum vel regi in persona sua ad ostendendum et probandum jura sic proposita et allegata
coram eo vel forsan si proposita insufficiencia et tanquam
probata reiceret ᶜ et cassaret et ulterius ad alia prejudicialia procederet contra regem et regnum Scocie.

Item si mittantur informaciones per litteras regias sub
regis sigillo si videretur expediens consilio deliberetur de
periculis que possent accidere; et timetur quod papa
informaciones hujusmodi et litteras tanquam insufficiencia documenta et munimenta reputabit, et ob hoc
procedens ad alia pronunciabit aliqua prejudicialia ut
supra. Et cavendum est summopere ᵈ ne aliquid ob-

ᵃ *to* ᵃ *om.* B, *by haplography, followed by* P ; *om.* C
ᵇ protestacionis B
ᶜ *Text corrupt in all MSS ?*
ᵈ *So* C (*corrector*) P ; sine opere AB

a risk that, because a letter of credence is wide in its terms and indefinite, this sort of envoy might, after subtle and clever questions put by the pope, go beyond his instructions, and perhaps say things which are prejudicial. Again, since an envoy bearing a full letter of credence is sometimes superior to any proctor, because of the general terms of his letter of credence, he may perhaps be forced to answer, and to say things other than he was instructed to say, and it would be impossible, or very difficult, to disavow them in future. Again, by thus sending an envoy, with such a statement bearing on the right which he has in the realm of Scotland, the king would appear, in a sense, to be obeying the papal mandate, and to be accepting the assignment of a date, and in a sense to be acknowledging him as judge, since it is said in the letter that ' he should send envoys with titles ' etc., within a certain time ; and protests to the contrary would not serve to nullify the effect of the action. Again, perhaps, if such an envoy made such a statement, the pope would assign a date for him, or for the king in person, to explain and to prove the rights so proposed and alleged before him, or perhaps if the propositions were insufficient and, so to speak, proved so, he might reject and quash them, and proceed further, to do other things harmful to the king and to the realm of Scotland.

Again, if a statement is sent by royal letter under the king's seal, if it should so seem expedient to the council, one must consider the dangers which might arise. It is to be feared that the pope will regard a statement of this sort, and a letter, as unsatisfactory documents, and for this reason he may proceed further, and make injurious judgments, as already said. And, above all, one must

scurum scrupulosum dubium vel prejudiciale quod
possit contra regem interpretari in dictis litteris insera-
bitur pro eo quod ipse littere si mittantur ad papam ad
perpetuam rei memoriam remanebunt.

Item sic mittendo et informando videtur quodammodo parere mandato et voluntati domini pape et sibi
obedire in temporalibus et ei tribuere facultatem exami-
nandi jura sua in eisdem informacionibus sibi missa et
forsan papa decreveret regem fore vocandum ad docen-
dum et ostendendum jura in hujusmodi litteris compre-
hensa et allegata.

Item papa intellegens in parte esse sibi paritum et
non plene precludet regi viam quicquam ulterius pro-
ponendi seu probandi.

Si vero rex Anglie nullo modo compareat nec mittat
procuratores nec nuncios nec informaciones extra-
judiciales nec se excuset nec judicium declinet, tamen
quia littere apostolice non videntur habere vim citacionis nec monicionis nec ipsum regem artare ad mittendum prout in ipsis litteris continetur, precipue cum papa
non reputetur judex in laico feudo; tanquam eciam
hujusmodi littere aspera insolita et inaudita ac juri
communi contraria videntur continere, in quo casu
eciam etsi papa esset judex competens videretur secunda
jussio expectanda, tunc forsan papa contra regem tanquam contra contumacem ᵃ et indefensum ad pronunciaciones preclusiones et juris ecclesie Romane declara-
ciones et ad alia procederet prejudicialia prout supra.¹

ᵃ contumacem B (*corrector*) P; contumacionem A; C *mutilated*

¹ The drift of this passage is not clear, and if the text is correct it seems to
mean that the pope's actions have been without precedent, and that it is
hard to foresee what he will do in future.

beware that nothing obscure, ill-expressed, doubtful, or prejudicial is inserted in the letter, which might be interpreted against the king, because if that letter is sent to the pope it will remain on record for ever.

Again, by so sending, and making a statement, one appears, to some extent, to obey the will and command of the lord pope, to bow to him in temporal matters, and to offer him the opportunity of examining his own claims in the light of the statement sent to him, and perhaps the pope would decree that the king should be called to show and to demonstrate the claims contained and alleged in a letter of this sort.

Again, when he understands that he has been obeyed in part, but not fully, the pope may close the door to any further proofs or proposals by the king.

If indeed the king of England makes no appearance at all, and sends no proctors, or envoys, or extra-judicial statement, and does not excuse himself, nor decline to receive judgment, yet, because the papal letter does not seem to have the force of a *citacio* or a *monicio*, nor to compel the king to send as the letter demands, especially since the pope is not reckoned to be a judge in a lay fee ; since also a letter of this sort appears harsh, unusual, and strange, and seems to contain things contrary to common law, in which case even if the pope were a proper judge, a second command would seem to be called for, then perhaps the pope would proceed against the king as against one contumacious and without defence, by making judgments, restrictions, and declarations of the law of the Roman church, and in the other harmful ways already described.[1]

30

Littere misse ad curiam Romanam super jure regi competente in regno Scocie.^a

SANCTISSIMO [1] in Christo patri domino B[onifacio] divina providencia sancte Romane ac universalis ecclesie summo pontifici, Edwardus ejusdem gracia Rex Anglie dominus Hibernie et dux Aquitannie devota pedum oscula beatorum. Infra scripta non in forma nec in figura judicii [2] set omnino extra judicium pro serenanda sancte paternitatis vestre consciencia vobis transmittimus exhibenda. Altissimus inspector cordium nostre scrinio memorie indelebili stilo novit inscribi, quod antecessores et progenitores nostri reges Anglie jure superioris et directi dominii [3] ab antiquissimis retro temporibus regno Scocie et ipsius regibus in temporalibus et annexis eisdem prefuerunt, et ab eisdem regibus pro regno Scocie et ejusdem regni proceribus a quibus habere volebant, ligia homagia et fidelitatis juramenta receperunt ; et nos juris et dominii possessionem continuantes hujusmodi pro

---

Text: P.R.O. Close Rolls (C 54), 118, ms. 10 d, 9 d (C), whence Rymer, I, ii, 932-3 (R).   Printed also in *Chron. Ed. I and II*, I, 112-20 (L).   Calendared in Bain, II, no. 1200.   A draft in French (perhaps made for Edward himself and his lay advisers) survives as P.R.O. Scottish Documents, Exchequer (E 39), 99/48, 50, 51, and 1/18 (E), and it throws some light on the preparation of the text.

^a *Title from margin of* C

[1] This letter (Edward's reply to no. 28) was given on 15 May 1301 to Thomas Wale and Thomas Delisle, who took it to the pope.   In view of pp. 93-4 above, it is unfortunate that we know nothing of their letters of credence.   They reached Boniface, at Anagni, on 2 July (P.R.O. E 101/308/29).   Wale's description of his mission is calendared in Bain, II, no. 1167, where 'St Peter's Day' means 'St Peter and St Paul's Day', a confusion which has caused some difficulty.   The historical section of this letter from Edward the Elder onwards is based on John of Caen's 'Great

30

Letter sent to the court of Rome concerning the king's rights in the realm of Scotland.

To [1] the most Holy Father in Christ lord Boniface, by divine providence the supreme pontiff of the Holy Roman and Universal Church, Edward, by grace of the same providence king of England, lord of Ireland, and duke of Aquitaine offers his humblest devotion to the blessed saints. What follows we send to you not to be treated in the form or manner of a legal plea,[2] but altogether extrajudicially, in order to set the mind of your Holiness at rest. The All-Highest, to whom all hearts are open, will testify how it is graven upon the tablets of our memory with an indelible mark, that our predecessors and progenitors, the kings of England, by right of lordship and dominion,[3] possessed, from the most ancient times, the suzerainty of the realm of Scotland and its kings in temporal matters, and the things annexed thereto, and that they received from the self-same kings, and from such magnates of the realm as they so desired, liege homage and oaths of fealty. We, continuing in the possession of that very right and dominion, have received the same acknowledgments in our time,

---

Roll' (Rymer, 1, ii, 769-70), but the notary Andrew de Tange, who was present at the Lincoln parliament, may have been the actual compiler. In general see Powicke, *Thirteenth Century*, pp. 705-6, and cf. above, p. xxviii.

[2] cf. above, p. 89.

[3] E has *par droit de sovereine seignourie de tres anciens temps.* The omission here, and in similar passages below (p. 104, *n.* 3, and p. 105, *n.* 1), of any equivalent for *directi* corroborates the view expressed by the present editor in *SHR*, xxxv, 104, *n.* 4, that the latter term is a piece of Romanist verbiage, introduced by the notaries who prepared the Latin texts of Edward I's *dossier* on Scotland.

tempore nostro eadem tam a rege Scocie quam ab ipsius regni proceribus recepimus, quinimmo tanta juris et dominii prerogativa super regnum Scocie et ejusdem reges gaudebant quod regnum ipsum suis fidelibus conferebant, reges eciam ex causis justis amovebant et constituerunt sub se, loco ipsorum, alios regnaturos, que proculdubio ab antiquo notoria fuerunt et existunt licet aliud forte paternis auribus per pacis emulos et rebellionis filios fuerit falsa insinuacione suggestum quorum machinosa et imaginaria figmenta vestra providencia, quesumus, aspernetur.

Sub [1] temporibus itaque Ely et Samuelis prophete vir quidam strenuus et insignis, Brutus nomine, de genere Trojanorum post excidium urbis Troje cum multis nobilibus Trojanorum applicuit in quandam insulam tunc Albion vocatam, a gigantibus inhabitatam, quibus sua et suorum devictis potencia et occisis eam nomine suo Britanniam sociosque suos Britones appellavit et edificavit civitatem quam Trinovantum [2] nuncupavit que modo Londonia nominatur.   Et postea regnum suum tribus filiis suis divisit, scilicet Locrino primogenito illam partem Britannie que nunc Anglia dicitur et Albanacto secundo natu illam partem que tunc Albania a nomine Albanacti nunc vero Scocia nuncupatur, et Cambro filio minori partem illam nomine suo tunc Cambria vocatam que nunc Wallia vocatur, reservata Locrino seniori regia dignitate.   Itaque biennio post mortem Bruti applicuit in Albania quidam rex

---

[1] E shows that passage *sub temporibus itaque Ely* to *fuere subjecti* (below, p. 98, *n.* 2) was an afterthought.   The historical narrative originally began, therefore (as in John of Caen's ' Great Roll '), with Edward the Elder.   The ultimate source of the insertion is Geoffrey of Monmouth, *Historia Britonum*, i, chapters xvi ff.   On Edward I's interest in Arthurian

both from the king of Scotland, and from the magnates of that realm ; and indeed such prerogatives of right and dominion did the kings of England enjoy over the realm of Scotland and its kings, that they have even granted to their faithful folk the realm itself, removed its kings for just causes, and constituted others to rule in their place under themselves. Beyond doubt these matters have been familiar from times long past and still are, though perchance it has been suggested otherwise to your Holiness' ears by foes of peace and sons of rebellion, whose elaborate and empty fabrications your wisdom, we trust, will treat with contempt.

Thus,[1] in the days of Eli and of Samuel the prophet, after the destruction of the city of Troy, a certain valiant and illustrious man of the Trojan race called Brutus, landed with many noble Trojans, upon a certain island called, at that time, Albion. It was then inhabited by giants, and after he had defeated and slain them, by his might and that of his followers, he called it, after his own name, Britain, and his people Britons, and built a city which he called Trinovant,[2] now known as London. Afterwards he divided his realm among his three sons, that is he gave to his first born, Locrine, that part of Britain now called England, to the second, Albanact, that part then known as Albany, after the name of Albanact, but now as Scotland, and to Camber, his youngest son, the part then known by his son's name as Cambria and now called Wales, the royal dignity being reserved for Locrine, the eldest. Two years after the death of Brutus there landed in Albany a certain king of

---

legend see R. S. Loomis in *Speculum*, xxviii, 114-27 ; but on pp. 121-2 Edward's personal letter to Boniface is confused with the Barons' letter.

[2] Here, and in some other instances, we translate the Latin name by the French form from E.

Hunorum nomine Humber et Albanactum fratrem
Locrini occidit, quo audito Locrinus rex Britonum pro-
secutus est eum qui fugiens submersus est in flumine quod
de nomine suo Humber vocatur et sic Albania revertitur
ad dictum Locrinum. Item Dunwallo rex Britonum
Staterium regem Scocie sibi rebellem occidit et terram
ejus in dedicionem [1] recepit. Item duo filii Dunwallonis
scilicet Belinus et Brennius inter se regnum patris sui
diviserunt ita quod Belinus senior diadema insule cum
Britannia Wallia et Cornubia possideret; Brennius vero
sub eo regnaturus Scociam acciperet, petebat enim
Trojana consuetudo ut dignitas hereditatis primogenito
perveniret.[a] Item Arturus rex Britonum princeps
famosissimus Scociam sibi rebellem subjecit, et pene
totam gentem delevit et postea quemdam nomine
Anguselum in regem Scocie prefecit et cum postea idem
rex Arturus apud civitatem Legionum festum faceret
celeberimum, interfuerunt ibidem omnes reges sibi subjecti inter quos Anguselus rex Scocie servicium pro regno
Scocie exhibens debitum gladium regis Arturi detulit
ante ipsum et successive omnes reges Scocie omnibus
regibus Britonum fuere subjecti.[2] Succedentibus [3] autem
regibus Anglis in predicta insula et ipsius monarchiam
et dominium optinentibus subsequenter [3] Edwardus [4]
dictus senior filius Elvredi regis Anglie Scotorum Cumbrorum et Stregwallorum reges sibi tanquam superiori
domino subjectos habuit et submissos. Adelstanus rex
Anglie Constantinum regem Scotorum sub se regna-

---

[a] *So* L; proveniret CR
[1] *e reprist sa terre en sa seignurie*, E
[2] The addition in E ends here (cf. p. 97, *n.* 1 above).
[3] to [3] E has nothing to correspond here.

the Huns, called Humber, and he slew Albanact, the brother of Locrine. Hearing this, Locrine, the king of the Britons, pursued him, and he fled and was drowned in the river which from his name is called Humber, and thus Albany reverted to Locrine. Again, Dunwal, king of the Britons, slew Stater, king of Scotland, who rebelled against him, and received his land in surrender.[1] Again, the two sons of Dunwal, Belin and Brenn, divided between themselves their father's realm, so that the senior, Belin, should possess the crown of the island with Britain, Wales, and Cornwall, and Brenn, who was to rule under him, should receive Scotland, for the custom of Troy demanded that the dignity of the inheritance should go to the first born. Again, Arthur, king of the Britons, a prince most renowned, subjected to himself a rebellious Scotland, destroyed almost the whole nation, and afterwards installed as king of Scotland one Angusel by name. Afterwards, when King Arthur held a most famous feast at Caerleon, there were present there all the kings subject to him, and among them Angusel, king of Scotland, who manifested the service due for the realm of Scotland by bearing the sword of King Arthur before him ; and in succession all the kings of Scotland have been subject to all the kings of the Britons.[2] Succeeding [3] kings of England enjoyed both monarchy and dominion in the island, and subsequently [3] Edward,[4] known as the elder, son of Alfred, king of England, had subject and subordinate to him, as lord superior, the kings of the Scots, the Cumbrians, and the Strathclyde Welsh. Athelstan, king of England, established Constantine, king of Scots, to rule under him, saying ' it is a

---

[4] E resumes here, its narrative being now based on John of Caen's ' Great Roll '.

turum constituit dicens 'gloriosius est regem facere
quam regem esse' et est dignum memoria quod idem
Adelstanus, intercedente sancto Johanne de Beverlaco
quondam archiepiscopo Ebor',[1] Scotos rebellantes ei
dimicavit [2] qui gracias deo devote agens deum exoravit,
petens quatinus interveniente beato Johanne sibi aliquod
signum evidens ostenderet quatinus tam succedentes
quam presentes cognoscere possent Scotos Anglorum
regno jure subjugari, et videns quosdam scopulos juxta
quemdam locum prope Dumbar in Scocia prominere,
extracto gladio de vagina, percussit in silicem qui lapis
ad ictum gladii, dei virtute agente, ita cavatur ut
mensura ulne longitudini possit coaptari, et hujus rei
hactenus evidens signum apparet et in Beverlac' ecclesia
in legenda sancti Johannis quasi singulis ebdomadis per
annum ad laudem et honorem sancti Johannis pro
miraculo recitatur, et de hoc exstat celebris memoria
tam in Anglia quam in Scocia usque ad presentem diem.

Item Constantinus rex Scottorum et Eugenius rex
Cumbrorum ad predictum regem Anglie Adelstanum
post aliqualem dissencionem inter eos habitam venientes
se cum suis regnis eidem Adelstano dedidere, cujus facti
gracia filium Constantini ipse Adelstanus de sacro fonte
suscepit. Item Edredo regi Anglie Scoti sine bello se
subdiderunt et eidem regi Edredo tanquam domino
fidelitatem debitam juraverunt, quodam Yricio rege
super ipsos Scotos statuto. Item cum Edgarus rex Anglie
regem Scotorum Kinadium et Cumbrorum Malculmum
regem plurimarum insularum Makkum aliosque quinque

---

[1] This story is derived, *via* Caen's 'Great Roll', from the anonymous
'Miracles' of St John of Beverley (see Raine, *Hist. of Church of York* (RS),
1, 296-7). The description of John as 'archbishop' is, of course, erroneous.
[2] *venqi* E

greater cause for pride to make a king than to be one ',
and it is worthy to be remembered that this same
Athelstan, on the intercession of St John of Beverley,
formerly archbishop of York,[1] overcame [2] the Scots who
were in rebellion against him. Devoutly giving thanks
to God, he besought Him in prayer that by the intervention of the blessed John he would show him some
manifest sign, by which men present and to come could
recognise that the Scots were rightly subject to the realm
of England. When he saw some overhanging crags at a
place near Dunbar, in Scotland, he drew his sword from
its scabbard and smote upon the rock, which at the blow
of the sword, by reason of God's providence, was so
hollowed out that the measure of an ell can be fitted in
the length of it, and it may still be seen as a manifest
record of this event. The deed is recited in the church
of Beverley, every week throughout the year, as a miracle
for the praise and honour of St John, when the life of
St John is read, and there exists to the present day a
solemn commemoration of it, both in England and in
Scotland.

Again, Constantine, king of Scots, and Eugenius,
king of the Cumbrians, came to Athelstan, king of
England, after a certain dispute had taken place between
them, and surrendered themselves, with their realms, to
Athelstan, and as a result of this act Athelstan himself
stood godfather to the son of Constantine. Again, the
Scots submitted themselves without warfare to Eadred,
king of England, and swore the fealty due to King
Eadred as lord, a certain Eric being installed as king
over the Scots. Again, when Edgar, king of England,
caused Kenneth, king of Scots, Malcolm, king of the
Cumbrians, Mack, king of many islands, and five other

subregulos, scilicet Duvenaldum Syferth Huwal Jacob
et Juchil regem ipsum Edgarum in navi quadam prope
proram sedentem per flumen Dehe remigare fecisset
fertur ipsum dixisse successores suos gloriari ᵃ se reges
Anglorum esse cum tanta honorum prerogativa fruerentur ut ᵇ subjectam habeant tot regum potenciam. Post
dictum Edgarum successive successerunt reges Anglie
sanctus Edwardus martir Egelredus frater ejus Edmundus
dictus Hirenside filius Egelredi et Knutus, qui eorum
temporibus regnum Scocie in sua subjeccione pacifice
tenuerunt, hoc dumtaxat excepto quod anno quindecimo
regni Knuti predicti idem Knutus Scociam rebellantem,
expedicione illuc ducta, regem Scocie Malcolmum parvo
subegit negocio, subditusque est ei idem Malcolmus,
quibus Haraldus filius Knuti et Hardeknutus frater ejus
unus post alium reges Anglie successerunt, qui eis sic
regnantibus sibi subjeccionem regni Scocie pacifice
habuerunt.   Item sanctus Edwardus rex Anglie regnum
Scocie dedit Malcolmo filio regis Cumbrorum de se
tenendum.

Item Willelmus dictus bastardus rex Anglie, cognatus
dicti Edwardi, a Malcolmo rege Scotorum tanquam a
suo homine sibi subdito homagium cepit.   Item Willelmo
Ruffo, regi Anglie, predictus Malcolmus rex Scotorum
juramento fidelitatis subjectus fuit.   Item predictus rex
Willelmus Dovenaldum de regno Scocie ex justis causis
amovit et loco ejus Duncanum filium Malcolmi regem
Scocie prefecit, et recepit ab eo fidelitatis juramentum,
dictoque Duncano dolose perempto dictus rex Willelmus
prefatum Dovenaldum qui iterum regnum Scocie in-

ᵃ *Perhaps read* posse gloriari ;   *cf. Rymer, 1, ii, 769.*   E *has* devoir se glorifier.
ᵇ ut subjectam habeant *interlineated in another hand* C

sub-kings, namely Dufnal, Siferth, Hywel, Jacob and
Juchil, to row him upon the River Dee, as he sat in the
prow of the ship he is said to have observed that his
successors should rejoice in being kings of England, for
they enjoyed so great a prerogative of honour in having
subject to them such powerful kings.   After this Edgar
there succeeded in order, as kings of England, the holy
Edward the martyr, Ethelred his brother, Edmund called
Ironside son of Ethelred, and Canute, who in their time
peaceably held the realm of Scotland in subjection, with
this exception, that in the fifteenth year of his reign,
Canute with little trouble conquered a rebellious Scotland, under Malcolm, its king, after leading an expedi-
tion thither, and Malcolm was subjected to him.   Harold,
son of Canute, and Hardicanute his brother, succeeded
one after the other as kings of England, and they, during
their reigns, peaceably had the realm of Scotland subject
to themselves.   Again, St Edward, king of England,
granted the realm of Scotland to Malcolm, son of the
king of the Cumbrians, to be held of himself.

Furthermore, William, styled the Bastard, king of
England, a kinsman of the said Edward, received
homage from Malcolm, king of Scots, as from a vassal
subject to him.   Again Malcolm, king of Scots, was made
subject to William Rufus, king of England, by an oath
of fealty.   Again, this King William, for just causes,
removed Donald from the realm of Scotland, and in his
place appointed Duncan, son of Malcolm, as king of
Scotland, and received from him an oath of fealty.
When this Duncan was slain by treachery, King William
removed Donald, who had once more invaded the realm

R

vaserat amovit ab eodem et Edgarum filium dicti Malcolmi regem Scocie constituit et eidem illud regnum donavit, cui successit Alexander frater ejusdem Edgari, concessu regis Anglie Henrici primi fratris dicti regis Willelmi Ruffi. Item Matildi imperatrici filie et heredi regis Henrici predicti rex Scocie David fecit homagium et fidelitatem. Item regi Anglorum Stephano Henricus filius dicti regis David homagium fecit. Item Willelmus rex Scotorum pro regno Scocie et David frater suus et comites et barones regni Scocie devenerunt homines Henrici, filii regis Anglie Henrici secundi, in crastino coronacionis predicti Henrici filii Henrici secundi patre vivente, et fidelitatem ei juraverunt contra omnes homines salva fidelitate debita patri viventi. Anno vero vicesimo regni regis Henrici secundi predicti, dictus Willelmus rex Scotorum rebellare incipiens venit in Northumbriam cum excercitu magno et excercuit in populo stragem magnam, cui occurrentes milites comitatus Ebor' apud Alnewyk' ipsum ceperunt et dicto Henrico regi Anglie reddiderunt, annoque sequenti, scilicet xv kal. Marcii est idem Willelmus permissus liber abire. Postea vero apud Eboracum anno eodem xvij kal. Septembris idem Willelmus rex Scotorum de consensu prelatorum comitum baronum procerum et aliorum magnatum regni Scocie domino suo regi Anglie Henrico filio Matildis imperatricis predicto suis litteris patentibus cavisse noscitur quod ipse et heredes et successores sui reges Scocie episcopi et abbates comites eciam et barones et alii homines regni Scocie de quibus dominus rex habere voluerit facient regibus Anglie homagium fidelitatem et

of Scotland, from the kingdom, and appointed Edgar, son of the said Malcolm, as king of Scotland, and granted him that realm ; and to him there succeeded Alexander, brother of Edgar, by the grant of Henry I, king of England, brother of King William Rufus. Again, David, king of Scotland, did homage and fealty to the Empress Matilda, daughter and heiress of the said Henry. Again, Henry, son of King David, did homage to Stephen, king of the English. Again, William, king of Scots (in his case for the realm of Scotland), and David, his brother, and the earls and barons of the realm of Scotland, became the men of Henry, son of Henry II, king of England, on the morrow of the coronation of the said young Henry, which took place in the lifetime of his father, and they swore fealty to him against all men, reserving the fealty due to his father while he lived. In the twentieth year of the reign of Henry II, William, king of Scots, began a rebellion, came into Northumberland with a large army, and inflicted great slaughter upon the people. The knights of the county of York met him and took him captive at Alnwick, and surrendered him to King Henry of England, and in the year following, on 15 February, William was granted permission to depart. Later, at York, on 16 August of the same year, this William, king of Scots, with the agreement of the prelates, earls, barons, nobles, and other magnates of the realm of Scotland, is recorded to have guaranteed by letter patent, to his lord, the king of England, Henry, son of the Empress Matilda, that he and his heirs and successors, the kings of Scotland, and the bishops, abbots, earls, and also the barons, and other men of the realm of Scotland from whom the lord king wished to have it, should render to the kings of England homage, fealty,

liganciam ut ligio domino contra omnem hominem. Et [1]
in signum subjeccionis hujusmodi idem Willelmus rex
Scocie capellum lanceam et sellam suos super altare
ecclesie beati Petri Eboracensis optulit que in eadem
ecclesia usque in hodiernum diem remanent et servantur.[1]
Item episcopi comites et barones dicti regni Scocie convencionaverunt, ut verbis ejusdem convencionis utamur,[2]
domino regi et Henrico filio suo predictis ' quod si rex
Scocie aliquo casu a fidelitate regum Anglie et convencione predicta recederet ipsi cum domino rege Anglie
tenebunt sicut cum ligio domino suo contra regem
Scocie quousque ad fidelitatem regis Anglie redeat ',
quam quidem composicionem felicis recordacionis Gregorius papa ix in diversis rescriptis regibus Anglie et
Scocie directis mandavit firmiter observari, continentibus
eciam inter cetera quod Willelmus et Alexander reges
Scotorum regibus Anglie Johanni et Henrico ligium
homagium et fidelitatem fecerunt que tenentur successores
eorum comites et barones regni Scocie ipsis et suis successoribus exhibere,[3] et iterum quod cum idem rex
Scocie homo ligius sit ipsius Henrici regis Anglie et
eidem fidelitatis prestiterit juramentum quo se princi-
paliter astrinxit quod in ipsius regis et regni Anglie
detrimentum nichil debeat penitus attemptare.[4] Et papa
Clemens scribens regi Anglie pro Johanne episcopo
sancti Andree, expulso ab episcopatu suo per regem
Scocie, inter cetera rogavit quod Willelmum regem
Scocie moneret et induceret et si necesse fuerit distric-

---

[1] to [1] This sentence (not in Caen's ' Great Roll ') comes from an
unidentified source.   Its French equivalent in E is interlineated.
[2] See above, p. 4.
[3] See above, p. 18.
[4] See Rymer, I, i, 199 (date should be 1236).

and allegiance as to their liege lord, against every man.
As [1] tokens of this subjection, William, king of Scotland,
offered upon the altar of the church of blessed Peter at
York his helmet, lance, and saddle, which remain, and
are kept in that church up to the present day.[1]   Again,
the bishops, earls, and barons of the realm of Scotland
agreed with the lord king, and Henry his son (to use the
words of the treaty) [2], ' that if the king of Scotland should
perchance withdraw from his fealty towards the kings
of England, and from the treaty, then they will adhere
to the king of England as their liege lord against the king
of Scotland, until he return to the fealty of the king of
England '.   Pope Gregory IX, of happy memory, in
various rescripts addressed to the kings of England and
Scotland, ordered this treaty to be strictly observed.
These rescripts also record, among other things, that
William and Alexander, the kings of Scotland, did liege
homage and swore fealty to John and Henry, the kings
of England, and that their successors, and the earls and
barons of the realm of Scotland, are bound to offer the
same to them and to their successors.[3]   These rescripts
also record that the same king of Scotland is the liegeman
of Henry, king of England, and has taken an oath of
fealty to him, whose chief provision was that he should
attempt nothing at all to the disadvantage of the king
himself and of the realm of England.[4]   Pope Clement,
writing to the king of England on behalf of John, bishop
of St Andrews, who had been driven out of his see by
the king of Scotland, asked, among other things, that he
should admonish and persuade William, king of Scotland, and if necessary compel him by the royal distress

cione regali qua ei preminet [1] et concessa sue regie celsitudini potestate compelleret, ut dicto episcopo omnem
rancorem remitteret et episcopatum suum eum habere
in pace permitteret.[2] Et post convencionem predictam
in ecclesia beati Petri Ebor' coram predictis regibus
Anglie et Scocie et David fratre suo et universo populo,
episcopi comites barones milites de terra regis Scocie
juraverunt domino regi Anglie et Henrico filio suo et
heredibus eorum fidelitatem contra omnem hominem
sicut ligiis dominis suis. Et idem Willelmus rex Scotorum
ad mandatum regis Henrici predicti venit apud Nor-
hampton ad parliamentum domini sui adducens secum
omnes episcopos abbates priores tocius regni sui et venit
eciam ad ejusdem regis Anglie mandatum in Norman-
niam. Et idem rex Willelmus, post decessum dicti regis
Henrici, veniens Cantuar' Ricardo regi Anglie filio et
heredi dicti Henrici fecit homagium,[3] quo Ricardo viam
universe carnis ingresso sepefatus Willelmus Johanni regi
Anglie, fratri et heredi predicti regis Ricardi, extra
civitatem Lincoln' supra quendam montem in conspectu
omnis populi fecit homagium, et juravit ei fedelitatem
[*sic*] super crucem Huberti tunc Cantuar' archiepiscopi,
et eidem Johanni tanquam domino suo per cartam suam
concessit quod Alexandrum filium suum sicut hominem
suum ligium maritaret, promittendo firmiter in carta
eadem quod idem Willelmus rex Scotorum et Alexander
filius suus Henrico filio regis Anglie Johannis tanquam
ligio domino suo contra omnes mortales fidem et fidelitatem tenerent,[4] a quo quidem Willelmo rege Scotorum
postmodum pro eo quod desponderat filiam suam comiti

---

[1] *par destresce reale qe il ad sus luy* E
[2] See Haddan and Stubbs, II, i, 268.

which he can bring to bear on him [1] and by the power
granted to his royal highness, to abandon all his wrath
against the bishop, and to allow him to hold his see in
peace.[2]   And after that agreement, the bishops, earls,
barons and knights from the territory of the king of
Scotland swore fealty, in the church of blessed Peter at
York, before the kings of England and Scotland, and
David, brother of the latter, and all the assembly, to the
king of England and Henry his son, and their heirs,
against every man, as to their liege lords.   The same
William, king of Scots, at the command of King Henry,
came to the parliament of his lord at Northampton,
bringing with him all the bishops, abbots and priors of
his whole realm, and he came also at the command of
the selfsame king of England into Normandy.

The same King William, after the death of King
Henry, came to King Richard of England, son and heir
of Henry, at Canterbury and did homage,[3] and Richard
having followed the way of all flesh, William did homage
to King John of England, brother and heir of King
Richard, outside the city of Lincoln, upon a hill, in the
view of all the people, and swore fealty to him on the
cross of Hubert, then archbishop of Canterbury.   To
the same John, as his lord, he granted by charter the
right to dispose of his son Alexander, as being his liegeman, in marriage and gave a firm promise in the same
charter that he, William, king of Scots, and Alexander,
his son, would maintain faith and fealty to Henry, son of
King John of England, as their liege lord, against all
mortal men [4] ; and from this William, king of Scots, who
had married his daughter to the count of Boulogne

---

[3] A very imperfect way of describing pp. 6-8 above
[4] See above, pp. 12-13.

Bolonie preter ipsius regis Johannis domini sui assensum pro transgressione et temeraria presumpcione hujusmodi debitam satisfaccionem accepit.[1] Item Alexander rex Scotorum sororius noster regi Anglie Henrico patri nostro pro regno Scocie et postea nobis homagium fecit.[2][a]

Vacante [a] deinde regno Scocie post mortem Alexandri regis illius, et subsequenter per mortem Margarete ejusdem regni Scocie regine et domine neptis nostre, episcopi abbates priores comites barones proceres et ceteri nobiles et communitates tocius regni Scocie ad nos tanquam ad legitimum defensorem ducem aurigam capitaneum et dominum capitalem ejusdem regni sic vacantis gratis et spontanea voluntate accedentes, prout tenebantur de jure, jus nostrum progenitorum et antecessorum nostrorum ac possessionem superioris et directi dominii [3] in regno eodem et ipsius regni subjeccionem ex certa sciencia pure simpliciter et absolute recognoverunt, et prestitis nobis ab eisdem tanquam superiori et directo domino Scocie debitis et consuetis fidelitatum juramentis ac civitatibus burgis villis castris ac ceteris municionibus regni ejusdem in manu nostra traditis, ad custodiam ejusdem regni certos jure nostro regio officiales et ministros deputavimus quibus ipsi tempore vacacionis hujusmodi concorditer fuerant obedientes et intendentes in nostris preceptis regiis et mandatis. Postmodum autem diverse persone super successione in dictum regnum Scocie jure hereditario inter se contendentes ad nos tanquam ad superiorem dominum regni Scocie

---

[a] E *has paragraph mark here*; C *written throughout without any paragraph divisions.*

[1] Dr A. O. Anderson has pointed out that there was no such marriage (*E.S.* II, 373).

without the consent of his lord, King John, King John
received due satisfaction for this trespass and rash pre-
sumption.[1] Again, Alexander, king of Scots, the husband
of our sister, did homage to the king of England, our
father Henry, for the realm of Scotland, and later to us.[2]

Then the realm of Scotland became vacant after the
death of King Alexander, and subsequently that of
Margaret, who was queen and lady of the realm of
Scotland, and our [great] niece. The bishops, abbots,
priors, earls, barons, magnates and other nobles, and the
communities of the whole realm of Scotland came freely
and spontaneously, and as they were bound by law, to us
as their rightful defender, leader, guide, captain, and as
chief lord of the realm thus vacant, and recognized of
their certain knowledge, purely, simply, and absolutely,
the right of ourselves, and of our progenitors and predecessors, and our possession of lordship and dominion [3]
therein, and the subjection of that realm. Oaths of
fealty were given by them to us, as due and customary
to the lord superior of Scotland, and the towns, burghs,
and villages, and the castles and other strong points of
the realm were surrendered into our hands, and for the
custody of the realm we, by our royal right, appointed
certain officials and ministers, to whom, during that time
of vacancy, they were content to be obedient, as they
were also attentive to our royal precepts and commands.
Afterwards various persons who were disputing among
themselves about the succession by hereditary right to
the realm of Scotland, came to us, as lord superior of the

---

[2] For the homage to Edward I see above, pp. 38-41 ; for the reference to
Henry III cf. Anderson, *S.A.*, pp. 365-6 (a passage which may have been
read by the clerk who drafted the above letter).

[3] *possession de sovereigne seignurie* E. cf. above, p. 96, *n.* 3.

accesserunt, petentes super jure succedendi in regnum predictum sibi per nos exhiberi justicie complementum, volentes et expresse consentientes coram nobis tanquam superiore et directo domino [1] regni Scocie stare juri. [2] Et demum earumdem parcium peticionibus et juribus coram nobis tanquam coram superiore et directo domino judicialiter propositis ac sufficienter auditis rimatis examinatis et diligenter intellectis, in presencia omnium prelatorum et nobilium quasi tocius regni Scocie et de voluntate et assensu expresse eorumdem procedentes, Johannem de Balliolo debite prefecimus in regem Scotorum [3] quem tunc in successione ejusdem regni heredem legitimum et jura habere invenimus potiora, qui quidem prelati comites barones communitates ac ceteri incole ejusdem regni hujusmodi sentenciam nostram expresse omologarunt acceptarunt et expresse approbarunt, et ipsum Johannem de mandato nostro virtute hujusmodi judicii in regem suum admiserunt.

Ac idem Johannes rex Scocie pro regno suo prestito nobis homagio debito et consueto ac fidelitatis juramento ad parliamenta nostra de mandato nostro veniens, eisdem tanquam noster subditus sicut alii de regno nostro interfuit, et nostris tanquam domini sui superioris dicti regni Scocie paruit beneplacitis et mandatis nobis in omnibus obediens et intendens quousque idem Johannes rex Scocie et prelati comites barones nobiles communitates ac ceteri incole majores regni ejusdem, ex preconcepta malicia et prelocuta ac preordinata prodicione, facciones confederaciones conspiraciones et conjuraciones in exheredacionem nostram et heredum nostrorum ac regni nostri contra debitum homagii sui et fidelitatis

---

[1] *come sovereign seignur* E.   cf. previous note.
[2] See above, p. 56.

realm of Scotland, asking that we should grant them the
completeness of justice in the matter of their right of
succession in the realm ; they being willing, and agreeing
expressly, to accept our jurisdiction [2] as lord superior [1]
of the realm of Scotland. In the end, after the petitions
and rights of these parties had been sufficiently set forth
and heard in form of law, and had been examined,
scrutinised and diligently considered before ourselves as
lord superior, in the presence of almost all of the prelates
and nobles of the whole realm of Scotland, we, acting
with their agreement and express assent, duly promoted
John Balliol, whom we found to be true heir in succession
to the realm, and to possess the best right to it, to be the
king of Scots.[3] The prelates, earls, barons, communities
and other inhabitants of the realm expressly adopted,
approved and accepted this our sentence, and by virtue
of this judgment, received John as their king at our
behest.

This John, king of Scotland, having rendered to us
the due and accustomed homage, and the oath of fealty,
came to our parliaments at our command and was
present in them as our subject, like the others of our
realm, and abided by our pleasure and commands, as
those of his lord, the superior of Scotland, being obedient
and subject to us in all things, until he and the prelates,
earls, barons, nobles, communities and other chief
inhabitants of the same realm, by preconceived and pre-
arranged malice, and by treachery deliberately planned,
contrary to the obligation of their homage and the oath
of fealty, and wickedly embarking upon the crime of
treason, entered into plots, confederations, conspiracies

---

[3] See above, p. 61.   Note use of ' debite ' in reply to Boniface's ' indebite ' (above, p. 84).

juramentum inter se inierunt in crimen lese majestatis nequiter incidendo. Unde cum premissa, ex fideli relacione fama publica consenciente ad aures nostras pervenissent, volentes futuris periculis precavere que ex hiis et aliis possent nobis regno nostro et regni nostri incolis verisimiliter provenire pro assecuracione regni nostri accessimus ad confinium regni utriusque pluries mandantes eidem Johanni tunc regi Scocie quod ad certa loca in confinio predicto ad nos accederet super premissis et aliis pro statu tranquillitate et pace utriusque regni assecuracionem facturus, et alia per nos et consilium nostrum sibi exponenda auditurus, et super hiis et ea contingentibus justiciam recepturus, qui spretis mandatis nostris contumaciter in sua persistens perfidia ad bellicos apparatus cum episcopis prelatis et clericis comitibus baronibus regni Scocie ac eciam aliis exteris conducticiis contra nos regnum nostrum et incolas regni nostri hostiliter se convertens accinxit, et ad hostiles aggressus et incursus procedens regnum nostrum invasit, quasdam villas regni nostri Anglie per se et suos depredatus est easque vastavit incendio homines nostros interfecit et nonnullis nautis nostris per eos peremptis naves hominum nostrorum regni Anglie comburi fecit, et e vestigio redditis nobis homagio et fidelitate per regem Scotorum tam pro se quam pro aliis quibuscumque regni sui incolis per verba effectum diffidencie exprimencia,[1] comitatus nostros Northumbr' Cumbr' et Westmerland regni nostri Anglie, congregato ingenti excercitu, hostiliter per se et suos invasit, stragem innumeram hominum nostrorum

---

[1] See above, p. 70.

and alliances for the disinheritance of ourselves, our heirs, and our realm. Therefore, when these things had come to our ears by a trustworthy account, which was consonant with the common rumour, we, wishing to guard against the dangers which might well arise in future from these and other things, to us, our realm, and the inhabitants of our realm, journeyed (for the protection of our kingdom), to the boundary between the two realms, repeatedly asking John, then king of Scotland, to come to us, at specified places on the border, to give security upon these and other things, in order to guard the well-being, the tranquillity, and the peace of either kingdom, and to hearken to other matters which were to be explained to him by ourselves and our council, and to receive justice in these matters, and others connected with them. He contumaciously spurned our commands, and continued in his perfidy, and aroused himself to warlike action, turning himself in hostile manner upon us and our realm and its people, in company with the bishops, prelates, clerks, earls and barons of the realm of Scotland, and also with others hired from without. Proceeding to hostile attacks and incursions, he invaded our realm, and both he and his followers plundered and laid waste by fire certain villages of our realm of England, slew our men, and when some of our sailors had been slain by his people, he caused the ships of our men of the realm of England to be burned, and forthwith he renounced homage and fealty to us, both on his own behalf and for the other inhabitants of his realm, in words of formal defiance.[1] After assembling a great army, he and his men made a hostile invasion of our counties of Northumberland, Cumberland and Westmorland in our realm of England, and indulged in

incendia monasteriorum ecclesiarum et villarum inhumane perpetrando et patriam undique depopulando
infantes in cunis mulieres in puerperio decubantes in-
misericordi et atroci sevicia trucidarunt, et (quod auditu
horrendum est) a nonnullis mulieribus mamillas atrociter
abciderunt parvos clericulos primas litteras et gramati-
cam addiscentes ad numerum circiter ducentorum in
scolis existentes, obstructis hostiis scolarum, igne supposito concremarunt,[1] nosque cernentes tot dampna
obprobria facinora et injurias in exheredacionem nostram
et destruccionem populi regni nostri prodicionaliter
irrogari nec volentes racione juramenti quo ad conservacionem jurium corone regni nostri sumus astricti [2]
tam execranda detestanda et nefanda facinora ulterius
tolerare, nec jura nostra relinquere indefensa, cum idem
Johannes et gens Scotorum nostri subditi per leges se
justificari minime permisissent, ipso regno Scocie quod a
longissimis temporibus, sicut superius exprimitur, nobis
et progenitoribus nostris feudale extitit ex causis premissis commisso; deinde bello juxta leges et consuetudines regni nostri contra eos de consilio procerum et
magnatum nostrorum indicto, contra dictum Johannem
et gentem Scottorum vires potencie nostre extendimus
prout de jure nobis licuit et processimus contra ipsos
tanquam notorie proditores contumaces et publicos [3]
hostes nostros. Subacto itaque regno Scocie jure proprietatis nostre dicioni, prefatus Johannes rex Scocie

---

[1] The burning of the school (at Hexham) is also recorded in *Chronicon de
Lanercost* (1839), p. 174.
[2] cf. H. G. Richardson in *TRHistS*, xxiii (1941), 131-5 ; P. E. Schramm,
The History of the English Coronation, pp. 197, 270-1.

slaughter of our people without number, and in a merciless burning of monasteries, churches and villages; on all sides they unpeopled the land, slaying children in the cradle and women lying in childbed with brutal and inhuman savagery and, terrible as it is to hear, vilely cutting off the breasts of women. Small school-children of tender years, learning their first letters and grammar, they burned, in the school where they were, to the number of about two hundred, by blocking the doors of the school and setting it on fire.[1] We perceived that these numerous losses, insults, crimes and injuries were being treacherously inflicted on us, causing us to be disinherited, and the people of our realm to be destroyed; and being unwilling, because of the oath which binds us to maintain the rights of our crown,[2] to endure any longer such execrable, detestable and unspeakable villainies, or to let our rights disappear without resistance, for this John, and our subjects, the people of Scotland, had furnished themselves with no justification in law, since the realm of Scotland, which from most ancient times, as is said above, has been feudally subject to us and our progenitors, and for the reasons explained, committed to us, we at length declared war against them, according to the laws and customs of our realm, and by the counsel of our nobles and magnates. We mobilised the resources of our power against John and the Scottish people, as the law allowed us, and proceeded against them as notoriously contumacious traitors, and as our open enemies.[3] So the realm of Scotland was subjected by right of ownership to our power, and John, king of

---

[3] *contre eaux sicom contre nos enemis et apertz traytres* E.   *Apertz* suggests rendering of *publicos* here.

ipsum regnum Scocie quatenus [1] de facto tenuit sponte
pure et absolute reddidit in manum nostram prodiciones
et scelera memorata coram nobis et proceribus regni
nostri publice recognoscens. [2]

Quo peracto prelati comites barones nobiles et communitates regni Scocie quos ad pacem nostram regiam
suscepimus subsequenter homagia et fidelitates nobis tanquam inmediato et proprio domino ejusdem regni Scocie
fecerunt ac eciam prestiterunt [3] ac redditis nobis ejusdem
regni civitatibus villis castris municionibus ac ceteris locis
omnibus ad dictum regnum spectantibus officiales nostros
et ministros ad regimen ejusdem regni Scocie prefecimus
jure nostro.   Cumque jure pleni dominii in possessione
ejusdem regni existere dinoscamur omittere non possumus
nec debemus quin insolenciam subditorum nostrorum
rebellium, si quos invenerimus, preminencia regia [4]
prout justum fuerit et expedire viderimus, reprimamus.
Quia vero ex premissis et aliis constat evidenter et
notorium existit quod prelibatum regnum Scocie tam
racione proprietatis quam possessionis ad nos pertinet
pleno jure nec quicquam fecerimus nec caverimus scripto
vel facto, sicuti nec possemus, per que juri aut possessioni
predictis debeat aliqualiter derogari, sanctitati vestre
humiliter supplicamus quatinus premissa provida medita-
cione pensantes, ex illis vestri motum animi dignemini
informare, suggestionibus contrariis emulorum in hac
parte vobis factis fidem, si placet, nullatenus adhibendo, [5]

---

[1] *Le roiaume Descoce sicome il le tendit de fet* E
[2] See above, p. 73.
[3] e.g. p. 68 above.   Between 1300 and 1306 the notary Andrew de
Tange transcribed the whole body of these homages in triplicate, in the
form of the ' Ragman Rolls ' (P.R.O. C 47/23/3-5).   No. 3 is printed in
Instrumenta Publica (Bannatyne Club), pp. 59-176.

Scotland, publicly admitting[2] before us and the magnates of our realm the above treasons and crimes, rendered into our hand freely, completely, and absolutely the realm of Scotland, so far as he had *de facto* [1] possession of it.

Upon this, the prelates, earls, barons, nobles and communities of the realm of Scotland, whom we received into our royal peace, offered homage and fealty[3] to us as the immediate and proper lord of the realm of Scotland, and the towns, villages, castles, and fortresses of the realm, and all other places belonging to the realm, were surrendered to us, and by virtue of our right we appointed our officials and ministers to govern the realm of Scotland.   And since we are acknowledged to be in possession of that realm, by right of full dominion, we cannot and must not fail to suppress the insolence of our rebel subjects, if such there be, by our royal majesty,[4] as may be just, and as may seem appropriate.   Since, indeed, from what has been said already, and from other evidence, it is perfectly clear and well-known that the realm of Scotland belongs to us of full right, by reason of property and of possession, and that we have not done and have not dared to do anything, as indeed we could not do, in writing or in action, by which any prejudice may be implied to our right or possession, we humbly beseech your Holiness to weigh all this with careful meditation, and to condescend to keep it all in mind when making your decision, setting no store, if you please, by the adverse assertions which come to you on this subject from our enemies,[5] but, on the contrary, retaining our

---

[4] *Par nostre sovereignte reale* E

[5] There is no doubt that Scottish interests at the papal curia had helped to inspire no. 28, and were still active.   cf. below, pp. 110-17.

S

quinimmo statum nostrum et jura nostra regia supradicta habere velitis, si placet, paternis affectibus commendata. Conservet vos altissimus ad regimen ecclesie sue sancte per tempora prospera et longeva.

Dat' apud Kemeseye septimo die Maii anno domini M⁰ CCC⁰ primo et regni nostri vicesimo nono.

welfare and our royal rights, if it so please you, in your
fatherly regard. May the Most High preserve you, to
rule his Holy Church through many years of prosperity.

Kempsey, 7 May 1301, the twenty-ninth year of our
reign.

31

SIRE, come nadgueres vous eez mandez vos enfourmementz a l'apostoille sur vostre droit d'Escoce, les Escoz
meismes les enfourmementz s'en enforcent pur anientir
par aucunes acheisons desouz escrites. Sires, enprimes
dient que l'apostoille est verrei juge de vous et de touz
Crestiens, et nomeement du debat qu'est entre vous et
les Escoz, et dient que vous ne poez dedire la conisance
de li en ce cas mesmement pur ce que lour querele touche
crime de sacrilege. Et dient, sire, que a vous ne devient
aider les enformementz pur ce q'il n'estoient liverez a
l'apostoille au jour assignez a vous par sa somonce mais
bien après, et ce par une lettre santz aide de prove, et
dient que en cele lettre vous fondez vostre droit par
ancienetez qui contienent diverses fausetez et mensonges
abregez et vuedez par faitz contraires suantz de vos
ancestres et de vous, en descolorant[1] tout le remenant de
la lettre paront hom ne deit doner foi a tiele escripture,
et si dient il uncore que vous enforcez par tiel foundement
descovenable et deble fuir la conizance de vostre droit
juge et verité esteindre, et voz veisins qui sont plus
fieble de vous envoier par poer contre droit et pur
destorber que l'apostoille ne puisse pursuire l'examine-
ment de la busoigne avantdite. Et après, sire, il mous-
trent aucunes reisons que l'apostoille deit avant aler en

Text: B.M. MS Cotton Vespasian F VII, ff. 15-16 (C). Printed in
appendix to *Chronicon de Lanercost* (ed. Stevenson, 1839), pp. 517-21 (L).
The text is manifestly a report to Edward I of Scottish arguments against
no. 30, but it is not in letter form (having neither salutations, date, nor
place); and though the hand of C is contemporary, the precise nature of
the MS is not clear, and its relation to the mission of Thomas Wale (above,
p. 96, *n.*) can only be conjectured. It is obvious, however, that C has a close
relation to the 'instructions' of the Scots to their proctors at the curia,
printed in *Scotichronicon*, II, 192-210 (S), to which a few references are given
in the notes.

31

[A report to Edward I.]

SIR, seeing that you have lately sent a statement to the pope concerning your right to Scotland, the Scots are making efforts to nullify that statement by certain objections which are given below. They say first, sir, that the pope is the true judge of you and of all Christian people, and expressly so in the dispute which there is between you and the Scots, and they say that you cannot deny his cognizance of it in this affair above all, because their complaint touches upon the crime of sacrilege. And they say, sir, that the statement cannot be of any help to you because it was not delivered to the pope by the day assigned to you by his summons, but well after, and then in a letter with no proofs in support; and they say that in that letter you ground your right on old chronicles, which contain various falsehoods and lies, and are abrogated and made void by the subsequent contrary actions of your predecessors and of yourself, which vitiate [1] all the remaining part of your letter, and therefore one should give no credence to such a document. And they say further, that with only this unworthy and feeble case to rely upon, you are striving to evade the cognizance of your true judge, and to suppress the truth, and unlawfully, by force of arms, to repel your weaker neighbours, and to prevent the pope from pursuing the examination of this case. After that, sir, they put forward certain reasons why the pope ought to proceed in the case

---

[1] cf. Ducange, *Glossarium*, *s.vv.* ' colorare ', ' colloratio '.

la dite busoigne entre vous et eux laquele il ad repelee et
rescruz [1] a li, noncontrestant vos enformementz avantdites, et conustre et juger, si come il dient, et que ende-
mentres il deit contredire a vous totes maneres de fetz
de gueres entre les parties et les roiaumes avantdites, et
s'aforcent de ce prover par cinq resons qui sont tieles :
Primerement dient que .². prince seculer ne deit
faire suggestion a .². lieutenant le Seint Espirit en
terre mais que de verité et [   ] [a] vostre suggestion
contient le contraire, si come il dient, endroit de ce que
vous escreites a l'apostoille que au temps de vos lettres
tramis vous estoiez en pleniere possession de tot le
roiaume d'Escoce, de sy come il i ont douze cités, sees
des .². evesques, des queux citez ou diocises vous n'aviez
possessioun entiere, mais soulement aucuns lieux en les
eveschés de seint Andreu et de Glasgu, et par tiel con-
traireté, si come il dient, corumpu est tout liel [3] de
vostre suggestion qui n'est creable.

Derechief [b] il dient qu'il ne fait mie acrere al tesmoignance de vostre dit par vos nues lettres, de si come
vous estes partie et soul, et nient jurez et mesment en
prejudice d'autri. Derechief [b] au terme assis a vous par
l'apostoille vous naviez cure pur moustrer vostre droit,
ne prover, paront vous ne devez mes estre oy sur ce.
Derechief [b] nul n'est covenable tesmoign et juge en sa
cause demeine, de queu digneté q'il soit, et vous efforcez
vostre droit demeisne tesmoigner. Derechief [b] dient il
que les auncienetez que vous amenez pur vostre droit ne

---

[a] *Illegible; probably a word deleted by the writer.*
[b] derechief *preceded each time by a paragraph mark in* C.
[1] The exact meaning of this word is uncertain.

between you and them, which he has recalled and
[reserved ?] [1] to himself, notwithstanding your aforesaid statement, and to take cognizance of and judge
it, as they allege, and they say that in the meantime
he should forbid you to take any kind of warlike action
in the dispute between the parties and kingdoms; and
this they endeavour to prove by the following five arguments :

First, they say that [2] a secular ruler should not make
any submission which is not a true one to the [2] vice-
gerent of the Holy Spirit on earth, and that your submission contains something contrary to truth, as they
say, because you wrote to the pope that at the time of
sending your letters you were in full possession of all the
realm of Scotland, whereas there are twelve cities, the
sees of [2] bishops, of which cities or dioceses you did not
have entire possession, but only of some places in the
dioceses of St Andrews and of Glasgow. By such a mis-
statement, they say, the whole [argument ?] [3] of your
submission is destroyed, and it cannot be credited.

Again, they say that by your letter alone, nothing can
be added to the authority of your statement, since you
are a party to the case, and unsupported, and in no way
under oath, and, above all, you are acting to the prejudice of another. Again, at the term assigned to you by
the pope you took no care to demonstrate your right, or
to prove it, wherefore you should not be given a hearing
at all in this case. Again, nobody is a suitable witness
and judge in his own case, however great be his degree,
and you are attempting to bear witness to your own right.
Again, they say that the old chronicles that you use as

---

[2] On the *gemipunctus* see above, p. 17 ; this seems to be a curious case
of the ' honorific ' use (cf. repetitions later in text).

[3] This unidentified word is probably corrupt.

vous poent aider, ja feussent il provez si come il ne sont
mie, a ce quil dient, pur ce que par autres gestes ensuantz
plus forcibles, et covenances et faitz contraires, et privileges d'apostoilles a meisme celes ancienetez est de-
rogez et destret de tout en tout notoirement. Et pur
ce sire, si come il dient, en vostre lettre enveiez au . . pape
vous ne fetes mencion de lour resons les queles le . . pape
vous escrit en sa bulle, mais les dissimulez par sourdz
orailles come non oyes sanz respons faire, par quoi il
piert que vostre lettre et vostre entencion au . . pape
envoicz devient estre reboutez et les auncienetez escrites
et meisme la vostre lettre n'ount force ne effect a fuir la
jurisdiccion le pape, ne a destorber son procés en la
busoigne d'Escoce avantdite. Et dient, sire, que ne vous
deit valer ce que fait est nadgueres vudant le roiaume
d'Escoce, et ausi par la vudance de l'eglise de Rome,[1] a
qui apent la seignurie de meisme le roiaume ne ne deit
nure a lour frank estat q'il ont avant eu, ne destorber
procés en la court de Rome en la cause entre vous et eux,
pur ce que quantque donques fust fait estoit fait par
oppressions, par poour et force, tant come le roiaume
estoit sanz deffendur, sur queux choses il offrent de faire
prove et pleinere foi devant le . . pape, et dient que
cestes choses sont publiques et notoires. Et aprés, sire,
que foi ne soit doné as gestes, estoires et faitz contenuz en
voz enfourmementz, il dient que tieux choses[2] sont
contez en voz enformementz, la verité tue,[2] et s'enforcent

---

[1] The Holy See was vacant from April 1292 to July 1294, but this is
hardly relevant, since the Scots had admitted Edward's overlordship as
early as June 1291 (above, pp. 56–7). Note, however, that (a) there was
no pope at the date of the decision in favour of Balliol in November 1292
(above, p. 61), (b) Nicholas IV had on 1 March 1292 refused to confirm
'submissionem in [Edwardum regem] factam' by the Competitors—referring

evidence of your right could not assist you, even if they were authenticated, as is not the case, they say, because it is notorious that these same old chronicles are utterly made naught and of no avail by other subsequent documents of greater significance, by contrary agreements and actions, and by papal privileges. For this reason, sir, as they say, in your letter to the pope you make no mention of their arguments of which the pope wrote to you in his bull, but ignore them with deaf ears as if unheard, and make no reply, from which it appears that your letter and your assertion sent to the pope can be refuted, and the old chronicles and your letter already mentioned have no force or effect in escaping the jurisdiction of the pope, or in disturbing his process in the matter of Scotland. And they say, sir, that you can gain no profit from what was done of late, during the interregnum in the realm of Scotland, and also by reason of the vacancy in the Roman church,[1] to which belongs the lordship of the realm, nor should it injure their free status which they have had hitherto, nor disturb the process in the court of Rome in the cause between you and them ; because whatever was done then, was done by oppression, violence, and force, inasmuch as the realm was without defender. Of these things they offer to give proof and full assurance before the pope, and they say that these matters are public and notorious. Then, sir, in order that credence be not given to the documents, histories, and deeds described in your statement, they say that allegations like those [2] recounted in your narrative are put out of court [2] by the true facts,

---

probably to pp. 56-7 above (Potthast 23934 ;   *Cal. Papal Letters*, I, 557, completely perverts the sense).

[2] to [2] ' La verité tue ' is taken as an ablative absolute, ' tue ' being the past participle of ' taire '.

moustrer par estoires et gestes contraires leur entendement, c'est assavoir que Brut entre ses treis filz devisa
l'isle jadis appelé Bretaine, ore Engl[eterre], a l'un dona
il Logres, a l'autre Gales, au tiertz Escoce ore nomez, et
les fist piers issint que nul ne fust a autre souzmis ne
sugiet; et aprés vint une femme, Scocia par noun, fille
Pharaon de Egipte, que vint par Espaine et occupa
Irland, et aprés conquesta la terre d'Albanie, laquele ele
fist apeler aprés son noun Escoce, et un lieu en meisme la
terre fist elle apeler aprés les nouns de son filz Erk et de
son baron Gayl, par quoi icele terre fist apeler Ergaill, et
achaceront les Bretons, et de cel temps les Escotz come
gentz noveux et de novel noun ne communerent ove les
Bretons mais les pursuirent touz jours come lour enemis,
et se menerent par diverses lieux et coustumes et par
diverse lange.   Et aprés s'acompaignerent a les Pictes,
par la force des queux il destrurent les Britons et la terre
qu'est ore apelee Engleterre, paront les Britons donerent
trieuage a Romeins pur aver aide de l'emperour de Rome,
qi out [a] noun Sever, contre les Escotz, par aide de qui
les Britons fesoient un mur entre eux et les Escotz a la
longure [1] de cent et trente lieux de longure [1] de l'une
mer jesques a l'autre, et par ce dient que piert que
Escoce n'estoit en nul temps en la seigneurie de Britons,
mais il ne nient point que le roi Arthour par poer ne
conquesta Denemarche, France, Norweye et ausi Escoce,
et les tint a temps jesques a tant que li et Mordrik
estoient ocis en bataille, et de cele houre retorna le
roiaume d'Escoce a son frank estat.   Et dient que les

---

[a] ont CL

[1] The second 'longure' is redundant.   The actual length of Hadrian's
wall was 73½ English (80 Roman) miles.

and they endeavour to demonstrate their assertion by chronicles and narratives of a contrary purport. Brutus divided between his three sons the island once called Britain, and now England, and gave to one son Loegria, to another Wales, and to the third what is now called Scotland, and made them peers, so that none of them was subject to another. Afterwards came a woman named Scota, daughter of Pharaoh of Egypt, who came via Spain and occupied Ireland, and afterwards conquered the land of Albany, which she had called, after her name, *Scotland*, and one place in that land she had called after the names of her son Erk and her husband Gayl, wherefore that district was called *Ergaill* [Argyll], and they drove out the Britons, and from that time the Scots, as a new race and possessing a new name, had nothing to do with the Britons, but pursued them daily as their enemies, and were distinguished from them by different ranks and customs, and by a different language. Afterwards they joined company with the Picts, by whose strength they destroyed the Britons, and the land which is now called England, and for this reason the Britons gave tribute to the Romans, to obtain the help of the Roman emperor, whose name was Severus, against the Scots, and by his help the Britons made a wall between themselves and the Scots, having a length [1] of 130 leagues in length [1] from one sea to the other, and they say that by this it appears that Scotland was not at any time under the lordship of the Britons. But they do not deny that King Arthur by his prowess conquered Denmark, France, Norway and also Scotland, and held them until he and Mordred were slain in battle, and from that time the realm of Scotland returned to its free status. They say that the Britons were then expelled by the

Britons puis furent en getetz par les Saxoneis, et puis les
Saxoneis par les Danois, et puis les Danois par les
Saxoneis, et que a touz temps des rois des Saxons
demorerent les Escotz franks santz estre sugietz a eux, et
en cel temps par les reliques de seint Andreu qui vindrent
de Grece se converterent a la foy, cinq cens aunz avant
que les Engleis esteient Crestiens, et de cel temps le
roiaume d'Escoce, ovesque le roi et le roiaume, estoient
de la seigneurie l'eglise de Rome sanz meen, et par li
furent deffenduz contre touz ses nusantz; et mettent
autres resons pur eux come de seint Aydan et de seint
Columb, seintz d'Escoce, qi converterent les contez de
Combr[eland] Norhumbr[eland] et de Westmerland, qui
donque appartenoient au roi d'Escoce, et dient que un
Gregoire le fuiz Dugad, roi d'Escoce, conquist tot Engleterre et la mist en subjeccion.   Et al miracle que vous
escrivez [1] de seint Johan de Beverlé, dient que rien ne
prove, pur ce que hom ne set si sun dit vint par revelacion
del bon espirit, ou par la deseite del mauveis espirit.   Et
si nient il quantque vous dites orendroit de la subjeccion
d'Escoce en temps des Saxoneis.   Et dient que tout feust
ensint come vous contez en vos lettres, nequedent par
faitz suantz contraires tot est anienty et defait.   Vostre
conte uncore, sire, content du darrein temps des rois
d'Engleterre Normans, et dient pur voir que nul roi
d'Escoce pur le roiaume d'Escoce ne fist unques subjeccion.   Et si aucun fist, ce fu pur aucunes terres que li
roi d'Escoce tint en Engleterre.   Et puis respont a les
faitz de Dovenald et de Donecan, si dient que le roi
d'Engleterre remist meisme celi Donecan en le roiaume

---

[1] See above, p. 99.

Saxons, and then the Saxons by the Danes, and then the
Danes by the Saxons, and that in the whole period of
the Saxon kings the Scots remained free without being
subject to them, and at that time, by the relics of St
Andrew which came from Greece, they were converted
to the faith 500 years before the English became Chris-
tians, and from that time the realm of Scotland, with the
king and the realm (*sic*), were under the lordship of the
Roman church without any intermediary, and by it were
they defended against all their enemies. They set forth
other arguments on their behalf, for example mentioning
St Aidan and St Columba, the Scottish saints, who converted the counties of Cumberland, Northumberland and
Westmorland, which then belonged to the king of Scotland, and they say that a certain Gregory, son of Dugald,
king of Scotland, conquered the whole of England and
reduced it to subjection. As for the miracle which you
recount [1] of St John of Beverley, they say that it proves
nothing, because nobody knows whether his words came
by revelation of a good spirit, or by the fraud of an evil
spirit. So they deny whatever you say at this point about
the subjection of Scotland in the time of the Saxons.
And they say that even if everything had been as you
assert in your letter, nevertheless it has all been annulled
and undone by subsequent actions which imply the
contrary. Your narrative, sir, includes the last period of
the Norman kings of England, and the Scots say for
certain that no king of Scotland ever made himself
subject for the realm of Scotland. And if any did make
himself subject, it was for certain lands that the king of
Scotland held in England. Then, replying about the
acts of Donald and Duncan, they say that the king of
England returned Duncan to the realm of Scotland and

d'Escoce et en jetta Dovenald non pas come soverein seigneur d'Escoce, mais come amy et affyn, et celi roy qui avoit esposé Mayraut la seur le dit Donecan,[1] et dient que David frere Donecan, ne Henri son filz, ne firent mie homages au roi d'Engleterre pur le roiaume d'Escoce, mais pur le contez de Huntindon' et meisme celi David, qui tint en cel temps les contez de Cumbr[eland] Westmerl[and] et Norhumbr[eland] se fesoit aporter de plus loinz [2] temps d'Escoce pur estre enterré a Cardoill [3] en tesmoignance de sa seigneurie, et ce que William roi d'Escoce, neveu du dit David, fesoit ne deit neure ne avoir fermeté de droit, par ce q'il les fist par poour et par force de prison.[4] Et outre ce, touz ses faitz estoient anientiz par autres faitz contraires suantz, car le roi d'Engleterre, Richard, totes les obligacions et les promesses faites a meisme celi William contre le frank estat le roiaume d'Escoce releissa pleinement,[5] et ce piert par ce que Alex[andre], filz meisme celi William, qui regna en Escoce cinquante [6] aunz ne fist homage ne feauté au roi d'Engleterre de tout son temps.[7] Et Alexandre, le darrein roy d'Escoce,[8] en fesant homage a vous, fist protestacion qu'il le fist pur les terres de Tyndale et de Penrithe qui sont en Engl[eterre], et ensint vous receutes son homage, et non pas pur le roiaume d'Escoce.[9] Et dient que ausi come il le fist, si deist homme entendre que les autres rois devant li firent homages en meisme la manere. Et pur ce, sire, respoinent il a les bulles d'apostoilles que selonc les deversetez des

---

[1] Henry I of England, who married Maud, is here confused with William II, who assisted Duncan. The same error occurs in S, p. 200.
[2] Corruption likely here; omit *temps*, as rendered in translation?
[3] An error; David I *died* at Carlisle, and was buried at Dunfermline.
[4] Refers to treaty on pp. 1-5 above.
[5] Pp. 6-8 above
[6] Alexander II in fact reigned for only 34½ years; S, p. 204, says 36.

expelled Donald, acting not as lord superior of Scotland, but as a friend and relative, and as the king who had married Maud, sister of Duncan,[1] and they say that neither David, brother of Duncan, nor Henry, his son, ever did homage to the king of England for the realm of Scotland, but only for the county of Huntingdon, and that David, who at that time held the counties of Cumberland, Westmorland, and Northumberland, directed that he should be brought from afar,[2] from Scotland, to be buried at Carlisle,[3] as evidence of his lordship ; and that what William, king of Scotland, kinsman of the said David did, ought not to cause prejudice or have the force of law, because he did these things by coercion, and while he was in prison.[4]   Furthermore, all of these deeds were annulled by other subsequent acts of contrary significance, for Richard, king of England, made a full release [5] of all obligations and promises made by William contrary to the free status of the realm of Scotland, and this is apparent because Alexander, son of that William, who reigned in Scotland for fifty years,[6] did no homage or fealty to the king of England in the whole of his reign.[7] Alexander, the last king of Scotland,[8] when he did homage to you, protested that he was doing it for the lands of Tynedale and of Penrith, which are in England, and so it was that you received his homage, and not for the realm of Scotland.[9]   And they say that it must be understood that the other kings before him did homage in the same manner as he did his.   Therefore, sir, their reply, as far as the papal bulls are concerned, is that

---

[7] Not strictly true (cf. Bain, I, no. 686, and above, p. 24).   S, p. 204, more guardedly says that homage was not done ' pro regno Scotiae '.

[8] Balliol is ignored altogether.   This is curious for an English writer, but the Scots regarded Balliol not as ' the last ' king, but as the present one.

[9] See pp. 38-41 above.

temps avanditz deist homme entendre les mandementz
d'apostoilles, c'est assavoir le mandement du pape
Gregoire le neuf et del pape Honoire tierz [1] et des autres,
que sont grantees par les suggestions des rois d'Engleterre et noun pas selonc la verité du fait, ne par examine-
ment, et dient que la composicion faite en le temps le dit
William ne se fist unques en nul de ses pointz,[2] et que
vous les munimentz et les escritz et les cronicles qu'il
avoient en Escoce vous [sic] les avez aportez a force, pur
tolir defens a eux et prove de lour verité.

Sire, finalment il s'en forcent de prover en cinq
maneres que le roiaume d'Escoce est franq en sey et
nient sugeit a vous, c'est assavoir par privilege d'apostoille, par droit commun, par prescripcion, par franq
estat en touz jours, par munementz et escriptz, lesqueles
il porront prover, si come il dient, et dient par eux que
le pape Honoire granta au royaume d'Escoce qu'il ne
fuissent tret par devant juges aliens sur terres ne possessions, sauve en cause d'apels faitz a la court de Rome, et
par ce vuillent il dire que le roiaume d'Escoce est sugget
a l'eglise de Rome sanz meen.[3]   Et si piert il par fait, a
ce qu'il dient, que le contez de Monetez fu mis en play
devant juges donez par l'apostoille contre le roi d'Escoce.[4]
Et Innocent le quart ne vout granter la supplicacion le
roy d'Engleterre qu'il le fist de ce que le roy d'Escoce ne
se porroit faire coroner ne enoyndre sanz li, ne ne li
voleit granter disme en Escoce, par acheison de ce que le
pape ne soleit granter disme d'autri roiaume a autri

---

[1] Edward's letter had mentioned bulls of Gregory IX (above, pp. 17-
18) but not of Honorius III.   The allusion here may be to an unidentified
bull cited in the ' Great Rolls ' (Rymer, I, ii, 771), or to the bull of 17 January 1217 (Theiner, no. iv).
[2] See above, pp. 1-5, and p. xxi, n. 1.
[3] Above, pp. 14-16

apostolic mandates must be interpreted according to the circumstances of the times, that is to say, the mandate of Gregory IX, and that of Honorius III,[1] and the other mandates, were granted at the instance of the kings of England, and not in the light of the true facts of the matter, nor after examination, and they say that the agreement made in the time of William [the Lion] was never put into practice, in any of its provisions,[2] and that you have removed by force the muniments and writings and chronicles that they had in Scotland, in order to deprive them of defence and of evidence of the truth.

Finally, sir, they endeavour to prove in five ways that the realm of Scotland is free in itself and in no wise subject to you : by papal privilege, by common law, by prescription, by its free status at all times, and by muniments and writings which, so they claim, they can prove authentic, and they say, on the strength of these, that Pope Honorius granted to the realm of Scotland that its inhabitants should not be summoned before alien judges in matters relating to lands or property, except on the occasion of appeals made to the court of Rome, and by this they wish to assert that the realm of Scotland is subject to the Roman church without intermediary.[3] And this is apparent, they say, because the earl of Menteith was impleaded, on appeal from the king of Scotland, before judges appointed by the pope.[4] Innocent IV would not grant the plea which the king of England made, that the king of Scotland might not have himself crowned or anointed without English permission, nor would he grant the king of England a tenth in Scotland because, he said, the pope was not wont to grant a tenth

---

[4] See *Complete Peerage*, VIII (1932), 661. S, p. 212, shows that the countess, not the earl, should be referred to. Possibly ' le countez ' means ' the earldom '.

T

royaume.[1] Et puis, sire, passent il en recordant courte-
ment les resons contenuz en la bulle liveree a vous par
. . l'ercevesque de Canterbir[ie] sur le fait d'Escoce.[2] Et
dient a ce que par celes reisones et autres piert que le
roiaume d'Escoce n'est pas sugiet a vous, mais est de la
seigneurie de l'eglise de Rome sanz meen. Et que s'il
firent arzons et homicides en vostre terre, vous lour
donastes acheison, car vous entrastes en lour terre
primierement [3] et feistes destruccions des bourgs et des
villes et des gentz santz nombre, et sacrilege notoire, et
prient que, si come l'apostoille ad totes choses repelees
a sa conizance, qu'il voille la busoigne examiner et faire
dreit entre vous et eux, et qu'il entredie a vous ende-
mentres totes maneres de faitz de guerre.

levied in one realm to another.[1] Then, sir, they proceed
to a brief account of the arguments contained in the bull
delivered to you by the archbishop of Canterbury on the
matter of Scotland.[2] And they say of this, that from
those arguments and others, it appears that the realm of
Scotland is not subject to you, but is under the lordship of
the church of Rome without intermediary. And if they
committed acts of arson and homicide in your land, you
gave them occasion, because you first entered their land,[3]
and wrought destruction of towns and villages, and of
people without number, and committed notorious sacrilege. They pray that since the pope has recalled this
whole question to his own cognizance, he will see fit to
examine the matter, and to do justice between you and
them, and that in the meantime he will inhibit you from
committing any manner of warlike act.

[1] Above, p. 29
[2] Above, pp. 81-7
[3] In fact the Scots invaded England in 1296, a few days before Edward
invaded Scotland (Ramsay, *Dawn of the Constitution*, pp. 424-5), but possibly
there is a reference to the allegation on p. 71 above.

32

FAIT [1] a remembrer que [si co]me [sire Ro]bert de Brus
le filz,[2] qui feut en l'omage e en la foy le roi d'Engleterre
de la / contee de Carrik, [se] le[va en] g[uer]re contre le
dit roi son [seig]neur par mauveis conseil, e il se soit
rendu a la / pees e a la volunté de [meisme * le ro]y en
esperance de sa bone grace, le dit roi pur les bons
services que les auncestres / e le lignage le dit Robe[rt
ount * fet * a]u roy e a ses auncestres, e pur le bon servise
que meisme celi Robert ad promis a faire / en temps a
venir, [a d]esclarz . . . . sa volunté e sa grace en
ceste manere. C'est assavoir que sauvez soient au dit
Robert / e a ses hommes e a ses te[nants de] Carrik vie
e membre, terres e tenementz, e qu'il soient quites
d'enprisonement. / E s'il avenoit que par l'ordenan[ce
d']apostoi[lle ou * par *] true, ou par pees taillee quant
a la guerre d'Escoce ou de France / le susdit Robert
feu[st grevé *] si [qu'il * n]e peust joir ses propres terres
dont il est ore seise en Escoce, le dit roi promet / d'avoir
rega[rd] a s[a perte,* si *] qu'il eit renable [3] sustenance,
come affiert a li. E le roy, tant come en li est, / grante
au dit Robert qu'il ne soit desheritez de nule terre que li
porra escheir par droit de par son peere, en Engleterre / ne
en Escoce. E le r[oi grante *] a meisme celi Robert la
garde e le mariage du filz e heir le conte de Mar.[4] / E pur

Text : P.R.O. Duchy of Lancaster, Cartae Miscellaneae (D.L. 36), I, f. 1.
This appears to be the original privy seal letter, which must have passed
into the Duchy records from the Bruce family muniments. Printed, with
commentary and notes, by E. L. G. Stones, in *SHR*, XXXIV (1955), 122-34.
Not calendared by Bain. MS is badly damaged ; for the symbols used
here in transcription see above, pp. xli-xlii.

[1] Bruce ' the younger ' (the future king) had been in rebellion since
1297. The present document, which probably dates from late in 1301 or

32

NOTE [1] that because Robert Bruce the younger,[2] who was in the homage and allegiance of the king of England for the earldom of Carrick, but, because of evil advice, rose up in war against the king his lord, has surrendered himself to the peace and the will of the king, in hope of receiving his mercy, the king, because of the good services done to the king, and his ancestors, by the ancestors and the kin of Robert, and because of the good service that Robert has promised to do in time to come, has declared . . . . his will and his grace in the following manner, that is to say : Robert, and his vassals, and his tenants in Carrick, shall be unharmed in life and limb, and in lands and tenements, and free from imprisonment. If it should happen that by a papal ordinance, or a truce, or a peace declared in the war with Scotland or with France, the aforesaid Robert were so hindered that he could not enjoy his own estates, of which he is now seised in Scotland, the king promises to take his loss into account, so that he may have a reasonable [3] income, as is appropriate to him. The king, so far as in him lies, grants to Robert that he be not disinherited of any land which may come to him by right of his father, in England or in Scotland. The king grants to Robert the wardship and marriage of the son and heir of the earl of Mar.[4] Because [Robert ? fears that the ?]

---

early in 1302, marks his return to the allegiance of Edward. From now until 1306 he held a position of considerable trust in Edward's counsels (cf. p. 120 below). For discussion see *SHR*, loc. cit. ; and cf. above, p. xxix.

[2] On the various Robert Bruces see above, p. 49, *n.* 1.

[3] More commonly spelt *raisnable* (from *rationabile*).

[4] Earl Gratney (Bruce's brother-in-law) died between 1297 and 1305, leaving a young son.

ce que le dit . . . . e roiaume d'Escoce porroit estre esloignez hors de la mein le roy, que Dieu deffende, / e liverez a monsieur Joha[n de * Baillol * ou *] a son filz,¹ ou que le droit porroit estre mis en debat, ou reversé e repelez en novel / jugement, le roi . . . . grante au dit Robert qu'il peusse suire son droit,² e le orra bonement e le tendra / a droit [en] sa co[urt; e si par au]cune avienture avenoit que le droit deust estre trié aillors que en la court le / roy, en celi cas le roi prom[et au dit] Robert aide e consail si avant come il porra en bone manere. E si, aprés ce que le / roiaume d'Escoce soit peisibl[ement e]n la mein le dit roy, aucunes gentz vousissent grever le susdit Robert par / . . . . ou a . . . . a de . . . . [r]oi le meintendra en son droit, e le deffendra tant avant come seigneur / devra son homme. E en [tesmoignance de] totes ces choses le dit roi ad fait faire cest escrit overt, sealé de / son privé seal.

---

¹ John Balliol had been in exile in France since 1299. We know from other sources that there was some fear in England, late in 1301, that Balliol would return to Scotland with French support (*SHR*, xxxiv, 130-1). His son was Edward, who revived the Balliol claim to the Scottish throne in 1332.

² At first sight it may appear that Edward is here agreeing to support a claim by Bruce to the Scottish throne. This, however, is not only improbable in the circumstances, but out of keeping with the whole trend of the document, which is to guarantee Bruce against the loss of what he holds, or may reasonably expect to inherit in the normal course of events. In the present sentence it will be noted that a rediscussion of ' le droit ' is for Robert an unpleasant prospect, equivalent to the return of Balliol to Scotland, and not an opportunity for gain. Further, the assumption of Edward is that Scotland will return peaceably into his own hands (line 12). There are certainly obscurities about the agreement, but Bruce's concern is for his estates, and those which he hopes to inherit from his father. For the clause ' aillors . . . roy ' (line 9), note the very interesting parallel below, in a charter issued later by Bruce himself (p. 171, line 18). I have discussed this matter with Sir Maurice Powicke, who concurs with the above view.

realm of Scotland might be removed from the hands of
the king, which God forbid, and delivered to John
Balliol, or to his son,[1] or that the right might be put in
question, or reversed and repealed in a new judgment,
the king . . . . grants to Robert that he may
pursue his right,[2] and he will give him a fair hearing,
and treat him justly in his court; and if by any chance it
happen that the right ought to be tried elsewhere than in
the king's court, in that case the king promises help and
advice to Robert, so far as he can properly give it. If,
after the realm of Scotland is at peace in the hands of the
king, any persons wish to vex Robert by . . . . the
king will support him in his right and defend him, so
far as a lord should do his vassal. As evidence of all
these things, the king has caused this letter patent to
be written, and sealed with his privy seal.

33

Ordinacio facta per dominum regem super stabilitate
terre Scocie.[a]

FAIT [1] a remembrer que, come nostre seigneur le roy de [b]
son parlement qu'il tynt a Westmoster en quarreme l'an
de son regne trentisme tierz eust fait asavoir par l'evesque
de Gla[s]gu, le counte de Carrik, monsire Johan de
Segrave adunques tenant le lieu le roy en Loeneis, et par
sire Johan de Sandale chamberleyn d'Escoce, a les bones
gentz [2] de la terre d'Escoce qu'il feisent assembler la
communalté de la terre, et que entre eux toutz eleusent
certeyn noumbre de gentz pur venir de par meisme la
communalté a Westmuster au parlement que nostre
seigneur le roy avoit ordené a tenir a treis semaynes
aprés la feste de la Nativité seynt Johan le Baptiste
procheyn suant, lequel parlement fust esloignez tantque
a la feste de l'Assumpcion de Nostre Dame par maunde-
ment de nostre seigneur le roy, et puis tantque as ustaves
de la feste de la Nativité Nostre Dame procheinement
suant; asquelx lieu et terme les evesques de seint Andreu
et de Dunkeldyn, l'abbé de Coupre et l'abbé de Meuros,
le counte de Boghan, monsire Johan de Mubray, monsire
Robert de Keth, monsire Adam de Gurdon, monsire
Johan de Inchemartyn vyndrent come ceux qui feurent
esleux et enveez de par la communalté de la dite terre
d'Escoce.   Et le counte Patrik qui fust esleu d'avoir

Text: P.R.O. Close Roll 33 Edward I (C 54/122), m. 13 d, *schedule* (C),
whence *APS*, I, 119-23 [red]; Prynne, pp. 1053-6; *Parliamentary Writs*, I,
160-3; *Rotuli Parliamentorum*, I, 267-9.

   [a] *Title from* C   [b] *read* en ?

33

An ordinance made by the king for the good order of Scotland.

NOTE [1] that our lord the king, in his parliament which he held at Westminster, in Lent, in the thirty-third year of his reign [1305], made it known, through the bishop of Glasgow, the earl of Carrick, John Segrave, then lieutenant of the king in Lothian, and John de Sandale, chamberlain of Scotland, to the good people [2] of the realm of Scotland that they should cause the community of the realm to assemble, and that in concert they should elect a certain number of persons to come, on behalf of the community, to the parliament at Westminster, which our lord the king had ordained to be held three weeks after the ensuing feast of St John Baptist [15 July 1305], which parliament was postponed until the feast of the Assumption of Our Lady [15 August 1305] by order of our lord the king, and then until the octave of the ensuing feast of the Nativity of Our Lady [15 September 1305]; and to that place and at that time came the bishops of St Andrews and of Dunkeld, the abbot of Cupar and the abbot of Melrose, the earl of Buchan, John Mowbray, Robert Keith, Adam Gordon, and John of Inchmartin, being those who were chosen and sent by the community of the realm of Scotland. Earl Patrick,

---

[1] This ordinance, which was prepared after twenty days of debate (see narrative in *Flores Historiarum* (RS), III, 124-5), appeared to offer the hope of lasting peace in Scotland. In fact it was made a dead letter by Bruce's murder of Comyn five months later. See Powicke, *Thirteenth Century*, pp. 712-13; Barrow, *Feudal Britain*, pp. 404-5; Dickinson, *Scotland*, p. 161; and cf. above, p. xxix.

[2] *Bones gentz*: cf. above, p. 53, *n.* 2.

este [a] le dissisme de venir de par meisme la communalté,
n'y vint mye, parquei par le commaundement nostre
seigneur le roy y fust assignez monsire Johan de Meneteth. E pur treiter des bosoignes d'Escoce ensemblement ove les gentz d'Escoce avant nomez feurent assignez
ascunes gentz d'Engleterre, dunt les nouns sont cy desuth,
e eux tutz, ausi bien les Engleis come les Escotz qui
feurent presentz au treitiz de celes bosoignes, et chescun
de eux severaument, par commaundement nostre seigneur le roy, feurent sermentez solonc le purport des
articles desouz escritz :

L'evesque de Cestre [1]	Monsire William Martyn
L'evesque de Wirecestre	Monsire Roger Brabazun [2]
L'abbé de Westmuster	Sire Rauf ' de Hengham [2]
L'abbé de Waverlé	Monsire William de Bereford [2]
Le counte de Nicole	Monsire Roger de Heghham
Le counte de Hereford	Monsire Johan de l'Isle
Monsire Hugh le Despenser	Mestre Philipe Martel [3]
Monsire Henry de Percy	Mestre Reynaud de Brandon
Monsire Johan de Hastingg	Frere Hugh de Mamecestre [4]
(mes il n'y poeit venir	
pur la maladie)	Sire Johan de Benstede [2]
Monsire Johan Boteturt	Sire Johan de Sandale

Et endroit des dites bosoignes entre ceux d'Engleterre et d'Escoce avantnomez, primerement treitié est sur
le governement de la terre d'Escoce. Et quant a mettre
gardein de la terre acordé est que monsire Johan de

---

[a] ester C

[1] More accurately, ' bishop of Coventry and Lichfield ' ; but this shorter
name was often used.

[2] Judges of the king's bench or the common pleas in England.

who was chosen as the tenth to come on behalf of the community, made no appearance, wherefore, by command of our lord the king, John of Menteith was assigned in his place. To treat of the business of Scotland, together with the aforesaid representatives of Scotland, there were assigned certain Englishmen whose names are given below, and all of them, both English and Scots, who were present at this discussion, and each of them severally, by command of our lord the king, were sworn according to the content of the articles written below:

The bishop of Chester [1]	William Martyn
The bishop of Worcester	Roger Brabazon [2]
The abbot of Westminster	Ralph de Hengham [2]
The abbot of Waverley	William de Bereford [2]
The earl of Lincoln	Roger de Heghham
The earl of Hereford	John Delisle
Hugh Despenser	Master Philip Martel [3]
Henry Percy	Master Reginald of Brandon
John Hastings	Brother Hugh of Manchester [4]
(who was too ill to come)	John de Benstede [2]
John Boteturt	John de Sandale

As regards the business discussed between the delegates of England and of Scotland who have been mentioned above, the first thing considered was the government of the realm of Scotland. And in the matter of setting a warden over the country, it was agreed that

---

[3] Martel was *custos processuum* (Cuttino, *English Diplomatic Administration*, pp. 22 ff.). ' Master ' = Master of Arts.
[4] On Brother Hugh see *Fritz Saxl 1890–1948*, ed. D. J. Gordon (1957), pp. 121-2.

Bretaine soit leutenant le roy en Escoce et gardeyn de la terre.

Item endroit de l'estat du chaunceller acordé est que sire William de Bevercotes demoerge chaunceller d'Escoce. Item que sire Johan de Sandale demoerge chamberlein d'Escoce, et que un contreroullur [1] soit assigné a li, c'est a savoir sire Robert Heron.

Puis est treitez et acordez de mettre quatre poire des justices en la terre d'Escoce, et pur ce que les choses soient mesnees de meillur array et plus a honur et au profit de nostre seigneur le roy et a l'aisement du poeple, est assentu que en Loeneys soient deux justices, c'est a savoir monsire Johan de l'Isle et monsire Adam de Gurdon; en Gaway monsire Roger de Kirkpatrik et monsire Wauter de Burghdon. Et pur les terres dela la mer d'Escoce, c'est a savoir entre la rivere de Forth et les montz,[2] monsire Robert de Keth et monsire William Inge. Et pur les terres dela les montz monsire Reynaud le chien et monsire Johan de Vaux du counté de Nor-thumbr'.[3]

Item, acordé est que les viscuntes qui demorront en la terre seient gentz neez de la terre d'Escoce ou Engleis, et soient mys et remuez par le lieutenant le roy et par le chamberlein solonc lur descrecion, et ceux viscuntes facent l'office d'escheterie si come les viscuntes soleient faire et que ceux qui seront mys viscuntes soient les plus suffisauntz, les plus covenables et les plus profitables que homme purra trover pur le roy, pur le poeple, et pur la pees garder et meintenir. Et quant a ore ordené est de viscuntes en la manere que s'ensuit:

---

[1] Not an overseer, but an official who kept a duplicate roll of accounts.
[2] i.e. 'the Mounth', or Grampians.

John of Brittany should be the king's lieutenant in Scotland and warden of the country.

Further, as regards the position of chancellor, it was agreed that William de Bevercotes remain chancellor of Scotland, and also that John de Sandale remain chamberlain of Scotland, and that a controller[1] be assigned to him, namely Robert Heron.

Then agreement was reached to appoint four pairs of justiciars in the land of Scotland, and so that the matter should be organized in a better way, and to the greater credit and advantage of our lord the king, and the convenience of the people, it was agreed that in Lothian there be two justiciars, namely John Delisle and Adam Gordon; in Galloway Roger Kirkpatrick and Walter de Burghdon; in the lands beyond the Scottish sea, that is between the River Forth and the mountains, Robert Keith and William Inge; and in the lands beyond the mountains,[2] Reginald Cheyne and John de Vaux, of the county of Northumberland.[3]

Further, it was agreed that the sheriffs of the country shall be natives of Scotland, or of England, and shall be appointed and dismissed by the king's lieutenant, and by the chamberlain, at their discretion, and those sheriffs shall perform the office of escheator as sheriffs are accustomed to do, and those who are made sheriffs shall be the most capable, suitable, and efficient that can be found for the good of the king and the people, and for keeping and maintaining the peace. And for the moment the arrangements for sheriffs are as follows:

---

[3] The four major officials (lieutenant, chancellor, chamberlain, controller) are all Englishmen; but the pairs of justiciars each consist of an Englishman and a Scotsman; and the sheriffs named below seem, outside the crucial lowland area, to be mainly Scottish.

Que le chamberlein qui aura la garde du chastel de Berewyk mette desoutz luy tiel pur estre viscunte de Berewyk pur qui il voudra respondre. D'Edeneburgh, de Hadington, de Lynliscu : monsire Ive de Aldeburgh viscunt. De Pebbles : Robert Hastang, vallett, viscunt. De Selkirk : celi qui est de fee viscunt.[1] De Dunfres : monsire Richard Syward viscunt. De Wygeton : Thomas Makhulagh viscunt. De Are : monsire Godefroi de Ros viscunt. De Lanark : monsire Henri de Seynt Cler viscunt. De Dumbretan : monsire Johan de Meneteth viscunt et con[estable]. De Stryvelyn : William Biset viscunt et con[estable]. De Clacmanan, De Ughtreardour [2] : monsire Maucolom de Inverpeffré viscunt. De Kynros : celi qui est de fee viscunt. De Fyf : monsire Co[n]stantyn de Loghore viscunt. De Perth : monsire Johan de Inchemartin viscunt. De Forfare : William de Herth viscunt. De Kynkardyn : monsire Richard de Dummor' viscunt. De Aberden : monsire Norman de Lethelyn viscunt. De Banf' : monsire Wauter de Berkelé [3] viscunt. De Elgyn : William Wyseman viscunt. De Foreis et de Invernarn : Alex[andre] Wyseman viscunt. De Invernis : monsire Johan de Estrivelyn viscunt. De Crombathyn : monsire William de Mohaut, qi est de fee, viscunt.

Item, endroit de coroners, acordé est que le lieutenant le roy, le chauncell[er] et le chamberlein veent queux coroners sont en la terre suffisantz, et ceux qu'il troveront suffisantz demoergent en lur offices et ceux qui ne seront trovez suffisantz et neent chartrés du doun des offices soient ostez, et que le lieutenant le roy et le

---

[1] On this hereditary sheriffdom, and those mentioned below, see W. Croft Dickinson, *Sheriff Court Book of Fife*, p. xxxv.

The chamberlain who shall have custody of the castle of Berwick shall appoint under him such a person to be sheriff of Berwick as he shall be prepared to answer for. For Edinburgh, Haddington, Linlithgow, Ivo of Aldeburgh as sheriff. For Peebles, Robert Hastang, esquire, as sheriff. For Selkirk, he who is of fee as sheriff.[1] For Dumfries, Richard Siward as sheriff. For Wigtown, Thomas MacCulloch as sheriff. For Ayr, Godfrey de Ros as sheriff. For Lanark, Henry Sinclair as sheriff. For Dumbarton, John of Menteith as sheriff and constable. For Stirling, William Biset as sheriff and constable. For Clackmannan and Auchterarder,[2] Malcolm of Innerpeffray as sheriff. For Kinross, he who is of fee as sheriff. For Fife, Constantine of Lochore as sheriff. For Perth, John of Inchmartin as sheriff. For Forfar, William of Airth as sheriff. For Kincardine, Richard de Dummor as sheriff. For Aberdeen, Norman Leslie as sheriff. For Banff, Walter of Berkeley[3] as sheriff. For Elgin, William Wiseman as sheriff. For Forres and Invernairn, Alexander Wiseman as sheriff. For Inverness, John of Stirling as sheriff. For Cromarty, William of Mowat, who is of fee, as sheriff.

Further, as regards coroners, it is agreed that the lieutenant of the king, the chancellor, and the chamberlain shall ascertain which of the coroners in the land are satisfactory, and those whom they find satisfactory shall remain in their office, and those who are not satisfactory, and have no charters of gift of their office shall be removed, and that the king's lieutenant, and the chan-

---

[2] Dickinson (op. cit. p. 367) was in doubt about the interpretation of the text here, but C makes it clear that Clackmannan and Auchterarder are placed under Malcolm of Innerpeffray.

[3] The modern Scottish form is ' Barclay '.

chauncell[er] et le chamberlein solonc lur descrecion y mettent autres, Engleis ou gentz d'Escoce neez, qui soient suffisantz, meis les coroners qui ne seront trovez suffisantz, et eent chartres du doun des offices ne soient remuez tantque le lieutenant le roy, le chaunc[eller] et le chamberlein eient sur ce certifiez le roy, et qu'il en eit dit sa volunté. Et acordé est que le lieutenant le roy et le chaunc[eller] et le chamberlein avisent et certifient le roy a son procheyn parlement a treis semaynes de Pasch[e] de ceux coroners qui ne seront trovez suffisantz, ausi bien de ceux qui unt chartres, come des autres qui ne les unt.

Item, endroit de chasteux ordené est que le lieutenant le roy eit en sa main les chastelx de Rokesburgh et de Jeddeworth si come le roy ad ordené.

Item, que monsire Johan de Kingeston demoerge conestable et gardeyn du chastel de Edeneburgh.

Item, que Pier' Lubaud demoerge gardein de Linliscu si come le chamberlein li ad la garde baillee.

Item, que William Byset demoerge conestable et gardein du chastel d'Estryvelyn, et viscunte, et la garneison du chastel soit ordenee par le lieutenant le roy et par le chamberlein a lur premere venue en Escoce.

Item, que monsire Johan de Meneteth [1] demoerge conestable et gardein du chastel de Dumbretan, et viscunt, et la garneison de ceu chastel soit ordiné par le lieutenant le roy et par le chamberlein a lur procheine venue en Escoce.

Et fait a entendre que le lieutenant le roy et le chaunc[eller] et le chamberlein puissent, solonc lur

---

[1] The only Scotsman, apart from Bruce, to be given charge of a castle. He is well known for his part in the capture of Wallace, in this same year.

cellor and the chamberlain at their discretion, shall install others there, of English or Scottish race by birth, who are satisfactory. But the coroners who are not found satisfactory, and have charters of gift of their office, shall not be removed until the king's lieutenant, the chancellor, and the chamberlain have certified the king of this, and he has stated his will in the matter. And it is agreed that the king's lieutenant, the chancellor, and the chamberlain shall inform and certify the king at his next parliament, three weeks after Easter [24 April 1306] about those coroners who are not found satisfactory, as well those who have charters, as the others who have not.

Further, as regards castles, it is ordained that the king's lieutenant shall have possession of the castles of Roxburgh and Jedburgh, as the king has ordained.

Further, that John of Kingston remain constable and warden of the castle of Edinburgh.

Further, that Piers Lubaud remain warden of Linlithgow, as the chamberlain has granted the custody of it to him.

Further, that William Biset remain constable and warden of the castle of Stirling, and sheriff, and that the defence of the castle be ordained by the king's lieutenant and by the chamberlain, at their first coming into Scotland.

Further, that John of Menteith ¹ remain constable and warden of the castle of Dumbarton, and sheriff, and that the defence of the castle be ordained by the king's lieutenant and by the chamberlain, at their next coming into Scotland.

And it should be understood that the king's lieutenant, and the chancellor, and the chamberlain may at their

U

descrecion, remuer les justices et viscuntes avantnomez et mettre y autres, Engleis ou gentz neez d'Escoce, tielx come il verront qui soient suffisantz, tutes les foitz que lur plerra et si come il verront que meutz soit a l'honur et au profit du roy et a l'aisement du poeple, et pur le meintenement de la pees.

Endroit des leis et usages pur le governement de la terre d'Escoce, ordené est que l'usage de Scot' et de Bret' desorendroit soit defendu, si que mes ne soit usez.[1]   Et ordené est ausint que le lieutenant le roy, de l'houre qu'il sera venuz en la terre d'Escoce, face assembler les bons gentz de la terre en aucun certeyn lieu lequel il verra que a ce soit covenable, et que illoeques en la presence de luy et des gentz qui [a] y seront assemblez soient rehercez les leis que le roy David fist, et ausint les amendementz et les addicions qui unt esté puis faites par les roys.   Et le lieutenant le roy entre li et le conseil qu'il y aura, ausi bien des Engleis come des Escotz, redrescent et amendent les leis et les usages qui sont apertement encontre Dieu et reison, solonc ce qu'il purront en si brief terme et si avant come il purront saunz l'avisement du roy.   Et celes choses qu'il ne purront redrecer ne n'oseront enprendre saunz le roy, ensemblement ove celes qu'il averont acordez, soient myses en escrit distinctement et apertement par commun assent du lieutenant le roy et des gentz qui y seront assemblez, et desouz le seal le lieutenant soient portez au roy a Westmoster a treis semaynes aprés la Pasch[e] procheynement avenir, par meisme le lieutenant et par certeynes gentz

---

[a] quil C

discretion remove the said justiciars and sheriffs, and replace them with others, whether English or Scots by birth, who in their view are satisfactory, as often as they please, and in such a way as, in their opinion, may be best for the credit and advantage of the king and the convenience of the people, and for the keeping of the peace.

As for the laws and customs to be used in the government of the land of Scotland, it is ordained that the custom of the Scots and the Brets be henceforward forbidden, so that it is never to be used.[1] And it is also ordained that the king's lieutenant, at the time that he comes to Scotland, shall cause the good people of the land to assemble in some definite place which shall appear suitable for this, and that there, in the presence of himself, and of the people who are there assembled, shall be read over the laws that King David made, and also the amendments and additions which have been made since by the kings. And the king's lieutenant, in concert with the council which shall be there, composed of English and of Scots, shall reform and amend the laws and customs which are clearly displeasing to God and to reason, as well as they can do in so short a time, and going as far as they may without asking the opinion of the king. And those matters which they cannot amend, or dare not undertake without the king, together with those that they have agreed on, shall be put in writing distinctly and clearly, with the agreement of the king's lieutenant and of the people who are there assembled, and taken, under the seal of the lieutenant, to the king at Westminster three weeks after next Easter [24 April 1306], by the lieutenant, and by certain people of Scot-

---

[1] See Dickinson, *Scotland*, p. 59.

d'Escoce tantz et tielx come les gentz de la communalté
de la terre qui seront a cele assemblé voudront eslire pur
meismes les choses porter au roy, as lieu et terme avantditz, et que celx qui y vendront eent ple[i]n poer de par
la communauté de la terre pur acorder et affermer ce
que en serra ordené, ausi avant come eux tutz de la communalté purront faire s'il y feusent presentz, si que
adunques entre eux qui y vendront et les gentz que le
roy voudra assigner a eux, puissent les dites choses estre
vewes et examinees, et que homme puisse ordener et
affermer tieu redrescement par quei la terre d'Escoce
puisse meutz estre guiee et governee a toutz jours mes.
Et vuet le roy que son dit lieutenant soit illoeques en
propre persone a meisme l'oure.   Puis [a] commanda le
roy et ordené est que le dit terme que feut mis a son
lieutenant et as gentz d'Escoce por venir au parlement
as trois semeines aprés Pasch[e] soit esloignez tantque
a l'Ascension.[a]

Item, endroit de remuer hors d'Escoce ceux par qui
la pees porreit estre troublee, ordené est que le lieutenant
le roy, quant il sera venuz en Escoce, eit sur ce conseil et
avisement ove les bones gentz de la terre, et ceux qu'il
trovera par le conseil qu'il y avera qu'il face [b] a remuer,
par tiele acheson envee en Engleterre au roy en corteise
manere, si que le roy puisse ordiner a les faire demurrer
en Engleterre decea Trente si come il verra que face a
faire.

Item,[1] ordené est que monsire Alexandre de Lyndeseie

[a] *to* [a] *added in a second hand* C
[b] *facent* C

land, such in kind and number as the people of the community of the realm, who are assembled for the purpose, desire to choose to take these things to the king at the place and time aforesaid. Those who come there shall have full power, on behalf of the community of the realm, to give consent to what shall be ordained in the matter, to the same degree as the whole community could do if it were present, so that these things can then be studied and examined by those who have come there, and by the people whom the king desires to join with them, and that a revision may be ordered and agreed by which the realm of Scotland may best be guided and governed, henceforth and always. The king desires that his lieutenant be present there in person at the same time. (Later the king commanded, and it is ordained, that the date which was arranged for his lieutenant and the people of Scotland to come to parliament, three weeks after Easter, be postponed until Ascension Day [12 May 1306].)

Further, for removing from Scotland those by whom the peace might be disturbed, it is ordained that the king's lieutenant, when he comes to Scotland, shall take counsel and advice on this from the good people of the realm, and those whose departure shall be found necessary, after such advice has been taken, for that reason, he shall send to the king in England, with due respect, so that the king may give orders for them to be made to live in England, south of the Trent, so far as it may seem needful.

Further,[1] it is ordained that Alexander Lindsay must

---

[1] Marginal note ' scribatur sibi, etc.' applies apparently to next two items as well.

demoerge hors d'Escoce par un demy an, si come autre foiz fust ordené.

Item, acordé est que commandé soit au counte de Carrik qu'il mette le chastel de Kyndromyn en la garde de tiel homme pur qui il meismes voudra respoundre.

Item, ordené est que monsire Symund Fraser soit prest et apparaillez le xx jour de Noel a mover desadunques pur venir au roy, et pur aler par ses journees de jour en autre tant qu'il soit hors du poer nostre seigneur le roy et hors du poer le roy de France, pur tenir exil par quatre anz, si come autre foitz feust ordené, c'est a savoir a la grace et au repel de nostre seigneur le roy.[1]

Endroit des bosoignes d'Escoce que deyvent estre treitees, quant au governement de la terre d'Escoce par les gentz a ce assignez, voet nostre seigneur le roy que aux tutz, ausi bien les Engleis come les Escotz, soient chargez et sermentez sur le corps Nostre Seigneur et sur seintes reliques et sur seintes Ewangeilles, c'est a savoir chescun severaument en la manere qui s'ensuit :

Que vous bien et loiaument dirrez et conseillerez ce que vous senterez que purra torner a meyntenement de la pees et de la quiete de la terre et de la seignurie et du poeple nostre seignur le roy, especialement en la terre d'Escoce. Et que les desturbances et les empeschementz que vous avez seu et savez ou purrez savoir, que unt esté et sont ou purront estre contre la pees et la quiete de la terre et de la seignurie et du poeple nostre seigneur le roy, et nomement en la dite terre d'Escoce, en quele chose que ce soit vous dirrez et desclorrez overtement solonc vostre entendement, loialment et en bone foy, et

---

[1] This order of banishment seems to have been remitted a few weeks later (Rymer, I, ii, 974).

live outside Scotland for half a year, as was previously
ordained.

Further, it is agreed that the earl of Carrick be
ordered to put the castle of Kildrummy in the keeping
of a man for whom he himself is willing to answer.

Further, it is ordained that Simon Fraser must be
ready, on or after the twentieth day after Christmas, to
set out to come to the king, and [then] to go on his
travels day by day, until he is out of the jurisdiction of
our lord king, and that of the king of France, and to
remain in exile for four years, as was previously ordained,
that is at the grace and call of our lord king.[1]

Concerning the business of Scotland which ought to
be handled—as regards the government of the land of
Scotland—by the people appointed for this, our lord the
king desires that all of them, both English and Scots, be
charged and sworn on the body of Our Lord, on holy
relics, and on the Holy Gospels, that is to say each of
them separately, in the following manner :

That you will speak rightly and loyally, and advise
what you think will be able to lead to the keeping of the
peace and quiet of the land, and of the lordship and of
the people of our lord king, particularly in the land of
Scotland. And that the disturbances and hindrances
that you have known, and know, or may know, which
there have been, and are, or may be, to the peace and
quiet of the land, and of the lordship and of the people
of our lord the king, and especially in the land of Scotland, in whatever matter arising, you will speak of and
disclose openly according to your understanding, loyally

comment la terre purra meltz estre guiee et governee.
Et si vous sachez lei ou usage par quei la pees et la
quiete de la terre, de la seignurie et du poeple nostre
seigneur le roy, et nomement en la terre d'Escoce, eit
esté ou soit ou purra estre troublé en nule manere, que
vous les dirrez as autres qui sont ausint assignez a ce
conseil, et sur ce dirrez vostre conseil et vostre avys entre
eux ensemble par commun acord par quei la defaute
puisse estre amendé si avant come vous saverez, car le
roy voet overir par voz conseilx.

Et que pur amur, ne pur haur, ne pur parenté, ne
pur affinité, ne pur chose que puisse avenir, ne pur
serment, ne pur alliance que vous avez fait avant ces
houres a qui que ce soit, vous ne lerrez de faire, de dire,
ne de conseiller les choses desus dites a tut vostre seu et
a tut vostre poer.   Et que de chose que soit faite ou dite
ou parlee entre vous et les autres qui sont entendantz a
cest conseil, vous ne aviserez nul autre, et que les choses
treitees et accordees vous tendrez secrees, si que eles ne
soient descovertes tantque vous les eez mustrez au roy
et a ceux qu'il y voudra apeler, et qu'il eit sur ce dit et
ordiné sa volunté.

Et si vous sachez nul qi demoere en la terre d'Escoce
[qui] purra torner a desturbance de la pees, et lequel
vausist melz a demorrer hors de la terre d'Escoce pur le
meyntenement de la pees, que vous les mustrez et dirrez
overtement qui c'est et toutz ceux qui vous saverez qui
soient tielx.   Et que tutes les choses susdites dirrez et
conseillerez a l'honur de nostre seigneur le roy et a
quiete et au profit de vous et des autres bones gentz de
son roiaume et de sa seignurie.

and in good faith, and also how the land may best be guided and governed. And if you know a law or custom by which the peace and quiet of the land, of the lordship, and of the people of our lord king, and especially in the land of Scotland, has been, or is, or may be troubled in any way, that you will speak to the others who are also appointed to this council, and on this give your advice and opinion among them together by common agreement, so that the fault can be corrected as soon as you know it, for the king wishes to act with your advice.

And that you will not neglect to do, to say, nor to advise the above things with all your knowledge and all your power, on account of love, or hate, or kindred or affinity or anything which may happen, or by reason of an oath or an alliance that you have made with any man whatsoever before this time. And that you will not tell anybody else of anything that was done, or said, or spoken between you and the others who are concerned in this council, and that the matters discussed and agreed you will keep secret, so that they cannot be revealed until you have declared them to the king, and those whom he wishes to call, and he has spoken and declared his pleasure upon them.

And if you know anyone dwelling in the land of Scotland who may embark on the disturbance of the peace, and whom it would be better to have dwelling outside the land of Scotland, for the maintenance of the peace, that you will reveal them and say openly who that man is and who are all those whom you know to be such. And that in all these matters you will give your advice for the honour of our lord the king, and for the tranquillity and advantage of yourselves, and of the other good folk of his realm, and of his lordship.

Et [1] fait a remembrer que le roi, a son parlement des dites oytaves de la Nativite nostre Dame, commanda devant son consail au chamberlein d'Escoce que les burgages de Berewyk [a] soient baillez et tenuz selonc les extentes que feurent faites par son commandement puis le conquest, et que nule chartre purchacée a tenir par meindre extente ne soit alloee.[b]

[a] Berewyk que soient C
[b] *This para. in C seems to be in the second hand of page 126, n. a.*

And note [1] that the king, at his parliament on the octave of the Nativity of Our Lady, ordered the chamberlain of Scotland, in the presence of his council, that the burgages of Berwick should be conveyed and held according to the valuations that were made by his command after the conquest, and that no charter obtained for holding by a lesser valuation be allowed.

[1] Marginal note ' breve etc.'

34

A [1] son tre[s] cher ami, si lui plest, quant q'il soit et poet de honours, reverens et chieres amistez. Sire, les nov[eles] / de cestes parties sont teles, qe le counte de Carrik tient les chasteux le roi de Domfres, de Are, et le chast[el] / de Dalswynton qui feust a monsire Johan Comyn, et le chastel de Tibres q'est [a mon]sire Richard Syward, et tient le / dit monsire Richard et monsire Willeam [*sic*] de Baillol en prisoun, si come avaunt fist. Et des vitailes que furent / en chastel de Are est en la vile, en meyns de marchaunz, bien a [cent tonn]eux [a] de vin, et autres vita[illes] / a grant plenté. Ad il fait vitailler son chastel de Loghendoun [2] en Carrik, et le chastel de Ananorby [3] en . . . . / pur grant temps, lequel chastel Dananerbi [3] apent au roi et a sa corone, mes le roi le graunta a un Ma[ucolom] / Coyllan par fause suggestion sauntz enquest, lequeil Maucolom l'ad chaungé of [4] le counte pur autre. / Et le counte de Carrik ad ostei[é] en Gaweye pur faire lever les gentz ove lui, mes eux l'ount respon[du en] / acord que jamés contre le roi ne leverount au nul vivant, [et ?] si il eynt par

---

Text: B.M. MS Cotton Tiberius E VI, ff. 201v-202 (C), a transcript in a register, badly damaged in the Cottonian fire of 1731, and partly illegible, especially at the ends of lines on f. 201v, and the beginnings on f. 202. Printed, incompletely and with many errors, in *Registra Johannis Whetham-stede* [etc.], ed. Riley (RS, 1873), pp. 347-53. The damaged portions of C may be slowly degenerating; at all events a transcript made by the present editor in 1953 (Z) has a few readings no longer decipherable even with an ultra-violet lamp. For the symbols used here in transcription see above, p. xli.

[a] cent tonn Z

[1] The importance of this document was first noted by Charles Johnson in *EHR*, xxxiii (1918), 366-7. The author and his correspondent are

34

To [1] his beloved friend, if it please him, all possible honour, reverence, and dear friendship. Sir, the news in these parts is this, that the earl of Carrick holds the king's castles of Dumfries and Ayr, and the castle of Dalswinton, which belonged to John Comyn, and the castle of Tibbers, which belongs to Richard Siward, and he holds this Richard, and William Balliol, in prison as he did before; and of the victuals which were in the castle of Ayr, there are, in the town in the hands of merchants, a good hundred casks of wine, and other victuals in great plenty. He has had his castle of Loch Doon [2] in Carrick, and the castle of [Dunaverty ?] [3] in [Kintyre ?] victualled for a long period. This castle of [Dunaverty ?] [3] belongs to the king and to his crown, but the king, as a result of treacherous advice, granted it without an inquest to a certain Malcolm Coyllan, and this Malcolm has exchanged it with [4] the earl for another. The earl of Carrick has made war in Galloway to cause the people to rebel with him, but they have answered in accord that they will never rebel against the king for any man living, and if they have help from the

---

unknown, but the letter was written only a few weeks after the murder of Comyn on 10 February 1306, and is a unique source of information about Bruce's movements in the period before his coronation. On the persons and places named see Bain, II, index, and Johnson, loc. cit. In general see above, p. xxix.

[2] Hardly Lochmaben, as suggested by Johnson.

[3] Professor Barrow has suggested to the present editor that ' Dananerbi ' is a copyist's blunder (palaeographically very simple) for ' Dunaverty ' in Kintyre, noting also that one of Bruce's supporters is known to have been ' Malcolm McCulian en lisle de Kentyr ' (Palgrave, *Documents*, pp. 309, 315). We should perhaps, therefore, read ' Kentyr ' in the space after ' en '.

[4] *of = ove*

temps aide du roi . . . . . / . . . . . ª se tendrount taunt qe
noveles les veignent du roi, et le conseil le roi lour ad
assigné q[uelques *] / gardeynes d'eux meismes et il se
tiegnent bien payés. Sire, le counte de Carrik ad esté a
Gla[scu et / Rother]glen, et en celes parties, et ad pris
feauté des gentz ou il est venuz, et les a chargé q . . . .
/ d'aler ove lui ov lour vivre de ix jours quele hure q'il
soient garniz de un jour et de une [nuit*]. / Le maveys
evesque ¹ se tient a Glascu son chief consailer, et le count
vient sovent et tiegn[ent] . . . . / et lour consail
ensemble, et quillent tot le pover q'il povent de totes pars.
Et monsire Robert B[oyd] ² / coroner de val de Clyd ad
emblé le chastel de Rothereseye par mer fesaunt entendre
a ceux d . . . . / pur vitailler le dit chastel de
par monsire Adam Gordon.³ Et le dit monsire Robert
Boyd ov tot le [pover] / de Conyngham ount assegé le
chastel d'Ynverkyp et monsire Adam Gordon [y est?]
. . . . / nient taunt que socour lui viegne par le
roi.⁴ Sire, monsire Johan de Moubray est en Lidesdale
[ove * Ing] / ram Domframvile, et ount quillé lur pover
et chivaucherount si tost com il averount noveles / que
serra bien par temps, qar il se tiegnent bien et loiaument,
et se aparaillent de chivaucher v . . . . / Le
counte de Boghan et le counte d'Azheles ᵇ sont accordez
et entrefiez ᶜ de vivre a la . . . . / lent quant q'il
povont, ensemblement ove monsire Alisaundre d'Abernethy et monsire David [et?] / lour pover, de chivaucher
bien par temps issint que eux. Monsire Johan de

ª roi *was doubtless followed by a lost word at the end of the line; the next line
begins with part of a word.*

ᵇ *For spelling with ' z ' cf. above, p. 59, note b.*

ᶜ entre miez C

king in time . . . . [they] will maintain themselves until word comes from the king, and the council of the king has assigned them [certain ?] wardens for themselves, and they hold themselves well paid. Sir, the earl of Carrick has been at Glasgow and Rutherglen, and in those districts, and has received the fealty of the people where he has come, and has charged them [to be ready ?] to go with him with rations for nine days, whenever they receive notice of a day and a [night ?]. The wicked bishop [1] remains at Glasgow as his chief adviser, and the earl comes often, and they take . . . . and their counsel together, and they are mustering all the support that they can from every quarter. And Robert Boyd,[2] coroner of Clydesdale, has seized the castle of Rothesay by sea, giving those within [?] to understand [that he was entering ?] to victual the castle on behalf of Adam Gordon.[3] This Robert Boyd, with all the [power ?] of Cunningham, has besieged the castle of Inverkip, and Adam Gordon [is there ?] . . . . until help comes to him from the king.[4] Sir, John Mowbray is in Liddesdale with Ingram de Umfraville, and they have gathered their power, and will ride as soon as they have news, which will be very soon, for they conduct themselves well and loyally and are preparing themselves to ride . . . . The earl of Buchan, and the earl of Athol, have agreed and sworn together to remain . . . . when they can, together with Alexander of Abernethy and David and their force, to ride very soon, as well as them. John Mowbray, and all the forces on this side

---

[1] Robert Wishart, bishop of Glasgow 1273–*c.* 1316.
[2] cf. Palgrave, *Documents*, p. 319; Bain, II, no. 1829.
[3] cf. above, p. 122.
[4] cf. Bain, II, no. 1807.

Moubrey, of tot [le * pover * de] / cea la mer ¹ ensemble-
rount ou il verront que mieut soit, par acord, de chivaucher hastive[ment, ove * l'aide * de *] / Dieu,
countre les enemis.

Sire, le counte Patrik est assigné gardeyn des countés
Rok[esburgh] / et Selkyrk.   Monsire Water de Borgh-
den ² ad enpris la garde du pel de Selkyrk et de la
for[est] . . . . . / . . . . . et ª monsire Simon Frisel ³ est
dever nous a Berewyk, of monsire Robert le fitz [Roger] ᵇ /
qui demorrount celes parties, ov cent hommes a pié de
Norhumbr[land] qui serront a Berewyk le ⁴ . . . .
[pur * / rester] cy ou aler qile part que mieutz soit au
profit le roi.   Les chasteux le roi Be[rewyk] / Jeddeworth,
Bothevile, Kyrcomtellagh, Edenebborghe, Lynlescu, et
[D ?]estrivelyn sont vi[taillés des *] / choses, issint q'il
ne averount gard[eins] taunt que noveles viegnent du
roi et . . . . leiser le ch . . . . / Sumes a
Berewyk en aforsaunt le pel et les gardes de la vile et du
chastel [hors * de *] / la vile, lesqueux nous trovoms de
boen volunté . . . . / que vous averez bones
noveles bien par temps, si ceux [qui tiegnent a foi le roi
soient] ᶜ . . . . / [prom ?]esses, a qeu chose jeo ne
me ose afier, mes si tost com [jeo * ai *] entendu, [le fait
je ferai vous sa ᶜ] / voir.   Sire, coment qe homme vous
face entendaunt du dit counte de Carrik, ne[quedant *
il *] / se afforce d'aproprier le roiaume d'Escoce, et
d'estre roi . . . . Le conseil le roi [lui * comanda *]
/ q'il fist deliverer les ministres le roi et les chasteux le

ª *Probably a word lost at the end of the line; then there is an illegible word at the*
beginning of the next line.
  ᵇ Rog . . . Z ; *not now legible in* C ; *but confirmed by Bain,* II, *no. 1751*
  ᶜ *Words in brackets exceedingly doubtful*

of the sea,¹ will assemble where they consider, by general agreement, that it is best to do so, to ride in haste, with God's help, against the enemy.

Sir, Earl Patrick is assigned as warden of the counties of Roxburgh and Selkirk. Walter de Burghdon ² has undertaken the keeping of the peel of Selkirk and of the forest . . . . and Simon Fraser ³ is with us at Berwick with Robert FitzRoger, and they will stay here, with 100 foot soldiers of Northumberland who will arrive at Berwick on ⁴ . . . . to stay here, or to go wherever may be best, for the advantage of the king. The king's castles of B[erwick ?], Jedburgh, Bothwell, Kirkintilloch, Edinburgh, Linlithgow and Stirling are victualled with stores, but they will have no keepers until word comes from the king . . . . We are at Berwick, reinforcing the peel, and the guards of the town and of the castle outside the town, whom we find of good will, [and we believe ?] that you will have good news very soon if those who remain on the side of the king are [true to their promises ?], on which matter I do not dare to pledge myself, but as soon as [I have ?] heard of . . . . [I will let you know ?]. Sir, however you are given to understand of the earl of Carrick, [he nevertheless ?] is attempting to seize the realm of Scotland and to be [king ?] . . . . The king's council [ordered him ?] to deliver the king's officers, and the king's castles in his

---

¹ ' The [Scottish] sea', in medieval texts, commonly means the River Forth, with its estuary.

² cf. above, p. 122.

³ cf. above, p. 127, and *n.* 1. He was taken in arms against Edward in June of this year, and the present allusion seems to be the latest reference to him as a supporter of the English cause before his second defection.

⁴ Probably the name of a day of the week is missing.

roi en sa mayn [a] / [et * les *] viles qe furent a monsire
Johan Comyn et deyvent estre au roi par la mort le dit
monsire Johan, que Dieux assoille, / [mes * a] ceo, sire,
n'ad il nul respons maundé. Sire, meismes la chose lui
maunda le chaumberleyn par sa lettre quant / [il * oit *]
les noveles, et il respoundi q'il prendroit chasteux, viles,
et gentz quant q'il pout, et q'il se aforcereyt / [quant]
q'il pout, taunt que le roi lui eust maundé sa volunté de
sa demande [1] ; et si il ne lui vout granter, il se / [def]en-
droit de plus lo[ng] bastoun q'il eust.

Sire, il fait trere hors des chasteux de Domfres, Are,
Dalswyngton [2] / et Tibres quant q'il treve que soit boen,
et fet garnir ses [b] chasteux demene, et bie a destruire les
avaunt / [ditz] chasteux au plus tost que le pover le roi
vendra celes parties. Le jour que ceste lettre fust faite,
monsire / [Johan de] Meneteth [3] me maunda que le
counte de Carrik fust passé la mer ove lx hommes
d'armes. Et sire / [si les gentz * de]la soient bons, a
queu chose jeo ne mefi pas, il avera entre eux petite
duree. Le samedi / [avant que ceste ?] lettre fust faite,
le counte de Carrik vient a Glascu, et l'evesque le dona
absolucion pleyniement / [de ses] pecchez, et le fist jurer
q'il esterroit a l'ordenaunce de la clergie de Escoce, et
l'asoutz come / . . . . ast bien purchacer son
heritage en totes les maneres q'il pout. Et mangeront
[*sic*] ensemble, et peus / [le * counte *] departi vers
Meneteth, pur passer l'ewe de Forth, et come il vient a

<hr/>

[a] *Folio ends here; thereafter damage is mainly at the beginnings of lines instead
of the ends.*
   [b] ces C

hands, and the towns which belonged to John Comyn, and should belong to the king because of the death of John, on whom may God have mercy, [but] to this, sir, he has made no answer. Sir, the chamberlain commanded him by letter to do the same thing when he heard the news, and he replied that he would take castles, towns and people as fast as he could, and strengthen himself as fast as he could, until the king had notified his will concerning his demand,[1] and if he would not grant it to him, he would defend himself with the longest stick that he had.

Sir, he is having taken from the castles of Dumfries, Ayr, Dalswinton,[2] and Tibbers whatever he has found to be good, and he is causing his own castles to be garrisoned, and he intends to destroy those other castles as soon as the power of the king reaches those parts. On the day that this letter was written, John of Menteith [3] informed me that the earl of Carrick had crossed the sea with 60 men-at-arms. And sir, if the people on the other side are trustworthy, which I do not misdoubt, he will have but a short stay with them. The Saturday [before] this letter was written, the earl of Carrick came to Glasgow, and the bishop gave him absolution fully for his sins, and made him swear that he would abide under the direction of the clergy of Scotland, and freed him [that he might go ?] to secure his heritage by all the means that he could. And they had a meal together, and then [the earl] left in the direction of Menteith to cross the River Forth, and when he came to Dum-

---

[1] i.e., for the throne of Scotland
[2] There may have been room for the name of another castle before ' et '.
[3] Sheriff and constable of Dumbarton (above, p. 124)

Dombritaigne [1] il maunda / [Alisa]undre de Lyndesaye
et monsire Water Logan a demaunder le chastel, et que
sir Johan de Mene/[teth irroit * de] hors en trewe de
parler ovesques eux, mes il ne se voleit assentir mes lour
graunta en trewe / [de venir *] si pres du chastel q'il
pout oyr dedenz ceo q'il voleynt dire dehors. Il vindrent,
et de/[manderent ?] le chastel a l'eos lour seigneur, et
monsire Johan les respoundi q'il avoit le chastel du beal
le / [roy et nu]l autre, ne le voleit il rendre mes a lui, si
il ne portast lettre du grante seal le roi, issint / [q'il soit]
deschargé en la manere q'il fust chargé. [Puis * il *]
s'en departirent saunz plus dire. A Dieu qui vous garde.
Escrite a Berewyk / . . . . [jour] de Marz.

   [1] The special interest of this passage is that it may describe Bruce's
journey towards Scone for his coronation on 25 March 1306 (see below,
p. 138). To go from Glasgow to Dumbarton in order to cross the upper
waters of the Forth is unorthodox; but Stirling was in enemy hands, and
Bruce may have hesitated to go in that direction. Unluckily our letter
cannot be precisely dated in March, but it may be that the crossing of 'the
sea' (the Forth) with 60 men-at-arms was the prelude to Bruce's coronation. (Johnson [op. cit.] read the figure as 60,*000* men, but there is no
doubt of the reading *lx*.)

barton [1] he ordered Alexander Lindsay and Walter
Logan to demand the surrender of the castle, and that
John of Menteith should [go ?] out under truce to
talk with them. He would not agree, but allowed them
[to come ?] under truce so close to the castle that he
could hear from inside what those outside wanted to say.
They came and [demanded] the surrender of the castle
for the use of their lord, and John replied that he held
the castle by commission from [the king and from ?] no
other person, and he would not render it except to
the king, if [the claimant] did not bear a letter under the
king's great seal, so that he should be acquitted in
the same manner in which he was commissioned. [Then
they ?] departed without saying anything more. Fare-
well, and may God keep you. Berwick . . . .
[day] of March [1306].

35

.... IDEM [1] episcopus, recepto suis in manibus scripto memorato [2] et diligenter inspecto, organo vocis sue bona fide cognovit omnia contenta in dicto scripto esse vera et factum suum, et de voluntate et consciencia sua dictum scriptum [2] processisse et fuisse sigillatum, et eidem appensum suum esse sigillum. Premissis itaque inter prefatos episcopum et clericos inter se, ut premittitur, ad invicem conferentes confessatis et dictis, quesivit ab eodem domino episcopo dictus dominus Robertus [3] quare idem episcopus prefato domino regi Anglie suove consilio dictam confederacionem per ipsum, ut predicitur, fuisse factam non intimaverat eo die quo vocatus fuit et admissus de consilio ipsius regis apud Schene juxta Kyngeston, pro sui observancia juramenti quod ibidem eidem domino [regi] prestitit, ut est moris, cum in eodem juramento inter cetera articuli certi contineantur, videlicet quod quicumque illud prestare debeat juramentum ad sancta dei evangelia jurabit quod ab illo tempore in [futurum?] nulli persone viventi absque dicti domini regis licencia se debeat confederare, et si quam cum quacumque persona prius fecerit confederacionem, eam ibidem in actu jurandi eidem domino regi

Text : Extract from P.R.O. Scottish Docts., Exchequer (E 39), 4/5, the original notarial instrument (E). Calendared by Bain, II, no. 1818; apparently never printed in full. Valuable especially because of its information about the coronation of Bruce in March 1306. The earlier part is much defaced ; we give here only the later part, and even there, the text is not everywhere legible with certainty.

35

[Concluding portion of the confession of Bishop Lamberton to representatives of Edward I.]

. . . . THE [1] bishop received the said document [2] in his hands, carefully examined it, and verbally admitted in good faith that everything contained in the document was true, and recorded his own actions, and that the text [2] had been issued and sealed in accord with his own will and conscience, and that the seal appended to it was his own. And so, after these matters had been admitted and discussed by the bishop and clerks conferring together, Robert [3] asked the bishop why the bishop had not observed the oath which he swore to the king, according to custom, on the day that he was summoned to be admitted to the king's council at Sheen, near to Kingston, by declaring to the king of England and his council, that the confederacy had been made by him as aforesaid ; since in the oath there are contained, amongst other things, certain articles, to wit that whoever has to take that oath will swear upon the Holy Gospels of God that from that time onwards he must ally himself with no living person without the leave of the king, and that if he has previously made a confederacy with any person he should notify it there to the king or his council, at the

---

[1] At this point the bishop of St Andrews is giving evidence at Newcastle before certain clerks of Edward I, concerning his association with Bruce, and has just been shown the text of a confederacy which he had made with Bruce in June 1304 (Palgrave, *Documents*, pp. 323-5). cf. above, p. xxix.

[2] The reference is to the bishop's confederacy with Bruce.

[3] Robert of Cottingham, one of the examining clerks

suove [?] consilio intimaret et hoc juramentum episcopus
juraverat super sancti dei evangelia, ut est moris. Et
predicta confederacio inter ipsum episcopum et dictum
Robertum de Brus inita, ut premittitur, nulli dub [a] . . . . .
ipsius episcopi in hac parte precessit juramentum de quo
sibi utpote facto proprio et satis recenti innotuit vel
debuit competenter. Cui memoratus episcopus respon-
dendo dixit, organo vocis sue, bona fide se dictam confederacionem in illo actu omnino tradidisse oblivioni, et
idcirco nullam ibidem de ea fecit mencionem.

Objectum fuit insuper eidem episcopo per prefatum
dominum Johannem de Sandale [1] quoddam, de quo
multum, ut dicebat, mirabatur, quod ex quo idem
episcopus inter alios de consilio domini regis Anglie in
partibus Scocie primus et major fuerat nominatus et
pacis regie conservator principalis per ipsum regem depu-
tatus, et eciam ut talis inter eosdem de consilio certis die
et loco convenerat super quibusdam ipsius domini regis
negociis [2] arduis et pacis conservacionem tangentibus
tractaturus, et aliquamdiu sedebat conferens cum eisdem,
quia statim intellegit voluntatem dicti Roberti de Brus
se regem Scocie facere proponentis, in contemptum et
exheredacionem ipsius domini sui, domini regis Anglie,
et quantum in eo fuit nitentis, noctanter et latenter,
relicto dicto domini regis Anglie consilio, ipse episcopus
non coactus non invitus set spontanea et libera sua
voluntate, mare Scoticanum transfretando versus eundem
Robertum de Brus gressus suos cum festinacione direxit
ad honorem sibi, die coronacionis sue, exhibendum;

---

[a] *Under ultra-violet light may possibly be read as* dubm̄.

time of swearing; and this oath the bishop had sworn on the Holy Gospels of God, as the custom is. And the confederacy made between the bishop and Robert Bruce, as the bishop could not doubt, preceded the oath, a fact which was known to him, or may reasonably be thought to have been, since the action was his own and a sufficiently recent one. To this the bishop replied in his own words, in good faith, that on that occasion he had utterly forgotten the confederacy and therefore made no mention of it there.

A further complaint was made to the bishop by John de Sandale,[1] concerning which, as he said, he felt great surprise. After the bishop was nominated head and chief of the council of the lord king of England in the land of Scotland, and was made by the king principal keeper of the king's peace, and also, in that capacity, had met with those of the council on a certain day and in a certain place to discuss certain difficult business [2] of the king, which concerned the maintenance of the peace, and had sat for some time conferring with them, because he suddenly realized the intentions of Robert Bruce, who was proposing to attempt, as far as in him lay, to make himself king of Scotland, in contempt of, and to the disinheritance of his lord the king of England, the bishop left the council of the king of England secretly and by night, not under pressure, or unwillingly, but of his own pure free will, and crossed the Scottish sea, and hastily directed his steps towards Robert Bruce in order to show him honour on the day of his coronation. He

---

[1] Another of the examining clerks

[2] Apparently this meeting was at Berwick, to take action after the murder of Comyn (Palgrave, *Documents*, p. 336).

respondit organo vocis sue bona fide, ut dicebat, quod
negare non potuit bono modo quin ipse mare Scoticanum
ut premittitur transfretavit versus eum cum ipso tantum
locuturus, adiciens quod propter ipsius graves com-
minaciones tam in persona quam rebus sibi factas, et non
ob aliam causam, ad ipsum accessit voluntati sue et
mandato [ob]temperando, de quo ad presens vehementer condolere et ex toto corde penitere se dixit, quia
jam perpendit quod credens se et sua salvare, omnem
suam perdiderat substanciam quam habebat.

Objectum ¹ fuit adhuc prefato domino episcopo per
predictum dominum Robertum de Cotingham quod
cum dominus rex Anglie eidem episcopo, tanquam illi
de quo pre ceteris terre sue Scocie tam nobilibus quam
prelatis confidebat, personam Andree filii et heredis
Jacobi Senescalli Scocie tradiderat custodiendam, audi-
toque demum tam de murdro ᵃ et interfeccione quondam
domini Johannis Comyn domini de Badenagh quam
infidelitate rebellione et excogitata nequicia Roberti de
Bruz et eidem adherencium, eidem episcopo per suas
litteras mandaverat quod statim visis suis litteris dictum
Andream eidem domino regi remandaret ; quare idem
episcopus regio mandato predicto recepto et intellecto
non paruit sed ipsum Andream dicto Roberto de Brus
ejusdem domini regis Anglie inimico notorio et proditori
liberavit ; palam et expresse cognovit organo vocis sue
episcopus prelibatus quod neg[are non ?] potuit bono
modo quin ipse eundem Andream dicto Roberto de
Brus, eciam postquam dictum mandatum regium receperat, ut premittitur, liberaverat, sed non potuit inde ᵇ

ᵃ modo E
ᵇ *The text seems corrupt.*

replied in his own words, and in good faith, as he said, that he could not well deny that he crossed the Scottish sea, as had been said, to meet him, but only to have speech with him, adding that because of Robert's severe threats made against him, both in regard to his person and his property, and for no other cause, he went to him to mollify his will and his command, for which he declared that he was now very sorry, and repented with his whole heart, because he now perceived that in thinking to save himself and his property, he had lost all the substance that he had.

Again,[1] complaint was made to the bishop by Robert of Cottingham that because the king of England gave into the keeping of the bishop, as one in whom he trusted above all others, both nobles and prelates, in the realm of Scotland, the person of Andrew, the son and heir of James the Steward of Scotland, and hearing at length of the brutal murder of the late John Comyn, lord of Badenoch, and of the infidelity, rebellion, and premeditated iniquity of Robert Bruce and his supporters, he gave orders to the bishop by letter, that immediately on seeing the letter he should restore Andrew to the king; why did the bishop not obey the royal mandate, which he had received and understood, but rather deliver Andrew to Robert Bruce, a notorious enemy of the king of England and a traitor? The bishop recognised, openly and expressly and in his own words, that he could not well deny that it was after he had received the royal mandate, as aforesaid, that he had delivered this Andrew to Robert Bruce, but that he could not [avoid it?].

---

[1] The next 21 lines were printed in a footnote by Hailes, *Annals of Scotland,* II, 14.

ut dicebat. Requisitus eciam adhuc dictus episcopus an ipse, postquam dictus Robertus de Brus dominum Johannem Comyn interfecerat, ut predicitur, et se regem Scocie fecerat coronari et eciam proclamari, missam sibi celebraverat pr [a] . . . . et ratificacione[m] [b] regii sui status vel honorem alium eidem ut domino fecerat, aut alio communionis genere communicaverat cum eodem, spontanea et mera sua voluntate, bona fide, ut dicebat, et palam cognovit quod cum eodem communicaverat, missamq[ue ?] sibi in pontificalibus die dominica in ramis palmarum, tercia videlicet die proximo sequente diem coronacionis [1] ipsius, celebraverat, fidelitatemque sibi pro temporalitate episcopatus sui fecerat, et juramentum fidelitatis ad sancta dei evangelia prestiterat.

Premissa omnia et eorum singula quia vera sunt et quia mentiri noluit idem episcopus se recognovisse dicebat. Act' apud Novum Castrum super Tynam, Dunolm' dioc', in camera ipsius episcopi, anno indiccione mense et die prenotatis, presentibus domino Johanne de Schefeld et Johanne de Donecastre, domino Johanne de Blockele [?] capellano, Arnaldo dicto le Baskle et Johanne de Tardze [?] cum magistro Johanne de Heselarton clerico et publico imperiali auctoritate notario, testibus ad premissa vocatis specialiter et rogatis.

---

[a] *One illegible word seems to follow the word beginning with* pr.
[b] *Inflexion uncertain because of gap before* et

Again, asked whether after Robert Bruce had slain John Comyn, as is mentioned above, and had had himself crowned and proclaimed king of Scotland, the bishop had celebrated mass for him . . . . and made ratification of his royal status, or done some other honour to him as lord, or had communicated with him in any other way, he agreed with spontaneous and pure free will and in good faith, as he said, and openly, that he had communicated with him, and had celebrated mass for him in pontificals on Palm Sunday [27 March 1306], that is the third day after his coronation,[1] and had offered fealty to him for the temporality of his bishopric, and had sworn the oath of fealty on the Holy Gospels of God.

The bishop declared that he acknowledged all and singular of the aforesaid as being true, for he was unwilling to tell falsehoods. Newcastle-upon-Tyne, diocese of Durham, in the chamber of the bishop, the year, indiction, month, and day aforesaid [9 August 1306], in the presence of John of Sheffield and John of Doncaster, John of Blockley, chaplain, Arnold le Baskle, and John de Tardze, with Master John of Heslerton, clerk and imperial public notary, as witnesses specially called and summoned to these proceedings.

---

[1] Palm-Sunday in 1306 fell on 27 March; Bruce's coronation appears, from this passage, to have taken place three days before, by liturgical reckoning, that is on 25 March. It seems curious that this document, giving the testimony of a person who was present, and recording it only a few months later, should not have been used in discussions of the matter; Bain's calendaring of the text, admittedly, is not helpful. For references see Dunbar, *Scottish Kings*, p. 129.

Et ego, Andreas,[1] quondam Guilielmi de Tange, clericus Eboracensis diocesis sacrosancte sedis apostolice publicus auctoritate notarius, qui premissis una cum dictis testibus et notario interfui eaque sic fieri vidi et audivi, rogatus super hiis presens confeci publicum instrumentum, inserendo in eodem dictarum litterarum domini episcopi sancti Andree tenores de verbo ad verbum nichil addens vel minuens quod sensum mutet vel viciet intellectum, et cum domino Johanne de Flete et dicto notario earum cum originalibus litteris tenores diligenter examinavi, et quia eos cum dictis originalibus inveni in omnibus concordare, presens instrumentum publicum manu mea confectum premissa sicut agebantur continens signo[2] meo consueto signavi, in fidem et testimonium premissorum.

[1] Andrew de Tange was a notary who acted for Edward I and Edward II on a great many occasions. He wrote triplicate copies of a ' Great Roll of Scotland ' which recorded the ' Great Cause ', and Edward I's subsequent relations with Balliol to 1296, and triplicate copies of the ' Ragman Rolls ' (see above, pp. lii, liv). On notarial instruments see above, p. 64, *n*. 1.

[2] See the illustration (reduced from original size) on this page. Another illustration of Tange's *signum* may be seen in G. F. Browne, *Echt-Forbes Charters*, plate XII.

And I, Andrew,[1] son of the late William de Tange, clerk, of the diocese of York, a notary public by authority of the Holy Apostolic See, who was present with the said witnesses and notary at the above transactions, and who therefore saw and heard them take place, have made on request the present public instrument about them, and inserted in it the text of the letter of the bishop of St Andrews, word for word, not adding nor taking away anything that might change its sense or alter its meaning. I have carefully compared the text with that of the original letters, assisted by John de Flete and the notary previously mentioned, and since I have found it to agree at all points with the original, I have marked the present public instrument (written in my own hand, and recounting these proceedings as they really took place) with my accustomed *signum*,[2] as trustworthy evidence of them.

36

Omnibus Christi fidelibus ad quorum noticiam presens scriptum pervenerit, episcopi abbates priores ac ceteri de clero in regno Scocie constituti salutem in salutis auctore. Noverit universitas vestra quod cum inter dominum Johannem de Balliolo dudum regem Scocie per regem Anglie de facto promotum et recolende memorie quondam dominum Robertum de Brus, avum domini Roberti regis qui nunc est, orta fuisset materia questionis quis eorum videlicet proximior esset jure sanguinis ad hereditandum et regnandum super populum Scoticanum, fidelis populus sine dubitacione semper tenuit, prout a suis antecessoribus et majoribus intellexerat, et credidit verum esse, quod dictus dominus Robertus avus post mortem regis Alexandri ejusque neptis filie regis Norwagie verus heres extitit, et cun[c]tis aliis ad regni regimen preferendus, licet humani generis inimico zizaniam seminante diversis machinacionibus emulorum et cautelis quas per singula longum esset enarrare in contrarium res sit versa, pro cujus eversione et carencia regie dignitatis dampna gravia regno Scocie et ejus incolis ex tunc evenerunt, prout facti experiencia rerum magistra, hactenus sepe repetita, manifeste declaravit.

Text: Original in H.M. Register House, Edinburgh (E) (facsimile in *Nat. MSS Scotland*, II, no. xvii), whence *APS*, I, 460 [red]. E has slits for twelve seals, presumably those of all the Scottish bishops. Though no seals remain, several tags survive, and some of these bear the names of sees, e.g. ' Glasguensis '. The document presents many difficulties, which are discussed by D. Hunter Marshall in *SHR*, XXIII (1926), 280-93. In particular, (a) Dundee seems to have been in English hands in February 1310, (b) for various reasons many of the Scottish bishops seem unlikely to have been able to attend such a council. We print the document, however, because the handwriting is probably of the time of Robert I, and it appears to contain the earliest statement of the story that ' the faithful people of Scotland ' had

36

WE, the bishops, abbots, priors, and other clergy in the realm of Scotland, give greeting, in the name of the Author of salvation, to all the faithful in Christ to whose notice the present document shall come. Be it known to all of you, that when there arose a subject of dispute between John Balliol, lately installed as king of Scotland *de facto* by the king of England, and the late Robert Bruce, of honourable memory, the grandfather of Robert who is now the king, concerning which of them had the better title, by right of birth, to inherit the rule over the people of Scotland, the faithful people always believed without hesitation, as they had understood from their ancestors and elders, and held to be the truth, that Robert, the grandfather, was the true heir, and was to be preferred to all others as ruler of the realm, after the death of King Alexander, and of his granddaughter, the daughter of the king of Norway. But because the enemy of the human race has sown tares, and because of the divers stratagems and tricks of Robert's rivals, which it would be tedious to describe one by one, the matter has turned out otherwise and, by his deprivation and loss of the royal dignity, grievous harm has since come to the realm of Scotland and to its inhabitants, as experience of events, our mistress in politics, now often repeated, has manifestly shown.

---

always believed that Robert I's grandfather was the true heir to the Scottish throne (though allegations had already been made, e.g. in 1299 (p. 84 above), against the propriety of Edward I's actions during the interregnum). The story is very dubious (see, e.g., Fordun, I, 312), but it has had some influence on historians even in modern times. On the Latin style, and possible authorship, of this text see T. M. Cooper, *Supra Crepidam* (1951), p. 54.

Y

Videntes igitur populus et plebs predicti regni Scocie multarum tribulacionum aculeis fatigati dictum dominum Johannem per regem Anglie pro diversis causis captum incarceratum, regno et populo privatum, ac regnum Scocie per ipsum perditum et in servitutem redactum, ingenti populacione vastatum, crebri doloris acerbitate respersum, pro defectu recti regiminis desolatum, omni periculo expositum, et occupanti concessum, populumque bonis spoliatum, bellis cruciatum captivatum vinculatum et incarceratum, stragibus immensis innocencium et continuis incendiis oppressum subjectum et mancipatum ac perpetue ruine proximum nisi divino consilio circa regni sic deformati ac desolati reparacionem et ejus regimen celerius tractaretur, Summi Regis providencia sub cujus imperio reges regnant et principes dominantur tot et tanta dampna gravia morte amariora rerum et corporum sepe contingencia pro defectu capitanei et fidelis ducis diucius ferre non valentes, in dictum dominum Robertum regem, qui nunc est, in quem jura patris avique sui ad predictum regnum judicio populi adhuc resident et vigent incorupta [*sic*] auctore divino convenerunt, ac de consciencia et consensu eorumdem assumptus est in regem ut regni deformata reformet, corrigendaque corrigat, et dirigat indirecta. Et ipsorum auctoritate regno prefectus, rex Scottorum sollempniter est effectus, cum quo fidelis populus regni vivere wlt [*sic*] et mori tanquam cum illo qui jure sanguinis et aliis virtutibus cardinalibus preditus aptus est ad regnandum ac

Therefore the whole people of the realm of Scotland, wearied with the stings of many tribulations (for this John was taken by the king of England, for various reasons, and imprisoned, and deprived of his realm and people, and the realm of Scotland was lost by him, and reduced to servitude, laid waste by great slaughter, and imbued with the bitterness of heavy sorrow, made desolate by the lack of true governance, exposed to every danger, and given up to the despoiler, the inhabitants deprived of their property, tortured with strife, made captive, bound and imprisoned, oppressed with untold killings of blameless people, and with continual burnings, subject and in bonds, and nigh to perpetual ruin unless by divine counsel speedy provision were made for the restoration of a realm so afflicted and desolate, and of its government, by the providence of the King most high, under whose authority kings rule, and princes govern), this people, being unable any longer to endure injuries so many and so great, and more bitter than death, which were being continually inflicted on their property and their persons for lack of a captain and a faithful leader, agreed, by divine prompting, on Lord Robert who now is king, in whom reside and remain uncorrupted, in the general opinion, the rights of his father and his grand-father to the kingdom ; and with their knowledge and approval he was received as king, that he might reform the defects of the realm, correct what had to be corrected, and direct what was without guidance. By their author-ity he was set over the realm, and formally established as king of Scots, and with him the faithful people of the realm wish to live and die, as with one who, by right of birth and by endowment with other [*sic*] cardinal virtues, is fit to rule, and worthy of the name of king and of

dignus regis nomine et honore regni, quia salvatoris
gracia injuriam propulsando regnum sic deformatum et
perditum gladio reparavit [1] prout multi retro principes
et Scottorum reges dictum regnum, olim sepe perditum,
per gladium reparaverant quesierant et tenuerant temporibus retroactis, ut in antiquis Scottorum gestis mag-
nificis plenius continetur, ac sudores bellici Pictorum
contra Britones et Scottorum contra Pictos de regno
fugatos cum multis aliis antiquitus ense fugatis victis et
expulsis manifeste testantur.

Et si aliquis ex adverso jus vendicet in predictum
regnum per litteras in preteritum sigillatas consensum
populi et plebis continentes,[2] sciatis hoc totum de facto
processisse per vim et violenciam quibus non poterat
tunc resisti et metus multiplices cruciatus corporum ac
terrores varios [3] qui sensus perfectorum et animos aver-
tere poterant et cadere in constantes.[4] Nos igitur . .
episcopi . . abbates . . priores et ceteri de clero pretaxati
premissa veritate subnixa scientes et corditer appro-
bantes, dicto domino Roberto regi nostro Scoc' illustri

---

[1] As Hunter Marshall observed (op. cit., p. 290), this is a considerable
exaggeration of Bruce's achievements by 1310.

[2] The reference is probably not to any one group of documents. The
' Ragman ' homages of 1296 (see above, pp. liv, 68) are the only ' sealed '
documents expressing the consent of ' the people '; but, on less strict terms,
we may include the ' Great Rolls ', the ' Award of Norham ' (above, pp.
56-7), and many others.

[3] cf. above, p. 71, *n.* 2.

[4] See above, p. 84, *n.* 4.

the honour of a realm since, through the grace of the Saviour, he has saved from injury and restored [1] with his sword the kingdom thus damaged and decayed, as many princes and kings of the Scots had formerly by the sword restored, gained, and held in ancient times the said kingdom, which of old was often in jeopardy, as is contained more fully in the ancient and splendid histories of the Scots, and as the warlike efforts of the Picts against the Britons, and of the Scots against the Picts, who were expelled from the realm, and many others who were put to fight, conquered, and expelled with the sword in olden days, clearly testify.

If anyone, however, defends his claim to the realm by producing sealed letters from the past, which record [2] the consent of the whole people, be it known that this entire business was in fact carried through by force and violence which nobody could then resist, and by intimidation and many tortures of the body, and by various threats [3] which were able to pervert the senses and the minds of even the best of men, and to afflict the steadfast.[4] We, therefore, the bishops, abbots, priors and other clergy aforesaid, knowing that these statements are founded upon the truth, and heartily approving of them, have sworn the fealty due to Lord Robert, our illustrious king of Scotland, and we agree, and bear

fidelitates debitas fecimus, ac sibi et heredibus suis per
successores nostros in posterum fore faciendas recog-
noscimus et tenore presencium profitemur. Et in signum
testimonii et approbacionem omnium predictorum, non
vi compulsi nec dolo inducti aut errore lapsi sed pura et
perpetua ac voluntate spontanea, huic scripto sigilla
nostra fecimus apponi. Dat' in concilio generali Scoti-
cano, in ecclesia fratrum minorum de Donde, xxiiij die
mensis Februarii, anno domini MCCC nono celebrato, et
anno regni ejusdem quarto.

witness by the text of this document, that the same should be done to him and his heirs, by our successors in future. And we have caused our seals to be added to this document, as a sign of our testimony, and in approval of all the aforesaid, being not constrained by force, or seduced by craft or lapsing into error, but acting with pure, perpetual, and spontaneous freewill. At a Scottish general council, celebrated in the church of the Friars Minor of Dundee, 24 February A.D. 1309 [1309/10], in the fourth year of the reign of the same [king].

37

FAITE [1] a remembrer que le xvj jour du mois d'August,
l'an de grace millisme trecentisme et duzime, accordé
feut et assentu et par bone foi establé entre le noble prince
monsire Robert par la grace de Dieu roi d'Escoce, de une
part,[a] et les gentz de la comunalté de l'evesché de
Duresme entre Tyne et Teyse, par monsire Richard
Marmeduke,[2] William de Denum,[3] Gilbert Gategange
et Johan de Alainsheles, messengers ordinez de par la
mesme comunalté de treiter et assentir sour suffrance de
guerre ; c'este a savoir que le dit roi ad otreié por lui et
touz les suens et ses aherdauntz as dites gentz une
suffrance de guerre et treve du dit xvj jour d'Aust tant
que la feste de la nativité de seint Johan le Baptiste
prochein a venir a durer, por une somme de avoir dont
quatre centz et cinquant mars sunt aprés a paier a la
feste de seint Michel prochein a venir sancz delay. Et
si aveigne que les ditz deners ne soient paiez en l'abbeie
de Holmecoltran ou aillours al dit roi ou a son attourné
portant sa lettre de acquitance a la feste avantdit ou
devant, que de cel oure en avant la dite suffrance et
treue soient rompuz, fraintz et pur nule tenuz et de
toutes defaite. Et si mesfesours d'Escoce entrent le dit
evesché por mal faire, bien list a les dites gentz de eux

Text: P.R.O. Duchy of Lancaster 3/1 (Bishop Kellawe's Register), f. 56
(K), whence *Registrum Palatinum Dunelmense* (RS), I, 204-5.

   [a] *The corresponding* de lautre part *seems to have been forgotten by the writer, or
omitted by the scribe of* K.

   [1] This document illustrates the levying of blackmail on the northern
counties of England by Bruce between 1311 and 1328. For a detailed study
see Jean Scammell, ' Robert I and the North of England ', *EHR*, LXXIII

37

NOTE [1] that on 16 August, in the year 1312, agreement was reached, and in good faith established, between the noble prince, Robert, by the grace of God king of Scotland, on the one hand, and the people of the community of the bishopric of Durham between Tyne and Tees [on the other] represented by Richard Marmaduke,[2] William of Deanham,[3] Gilbert Gategange, and John de Alainsheles, the envoys appointed on behalf of the community to negotiate and make agreement, on the following truce : the king has granted to the said people, on behalf of himself, and of all his own followers and his adherents, a truce and armistice from the 16 August aforesaid until the feast of the nativity of St John Baptist next [24 June 1313] in return for a sum of money, of which 450 marks are later to be paid at the feast of St Michael next [29 September 1312] without any delay. And if it should happen that the money is not paid, in the abbey of Holmcultram, or elsewhere, to the king or to his attorney bearing his letter of acquittance, on the feast aforesaid, or before, then from that time onwards the truce and armistice shall be broken, cancelled, and considered as null and of no effect at all. And if evil-doers from Scotland enter the bishopric to do wrong, it is fully allowed to the people to arrest them by force. The

---

(1958), 385-403. It is on record that the city of Durham was burned by the Scots in 1312, the year of our text (Fordun, I, 346).

[2] Steward of the bishopric of Durham ; see Scammell, art. cit., p. 393.

[3] A local clerk, and also an eminent common lawyer and diplomatist ; cf. Scammell, art cit., p. 399, *n.* ; G. O. Sayles, *Select Cases in King's Bench under Edward III* (Selden Soc., 76), p. xlvii and *n.* 8.

par force arresteer. Et que les gentz de la dite comunalté ne se leverunt de guerre contre le dit roi d'Escoce
ne encountre les suens deinz son poer ove nul homme
fors ove le roi d'Engleterre ou ascun que avera roial poer,
et s'il le facent ove le dit roi ou ove nul autre, de lours
soit la dite treue voide et por nul tenuz. En tesmoignance de quele chose a la partie de ceste endenture vers
le dit roy demorancz les ditz Richard, William, Gilbert
et Johan ount mis lour seals, et a l'autre partie de cele
endenture demoraunt vers les gentz de la dite comunalté
le dit roi ad mis son privé seal. Don[é] a Hextildeham,
le jour et l'an avantditz.

people of the community shall not rise in war against the
king of Scotland, or against his followers within his realm,
under anyone except the king of England, or someone
who has royal authority; and if they do so with the
king or with any other, from that time the truce shall
be considered as null and void. As evidence of this,
Richard, William, Gilbert, and John have affixed their
seals to the portion of this indenture which remains with
the king, and the king has affixed his privy seal to the
portion of the indenture which remains with the people
of the community. Hexham, the day and year aforesaid.

38

(a) [45/197]

EDWARD,[1] par la grace de Dieu roi d'Engleterre, seigneur d'Irlaunde, e ducs d'Aquitaine a noz chers e foialx par la meisme grace T[homas] evesque de Wirecestre e J[ohan] evesque de Cardoill, Berthelmeu de Badelesmere, e noz autres messagés envoiez [2] as parties de Noef Chastel sur Tyne, saluz. Nous avoms [bien] entendu les lettres que vous, mestre Robert de Baudak, nous avez enveez, contenauntes ce q'estoit fait a la fesaunce d'yceles es busoignes pur queles vous estés envoiez celes parties ; et pur ce que contenuz est en les dites lettres que vous avez pris (?) jour de tretiz le meskerdy aprez la quinzene de la Chandelour, a queu jour nous savoms bien que les messagés nostre seint piere le pape,[3] qi sount uncore a Loundres, ne les messagés nostre cher frere le roy de Fraunce,[4] qi sen partirent nadgaires et qi sount venuz pur le tretiz, ne y purrount en nulle manere estre, si voloms et vous maundoms que meisme le tretiz faitz purloigner, ou en negoceaunt et debataunt les choses od ceux d'Escoce, ou par voie de continuance de quinze jours ou trois symaynes, que les dites messagés y puissent venir, et endementiers esperoms que nostre cher cousin

---

Texts : P.R.O. : (a) to (c) and (e) to (h), Ancient Correspondence (S.C. 1), 45/197, 198; 32/87; 45/199, 200, 201 ; 21/164 : (d) and (j) extracted from Exchequer (K.R.), Memoranda Rolls (E 159), 93, m. 77. Apparently none has been printed before, but (d) calendared in Bain, III, no. 728, with mention of (j).

[1] The interest of these texts lies in the great rarity, among the archives of Anglo-Scottish relations in the Middle Ages, of any such collection of letters between envoys and their government. Notice the employment of the ' process of Scotland ', i.e., the ' Great Roll ' of Andrew de Tange, written for this kind of use as recently as 1315–18.

38

(a) [Edward II to his ambassadors]

WE,[1] Edward, by the grace of God king of England, lord of Ireland, and duke of Aquitaine, give greeting to our beloved and faithful Thomas and John, by the same grace bishops of Worcester and of Carlisle, Bartholomew Badlesmere, and our other envoys sent [2] to the region of Newcastle-upon-Tyne. We have duly received the letters which you, Master Robert Baldock, have sent us, containing a report of what had been done, at the time when those letters were written, in the business for which you were sent to those parts. We note in those letters, that you have arranged a meeting for negotiations, on the Wednesday after the quinzaine of Candlemas [18 February 1321], a day on which we well know that the envoys of our Holy Father the pope,[3] who are still in London, and the envoys of our dear brother the king of France,[4] who are coming for the discussions, and have but lately set out, cannot possibly be there; and so it is our will and desire that you cause the proceedings to be prolonged, either by discussing and debating matters with the Scots, or by means of an adjournment of a fortnight or three weeks, so that these envoys may come there. Meanwhile we hope that our beloved cousin the

---

[2] On 19 January 1321, English envoys were appointed to negotiate with the Scots for a peace or a prolongation of the truce then in force (Rymer, II, i, 441). They were occupied in this work until May (see payments of expenses in B.M. MS Add. 9951, ff. 6, 8, 20, 22).

[3] For these papal envoys see text (b) below.

[4] i.e. Bertrand Boniface, John, lord of Varens, and William, bishop of Mende. Edward wrote commendatory letters to the pope and cardinals about their work (Rymer, II, i, 435, 442, 450).

le counte de Pembrok vendra en Engleterre, et de
l'houre q'il serra [venuz] nous lui feroms h[aster] devers
vous taunt [que] nous purroms issint que, od leide de
Dieu il y serra si . . . . .ᵃ les messagés le pape ou le
roi de Fraunce, les [queux nous ?] volums que vous enfourmez de nostre droit a la terre d'Escoce et del proces ¹
ent eu et fait en temps nostre cher piere, que Dieux
assoille, si avaunt come vous [porrez ?] que soit affaire
pur nostre honur et profit. Et sovent nous mandez quel
esploit vous y trovez, et les novelles devers celes parties.
Don[é] souz nostre privé seal, a Westmoustre, le xvij
jour de Fevrier, l'an de nostre regne quatorzime.

(b) [45/198]

Edward, par la grace de Dieu roi d'Engleterre,
seignur d'Irlaunde, et ducs d'Aquitaine a noz chers e
fealx les honurables pieres en Dieu, par la meisme grace
T[homas] evesque de Wirecestre J[ohan] evesque de
Cardoill, et a noz autres messagés envoiez as parties
du north' saluz. Por ce que l'onurable piere en Dieu
l'evesque de Wincestre et frere Guilliam de Landun,
messagés nostre seint piere le pape, vienent vers vous pur
estre a ce tretiz que se tendra entre vous et les gentz
d'Escoce, vous mandoms que vous les enfourmez et com-
munez ovesques eux de noz busoignes touchantes le dit
tretiz, car il nous ont certeinement promis de mettre en
meismes les busoignes tote l'eide et le bon conseil q'il
porront pur nostre estat et nostre honur, selonc ce q'il
serront enfourmez par vous.² Don[é] souz nostre privé

ᵃ *Holes in MS make two or three words illegible.*

¹ i.e., the ' Great Cause ' under Edward I, see above, p. xxv.
² Rigaud of Assier, bishop of Winchester, and William de Landun, in

earl of Pembroke will reach England, and from the moment that he arrives we shall cause him to hasten towards you as fast as possible, so that, with God's help, he will be there as [soon as] the envoys of the pope or of the king of France, [whom] we desire you to inform about our right in the realm of Scotland, and about the suit [1] which was held concerning that matter in the time of our beloved father, on whom God have mercy, as soon as you [can] do so with due regard to our honour and welfare. Inform us frequently of what success you have there, and of all that is going on. Westminster, attested by our privy seal, 17 February in the fourteenth year of our reign [1321].

(b) [Edward II to his ambassadors]

We, Edward, by the grace of God king of England, lord of Ireland, and duke of Aquitaine, give greeting to our beloved and faithful subjects, the honourable fathers in God Thomas and John, by the same grace bishops of Worcester and of Carlisle, and to our other envoys sent to the regions of the north. Because the honourable father in God the bishop of Winchester, and Brother William de Landun, the envoys of our Holy Father the pope, are coming to join you in the negotiations which are to take place between you and the Scots, we order you to instruct them, and have discussions with them, concerning our interests in the negotiations, for they have given us a firm promise to furnish all the help and good counsel that they can in that business, for our welfare and our honour, according to the information that you shall give them.[2] Westminster, attested by our privy

---

fact brought with them a papal letter which could not be shown to Bruce, because of some indiscretion in it (Rymer, II, i, 450).

seal, a Westmostre, le xix jour de Fevrier, l'an de nostre
regne quatorzime.

(c) [32/87]

Edward, par la grace de Dieu roi d'Engleterre,
seigneur d'Irlaunde, e ducs d'Aquitaine a noz chers e
foialx par la meisme grace T[homas] evesque de Wirecestre J[ohan] evesque de Cardoill, Berthelmeu de
Badelesmere, et a noz autres messagés au tretiz devers le
north' saluz. Por ce que nostre cher cousin et foial
Aymer de Valence conte de Pembrok, qi nous aviens
ordenez d'estre au dit tretiz, est tant occupez entre
grosses busoignes qi li touchent es parties de Fraunce
que nous ne savoms uncore nulle certeineté de sa venue,
et d'autre part nostre cher e foial Humfrei de Bohoun
counte de Hereford qi feust aussint ordeinez d'estre a
meisme le tretiz ne y vient point, par aucunes enchesons,
et nous harriens molt que les busoignes du dit tretiz
feussent destourbees ou trop delaiees par lour absence, si
avoms ordenez d'envoier au dit tretiz nostre cher cousin
et foial Johan de Bretagne, counte de Richemond, qi est
en venant vers celes parties a tote la haste q'il poet
bonement, et vous mandoms et chargeoms que vous
tretez et parlez sur les dites busoignes a l'esploit que vous
porrez en attendantz sa venue, qi serra procheinement,
a l'eide de Dieu. Et de l'oure q'il y serra venuz, entre li
et vous aillez avant en meismes les busoignes, selonc ce
que vous verrez que face affaire a l'honur et profit de
nous, si avant come si touz les autres y feussent sanz
attendre la venue de nul autre. Don[é] souz nostre
privé seal, a Westmostre, le xxiij jour de Fevrier, l'an de
nostre regne quatorzime.

seal, 19 February in the fourteenth year of our reign [1321].

(c) [Edward II to his ambassadors]

We, Edward, by the grace of God king of England, lord of Ireland, and duke of Aquitaine, give greeting to our beloved and faithful Thomas and John, by the same grace bishops of Worcester and of Carlisle, Bartholomew Badlesmere, and our other envoys at the negotiations in the north. Since our beloved and faithful cousin Aymer of Valence, earl of Pembroke, whom we have ordained to be present at the negotiations, is so occupied with serious business of his own in the realm of France that as yet we have no certainty of his coming, and on the other hand our beloved and faithful Humphrey de Bohun, earl of Hereford, who was also ordered to be present at the negotiations is not coming at all, for certain reasons, and we are much perturbed lest the progress of the negotiations should be impeded or too much delayed by their absence, we have accordingly given orders for sending to the negotiations our beloved and faithful cousin John of Brittany, earl of Richmond, who is on his way to the north as fast as he can. We order and charge you, that you negotiate and discuss the business with what success you can while awaiting his arrival, which will be soon, with God's help. From the moment that he arrives, you and he together should carry on the business according to what you see to be necessary for our honour and advantage, just as if all the others were there, and without waiting for the arrival of anyone else. Westminster, attested by our privy seal, 23 February, in the fourteenth year of our reign [1321].

z

(d) [Extract from E 159/93/m.77]

.... Die Jovis proximo ante festum Cinerum anno xiiij°, processus Scocie predicti, una cum instrumento predicto,[1] liberantur Johanni de Britannia comiti Richem', eunti usque Novum Castrum super Tynam ad tractandum de pace reformanda inter regem et Scotos, una cum archiepiscopo Ebor' episcopo Wygorn' et aliis ibidem inde tractantibus, per breve de privato sigillo residens ad receptam scaccarii, ad liberandum magistro Roberto Baldok' et Willelmo de Ayermynne.

(e) [45/199]

Edward, par la grace de Dieu roi d'Engleterre, seigneur d'Irlaunde, e ducs d'Aquitaine, a nostre cher clerc William de Ayremynne saluz. Por ce que nostre cher cousin et foial le counte de Richemund est en venaunt vers les parties du north' pur estre au tretiz, vous maundoms et chargeoms que vous soiez entendaunt a lui si avaunt come vous seriez a nous meismes si nous y feussions. Et ce en nulle manere ne lessez. Don[é] souz nostre privé seal a Westmoustr' le xxvj jour de Fevrier l'an de nostre regne quatorzime.

(f) [45/200]

Edward, par la grace de Dieu roi d'Engleterre, seignur d'Irlaunde, et ducs d'Aquitaine, a noz chers e fealx les honurables pieres en Dieu par la meisme grace T[homas] evesque de Wirecestre J[ohan] evesque de

---

[1] The preceding passage, not given here, describes exemplars of Andrew de Tange's ' Great Roll ' and ' Ragman Roll ' (i.e., ' the processes of Scotland ') and an instrument by Tange recording the ' award of Norham ' of

(d) [A note by the exchequer clerks]

On Thursday before Ash-Wednesday in the four-teenth year [26 February 1321] the said processes of Scotland, together with the said [notarial] document,[1] were delivered to John of Brittany, earl of Richmond, who was going to Newcastle-upon-Tyne to negotiate for the making of a peace between the king and the Scots, along with the archbishop of York, the bishop of Wor-cester, and others [already] negotiating there, by authority of a writ of privy seal which has been kept at the receipt of the exchequer, for delivery to Master Robert Baldock and William Airmyn.

(e) [Edward II to one of his ambassadors]

We, Edward, by the grace of God, king of England, lord of Ireland, and duke of Aquitaine, give greeting to our beloved clerk William Airmyn. Since our beloved and faithful cousin, the earl of Richmond, is on his way to the north, in order to be present at the negotiations, we command and enjoin you to be as attentive to him as you would be to ourselves if we were there. And this you shall in no wise neglect. Westminster, attested by our privy seal, 26 February in the fourteenth year of our reign [1321].

(f) [Edward II to his ambassadors]

We, Edward, by the grace of God king of England, lord of Ireland, and duke of Aquitaine, give greeting to our beloved and faithful subjects, the honourable fathers in God Thomas and John, by the same grace bishops of

---

1291 (the text on pp. 56-7 above). These are now P.R.O. C 47/23/2 and 4, and E 39/16/12 (or 17).

Cardoill, Barthelmeu de Badlesmere, et noz autres messagés envoiez au tretiz as parties du north, saluz. Nous avoms bien et diligeaument entenduz les lettres que vous, avantdit Berthelmeu, et noz chers clercs mestre Robert de Baldok et William de Ayremynne nous envoiastes par Richard Blundel, porteur de cestes, sur l'esploit de noz busoignes devers vous adonques, et vous savoms molt bon gré de la bone diligence que vous y avez mis, et vous fesoms savoir que avant que voz dites lettres nous vindrent, pur la longe demoere que nostre cher cousin et foial le counte de Pembrok fait es parties de France pur grosses busoignes que li touchent illoeques, si aviens envoiez vers vous pur le dit tretiz nostre cher cousin le counte de Richemond, lequel se party de Londres en alant vers celes parties yce joedi le xxvj jour de ce mois de Fevrier, et li avoms ja excitez par noz lettres q'il se haste vers vous a tout l'esploit q'il porra, et q'il vous certifie par ses lettres et par le dit Richard queu jour il entend d'estre a Noef Chastel, si que entre vous eue consideracion du dit jour et du temps q'il vous covendra mettre d'illoeques jusques a Baumburgh, facez garnir ceux d'Escoce de venir illoeques a un covenable jour pur treter ovesques vous, selonc l'acord q'est pris entre vous et eux, issint que les messages nostre seint piere le pape et le roi de Fraunce nostre cher frere ne s'ennoient de lour longe demoere celes parties. Et vous mandoms et chargeoms que de l'houre que nostre dit cousin de Richemond sera venuz a vous, aillez avant en les dites busoignes ovesques lui si avant come vous seriez si nostre dit cousin de Pembrok et tous les autres nomez en nostre commission y feussent, aussi bien en tretiz de finale pees,

Worcester and of Carlisle, Bartholomew Badlesmere, and our other envoys sent to negotiate in the north. We have given very careful attention to the letter which you, Bartholomew, and our beloved clerks, Master Robert Baldock and William Airmyn, have sent us by Richard Blundel the bearer of this letter, concerning the progress of our affairs in your hands up till then, and we feel deeply grateful for the great diligence that you have shown in the matter. We have to inform you that before your letter reached us, in view of the long stay which our beloved and faithful cousin the earl of Pembroke was making in the realm of France, on serious business which concerns him there, we had sent to you, for these negotiations, our beloved cousin the earl of Richmond, who left London on the way thither, this Thursday, 26 February; and we have urged him already, by our letter, to hasten towards you with all the urgency that he can, and to inform you, by his letter, and by the said Richard, of the day on which he expects to be at Newcastle, so that after you have considered between you the day and time on which it will suit you to move from there to Bamburgh, you will cause the Scots to be warned to come there on a suitable day to treat with you, according to the agreement which has been undertaken between you and them, so that the envoys of our Holy Father the pope, and of our beloved brother the king of France, will not weary of their long stay in those parts. We command and enjoin you, that from the moment when our cousin of Richmond reaches you, you proceed with him in the business as actively as you would if our cousin of Pembroke and all the others named in our commission were present there, both for negotiating a final peace, and for an extension of the

come de eloignance de trieue, et de totes autres busoignes
que nous purront [?] toucher celes parties. [Por] ce
que nous avoms entenduz par voz dites lettres, que les
Escotz ont chalangé la seurté que entre [1] vous avez fait
a lour messagés, pur ce que elle ne est mie efforcee par
serment fait en nostre alme,[2] et nous ne voloms mie que
les choses qui se devient treter par bone foy soient mises
en escrupule ne en suspecion, si vous enveoms commission d'affermer la dite seurté par serment en nostre
alme, et voloms que vous usez cele commission selonc ce
que vous verrez que face affaire a nostre honur, et a
l'esploit de nos busoignes ; et pur ce que les commissions
originales sont de diverses fourmes, si vous enveoms
quatre commissions acordantes a les autres [et] soiez
avisez de user cele que mielz sera acordante a l'estat [?]
des busoignes quant vous les averez bien examinez.
Don[é] souz nostre privé seal a Westmostr', le premier
jour de Marz, l'an de nostre regne quatorzime.

(g) [45/201]

Edward, par la grace de dieu roi d'Engleterre,
seigneur d'Irlaunde, e ducs d'Aquitaine, a noz chers
clercs mestre Robert de Baldok', ercedekne de Midd', et
William de Ayremynne saluz. Nous vous mandoms que
le procés d'Escoce, lequel nous avoms fait livrer a nostre
cher cousin et foial le counte de Richemound pur prendre
ent l'avisement que vous porrez sur le tretiz, resceivez
de lui, et le facez bien et sauvement reporter a nous.
Don[é] souz nostre privé seal a Westm', le primer jour
de Marz, l'an de nostre regne quatorzime.

---

[1] *entre[mentiers]* ?
[2] See above, p. 24, *n.* 3.

truce, and for all other business which may concern us in those parts. Because we have gathered from your letter that the Scots have questioned the safe-conduct that you have granted in the meantime [1] for their envoys, on the ground that it is not enforced by oath made upon our soul,[2] and we do not in the least desire that any matter which has to be negotiated in good faith should be subject to uncertainty or suspicion, we accordingly send you a commission to affirm the safe-conduct by oath upon our soul, and we desire that you use this commission in whatever way, in your opinion, may bring increase to our honour, and advantage to our business; and because the original commissions are in divers forms, we send you four commissions agreeing with the others. Use your discretion, when you have well examined them, in employing the one which may best suit the state of the negotiations. Westminster, attested by our privy seal, 1 March, in the fourteenth year of our reign [1321].

(g) [Edward II to his ambassadors]

We, Edward, by the grace of God, king of England, lord of Ireland, and duke of Aquitaine, give greeting to our beloved clerks master Robert Baldock, archdeacon of Middlesex, and William Airmyn. With regard to the process of Scotland, which we have caused to be delivered to our beloved and faithful cousin the earl of Richmond, so that you may refer to it as far as possible in the negotiations, we command that you receive it from him, and cause it to be returned safe and sound to us. Westminster, attested by our privy seal, 1 March in the fourteenth year of our reign [1321].

(h) [21/164]

Trespussant e tresredoté seignur, pleise a vostre seignurie saver que nous [venismes ᵃ a Baumburgh joedi l'endemein de la feste de l'Annunciacion nostre dame, e si fumes nous hasté come nous poioms, mes nous trovasmes les eawes molt desrivees par la ou nous passasmes, e puis que nous venismes a Baumburgh, si] ᵃ avoms esté entendantz a l'espleit des bosoignes touchantes le tretiz a tote la diligence que nous avoms peu, e ont esté les bosoignes mené pur vous e pur vostre dreit bien e covenablement, la Dieu merci, et des Escotz avoms oi moltz des paroles q'il ont dit, q'il desiront la pees sur tote rien, mes en fait mostront il rien qui touche a la pees eintz le contraire, et finaument aprés grantz delais q'il fesoient il ne voleient acorder forque a une trieue longe come de xxvj auntz, a quei nous e vos autres messages ne volioms acorder santz vous aviser, e avoms parlé du primer jour du mois de Septembre que les Escotz serront certifié a Baumburgh de vostre volenté sur la dite bosoigne, si sire Robert de Brus se voille a ceo acorder, de quoi les Escotz ont encovenant q'il nous certefieront procheinement.¹ Sire, nostre seigneur vous sauve e gard touz jours par sa pussance, e vous doint bone vie e longe, e victoire de vos enemis. Escript a Wodham,² le viij jour de April.

ᵃ *Passage in brackets afterwards deleted in MS.*

¹ There seems to be no evidence that this meeting took place or that the truce *was* renewed; which is not surprising, since by September 1321 Edward was preoccupied with domestic affairs (cf. *Vita Edwardi Secundi*, ed. Denholm-Young, 1957, p. 120).
² Near Bishop Auckland, Co. Durham

(h) [The ambassadors report to Edward II]

Most powerful and most dread lord, may it please your lordship to know that we [came to Bamburgh on Thursday, the morrow of the feast of the Annunciation of our Lady and we made such haste as we could, but we found the waters risen high on the road where we passed, and since we came to Bamburgh we] have been attending to the progress of events in these negotiations with all the diligence that we could, and (thanks be to God) the affair has been very properly conducted in the interests of yourself and of your right. From the Scots we have heard many declarations that they desire peace above all things, but in practice they have little to say which suggests it, rather the contrary, and finally, after they had caused great delays, they would agree only to a long truce, for example of twenty-six years, to which we and your other envoys would not agree without informing you, and we have suggested that on the first day of the month of September the Scots will be informed at Bamburgh of your wishes in the matter, if Robert Bruce is willing to agree to this, as to which the Scots have undertaken that they will inform us shortly.[1] Sir, may our Lord save and protect you always by his power, and grant you a happy and a long life, and victory over your enemies. Woodham,[2] 8 April [1321].

(j) [Extract from E 159/93/m.77]

De Processu Scocie Restituto ad Scaccarium [a]

Memorandum quod Willelmus de Ayrmynne, custos rotulorum cancellarie, venit hic quinto die Maii, videlicet in vigilia sancti Johannis ante portam Latinam anno xiiij°, et restituit hic tria instrumenta publica facta super jure regis ad regnum Scocie, que liberata fuerunt Johanni de Britannia comiti Richem', nuper eunti usque Novum Castrum super Tynam ad tractandum de pace inter regem et Scotos, una cum aliis per dominum regem missis, sicut superius continetur.[1] Et eodem die instrumenta predicta liberantur magistro Willelmo de Maldon, uni camerariorum etc., custodienda in thesauraria regis, etc.

[a]   Title as in MS

(j)

The Process of Scotland Restored to the Exchequer.

Note that William Airmyn, keeper of the rolls of chancery, came here on 5 May, that is on the eve of St John before the Latin gate, in the fourteenth year [1321] and restored here three public instruments made about the king's right to the realm of Scotland, which had been delivered to John of Brittany, earl of Richmond, who lately went to Newcastle-upon-Tyne to treat for peace between the king and the Scots, with others sent by the king, as is described above.[1]   And on the same day these instruments were handed to master William of Maldon, one of the chamberlains, etc., to be kept in the treasury of the king, etc.

[1] cf. text (d), p. 149.

39

De Pace Formata cum Scotis per Andream de Harcla.ᵃ

Dᴏᴍɪɴᴜꜱ ¹ rex mandavit hic breve suum de privato sigillo quod est inter communia ² de hoc anno in hec verba :

Edward, par la grace de Dieu roi d'Engleterre, seignur d'Irlaunde, e ducs d'Aquitaine a noz chers e foials nostre tresorier e a son lieutenant, e as barons de nostre escheqier, e as autres de nostre conseil a Everwyk, saluz. Nous vous envoioms cy dedeinz enclos le transcrit d'une endenture ³ faite sur l'acord pris entre Andreu de Harcla counte de Cardoil e Robert de Bruys, queu chose semble a nous e a nostre conseil comencement de grant mal, par quoi nous avoms ordinez nostre cher e foial William le Latymer a demorer en nostre dite citee ⁴ ove certeines gentz d'armes sur la sauveté de ycele. Si vous mandoms qe entre ⁵ vous soiez de bon confort e confortez noz bones gentz de meisme nostre citee, e au dit William, en quantque a la sauveté de

---

Text :   The textual problems of this ' treaty ' seem at the moment insoluble, and we aim only to assist the study of them by printing the important unpublished version in P.R.O. Exchequer (K.R.), Memoranda Rolls (E 159), 96, m. 70 (E), calendared in Bain, ɪɪɪ, no. 803.   A Latin text, half as long again, and different in many important points, was printed from a Register of the see of Bergen in *Proc. Society of Antiquaries of Scotland*, ɪɪɪ (1857–60), 458-61 (P).   The relation of E to P is unknown, and is made more puzzling by the absence of a date from E.   Incomplete, but textually important, Latin versions occur in *Chron. Edw. I and II* (RS), ɪɪ, 82-3 (B) ; *Chronicon de Lanercost* (ed. Stevenson, 1839), pp. 248-9 (L) ; and Stevenson, *Illustrations of Scottish History* (Maitland Club, 1834), from MS Harley 655, pp. 8-9 (H).   Since E has never been printed, and P has gone almost unnoticed, most discussions of the agreement have been based only on B and L, and must be treated with caution.

ᵃ *Title from margin of* E

39

The Peace made with the Scots by Andrew Harclay.

THE [1] king sent here his writ of privy seal (filed among the *communia* [2] of this year) which reads as follows :

We, Edward, by the grace of God, king of England, lord of Ireland, and duke of Aquitaine, give greeting to our beloved and faithful subjects, the treasurer and his lieutenant, the barons of our exchequer, and the others of our council who are at York. We are sending you enclosed here a copy of an indenture,[3] made to record an agreement undertaken between Andrew Harclay, earl of Carlisle, and Robert Bruce, a thing which seems to us, and to our council, to bode great evil. We have therefore ordered our beloved and faithful William Latimer to stay in the city,[4] with some men-at-arms, to look after its safety. We command you, accordingly, to be in good heart in the meantime [5] and to reassure our good people in the city, offering help and advice in every way that you know, or can contrive (as we trust you to do) to William, in matters which affect the safety of our

---

[1] For his part in this agreement, unauthorised by his own king, Harclay was executed as a traitor on 3 March 1323, but he pointed the way towards the thirteen-year truce of 30 May 1323 (Rymer, II, i, 521), and in some ways our text even resembles the ' final peace ' of 1328 (pp. 164-70 below). See above, p. xxix, and Ramsay, *Genesis of Lancaster*, I, 134-7.

[2] The section of the exchequer records where this royal writ was filed.

[3] L, H, and P say that the counterparts were sealed by Harclay and the earl of Moray.

[4] i.e. York

[5] cf. above, p. 151, *n.* 1.

nostre dite citee e de noz places e de nostre tresor qe y sont e des parties enviroun appent, soiez eidantz e conseillantz par toutes les voies qe vous saverez ou purrez, sicome nous nous fioms de vous. Don[é] souz nostre privé seal a Stowe Park, le xix jour de Janev[er], l'an de nostre regne seszisme.

Et quandam cedulam dicto brevi interclusam cujus tenor talis est :

Ces sont les pointz de l'acord fait par entre sire Robert de Bruys, d'une part e le counte de Cardoil d'autre part, pur touz ceux d'Engleterre qi volont estre desportez e sauvez de guerre del dit sire Robert de Bruys e de touz les seons :—

Premerement,[a] pur ce qe l'un roialme e l'autre furent en bon point tant come chescun roialme avoit roi de sa nacion e par soi feust meintenuz en ses leis e ses custumes severalement, qe unqore soit en meisme la manere. Et pur ce, [qe] touz ceux de lour acord soient conseillant e eidant ove tut lour poer a lui e a ses heirs q'ils peussent tenir le roialme d'Escoce franchement, entierement, e quitement, e curront sur toutz ceux qi ne se volont a ce assentir, come sur enemys de comun profit de l'un roialme [e] de l'autre. Et ceux qe [*sic*] se volent a ce obliger, se volont le roi e le counte avantditz afermer e asseurer q'il lour seront conseillant e meynteignant e eidaunt en toutes choses qe purront estre au comun profit du roialme d'Engleterre, selonc le dit des dusze persones a ce jurez, dont les sys seront esluz des gentz au dit roi, et sys seront esluz par le dit counte, par les queux dusze[1] ou par la greignur partie de eux, si mestier soit,

---

city, and of our courts and our treasury, which are there, and of the surrounding districts. Stow Park, attested by our privy seal, 19 January, in the sixteenth year of our reign [1323].

[The king sent also] a schedule enclosed with the writ, whose text is as follows :

These are the details of the agreement made between Robert Bruce, on the one hand, and the earl of Carlisle, on the other, on behalf of all those in England who wish to be spared and saved from war with Robert Bruce and all his followers :

First, because both kingdoms prospered so long as each kingdom had a king from its own nation, and was maintained separately, with its own laws and customs, let it again be done in the same manner. For this reason, all those who are parties to this agreement [?] shall give all possible counsel and aid to Robert, and his heirs, so that they may be able to hold the realm of Scotland freely, entirely, and in liberty, and they shall pursue all those who are unwilling to agree to this, as enemies of the common good of the one realm and of the other. The king and the earl wish to assure and to satisfy those who are willing to commit themselves to this, that they will advise, maintain, and assist them in everything that can be to the common profit of the realm of England, according to the decision of twelve persons sworn for this purpose, six of whom shall be chosen from the people of the king, and six chosen by the earl. By these twelve,[1] or the majority of them, if need be, everything that has

---

[1] In P the function of the twelve is to decide cases where Bruce and Harclay disagree.

toutes choses qe seront affere pur le commun profit de ambedeux les roialmes soient tretez, ordinez, a determinez. Et seront les principals seignurs tenuz a faire execucion de leur dit e de leur ordinance en touz pointz. Et touz ceux qi de cest acord voedront estre, averont du dit roi d'Escoce e del counte tele seurté [1] come les dites dousze persones dirrount qe soit a avoir. Et qe a cest acord ne se volent assentir, qe touz li autres qi sont de l'acord li curront sur, e les ditz roi e counte ovesques. Et si le roi d'Engleterre se voet assentir dedeinz un an acomptez aprés la faccion de ces covenances, qe le dit roi d'Escoce eit son roialme frank et quit a lui et a ses heirs come desus est dit, le roi d'Escoce lui fera les choses qe s'ensuyent, c'est assavoir q'il fera fere un[e] abbeye en Escoce de la rente de cinq cents marcz d'esterlings pur les almes de ceux qi sont mortz en la guerre, e lui durra auxint dedeinz dys aunz qarante mille mars d'esterlings, c'est assavoir chescun an qatre mille mars, et qe le dit roi d'Engleterre avera le mariage de l'heir mal [2] du dit roi d'Escoce a marier en covenable lieu en son sanc,[3] s'il est avys as dousz persones avantdites qe ce soit a faire pur le comun profit de ambedeux.[a] Et si le roi d'Engleterre ne voet ces offres dedeinz un an accepter, qe le roi d'Escoce ne soit plus obligez, mes ovreront[b] les dites dusze persones selonc lour avisement a comun profit de l'un roialme e de l'autre. Et fait assavoir qe si l'acord se face par entre les ditz rois, qe Dieux deynt, nul de eux

---

[a] B *ends here*.

[b] averont E ; operarentur H, *whence conjecture in text*

[1] In B and P, Bruce also is to have security from those who wish to take part in the agreement.

[2] cf. these financial and matrimonial provisions with those of 1327–8 (below, pp. 158-9, 165-9). At the present date Bruce had still no legitimate

to be done for the common profit of both realms shall be negotiated, ordained, and settled. And the magnates shall be bound to execute their decisions and their ordinances in every detail. All those who wish to take part in this agreement shall have, from the king of Scotland and the earl, such security [1] as the aforesaid twelve persons shall say that there should be. As for those who do not wish to consent to this agreement, all the others who partake in it shall pursue them, and the king and the earl [shall act] likewise. If the king of England is willing to consent, within one year after the making of this agreement, that the king of Scotland shall have his realm, free and quit for himself and his heirs, as is said above, the king of Scotland shall do for him the things which follow, that is to say: he will found an abbey in Scotland with a rent of 500 marks sterling for the souls of those who were slain in the war, and within ten years he will grant him also 40,000 marks sterling, that is 4,000 marks each year; and the king of England shall have the marriage of the heir male [2] of the king of Scotland, to be married, in some suitable place, to one of his kindred,[3] if it is the opinion of the twelve persons aforesaid that this should be done, for the common advantage of both [realms]. If the king of England does not wish to accept these offers within a year, the king of Scotland shall be bound no further, but the twelve persons shall act according to their judgment for the common profit of one realm and the other. And note that if agreement is reached between the kings, as God

---

son; his heir male was Robert, son of Bruce's daughter Marjorie, born in 1316, and later King Robert II.

[3] *In congruo loco in sanguine suo* P; *loco conveniente in sanguine suo pro regni utriusque utilitate maritandi* H.

2 A

pur ce sera tenuz de receyvre en son roialme homme qi
ad esté encontre lui, ne de lui rendre ses terres qe lui ou
ses auncestres avoient en son roialme, s'il nel voet faire
de sa grace especiale.[1]

Et le counte de Murreve ad juré en l'alme le roi
d'Escoce q'il meyntendra touz ceux qi volent estre de
ceste acord encontre toutes gentz, et qe le roi d'Escoce
ne prendra jamais pees ove le roi d'Engleterre saunz ce
qe touz ceux qe sont de l'acord ne seront compris
dedeinz sa pees. Et aussint le counte de Cardoil est
jurez de meyntenir touz ceux qi sont de l'acord.[2]

[1] cf. below, pp. 158, *n*. 3, 171, *n*. 1.
[2] P and L are dated at Lochmaben, 3 January 1322/3.

grant, neither of them on this account shall be bound to receive in his realm a man who has been opposed to him, nor to render him the lands that he or his ancestors had in his realm, if he does not wish to do it of his special grace.[1]

The earl of Moray has sworn on the soul of the king of Scotland that he will maintain all those who wish to take part in this agreement against all men, and that the king of Scotland will never make peace with the king of England, unless all those who are concerned in this agreement are included in his peace. Likewise the earl of Carlisle has sworn to maintain all those who are concerned in the agreement.[2]

40

Peticiones ex parte regis Scocie concesse per regem Anglie.[a]

Edward,[1] par la grace de Dieu roy d'Angleterre seigneur d'Irlande, et ducz d'Aquitaine, a les nobles d'Escosse saluz. Nous avons veus desouth le seal sire Robert de Brus les pointz que s'ensuent.

Ces sont les pointz que le dit sire Robert demande avoir ensealés du grand seal le roy d'Angletere. Primierement, que le roy et son barnage se sont assentuz que ledit sire Robert eit [b] le roy[a]lme d'Escosse frank, quit, et entier, sans nulle maniere de bernage,[2] a luy et ses hoirs pour tousjours. Item, que le mariage du filz et hoir ledit sire Robert se face a la seur le roy d'Engleterre, et que dower soit faicte a la damoyselle selon ce que home pourra accorder, od autres [c] pointz qi appendent au dict mariage. Item, que null que soit a la foy le roy d'Angleterre ne de ses adherentz ne peusse terre ne tennement demander dedans le royalme d'Escosse od les apurtinances, ne null home d'Escosse ne des adherdantes ledit sire Robert ne peusse terre ne tenement demander dedans le royalme d'Angleterre.[3] Item, que ledit sire Robert et ses hoirs soient tenuz d'ayder au roy d'Angleterre et ses hoirz en son royalme d'Angleterre contre toutz, sauve l'aliance faicte entre ledit sire Robert et le roy de France, et que le roy d'Angleterre et ses hoirs

---

Text: B.M. MS Harley 4637 C, f. 87 (H), a sixteenth-century transcript, with some errors. Printed, with introduction and notes, by E. L. G. Stones in *SHR*, xxx (1951), 49-54.
  ^a *Title from* H
  ^b cict ? H
  ^c ancores H

40

Requests on behalf of the king of Scotland, granted by the king of England.

WE,[1] Edward, by the grace of God king of England, lord of Ireland, and duke of Aquitaine, give greeting to the nobles of Scotland. We have examined the following terms, which have been issued under the seal of Robert Bruce :

These are the terms which Robert requests to have sealed with the great seal of the king of England. First, that the king and his baronage are agreed that Robert shall have the realm of Scotland free, quit, and entire, without any kind of subjection,[2] for himself and his heirs for ever. Also that the son and heir of Robert shall be married to the sister of the king of England, and that dower shall be provided for the lady according to what can be agreed, with other details which relate to the marriage. Also that nobody who is in the allegiance of the king of England, or of his adherents, can demand land or tenement within the realm of Scotland or its appurtenances, nor can any man of Scotland, nor of the adherents of Robert, demand land or tenement within the realm of England.[3] Also that Robert and his heirs shall be bound to help the king of England and his heirs in his kingdom of England against everyone (saving the alliance made between Robert and the king of France),

---

[1] Our text gives the preliminary agreement which led to the ' final peace ' of 1328 (pp. 161-70 below). For details see E. L. G. Stones, art. cit.

[2] See Ragueau, *Glossaire du droit françois* (1704), s.v. ' barnage '.

[3] This matter is strangely ignored in the treaty on pp. 161-70 below ; for its subsequent history see pp. 171-2 below, and notes.

soient tenuz d'ayder audit sire Robert et ses hoirs en Escosse contre toutz en mesme la maniere, comme bons aliés. Et ledit sire Robert veult donner vingt mille livres d'esterlinges, dedans trois ans apres la paix affermé, proportionaument par suffisante seurté. Item, que ordiné soit par le roy d'Engleterre et son conseil et par ledit sire Robert et son conseil, que la sentence [1] pronuncée a la court de Rome contre ledit sire Robert et les siens soit duement repellé a plutost que home peult, et ce faire [a] le roy d'Angleterre mettra ayde et conseil et poer sans faintise. Et s'il plaist au roy d'Angleterre mander par son grand seal a les nobles d'Escosse q'il voille les choses avantditz affermer et en celle maniere avoir tretez pur bien de paix, il plaist audit sire Robert de mander les siens a Neuf Chastel sur Teyne par suffisaunt conduyt du roy d'Angleterre de treter od les messages le roy d'Angleterre des choses avantdictes en la forme avantdite au jour que sera accordé. Escrite a la ville de Berwik, le xviij jour d'octobre.

Et plaist a nous avantdit roy d'Angleterre de avoir et tenir tretiz par les noz od vous nobles les grantz et les messages d'Escosse, a nostre ville de Noef Chastel sur Teyne, au jour que sera sur ce accordés sur paix finale, issint que le mariage du filz et hoir dudit sire Robert nous soit assuré pour nostre seur, et convenable dower luy soit ordenez, selon ce que home pourra accorder, od autres [b] pointz que appendent audit mariage, et que suffisante seurté nous soit faite de vingt mille livres avantdictes, a payer deinz le terme susdicte au lie[u]

---

[a] *read* et pur ce faire ?   [b] ancores H

[1] Bruce was excommunicate at this date, but curiously little seems to be known of the details of his relations with the Holy See, and of the ' processes against him (see p. 168 below).

and that the king of England and his heirs shall be bound
to help Robert and his heirs in Scotland against everyone, in the same manner, like faithful allies. Robert is
prepared to give £20,000 sterling within three years
after the confirmation of the peace, by instalments,
[secured by] sufficient surety. Also that it be ordained
by the king of England and his council, and by Robert
and his council, that the sentence [1] pronounced at the
court of Rome against Robert and his followers shall be
repealed in due form as soon as possible ; and to achieve
this the king of England shall furnish help and counsel
and support, without dissimulation. And if the king of
England is prepared to send his writ under the great seal
to the nobles of Scotland, saying that he is willing to
confirm the above, and on these premises to negotiate
for the sake of peace, Robert is prepared to send his
envoys to Newcastle-upon-Tyne (under an adequate safe-
conduct from the king of England) to negotiate with the
envoys of the king of England about the things aforesaid,
on the terms aforesaid, on a day to be agreed. At the
town of Berwick, 18 October [1327].

We, the king of England, agree to enter into negotiations, through our representatives, with you, the nobles,
magnates and envoys of Scotland, at our town of Newcastle-upon-Tyne, on a day to be agreed, concerning final
peace, in such a way that the marriage of the son and
heir of Robert be assured to us for our sister, and a suitable dower be ordained for her according to what can
be agreed, with other details which relate to the marriage,
and that a sufficient surety be given to us for paying the
£20,000 within the stated period, at a place to be agreed

que sur ce serra accordez. Et quant a eyde faire les uns aus autres, accordoms que parlaunce teigne entre ledit sire Robert et noz chers et feals Henré de Percy nostre cous[i]ng et William de Denum,[1] e auxint de ce que gentz d'Engleterre ne demandent terre en Escose ne gentz d'Escosse en Angletere, et ce que par eulx sera accordez soit reporté devant les solempnes messages au tretiz, et illoques[a] terminé par commun assent. Et comme les offres et les chosez susdictez nous soient suffisamment asseurés, nous promettons en bonne foy de assurer ledit sire Robert suffisamment le royalme d'Escose, a tenir quitement a luy et a ses hoirs sans service ou bernage a tousjours, sans quere encheson que les choses susdites soient desturbez, ou nul poinct de les mys en delay. Et lesditz choses issint mises a point,[2] promettons de prier [par] noz lettres a nostre saint piere le pape que ladite sentence soit relessé. En tesmoignance de qeu chose nous avons fait faire cestez noz lettres overtez. Don[é] a Notinghame, le trentiesme [jour d']Octobre, l'an de nostre regne premier.

---

[a] allegees H

[1] See above, p. 144, *n.* 3.
[2] *mettre à point* : see Godefroy, *Dictionnaire*, *s.v.* ' point '.

on for this purpose. As for giving help to each other, we agree that discussions shall take place between Robert, and our beloved and faithful Henry Percy, our cousin, and William of Deanham,[1] and also on the proposal that Englishmen may not demand land in Scotland, nor Scotsmen in England; and that what is agreed by them shall be reported to the official envoys at the negotiations, and there determined by common agreement. When the above offers and terms have been sufficiently guaranteed to us, we promise in good faith to afford Robert a sufficient assurance of holding the realm of Scotland freely, for himself and his heirs, without service or subjection, for all time to come, without our ever seeking occasion to disturb this agreement, or to cause any part of it to be delayed. When these things have been settled,[2] we promise to beseech our Holy Father the pope by letter, that the sentence which has been referred to may be repealed. As evidence of all this, we have caused this our letter patent to be written. Nottingham, 30 October, the first year of our reign [1327].

41

(a)

UNIVERSIS [1] presentes litteras inspecturis Edwardus dei gracia rex Anglie, dominus Hybernie, et dux Aquitanie salutem in domino sempiternam. Cum nos nonnullique predecessores nostri reges Anglie jura regiminis dominii seu superioritatis regni Scocie conati fuerimus obtinere, ob hocque motarum dira guerrarum discrimina Anglie et Scocie regna diucius afflixissent, nos attendentes cedes occisiones scelera ecclesiarum destrucciones et mala innumerabilia que hujusmodi occasione guerrarum regnicolis utriusque regni multipliciter contingebant, bonaque quibus regnum utrumque mutuis compendiis abundaret perpetue pacis stabilitate connexum, ac per hoc contra conatus noxios rebellare vel impugnare volencium interius vel exterius majori firmitate securum, volumus et concedimus per presentes pro nobis heredibus et successoribus nostris quibuscumque, de communi consilio assensu et consensu prelatorum et procerum comitum et baronum ac communitatum regni nostri in parliamento nostro, quod regnum Scocie per suas rectas marchias prout temporibus bone memorie Alexandri regis Scocie ultimo defuncti fuerunt habite et servate, magnifico

---

Text :   (a) Extracted here from lost notarial copy, printed in Thomas Innes, *Critical Essay* [etc.] (1729), II, 828-31 (N). It seems unnecessary to name here, or give variants from, the numerous MSS and printed texts, except for Rymer, II, ii, 730.
(b) P.R.O. Scotch Rolls (C 71), no. 12, m. 5 (C).   Printed by E. L. G. Stones in *SHR*, XXIX (1950), 39-40.
(c) From original indenture in S.R.O. (E), of which there is a facsimile in *Nat. MSS. Scotland*, II, no. xxvi.   Copy in P.R.O. Scotch Rolls (C 71), no. 12, m. 4.   Printed in Rymer, II, ii, 734-5, and elsewhere.

41

(a) [Quitclaim by Edward III]

WE,[1] Edward, by the grace of God king of England, lord of Ireland, and duke of Aquitaine, give eternal greeting in the Lord to all who shall inspect the present letter. We, and certain of our predecessors as kings of England, have tried to assert rights of rule, dominion, or superiority over the realm of Scotland, and in consequence a grievous burden of wars has long afflicted the realms of England and Scotland; therefore, considering the killings, slaughters, crimes, destructions of churches, and ills innumerable which so often befell the inhabitants of each realm, by reason of these wars, and the advantages which would accrue to each kingdom, to their mutual gain, if they were joined by the stability of perpetual peace, and thus enjoyed greater security against the evil attempts of those within or without desiring to rebel or to attack them, we wish, and grant by the present letter, on behalf of ourselves, our heirs, and all our successors, with the common counsel, assent, and consent, of the prelates, magnates, earls, barons, and communities of our realm assembled in our parliament, that the realm of Scotland, defined by its true marches as they existed and were maintained in the time of Alexander, of worthy memory, the late king of Scotland,

---

[1] These texts belong to the famous treaty of 1328, usually known by the name of Northampton, where it was confirmed, though (a) was actually issued at York, and the remaining terms were settled at Edinburgh. For the circumstances see articles by E. L. G. Stones in *SHR*, xxviii (1949), 121-32, xxix (1950), 23-51, and in *History*, xxxviii (1953), 54-61; and above, p. xxx. The Latin indenture made on the same day as (c) is not given here; for its place in the transaction see *SHR*, xxix, 23-51.

principi domino Roberto dei gracia regi Scottorum illustri confederato ac amico nostro carissimo suisque heredibus et successoribus, divisum in omnibus a regno Anglie integrum liberum ac quietum remaneat in perpetuum absque qualicumque subjeccione servitute clameo vel demanda, et si quod jus nos vel antecessores nostri in regno Scocie retroactis temporibus pecierimus vel pecierint quoquo modo, prefato regi Scocie heredibus et successoribus suis renunciamus et dimittimus per presentes. Omnes autem obligaciones convenciones et pacta initas vel inita qualitercumque cum nostris predecessoribus quibuscumque, quibuscumque temporibus, super subjeccione regni Scocie vel incolarum ejusdem per quoscumque reges vel incolas clericos vel laicos ipsius regni Scocie, pro nobis heredibus et succesoribus nostris remittimus penitus et omnino. Et si que littere carte munimenta vel instrumenta reperiantur de cetero ubicumque super hujusmodi obligacionibus convencionibus et pactis confecte vel confecta, pro cassis irritis inanibus et vacuis habeantur nulliusque valoris esse volumus vel momenti.

Et ad premissa omnia plene pacifice et fideliter perpetuis temporibus observanda, dilectis et fidelibus nostris Henrico de Percy consanguineo nostro et Willelmo la Zousche de Assheby et eorum alteri ad sacramentum in animam nostram prestandum per alias litteras nostras patentes plenam dedimus potestatem ac mandatum speciale. In cujus rei testimonium has litteras nostras fieri fecimus patentes. Datum apud Eboracum primo die Marcii anno regni nostri secundo.

Per ipsum regem et consilium in parliamento.

Sigillabantur [1] *autem dicte littere sigillo magno et rotundo de*

shall remain for ever to the eminent prince Lord Robert, by the grace of God the illustrious king of Scots, our ally and dearest friend, and to his heirs and successors, divided in all things from the realm of England, entire, free, and quit, and without any subjection, servitude, claim, or demand. Any right in the realm of Scotland which we or our ancestors have sought in past times, in any manner, we renounce and surrender, by the present letter, to the king of Scotland and his heirs and successors. We remit utterly and entirely, on behalf of ourselves, our heirs, and our successors, all obligations, agreements, and treaties undertaken in any way, with any of our predecessors, at any time, concerning the subjection of the realm of Scotland or its inhabitants, by any kings or inhabitants of the realm of Scotland, whether clerks or laymen. If any letters, charters, muniments, or instruments are found anywhere in future concerning obligations, agreements, and treaties which have been made, let them be regarded as quashed, vain, null, and of no effect, and we wish them to be of no value or moment.

We have given full powers, and a special mandate, to our beloved and faithful Henry Percy our cousin, and William la Zouche of Ashby, and to each of them, by another letter patent of ours, to take an oath upon our soul for perpetually observing all these things fully, peaceably, and faithfully. In testimony of this we have caused this our letter patent to be made. York, 1 March, in the second year of our reign [1328].

By the king himself and the council in parliament.

The letter was sealed [1] *with a large round seal in white wax, on*

---

[1] Details of sealing from N, which describes an exemplar extant in the Scottish archives in 1416.

*cera alba in cujus una parte erat forma cathedre in qua erat
ymago regis sedentis induti quasi regalibus vestibus cum corona
in capite et sceptro in manu dextra et ex utraque parte cathedre
flos lilii et in circumferencia scriptum erat litteris legibilibus*
EDWARDUS DEI GRACIA REX ANGLIE DOMINUS
HYBERNIE DUX ACQUITANIE. *Ex altera autem parte
sigilli erat ymago regis armati sedentis super equum gladium
ferentis evaginatum elevatum in manu dextra et super humerum
sinistrum erat scutum in quo erant tres ymagines leopardi
gradientis et in circumferencia erat scriptum litteris legibilibus*
EDWARDUS DEI GRACIA REX ANGLIE DOMINUS
HYBERNIE DUX ACQUITANIE.

(b)

Rex [1] universis ad quos presentes littere pervenerint
salutem. De fidelitate probata et circumspeccione provida venerabilium patrum Henrici Lincoln' episcopi
thesaurarii nostri et Willelmi Norwycen' episcopi ac di-
lectorum et fidelium nostrorum Henrici de Percy con-
sanguinei nostri Willelmi la Zousche de Assheby et
Galfridi le Scrope [2] plenam fiduciam reportantes, ad
tractandum cum Roberto de Bruys vel deputand' ab
ipso de finali pace et concordia inter nos et nostros subditos ex parte una et ipsum Robertum et suos subditos de
Scocia ex altera super guerris et discordiis hincinde motis
ineundis, et ad easdem pacem et concordiam modis et
viis quibus expedire videbitur vallandas et firmandas ac

---

[1] Printed as a specimen (the only one in this volume) of the ' credentials '
of medieval envoys. In the sealed engrossment, of course, the initial *rex*
and the concluding *in cujus* would be extended to the forms used on pp. 161
and 162.

[2] The bishop of Norwich, and Scrope, had much previous experience of
Anglo-Scottish diplomacy ; for Scrope in particular see E. L. G. Stones in
EHR, LXIX (1954), 7, 16.

one face of which there was the figure of a throne, in which there was a representation of a king seated, clad, as it were, in royal robes, with a crown on his head, and a sceptre in his right hand, and on either side of the throne a fleur-de-lys, and on the circumference was written in legible letters EDWARD BY THE GRACE OF GOD KING OF ENGLAND LORD OF IRELAND DUKE OF AQUITAINE. *On the other face of the seal was a representation of a king in armour, seated on a horse, and bearing an unsheathed sword raised in his right hand, and on his left shoulder was a shield, on which were three representations of a lion 'passant', and on the circumference was written in legible letters* EDWARD BY THE GRACE OF GOD KING OF ENGLAND LORD OF IRELAND DUKE OF AQUITAINE.

(b) [Credentials for the English ambassadors]

The king [1] greets all those to whom the present letter shall come. Having full confidence in the approved fidelity and prudent caution of the venerable fathers Henry, bishop of Lincoln, our treasurer and William, bishop of Norwich, and of our beloved and faithful Henry Percy, our cousin, William la Zouche of Ashby, and Geoffrey le Scrope,[2] we commit and grant to the said bishops, and Henry, William, and Geoffrey, or to four or three of them, by the text of this letter, the power to treat with Robert Bruce, or his representatives, for a final peace and settlement to be reached between ourselves, and our subjects, on the one hand, and Robert himself, and his subjects of Scotland, on the other, after the wars and disputes arising between them, and to establish and confirm the peace and settlement by such ways and means as seem expedient, and to perform such

omnia et singula que ad hujusmodi pacem et concordiam pertinere poterunt facienda ; prefatis episcopis Henrico Willelmo et Galfrido quatuor vel tribus ex eis tenore presencium committimus et concedimus potestatem, promittentes nos ratum et firmum habituros quicquid per predictos episcopos Henricum Willelmum et Galfridum quatuor vel tres ex eis tractatum vallatum et firmatum fuerit in premissis. In cujus etc. Teste rege apud Eboracum primo die Marcii.

(c) Convenciones facte per nuncios regis Anglie apud Edeneburgh[a]

Coneue chose soit a touz ceus queus cestes lettres verrunt qe le dys et septesme jour de Martz, l'an de grace mille troys centz vynt et septisme, selonc le cours de l'esglise d'Engleterre,[1] entre le tres excellent prince Robert par la grace de Dieu roi d'Escoce, dune part, et les honurables pieres en Dieu Henri par la seofrance de Dieu evesque de Nichole, William par mesme la soefrance evesque de Norwitz, Henri de Percy, William la Zouche de Assheby et Geffrei le Scrope, messages et procurers par especiale commissioun de tres excellent prince Edward, par la grace de Dieu roi d'Engleterre, seigneur d'Irlande, et ducs d'Aquitaine, a treter sur pees finale et a la dite pees affermer et asseurer entre le dit roi d'Engleterre et l'avantdit roi d'Escoce sur guerres mues entre les roiaumes de Engleterre et d'Escoce d'autrepart, treteez et acordeetz furent les choses soutzescriptes en la forme soutze-scripte, c'est assaver :

Primerement qe bone pees finale et perpetuele soit entre les ditz rois, lour heirs et successors et lour roiaumes

---

[a] *Title from endorsement on* E

acts, all and singular, as pertain to the peace and settlement. We promise to hold as settled and firm whatever is negotiated, agreed, and affirmed in these matters by the bishops, and Henry, William, and Geoffrey, or by four, or three of them. In [testimony] of which etc. Witness the king, at York, 1 March [1328].

(c) Agreement made at Edinburgh by the ambassadors of the king of England

This is to inform all those who shall see this letter, that on 17 March in the year A.D. 1327, according to the reckoning of the church of England [1327/28] [1] the following matters were discussed and agreed, in the form given below, between the most excellent prince, Robert, by the grace of God king of Scotland, on the one hand and the honourable fathers in God Henry, by divine permission bishop of Lincoln, William, by the same permission bishop of Norwich, Henry Percy, William la Zouche of Ashby, and Geoffrey le Scrope, the envoys and procurators, by special commission, of the most excellent prince Edward, by the grace of God king of England, lord of Ireland, and duke of Aquitaine, on the other hand, to negotiate for a final peace, and to affirm and confirm it between the king of England and the king of Scotland, after the wars arising between the realms of England and Scotland. That is to say :

First that there be a true, final, and perpetual peace between the kings, their heirs and successors, and their

---

[1] ' According to the reckoning of the church of England ' (and of Scotland) at this period, the year began on 25 March; hence 17 March 1327 must be interpreted as in the year 1328 by modern reckoning.

et terres, et entre lour soutzmis et peoples d'une part et
d'autre selonc la forme qe s'ensuyt. Et a la seurance et
affermance de cele pees est tretee et acordee qe entre
David, fitz eisné et heir le dit roi d'Escoce, et Johane,
soer de l'avantdit roi d'Engleterre qe unqore sunt de si
tendre age q'ils ne pount contract de matrimonie faire,
mariage se face a plus tost qe duement se porra faire. Et
a la seurance du dit mariage est fait serment en les almes
des ditz rois par les persones desoutz nomeetz, et des
prelatz et autres grauntz du roiaume d'Escoce. Et qe
l'avantdit roi d'Escoce doit doner et assigner a la dite
Johane en leus covenables denz son roiaume d'Escoce,
deux mille livereez de terre et de rente par an par
resnable extente a avoir ove feetz des chivalers, avoesons
des esglises et totes autres fraunchises apurtenauntes a
cele terre, a terme de la vie la dite Johane, sauve au dit
roi d'Escoce ses heirs et ses successors, avoesons des
abbeyes, priories et hospitals et les droitz de sa coroune,
issint qe si le dit David, aprés le dit matrimonie fait,
devie vivante la dite Johane qe mesmes les deux mille
liverez de terre ove les dites apurtenaunces demoergent
a la dite Johane a terme de sa vie en noun de dowere, si
qe ele ne puse demander autre dowere. Et qe de tiel
doun et assignement l'avantdit roi d'Escoce durra ses
lettres patentes generales,[1] et avant la feste de l'Ascen-
sioun prochein a venir ferra issint extendre cele terre en
presence de ceux queux le dit roi d'Engleterre voudra
pur sa dite soer a ceo deputer. Et aprés cele extente
faite, le dit roi d'Escoce ferra faire ses chartres avant la
dite feste des parceles extendues et nomees en due forme,

---

[1] The text of this letter is printed in *SHR*, xxix (1950), 43-4 (dated
17 March 1327/8).

realms and lands, and their subjects and people, on the
one side and the other, according to the form which
follows. And for the security and permanence of that
peace it is settled and agreed that a marriage take place,
as soon as properly can be, between David, the eldest
son and heir of the king of Scotland, and Joan, the sister
of the king of England, the two being still of such tender
age that they cannot make a contract of matrimony.
And for assurance of the marriage an oath was taken,
upon the souls of the kings, by the persons named below,
and by the prelates and other magnates of the realm of
Scotland. The king of Scotland shall grant and assign
to Joan, in suitable places in his realm of Scotland, two
thousand pounds' worth of land and rent annually, by
a just extent, to be held with knights' fees, advowsons
of churches, and all other franchises belonging to that
land, for the term of Joan's life, saving to the king
of Scotland and his heirs and successors, the advowsons
of abbeys, priories and hospitals, and the rights of his
crown. If David die after the marriage, and while Joan
is alive, the same two thousand pounds' worth of land,
with the appurtenances, shall remain with her for the
term of her life in name of dower, so that she can not
demand any other dower. This gift and assignment the
king of Scotland shall grant by his letter patent general,[1]
and before the next feast of the Ascension [12 May
1328] he shall cause an extent to be made of that land,
in the presence of those whom the king of England may
wish to appoint for this, on behalf of his sister. After the
extent is made, the king of Scotland shall have charters
made, before the said feast, specifying the extended
parcels of land designated in due form, [and granting

pur terme de la vie la dite Johane, et liverer mesmes les chartres et la seisine des dites terres a les ditz deputeez par le dit roi d'Engleterre. Et si par cas Dieu feit sa volenté [1] de la dite Johane avant qe le dit mariage feust affermé ou acompli, qe adunqes le dit roi d'Engleterre, ses heirs ou ses successors, eient le mariage le dit David pur autre plus prochein et covenable de lour saunc, et qe cele a qi il serra issint mariez eit les dites deux mille livereez de terre a terme de sa vie en noun de dowere en la forme susdite. Et si par cas Deu feit sa volenté [1] du dit David avant le dit mariage affermé ou accompli, qe adunqes le dit roi d'Engleterre, ses heirs ou ses successors eient mariage de le heir masle prochein de l'avantdit roi d'Escoce pur la dite Johane, si la lei de seinte esglise le seofre ou qe le pape le purra et voudra faire par dispensacioun. Et en ceo cas les ditz rois, lour heirs et successors, joyntement travailerunt pur cele dispensacioun purchacer. Et si ceo ne se purra faire en la persone la dite Johane par ascune cause, qe adunqes ceo mariage soit fait a autre du saunc du dit roi d'Engleterre plus prochein et covenable. Item il est tretee et acordee qe la dite Johane vendra en Escoce a Berwyk sur Twede le quinzisme jour du mois de Juyl prochein avenir, et illoqes serra baillee au dit roi d'Escoce, ou a celui ou ceus qe i vendront de part lui. Item il est tretee et acordee qe en cas qe Dieu feit sa volenté du dit David avant le matrimonie affermé ou acompli, qe la dite Johane, saunz desturbaunce et enpechement, puse demorer et returner au dit roi d'Engleterre, son frere, solonc ceo q'il plerra au dit roi soun frere et a lui, si ensi n'aveigne q'ele soit enceinte en quel cas ele ne passera pas hors du roiaume saunz congee du roi et du barnage.

---

[1] A euphemism, of course, for death

them] for the term of the life of Joan, and shall deliver the charters and the seisin of the lands to the persons appointed by the king of England. If by any chance God performs his will [1] for Joan before the marriage is affirmed or accomplished, then the king of England, or his heirs or successors, shall have the marriage of David for another close relative of their blood who is suitable, and she to whom he is so married shall have the two thousand pounds of land for the term of her life, in name of dower, in the above form. If by any chance God performs his will [1] for David before the marriage is affirmed or accomplished, then the king of England, or his heirs, or successors, shall have the marriage of the next heir male of the king of Scotland for Joan, if the law of Holy Church allows, or if the pope can and will do so by dispensation. In that case, the kings, or their heirs and successors, shall jointly strive to gain that dispensation. And if that cannot be done for Joan herself, for any reason, this marriage shall be made to another suitable close relative by blood of the king of England. Again, it is settled and agreed that Joan shall come into Scotland at Berwick-upon-Tweed on 15 July next [1328] and be there committed to the king of Scotland, or to him or to those who come there on his behalf. Again, it is settled and agreed that if God performs his will for David before the marriage is affirmed or accomplished, Joan may remain without disturbance and hindrance, and return to her brother the king of England, according to the pleasure of the said king her brother and herself, unless it should happen that she is pregnant, in which case she must not pass outside the realm without the leave of the king and the baronage.

Item, il est tretee et acordee qe les ditz rois, lour heirs et successors, serrunt bons amitz et loiaux allietz, et qe les uns aiderunt a les autres covenablement com bons allietz, sauve de part le dit roi d'Escoce l'alliaunce faite entre lui et le roi de France.[1] Mes s'il aveigne qe le dit roi d'Escoce, ses heirs ou ses successors, par cause de la dite alliance ou par ascune autre quecumque cause face guerre au dit roi d'Engleterre, ses heirs ou ses successors, qe le dit roi d'Engleterre, ses heirs et ses successors, peusent guerroier l'avantdit roi d'Escoce, ses heirs et ses successors, nient countreestant la pees qe ore se fait entre eaux ne chose qe i soit contenue. Item, il est tretee et acordee qe si nul leve de guerre en Irlande countre le dit roi d'Engleterre, ses heirs ou ses successors, qe l'avandit roi de Escoce, ses heirs et ses successors, nen aiderunt a les ditz enemitz le dit roi d'Engleterre. Auxint est il tretee et acordee qe si nul leve de guerre contre l'avandit roi d'Escoce, ses heirs ou ses successors, en l'isle de Manne ou es autres Illes de Escoce qe le dit roi Dengleterre, ses heirs et ses successors, nen aiderunt a les ditz enemitz.

Item, il est tretee et acordee qe toutz escriptz, obligaciouns, instrumentz et autres munimentz tochauntz la subjeccioun des gentz ou de la terre d'Escoce au roi de Engleterre lesqueux sunt adnulletz et defaitz par les lettres[2] le dit roi d'Engleterre, et toutz autres instrumentz et privilegies tochantz la franchise d'Escoce qe porrunt estre troveez en bone foi devers le dit roi d'Engleterre, soient rendutz et restitutz a l'avandit roi d'Escoce a plus tost q'ils purrunt bonement selonc ceo q'ils serrunt

---

[1] The ' auld alliance ', dating back formally to 1295. Cf. above, pp. 73, 158.

[2] i.e., pp. 161-3 above

Again, it is settled and agreed that the kings, and their heirs and successors, shall be true friends and loyal allies, and that the one shall help the other properly, as a good ally, saving, on the part of the king of Scotland, the alliance made between him and the king of France.[1] If it should happen that the king of Scotland, or his heirs or his successors, by reason of the said alliance, or for any other cause whatever, make war on the king of England or his heirs or his successors, then the king of England, or his heirs and his successors, may wage war on the king of Scotland, or his heirs and his successors, notwithstanding the peace which is now made between them, or anything which is contained in it. Again, it is settled and agreed that if anyone wage war on the king of England, or his heirs or successors, in Ireland, that the king of Scotland, or his heirs and successors, will not assist the enemies of the king of England. And likewise it is settled and agreed that if anyone wage war on the king of Scotland, or his heirs or successors, in the Isle of Man, or the other isles of Scotland, that the king of England, or his heirs and successors will not help the said enemies.

Again, it is settled and agreed that all writings, obligations, instruments, and other muniments concerning the subjection of the people of Scotland, or of the land of Scotland, to the king of England, which are annulled and undone by the letter[2] of the king of England, and all other instruments and privileges touching the freedom of Scotland which may be found in good faith in possession of the king of England, shall be rendered up and restored to the king of Scotland as soon as they well can be, when found, in such a way that

troveez, issint qe de cele livree seit faite endenture de chescun escript, obligacion, instrument et muniment qe livree serra.[1] Auxint il est tretee et acordee qe, en cas qe la dite lettre du dit roi d'Engleterre par la quele les ditz escriptz, obligaciouns, instrumentz et munimentz sunt defaitz et adnullez deust estre nulle et restitué au dit roi d'Engleterre, que adonqes touz escriptz, obligaciouns, instrumentz, et munimentz ensi livreez au dit roi d'Escoce par endenture soient restitutz et rebailleez au dit roi d'Engleterre, ses heirs ou ses successors, saunz countredit du dit roi d'Escoce, ses heirs ou ses successors.

Item, il est tretee et acordee qe le dit roi d'Engleterre eidera en bone foi qe les procés, si nuls sunt faitz en la court de Rome et aliors par auctorité nostre seint pere le pape countre le dit roi d'Escoce, son roiaume et ses soutzmis, clerz ou lais, soient repellez aveqes lour effect,[2] et a ceo faire et acomplir il envoiera ses lettres especiales de priere au pape et as cardinals.[3]

Item, treté est et acordé qe coment qe le dit roi d'Escoce, prelatz et autres grauntz de son roiaume soient obligez au dit roi d'Engleterre en vynt mille livres d'esterlings a payer en trois auns a trois termes a Twedemouthe,[4] et de ceo payement issint faire se soient submys a la jurisdiccioun de la chambre le pape si com en les lettres patentes du dit roi d'Escoce et des autres prelatz

---

[1] This clause has been strangely misunderstood. Bruce was not making a general demand for the ' restoration ' of *Scottish* archives removed by Edward I. He was asking only for documents which concerned Scottish independence, and the majority of these were not Scottish archives at all, but documents of English origin, like the ' Ragman Rolls '. This is made evident by the careful provision for listing the documents, so that they could be *returned to England* if the present treaty were not finally executed (see the next sentence of text). To speak of the transfers of documents from the P.R.O. to the S.R.O. in 1937, and subsequently, as a ' tardy fulfilment of the Treaty of Northampton ', is therefore a confusion of the issue. cf. E. L. G. Stones, in *History*, xxxviii, 59-61.

an indenture shall be made of this deliverance, enu-
merating each document, obligation, instrument, and
muniment that shall be handed over.[1] Also it is settled
and agreed that in case the letter of the king of England,
by which the said writings, obligations, instruments, and
muniments are annulled and cancelled, has to be
nullified, and restored to the king of England, then all
writings, obligations, instruments, and muniments so
delivered to the king of Scotland by indenture shall be
restored and handed back to the king of England or his
heirs or his successors, without dispute, by the king of
Scotland, or his heirs or successors.

Again, it is settled and agreed that the king of England will in good faith lend assistance, so that the law-
suits, if any such have been instituted at the court of
Rome, and elsewhere, by authority of our Holy Father
the pope, against the king of Scotland, his realm and his
subjects, whether clerks or laymen, may be revoked, with
all their consequences [2] [?], and in order to do this, and
to bring it about, he will send a private letter of request
to the pope and to the cardinals.[3]

Again, it is settled and agreed that although the king
of Scotland, the prelates, and the other magnates of his
realm, are committed to pay to the king of England a
sum of £20,000 sterling, over three years, in three instalments, at Tweedmouth,[4] and for making this payment
thus, they have submitted to the jurisdiction of the papal
camera, as is fully explained in the letter patent of the
king of Scotland, and of other prelates and magnates of

---

[2] Conceivably the meaning may be analogous to that of *cum effectu* =
urgently, as above, p. 45, *n.* 4.
[3] See Rymer, II, ii, 739-40.
[4] The £20,000 was all paid by Jan. 1331 ; a very considerable achievement by the Scots. On the *raison d'être* of the payment see Stones, *SHR*,
XXIX, 29, and above, pp. xxix-xxx.

et grauntz de son roiaume et instrument publyc de ceo
fait est pleynement contenuz,[1] nientmeynz les ditz
messages et procurers du dit roi d'Engleterre en noun
de lui voillent et grauntent par certeins resons qe nulle
execucioun, condempnacioun ne denunciacioun se face
par nul juge de la chambre le pape countre le dit roi
d'Escoce ne les autres obligeez, devant la fin de deus mois
aprés chescun des ditz trois termes.

Item, il est tretee et acordé qe les leis des marches
entre les ditz roiaumes soient bien gardeez et qe rede [2]
droit et justice soit fait des trespas qe en surderunt [3]
d'une part et d'autre, et si par cas defaute soit trovee en
les leis de la marche ou debat sourde qe ne poet estre
terminé par les ministres les rois, soient reporteez as ditz
rois et par eux et lour conseaus ou ceus q'ils voudrent
deputer d'une part et d'autre soient redresceetz et
amendeetz.

Item, les ditz messages et procurers ont promis[a] et
empris en bone foi en noun du dit roi d'Engleterre, q'il
toutes les choses sus escriptes et soutz escriptes par ses
lettres patentes sealeez de son seal, pur lui, ses heirs,
successors et soutzmis, ratefiera, approvera et confermera
et les dites lettres en Escoce envoiera, et dedenz l'Ascension prochein avenir au meir de Berwyk les ferra livrer.
Et est l'entencioun du dit roi d'Escoce et des avauntditz
messages et procurers le dit roi d'Engleterre qe par le[s]
tretiz qe ore se funt, nule manere de prejudice soit faite
au droit de seinte esglise en l'un roiaume ne en l'autre.

Et sur la seurance du dit mariage ad monsire Hughe

---

[a] promis *ed.* ; premis E C (*including confirmation of May 1328*)
[1] See *SHR*, xxix, 43-50.
[2] Mod. Fr. *raide*
[3] *sordre*, from *surgere*

his realm, and in the public instrument made on this subject [1] ; nevertheless the envoys and procurators of the king of England, acting in his name, desire and grant for certain reasons, that no execution, condemnation, or denunciation, be made by any judge in the papal camera against the king of Scotland, nor the other parties so bound, before the end of two months after each of the three terms mentioned.

Again, it is settled and agreed that the laws of the marches between the realms be well kept, and that strict [2] right and justice be done against trespasses which take place [3] on one side and the other, and if by chance a defect be found in the laws of the march, or a dispute arise which cannot be ended by the officials of the kings, let them be reported to the kings, and be redressed and amended by them, and their councils, or those whom they wish to appoint as deputies on the one side or the other.

Again, the envoys and procurators have promised in good faith, in the name of the king of England, that he will ratify, approve, and confirm, all the things written above and below by a letter patent, sealed with his seal, on behalf of himself and his heirs, successors and subjects, and will send this letter to Scotland, and cause it to be delivered to the mayor of Berwick before next Ascension Day [12 May 1328]. It is the intention of the king of Scotland, and of the envoys and procurators of the king of England, that by the agreement which is now made no manner of prejudice shall be done to the right of Holy Church in the one realm or the other.

For assurance of the marriage, Hugh earl of Ross, in

counte de Ros, en la presence du dit roi d'Escoce et par especial comandement de lui et en sa alme, et a garder, tenir et acomplir en bone foi saunz venir a l'encountre totes les choses susdites et chescun de iceles, si ad monsire Robert de Lawedre, justice de Loeneys, en la presence de mesme celi roi d'Escoce, et par especial comandement de lui et en sa alme, faitz sermens as seintes evangelies.[1] Et sur l'aseurance du dit mariage, et a garder, tenir et acomplir en bone foi saunz venir a l'encountre totes les choses susdites et chescun de iceles, si ad le dit monsire Henri de Percy en noun du dit roi d'Engleterre et par especial poer de lui et en sa alme fait serment as seintes evangelies. Et nous, Robert, par la grace de Dieu roi d'Escoce, totes les choses sus escriptes a nous moustrez et chescun de iceles agreoms, ratefioms, et approvoms pur nous et pur nos heirs et nos successors et pur notz soutzmis, saunz venir jammés a l'encountre.

En tesmoignance de queus choses, a l'une partie [2] de ceste endenture demorant vers les ditz messages et procurers avoms fait mettre nostre seal. Et nous avanditz messages et procurers a l'autre partie [3] de mesme l'endenture demorant vers le dit roi d'Escoce avoms mis nos seals. Doné a Edinburghe, le dys et septime jour de Marz, l'an de grace mille trois centz vynt et septime susdit.

[1] These oaths sworn by deputy are eloquent proof of Bruce's status as king in full sovereignty. cf. above, p. 24, *n.* 3.
[2] This counterpart, bearing the seal of Bruce, is not extant.
[3] This counterpart is E. It has lost all its seals.

the presence of the king of Scotland, and by his special command, and on his soul, and for keeping, holding and accomplishing, in good faith, without infringement, all the above things, and each of them, Robert of Lauder, justice of Lothian, in the presence of the king of Scotland, and by his special command, and on his soul, have taken oath on the Holy Gospels.[1] And for assurance of the marriage, and for keeping, holding, and accomplishing in good faith, without infringement, each and all of these things, Henry Percy, in the name of the king of England, and by powers specially granted by him, and on his soul, has taken oath upon the Holy Gospels. And we, Robert, by the grace of God, king of Scotland, confirm, ratify and approve, on behalf of ourselves and of our heirs and our successors and of our subjects, all the terms written above, which have been shown to us, and each of them, and we intend never to infringe them.

As evidence of these things we have caused our seal to be affixed to one counterpart [2] of this indenture, which belongs to the said envoys and procurators. And we, the envoys and procurators, have affixed our seals to the other counterpart [3] of the same indenture, which belongs to the king of Scotland. Edinburgh, 17 March 1327 [1327/8].

42

Robertus,[1] dei gracia rex Scottorum, omnibus probis hominibus tocius terre sue salutem. Sciatis nos de gracia nostra speciali [2] dedisse, concessisse, et hac presenti carta nostra confirmasse Henrico de Percy militi, filio et heredi quondam Henrici de Percy militis, omnes terras et tenementa ac redditus que fuerunt dicti quondam Henrici patris sui vel sua esse debuerunt jure hereditario, vel alio quovis justo et legitimo modo, infra regnum nostrum Scocie cum pertinenciis suis et cum omnibus libertatibus ad predictas terras tenementa et redditus quoquo modo pertinentibus, nulla guerre forisfactura eidem Henrico vel heredibus suis in aliquo obstante ; tendenda et habenda prefato Henrico et heredibus suis de nobis et heredibus nostris faciendo inde servicium debitum et consuetum.

Concedimus eciam eidem Henrico, pro nobis et heredibus nostris, quod predicti Henricus et heredes sui in prosecucione juris sui in curiis nostris, vel alterius cujuscumque infra regnum nostrum quod eis jure hereditario vel alio quovis modo competere possit per aliquam guerre forisfacturam in aliquo non excludantur. In cujus rei testimonium presenti carte nostre

Text: From the original charter in Alnwick Castle, reference ' Sherborne Missal Case no. 15 ' (A), complete with an almost perfect Great Seal of Robert I, *sur double queue*. I am grateful to His Grace the Duke of Northumberland for permission to photograph it. Printed, from A, in C. H. Hartshorne, *Feudal and Military Antiquities of Northumberland* [etc.] (1858), p. clv ; and (incompletely) from a cartulary text in *Percy Cartulary* (Surtees Soc., cxvii), p. 155.

[1] The numerous documents which together constitute the treaty ' of Northampton ' totally ignore the difficult question of restoring lands forfeited during the War of Independence. This charter, printed here because

42

Rᴏʙᴇʀᴛ,[1] by the grace of God king of Scots, gives greeting to all the worthy men of the whole of his realm. This is to inform you that we, by our special grace,[2] have given and granted, and by this our present charter confirmed, to Sir Henry Percy, son and heir of the late Sir Henry Percy, all the lands, tenements and rents which belonged to the late Sir Henry his father, or which should have been his by hereditary right, or by any other just and rightful title, within our realm of Scotland, with their appurtenances and all liberties belonging in any way to the aforesaid lands, tenements, and rents. No forfeiture resulting from war shall impede Henry, or his heirs, in any way. These lands shall be had and held, by Henry and his heirs, of us and our heirs, by performing the service which is customary and due for them.

We grant also to Henry, for ourselves and for our heirs, that Henry, and his heirs, shall not be debarred, by any forfeiture caused by war, from seeking before our courts, or the courts of anyone else in our realm, the rights which may belong to them by hereditary right, or by any other kind of title. As evidence of this, we have

---

its existence seems to have been virtually unknown (as it was to the present editor at the time when he wrote in *SHR*, xxix (1950), 34-5), shows that restoration was actually granted to Percy within a few months of the treaty ; and there is evidence to show that Robert I at least promised the same favour to Thomas Wake and to Henry of Beaumont (Rymer, ɪɪ, ii, 804). Possibly these concessions were obtained by Queen Isabella, on the occasion of the royal wedding at Berwick in July 1328 (*SHR*, xxix, 34). In general, see above, p. xxx.

[2] ' By grace ' because this was not a provision of the recent treaty.

sigillum nostrum precepimus apponi. Testibus Waltero
de Twynham cancellario nostro, Thoma Ranulphi
comite Moravie domino vallis Anandie et Mannie,
Malisio comite de Stratheryn, Jacobo domino de Duglas,
Roberto de Brus filio nostro dilecto,[1] Roberto de Lawedre
patre, Roberto de Meyners, et Hugone Flemyng militibus; apud Glasgu, vicesimo octavo die mensis Julii,
anno regni nostri vicesimo tercio.

[1] A bastard son of Robert I

ordered our seal to be affixed to this charter. Witnesses :
Walter de Twynham, our chancellor, Thomas Randolph,
earl of Moray and lord of Annandale and Man, Malise,
earl of Strathearn, James, lord of Douglas, Robert
Bruce, our beloved son,[1] Robert of Lauder senior,
Robert de Meyners and Hugh Fleming, Knights.
Glasgow, 28 July, the 23rd year of our reign [1328].

Supplementary Document

IN ¹ nomine domini Amen. Anno a nativitate ejusdem M°CCCC^{mo} primo, indiccione nona, pontificatus sanctissimi in Christo patris et domini nostri, domini Bonifacii divina providencia pape noni anno xij°, mense Octobris, die lune xvij eiusdem,ᵃ in mei notarii, parcium ᵇ et testium subscriptorum presencia personaliter constitut', commissarii regnorum Anglie et Scocie convenerunt, videlicet pro rege et regno Anglie reverendus in Christo pater et dominus, dominus Ricardus, permissione divina episcopus Bangorensis, magnifici ac strenui viri Henricus Percy [Nor]thhumbr' constabularius Anglie, Radulfus Nevyle Westmerland' ejusdem regni marescallus, comites, Ricardus dominus de Grey, Radulfus Evyr, Gerardus Heron, milites, Johannes Cursoun domicellus et magister Alanus Newerk ² clericus, et pro parte regis et regni Scocie, quidam Matheus episcopus Glascuensis, nobiles viri Archibaldus de Douglas et Georgius de Angous comites, Johannes de Merton ³ decretorum doctor ac Johannes de Swynton, Willelmus Styward milites et Adam Forster domicellus, in quodam campo prope Jhethamkyrke, Glascuensis diocesis, et primo ostenderunt hincinde commissiones eorum, quorum

---

Text : B.M. MS Cotton Vitellius E XI, ff. 239v–241v (C). Apparently as yet unprinted. The MS has been damaged by fire, so that some words are illegible at the beginning and at the end of the line. The extension of the abbreviations is more than usually uncertain, and the Latin at some points almost defies translation.

  ᵃ *After* ejusdem, anni ' *expunged* ' C
  ᵇ presencia C, *probably misreading abbreviation in exemplar*

  ¹ We give this text as perhaps the only surviving medieval description of the full proceedings when commissioners of the two realms met to

Supplementary Document

In [1] the name of the Lord Amen. In the year of the Nativity 1401, the ninth indiction, the twelfth year of the pontificate of the most Holy Father in Christ our lord Boniface IX, pope by divine providence, in the month of October, on Monday the 17th day, in the personal presence of myself, the notary, of the parties, and of the witnesses named below, the commissioners of the realms of England and Scotland met together. On behalf of the king and the realm of England there were the reverend father and lord in Christ Richard, by divine permission bishop of Bangor, the eminent and valiant Henry Percy, earl of Northumberland, constable of England, Ralph Neville, earl of Westmorland and marshal of the realm, Richard lord Grey, Ralph Evyr and Gerard Heron, knights, John Curzon, esquire, and master Alan Newark,[2] clerk, and on behalf of the king and realm of Scotland there were Matthew, bishop of Glasgow, the noble Archibald, earl of Douglas, and George, earl of Angus, John of Merton,[3] doctor of canon law, John of Swinton and William Styward, knights, and Adam Forster, esquire. The meeting took place in a field near Kirk Yetholm, in the diocese of Glasgow, where they began by showing their commissions

---

negotiate peace. It also illustrates the persistence of the English demand for homage long after 1328. The reader who wishes to study it in detail should do so in conjunction with the other texts cited in the notes, plus the two letters of February 1402 (not 1401, as the editor states) in *Royal and Historical Letters, Henry IV* (ed. Hingeston (RS, 1860)), 1, 52-6 and 58-65.

[2] Newark was obviously the technical expert on the English side. He had been in the royal service for ten years and possessed great diplomatic experience.

[3] On Merton see below, p. 177, *n.* 1.

tenores inferius annotantur,[1] et utriusque datis copiis et factis collacionibus earumdem, voluerunt et consencierunt [hin]cinde, quod ibidem in ipso loco ad tractandum de contentis in dictis commissionibus in crastino, videlicet die Martis xviij mensis suprascripti invicem convenirent, quibus die et loco commissarii pro parte regis Anglie videlicet reverendus pater episcopus Bangorensis, Ricardus dominus de Grey, Radulfus Evyr, Gerardus Heron, Johannes Curson, et Alanus Newerk, ac regis Scocie episcopus Glascuensis, Johannes de Merton, Johannes de Swynton, Willelmus Styward, et Adam Forster predicti hincinde convenerunt, et premissis aliquibus altercacionibus petitum fuit pro parte regis Anglie quod rex Scocie serviret regi Anglie tanquam homo et vassallus suus ligius, sicut eciam ab antiquissimis temporibus reges Scocie tenebantur facere et fecerunt, vel quod ostenderent quare ad hoc minime [?] tenerentur.

Ad que pro parte regis Scocie fuit responsum simpliciter quod ad hoc nunquam tenebantur reges Scocie, et quod propterea non tenebantur aliquid ostendere nisi prius pro parte regis Anglie fuisset aliquid ostensum quare ad hoc tenerentur, et postea, nonnullis altercationibus interpositis, dictus reverendus pater Ricardus episcopus Bangorensis, unus commissariorum pro parte regis Anglie, mandavit discreto ac circumspecto viro magistro Alano Newerk clerico in ea parte suo college predicto, quatenus recitaret commissariis regis Scocie cronicas et scripturas antiquas in illa parte loquentes,

---

[1] These commissions are *not* given in C, but see *Rotuli Scotiae*, II, 159 for those to the English envoys, and their confidential instructions in Nicolas, *Proceedings of Privy Council*, I, 168 ff. (cal. in Bain, IV, no. 589).

to each other, the texts of which are recorded later,[1] and after copies had been exchanged, and collations made of them, they agreed and consented mutually that they should meet there, in that very place, on the morrow, that is Tuesday the 18th of the month, to negotiate on the matters contained in the commissions. At that date and place, the commissioners on the part of the king of England, that is the reverend father the bishop of Bangor, Richard, lord Grey, Ralph Evyr, Gerard Heron, John Curzon and Alan Newark, and of the king of Scotland, [that is] the bishop of Glasgow, John of Merton, John of Swinton, William Styward, and Adam Forster met together, and after certain preliminary disputes, the request was made on behalf of the king of England that the king of Scotland should serve the king of England as his man and liege vassal, as indeed the kings of Scotland had been bound to do from the most ancient times, and so did; or that they should show reason why they were in no way bound to do so.

To this it was answered simply, on behalf of the king of Scotland, that the kings of Scotland had never been bound to do this, and that therefore they were not compelled to show any reason, unless some ground had first been shown, on the part of the king of England, why they were bound to do so. Later, with some discussion intervening, the reverend father Richard, bishop of Bangor, one of the commissioners on the part of the king of England, instructed the discreet and circumspect clerk master Alan Newark, his colleague in that matter, to recite to the commissioners of the king of Scotland the chronicles and ancient writings bearing on the argument,

qui tunc incontinenter recitavit coram eis quomodo sub temporibus Ely et Samuelis prophete vir quidam strenuus et insignis, Brutus nomine, de genere Trojanorum post excidium urbis Troje cum multis nobilibus Trojanorum applicuit in quandam insulam tunc Albion vocatam, partes nunc Anglie Scocie et Wallie vocatas in se integraliter continentem, a gygantibus inhabitatam, quibus sua et suorum devictis potencia et occisis, eam nomine suo Britanniam sociosque suos Britones appellavit, et postea regnum suum tribus filiis suis divisit, scilicet Locrino filio suo primogenito illam partem Britannie que nunc Anglia dicitur, et Albanacto secundo filio suo nato illam partem que tunc Albania, ab Albanacto, nunc vero Scocia nuncupatur, ac Cambro filio juniori partem illam a suo nomine tunc Cambriam nunc Walliam vocatam. Ac voluit tunc expresse et ordinavit quod dicto Locrino suo primogenito et suis successoribus dicti fratres sui et eorum successores pro hujusmodi terris sibi assignatis facerent homagium ligium et servicia inde debita imperpetuum, et quod in eos et eorum terris hujusmodi haberet prerogativam et superioritatem. Deinde idem Alanus summatim [?] recitavit coram eis quomodo ab illo tempore reges Scocie fecerunt homagium ligium regibus Anglie, exceptis paucis temporibus rebellionum ipsorum Scotorum usque ad moderna tempora, et continuacionem [?] rebellionis ipsorum Scotorum in ea parte. Et subjungendo dixit eis quod de hiis omnibus fuerunt et sunt nonulle cronice in nonnullis monasteriis [1] Anglie reperte et remanentes fide-

---

[1] It is clear that what Alan Newark recited came from Andrew de Tange's ' Great Roll ' (see Prynne, pp. 489-96). In essentials, the story is found above, in Edward I's letter to Boniface VIII (pp. 97 ff.). There is evidence, however, that Henry IV had, like Edward I, investigated monastic chronicles in search of justification for his claims in Scotland, and

and he forthwith recited before them how in the days
of Eli and Samuel the prophet, a certain valiant and
illustrious man called Brutus, of the Trojan race, landed,
after the destruction of the city of Troy, with many noble
Trojans, upon an island called at that time Albion,
which comprised the whole of what are now styled
England, Scotland, and Wales. It was then inhabited
by giants, and, when he had defeated and slain them, by
his might and that of his followers, he called it, after his
own name, Britain, and his people Britons, and afterwards he divided his realm among his three sons, that is
he gave to his first born, Locrine, that part of Britain now
called England, to the second, Albanact, that part then
known as Albany, after Albanact, but now as Scotland,
and to Camber, his youngest son, the part then known
by his son's name as Cambria, and now called Wales.
And he then expressly desired and ordained that the
brothers and their successors should do liege homage,
and the services thereby due, to Locrine his eldest son,
and his successors for ever, for the lands assigned to
them, and that he should have such a prerogative and
superiority over them and their lands. Thereupon Alan
briefly recited to them how from that time the kings of
Scotland did liege homage to the kings of England, except
for a few periods of rebellion by the Scots, until modern
times, and described the continuation of the rebellion of
the Scots in that matter. And furthermore he said to
them that concerning all these matters there were, and
are, certain chronicles extant, in certain monasteries [1]
of England, and still faithfully kept, which were written

had had the royal archives scrutinised. cf. Nicolas, I, 122-3; Palgrave,
Kalendars, II, 62 and III, 361-3; P.R.O. Issue Roll 564, s.d. 1 December
1399; and E. L. G. Stones in *SHR*, xxxv (1956), 98-9.

[liter] conservate et [a] conscripte per quendam Scotum nomine Marrianum.[1] Et tunc incontinenti magister Johannes de Merton predictus ibidem dixit [quod?] fatebatur quod ille Marrianus fuit tempore quo vixit fidelissimus homo, sed subjunxit quod fuit Scotus de Hibernia et non natus in eorum Scocia. Quibus dictis et recitatis, prefatus dominus [episcopus] Bangorensis dixit et asseruit quod propter hujusmodi cronicas, intencio domini regis Anglie super premiss[o] homagio de jure fuit plene probata, cum hujusmodi cronice fuerunt a fidedignis et nonnullis [re]ligiosis non suspectis, et presertim per dictum Marrianum, conscripte, ac in monasteriis et aliis locis non suspectis fideliter conservate [et] fama [est] de [b] hujusmodi homagio facto regibus Anglie a regibus Scocie a dictis temporibus, et per dicta tempora, nedum in dictis regnis Anglie et Scocie, verum eciam in omnibus regnis ac terris convicinis et [c] in Romana curia, in cujus eciam archivis de ipso homagio fit mencio et frequens memoria, vulgari [2] ad premissa communiter concurrente; et quod cronice de longissimo vetustissimo ac antiquissimo hujusmodi tempore loquentes, dummodo in antiquis libris et cartis, prout sunt conscripte, reperte et fideliter ac secure conservate fuerunt, faciunt plenam fidem de jure. Idem dominus Bangorensis allegavit nonnulla jura similia, decretales, et canones decretorum, et inter alia dixit quod fuit unum capitulum Extra *De Probacionibus* quod fecit bene ad materiam, sed asseruit se protunc non habere memoriam de capite ipsius,[d] ac interrogavit prefatum magistrum

---

[a] ec' C
[b] et fama est *ed.*; conservate fama de C
[c] eciam C
[d] lipius C

by a certain Scot called Marianus.[1] At this point master
John of Merton at once intervened, remarking that
Marianus was a very trustworthy person for the time
when he lived, but adding that he was a Scot of Ireland,
not a native of their Scotland. After these observations
had been made, the bishop of Bangor spoke, asserting
that because of such chronicles, the premise of the king
of England concerning the homage was fully established
in law, for such chronicles were written by trustworthy
persons, some of them monks, who were above suspicion,
and especially by this Marianus, and were kept carefully
in monasteries, and other places, which were also above
suspicion, [and that there is] a tradition that this sort of
homage was done to the kings of England by the kings
of Scotland from those times, and in those times, to be
found not only in the realms of England and Scotland,
but also in all the neighbouring realms and territories,
and also in the Roman curia, in whose archives it is also
mentioned and frequently recorded, common [opinion] [2]
concurring generally with the aforesaid ; and that the
chronicles, speaking of a very distant, ancient, and remote
time, provided that they are found in ancient books and
charters, and are faithfully and securely kept, as they
were written, bear full credit at law. The lord of Bangor
cited other similar laws, decretals, and collections of
decrees, and said, amongst other things, that there was
a chapter of the decretals ' On Proofs ' which told in
favour of his case, but that at the moment he could not
remember how it began, and he asked master John of

---

[1] i.e., Florence of Worcester, whose chronicle was based on that of
Marianus Scotus, an Irish monk of the eleventh century
[2] As a noun, *vulgaris* is usually plural, but recorded also in the singular.

Johannem de Merton, al[iquando?] [a] in scolis Oxon'
bene sibi notum, [1] quomodo incepit hujusmodi capitulum, qui statim capitavit [2] et dixit quod incepit 'Cum
causam '.[3] Et tunc dominus Bangorensis sibi dixit quod
verum dixisset in ea parte.

Et subsequenter, commissarii utriusque regis qui
protunc fuerunt ibi, videlicet pro parte regis Anglie
reverendus pater dominus episcopus Bangorensis, Ricardus dominus de Grey, Radulfus Evyr, Gerardus Heron,
Johannes Cursoun, et Alanus Newerk, et pro parte regis
Scocie episcopus Glascuensis pretensus,[4] Johannes de
Merton, Johannes de Swynton, Willelmus Styward et
Adam Forster prefati utrimque convenerunt, et con-
senserunt expresse quod in crastino, que [sic] erat
mercurii xix Octobris mens' [sic] sepedicti, descenderent
et convenirent ad tractandum tractanda apud ecclesiam
de Carram Dunolmensis diocesis. Inter alia prefati
commissarii regis Scocie expresse dixerunt quod volebant
ibidem ostendere relaxacionem juris [5] dicti homagii, et
defensiones eorum super eorum libertate in ea parte,
et ulterius dicere ac audire et allegare hincinde de jure
utriusque regni. Et statim postea omnes commissarii
predicti hincinde convenerunt expresse, quod cum
pluribus in crastino ibidem non convenirent nisi cum
quinquaginta lanceatis, et totidem ad custodiam equorum
ipsorum, et sic abinvicem recesserunt et ad propria

---

[a] *Or* aliqualiter?

[1] Doubtless this is the John de Merton recorded in Emden, *Biographical
Register . . . of Oxford*, III, 1267–8, as coming from Scotland to Oxford
c. 1378, and graduating B.Can.L. by 1387. See Emden, loc. cit., for
further details. Richard Young, bishop of Bangor, is noted by Emden
(III, 2137) as a probable Oxford man; this passage places the matter
beyond doubt.

Merton, whom he had at one time known well in the schools of Oxford,[1] how that chapter began, and John at once quoted the beginning,[2] and said that it began ' Cum causam ',[3] and then the lord of Bangor told him that he had answered truly in that matter.

Subsequently the commissioners of each king who were present at the time, namely on behalf of the king of England the reverend father the bishop of Bangor, Richard lord Grey, Ralph Evyr, Gerard Heron, John Curzon, and Alan Newark, and on behalf of the king of Scotland the pretended [4] bishop of Glasgow, John of Merton, John of Swinton, William Styward, and Adam Forster met together, and agreed expressly that on the morrow, Wednesday 19 October, they should go down, and meet to negotiate business at the church of Carham, in the diocese of Durham. Amongst other things, the commissioners of the king of Scotland said expressly that on that occasion they wished to show a ' release ' [5] of the right to the homage, and their defences of their liberty in that regard, and to speak further, and to hear and explain matters concerning the right of each kingdom. And immediately after this, all the commissioners agreed expressly that they would meet there on the morrow with not more than fifty spearmen, and as many more for the custody of their horses, and so they separated from each other and went to their own quarters. When

---

[2] *Capitare* in the sense appropriate here seems unrecorded ; we assume that it is connected with ' caput ' in the sense of ' head of a chapter '.

[3] C reads *Cum tamen*; but it is certain that his exemplar referred to *Decretals, Lib. II, Tit. xix*, cap. 13, *Quum causam*, where it is laid down that in a dispute concerning diocesan boundaries, regard is to be had to the evidence of *libri antiqui*, as well as of *testes* and *fama*.

[4] ' Pretended ' because provided to the see of Glasgow by a pope not acknowledged in England, on account of the Great Schism of 1378–1417.

[5] i.e., to produce an exemplar of no. 41 (a) above ?

remearunt. Qua die adveniente prefati dominus Bangorensis et Alanus, alios dominos et collegas eorum pre-
cedentes, intrarunt ecclesiam de Carram predictam, et
diu expectarunt tam prefatos dominos et collegas eorum
quam commissarios regis Scocie antedictos, et tandem
dictam ecclesiam, ex certis causis eos monentibus,
exeuntes equitaverunt ad quendam montem aliqualiter
ab ipsa ecclesia distantem, in cujus cacumine [?] in-
venerunt tam dictos dominos eorum collegas quam commissarios regis Scocie supradictos, et prope eos ad latus
totum exercitum quem [?] ibi habebant Scoti illis diebus, ut mihi apparuit, simul coadunatum et congloba-
tum, aciem faciendo quasi ad bellum, gente nostra quasi
pauca tunc al[iqualiter?] remocius agente. Et tunc
comes de Douglas,[1] unus commissariorum regis Scocie,
non satisfacto termino prout f[uit] assignatus, peciit
quod treuge eis prorogarentur et servarentur a festo
sancti Martini tunc proxime futuro usque ad idem
f[estum] tunc ad annum, quas asseruit literatorie sibi
per nobilem virum dictum dominum comitem North',
tunc ibidem presentem, antea fuisse promissas et concessas et literam ipsius comitis North', ut asseruit, sibi
al[ias?] destinatam super hoc ibidem publice [?]
ostendit; et propterea cum instancia vehementi postu-
lavit quod hujusmodi treugarum prorogacio et con-
cessio ibidem statim coram eorum exercitu et gente
nostra predicta proclamaretur, ut ad noticiam dominorum et regnicolarum utriusque regni posset devenire;
et al[iter?] protestabatur et dixit quod idem dominus
comes North' [nec] suum proprium, nec eciam ipsius, eo

---

[1] The dispute which follows is made somewhat clearer by reference to
Royal Letters, Henry IV (above, p. 173, *n.* 1).

that day came, the lord of Bangor, and Alan, preceded
the other lords, their colleagues, and entered the church
of Carham, where for a long time they awaited both the
lords, their colleagues, and the commissioners of the king
of Scotland. At length, after receiving certain information, they went out and rode to a hill, at some distance
from the church, on the top of which they found both
the lords, their colleagues, and the commissioners of the
king of Scotland, and nearby, on one side, the whole
army which the Scots had there at that time, as it seemed
to me, drawn up together and arrayed, assembled in line
as if for war, our own very small company being assembled
some distance further off. Then the earl of Douglas,[1]
one of the commissioners of the king of Scotland (though
the period which was arranged had not yet expired),
asked that the truce be prolonged and maintained for
them from Martinmas next [11 November] until that
same feast a year hence [?]. This truce, he said, had
been previously promised and granted to him, in writing,
by the noble lord the earl of Northumberland, who was
now present, and he showed there publicly a letter of the
earl of Northumberland, sent to him, as he asserted,
already about this matter, and therefore he demanded,
with great importunity, that such an extension and grant
of a truce should be proclaimed there at once, in the
presence of their army and of our own people, in order
that it might come to the notice of the lords and inhabitants of both realms ; and he protested that otherwise
the earl of Northumberland would not be maintaining

quod regem suum et regnum Scocie de hoc certificavit, honorem conservaret.

Ad quas peticionem et literam idem dominus comes North' dixit quod in crastino, deliberatus super hiis, dicto comiti de Douglas et suis collegis in eodem loco plene et clare vellet respondere quod de eorum consensu, nonullis aliis altercacio[nibus] ac responsionibus eciam hiis que i[nfra?] de dat' diei crastine statim annectuntur prius interpositis, vix potuit impetrare.[1] Deinde vero die Jovis xx^a sepedicti mensis Octobris crastina adveniente, modico ultra dictam ecclesiam de Carram in campo juxta latus aque de Twede convenientibus pro parte regis Anglie domino episcopo Bangorensis, Radulfo Evyr, Gerardo Heron, Alano Newerk, et Johanne Curson; et pro parte regis Scocie Glascuensi episcopo, Johanne de Merton, Johanne de Swynton, Willelmo Styward, ac Adam Forster, commissariis predictis, dicto domino comite North' cum sua gente in villa de Carram et dicto comite de Douglas in alia parte dicte aque de Twede super ipsius ripam cum sua gente remanentibus, dicti commissarii regis Scocie peticionem quam fecerat [?] supradictus comes de Douglas die immediate precedente repetentes, pecierunt responsum ad peticionem hujusmodi et ad literam supradictam, prout dicta die precedente per dictum comitem North' fuit eis promissum.

Et tunc incontinenti magister Alanus sepefatus de mandato collegarum suorum predictorum ibidem presencium interrogavit eos si vellent parere condicionibus in dicta litera contentis, et inter alia specialiter si vellent restituere omnes terras et possessiones pertinentes ad

---

[1] The passage from *nonnullis* to *impetrare* is obscure.

either his own honour or that of Douglas, in that he had assured [?] his king and the realm of Scotland of this.

To this petition and letter the earl of Northumberland said that on the morrow, when he had considered these matters, he would give his reply, fully and clearly, to the earl of Douglas and his colleagues, in the same place; and this postponement he was only able to obtain with their agreement after several other exchanges, and after the replies which are annexed immediately below, in the account of the following day.[1] Then verily the morrow came, Thursday the 20th of the month of October, and a little beyond the church of Carham, in a field by the side of the River Tweed, there met, on behalf of the king of England, the lord bishop of Bangor, Ralph Evyr, Gerard Heron, Alan Newark, and John Curzon, and on behalf of the king of Scotland, the bishop of Glasgow, John of Merton, John of Swinton, William Styward, and Adam Forster, the commissioners. The earl of Northumberland, with his retinue, remained in the town of Carham, and the earl of Douglas, with his retinue, on the other side of the river Tweed, upon the bank. The commissioners of the king of Scotland repeated the request which the earl of Douglas had made on the day immediately before, and asked for an answer to that request, and to the letter, as had been promised them, on the day before, by the earl of Northumberland.

Then straightway master Alan, at the request of his colleagues there present, asked them if they were willing to accept the terms contained in the letter, and, amongst other things, particularly if they were willing to restore all the lands and possessions pertaining to the castles of

castra de Jedworth Roxburgh et Bere[wik] ac cetera
castra que habet et possidet dominus rex Anglie super
marchias inter Anglie et Scocie regna secundum formam
et effectum treugarum tam novarum inter ipsa regna
Anglie et Scocie quam originalium inter regna Anglie
et Francie captarum,[1] ad quas hujusmodi nove treuge
cicius [?] recepte se referunt [?] easque ac earum limites
fines confrontaciones et bundas ad omnia dubia tollenda
declarare ceteraque attemptata reparare et emendare in
quibus contra ipsas treugas interim forisfecerunt. Que
omnia et eorum singula ec[ontra ?], aliquibus inhon[estis]
verbis ex parte eorum interpositis, penitus recusarunt ac
eciam declinarunt, licet simplici ac nudo v[erbo ?]
ventoso hujusmodi attemptata [a] dumtaxat, sed nullo
modo predictas restitucionem et declaracionem facere
dixerunt se bene . . . .[b] reparare, sed hiis non
obstantibus prefati commissarii regis Anglie tunc abinvicem presentes, ad satisfaciend' pertinacie [c] ipsorum
Scotorum, et ad ipsorum maliciam plenius ut apparuit
convincend', obtulerunt eis simpliciter prorog[acionem]
dictarum treugarum a dicto festo sancti Martini tunc
proxime sequente usque ad xx^{mum} diem post festum
nativitatis domini tunc proxime futurum, ad finem et
effectum quod interim possent eorum dominum regem
Anglie cerciorare an placeret quod haberent hujusmodi
treugas per eos petitas vel non, et quia de hujusmodi
domini regis voluntate interim [2] volebant eis clare et
distincte certificare. Quod consimiliter, ut supra,
omnino recusarunt.

---

[a] attep^{ta} C
[b] *End of line mutilated* C
[c] pertinacie *ed.*; proterv . . . . *or* protern . . . . C (*dots indicate mutilation
at end of line*)

Jedburgh, Roxburgh, and Berwick, and the other castles which the lord king of England holds and possesses on the marches between the realms of England and Scotland, according to the form and effect of the truces, both the new truce between the realms of England and Scotland, and the original truce between the realms of England and France,¹ to which the new truce recently received makes reference [?], and to declare them and their limits, frontiers, boundaries, and borders for the removal of all doubt, and to make reparation and amends for the other attacks by which, in the meantime, they had offended against the truce. These proposals one and all they utterly rejected and declined, with the addition of some very undiplomatic language, though on no better grounds than airy words, simple and unsupported, but in no wise, they said, were they [willing] properly to make this restoration and declaration. . . . Notwithstanding, the commissioners of the king of England who were then present, to satisfy the importunity of the Scots, and to overcome their malice more fully (as it appeared), offered to them simply a prolongation of the truce, from Martinmas next until the 20th day after Christmas, with the intention that in the meantime they might report to the king of England, [and ascertain] whether the Scots might have such a truce as they were asking for, or not, and because ₁[meanwhile] ² they wished to inform them clearly and distinctly of the will of the king in this matter. And this proposal, as before, the Scots again utterly refused.

---

¹ The ' original ' truce is presumably that of 1396 (Cosneau, *Grands Traités de la Guerre de Cent Ans*, 1889, pp. 69-99), though the point argued here is not obvious ; the ' new ' does not survive, but is known in general terms, Bain, IV, no. 589, para. 8.

² ' interim ' should perhaps be deleted.

2 D

Et tunc dicti domini commissarii domini regis Anglie, considerantes quod prefati regis Scocie commissarii nolebant adquiescere alicui, ut eis visum fuit in ea parte, racioni ac nolentes libenter abinvicem discedere in discordia et sine aliqua conclusione fructuosa, interrog-[abant] prefatos regis Scocie commissarios [numquid] ᵃ propter perpetue pacis stabilitatem fiendam inter dicta regna et detestabilem Christianorum sanguinis effusionem vitandam, in ea parte vellent questionem prefatam ponere in judicio alicujus viri sapientis et non suspecti deum ac conscienciam timentis, quoniam [?] per hoc venietur ad perpetuam pacem, de qua fit mencio in commissionibus nostris.¹ Nam si judicabitur pro domino nostro rege Anglie et ejus regno tunc, domino concedente, servietur [?] sibi et regno suo fideliter, et ipse pro se et regno suo tractabit regem et regnum vestrum ut dominus tenetur [?] hoc . . . . .ᵇ tractare vassallum suum de jure. Et sic erit perpetua pax et amicicia inter ipsos reges et regna. Si vero judicabitur pro libertate regis et regni Scocie, tunc eciam erit hujusmodi pax et amicicia, et nihilominus, in illis eve[ntibus], rex et regnum Anglie propter uberiorem et majorem stabilitatem hujusmodi pacis et amicicie fiendam intendit (*sic*) cum rege et regno Scocie taliter tractare et pacisci qualiter in ea parte merito reputabunt se contentos.

Ad quam interrogacionem prefatus episcopus Glascuensis pretensus incontinenti respondit an vellent ipsi commissarii regis Anglie ponere jus regni Anglie

---

ᵃ numquid *Mr R. E. Latham conj., for an indecipherable word in* C
ᵇ *A word or two lost at end of line* C

¹ Observe the change of person.

Then the commissioners of the king of England, considering that the commissioners of the king of Scotland were unwilling to agree to any proposal, as it seemed to them, in that matter, and not wishing readily to depart thence in disagreement, and without any fruitful result, asked the commissioners of the king of Scotland [whether] for the purpose of securing a perpetual peace between the said realms, and avoiding the deplorable shedding of Christian blood, they were ready, for their part, to place the whole question under the judgment of some wise individual, who was above suspicion, and who feared God and his own conscience, since by this means one may arrive at the perpetual peace, of which mention is made in our commissions.[1] For if judgment is given for our lord the king of England and his realm, then (with the Lord's help) faithful service will be done to him and his realm and he, on behalf of himself and of his realm, will treat your king and realm as a lord is bound . . . . to treat his vassal by law. And so there will be perpetual peace and friendship between those kings and realms. But if judgment is given for the liberty of the king and realm of Scotland, then also there will be such peace and friendship, and in that case, moreover, the king and realm of England, in order to provide a larger and ampler security for that peace and friendship, intend to treat with, and placate the king and realm of Scotland in such a way that in that matter they will with reason hold themselves content.

To this enquiry the pretended bishop of Glasgow replied straightway, asking whether the commissioners of the king of England were willing to place the right to

[eciam ?] [a] in arbitramento, cui tunc respondit prefatus dominus episcopus Bangorensis quod casus non essent similes.[1] Et dum incepit cum [eo] [b] super hoc raciocinari, alii college dicti pretensi Glascuensis episcopi trahentes ad partem aliter responderunt, dicentes quod super [hoc] volebant eorum regem consulere an sibi hoc placeret necne. Et tunc prefati commissarii domini regis Anglie eis dix[erunt] quod super hoc eciam volebant dictum dominum eorum regem Anglie plenius consulere, et sic abinvicem recesserunt et ad propria, ut creditur, hincinde remearunt.

Presentibus in omnibus et singulis supradictis nobilibus viris Willelmo Fulthorp, milite, J[ohanne] Mutford, et Ricardo de Ask, domicellis, Ebor' et Dunolm' dioc', testibus ad premissa vocatis specialiter et rogatis, tenentibus vero commissiones [c] de quibus supra fit mencio sequuntur [*sic*] [d] et sunt tales etc. Deinde vero dominica die xxiij mensis Octobris [predicti ?], in castro suo de Alnwyk, prefatus strenuus dominus, dominus H[enricus] comes North' ostendebat copiam prefate litere quam comes de Douglas asseruit, ut supra, per dictum dominum comitem North' sibi fuisse al[ias ?] destinatam prefato domino episcopo B[angorensi], et illam sibi liberavit copiandam, cujus tenor sequitur [2] et est clericis etc. Presentibus tunc ibidem discretis et nobilibus viris Willelmo Bryghtwell, Johanne Ibery presbiteris, Nicholao Darcy et Tho[me] Constable domicellis Linc' Dublin ac E . . . .[e] dioc', testibus ad premissa vocatis specialiter et rogatis.

---

[a] eciam, *ed. conj., for word probably lost at end of line*
[b] eo, *ed. conj., as previous note* ; eis *also possible*
[c] commissionu C
[d] *Read* specialiter ?
[e] *If an English diocese, this must be* Exon', Ebor', *or* Elien'.

the realm of England also [?] under arbitration, to which the bishop of Bangor replied that the cases were not similar.[1] And while he began to argue on this point with [him], the other colleagues of the pretended bishop of Glasgow drew aside, and replied otherwise, saying that on this they wished to consult their king, to discover whether this was his pleasure or not. Then the commissioners of the lord king of England said to them that on this they also wished to consult their lord the king of England more fully, and so they all departed, and returned to their own countries, as far as is known.

There were present at all of the above proceedings the noble William Fulthorp, knight, and John Mutford and Richard of Aske, esquires, of the dioceses of York and Durham, specially called, and invited, as witnesses to the aforesaid, and holding the king's commissions, of which [special ?] mention is made above and they are such, etc. Then, on Sunday, 23 October, in his castle of Alnwick, the valiant lord Henry, earl of Northumberland, showed a copy of the letter (which, as the earl of Douglas asserted above, had been sent to him elsewhere by the earl of Northumberland) to the bishop of Bangor, and gave it to him to be copied, and its text follows,[2] and it was [handed] to the clerks etc. There were present there on that occasion the discreet and noble William Brightwell and John Ibery, priests, and Nicholas Darcy and Thomas Constable, esquires, of the dioceses of Lincoln, Dublin and E . . . . who were specially called and invited as witnesses to the aforesaid.

---

[1] Referring to Henry IV's claim to the throne of England, which was still not recognised in all quarters.
[2] Not copied in C.

INDEX

*Places and persons named in the text are indexed only
under the form given in the translation.*

KING ALFRED'S COLLEGE
LIBRARY